D0847682

OMNIVM
LVX
CIVIVM
MDCCCLII
MDCCC
LXXVIII
BOSTON
PUBLIC
LIBRARY

The European Crisis of the 1590s

THE EUROPEAN CRISIS OF THE 1590s

Essays in Comparative History

Edited by
PETER CLARK

London
GEORGE ALLEN & UNWIN
Boston Sydney

**George Allen & Unwin (Publishers) Ltd,
40 Museum Street, London WC1A 1LU, UK**

George Allen & Unwin (Publishers) Ltd,
Park Lane, Hemel Hempstead, Herts HP2 4TE, UK

Allen & Unwin Inc.,
Fifty Cross Street, Winchester, Mass 01890, USA

George Allen & Unwin Australia Pty Ltd,
8 Napier Street, North Sydney, NSW 2060, Australia

First published in 1985.

British Library Cataloguing in Publication Data

Clark, Peter, 1944
The European crisis of the 1590s.
1. Europe——History——1517–1648
I. Title
940.2'32 D228
ISBN 0-04-940074-6

Library of Congress Cataloging in Publication Data

Main entry under title:
The European crisis of the 1590s.
Includes index.
1. Europe——History——1517–1648——Addresses, essays, lectures. 2. Europe——Social conditions——16th century——Addresses, essays, lectures. I. Clark, Peter, 1944–
D231.E95 1984 940.2'32 84–12371
ISBN 0-04-940074-6 (alk. paper)

Set in 10 on 12 point Bembo by Computape (Pickering) Ltd
and printed in Great Britain by
Butler & Tanner Ltd, Frome and London

Contents

PART TWO

Maps

Abbreviations

AD	Archives Départementales (France)
AM	Archives Municipales (France)
AN	Archives Nationales (France)
APC	*Acts of the Privy Council*
AS	Archivio di Stato (Italy)
BL	British Library, London
BN	Bibliothèque Nationale, Paris
CSPD	*Calendar of State Papers Domestic*
GA	Gemeentearchief (Netherlands)
PRO	Public Record Office, London

Preface

This collection stems from a small conference on the 'European Crisis of the 1590s' which was held at Leicester University in July 1981. The aim of the conference was to bring together historians working on the principal European countries in the late sixteenth century in order to investigate systematically a period which has often been seen as one of critical difficulty in the post-Reformation era. In the event the conference was a very lively and fruitful exercise in comparative history. The papers and commentaries generated a wide-ranging discussion not only on the problems of the 1590s, their origin and impact, but also about longer-term structural and institutional changes in western Europe in the late sixteenth and seventeenth centuries.

The format of this volume follows the broad lines of the conference: specific regional studies of the principal countries are followed by more general surveys analysing major themes in a European context. The collection includes revised versions of virtually all the papers presented in 1981.

We are particularly grateful to the Nuffield Foundation which took over the funding of the conference at relatively short notice. We are also indebted to the custodians of national, town and local archives across Europe, without whose patient help many of the papers could not have been written. Peter Burke and Bob Scribner gave valuable advice on the organisation of the conference and the preparation of the collection. Gillian Austen has furnished invaluable secretarial support at Leicester University, while Jenny Clark has acted as midwife once again to the lengthy editorial labours.

P.A.C.

PART ONE

1 *Introduction*

PETER CLARK

I

One of the more durable historical debates in modern times has been over the so-called 'General Crisis of the seventeenth century'. In its original formulation, in essays by H. R. Trevor-Roper, Eric Hobsbawm and others collected in *Crisis in Europe 1560–1660* (1963), the controversy had two, interconnected, themes: first a concern to explain the explosion of political instability in Europe in the mid-seventeenth century; secondly an attempt to establish whether this period of crisis marked the economic and social turning point in the long march from feudalism to capitalism.[1] Hopes of providing a general explanation of the political crisis have proved elusive, however, while the argument over the onset of capitalism has tended to shift away from the seventeenth century.[2] Recently the main thrust of the discussion has concentrated on trying to date the origin of the economic recession and to assess its general applicability and significance in western Europe. A number of these contributions to the debate are reprinted in *The General Crisis of the Seventeenth Century* (1978), edited by Geoffrey Parker and Lesley Smith.[3]

The General Crisis debate is rather like an elderly car with a defective battery and dirty points. There are times where one has a sense that it is going nowhere; then with a splutter and a start it comes to life and some rather frantic progress is made before it subsides into taciturnity. There can be little question that the arguments about the General Crisis have often been diffuse and inconclusive. There have been serious problems with trying to establish a common chronology and causation for the phenomenon which is meaningful, given the conventional definition of 'crisis' as short-term and interrelated economic, social and political upheavals precipitating longer-term structural changes in society. There are some obvious reasons for the confusion. First, because of the wealth of national, regional and subregional variations in European experience. As Michael Roberts has commented, while recent work on the general crisis has made the picture 'clearer, the increase in clarity serves only to reveal greater complexity and diversity'.[4] Ivo Schoffer has demonstrated that the Netherlands was a powerful, prosperous exception to the scenario of economic depression and England may also be classed as another exceptional case by the late seventeenth century.[5] Even more serious, the debate has suffered from the extended time-frame of discussion, sprawling backwards into the late sixteenth century and onwards into the eighteenth (becoming almost a general crisis of early modern times). Finally, there is the problem of disparities in the documentation accessible to historians of different countries.

None the less, like all good debates, the controversy has bred a new generation of research on European countries in the sixteenth and seventeenth centuries, while also establishing the undoubted value of the comparative approach. No less important, it has suggested that one of the ways forward may be to examine some of the major economic, social and other problems affecting parts of Europe in the late sixteenth and seventeenth centuries through a detailed investigation of one of the more notably critical or climactic decades within the General Crisis. By concentrating on a more limited period we may be able to avoid some of the methodological problems of the General Crisis debate: the beam of light will be narrow, but arguably more directed and better focused, more able to examine the context of the problems facing European society, to explore the possible connection between short-term difficulties and the longer-term processes of transformation.

Though there were other decades of upheaval and difficulty in the period,[6] the 1590s are an obvious candidate for this kind of investigation. Observers in France, England, Italy and Spain in the last years of the sixteenth century referred to it as a time of great upheaval. A Spanish writer declared in 1592: 'England without God, Germany in schism, Flanders in rebellion, France with all these together.'[7] It was a time when the outriders of the apocalypse were on the loose in much of Western Europe: years of terrible famine, plague, war and disorder. There were repeated prophecies of the end of the world in 1600.[8] More recently, a number of historians have emphasised the critical disruption of the 1590s. John Elliott (in 1963) wrote of the 'crisis of the 1590s' in Spain which was dominated by financial collapse, depopulation in the north and a sense of national failure; Bartolomé Benassar wrote in a similar vein on Spain a few years later.[9] For France Jean Jacquart has described the devastating impact of 'les années terribles' between 1589–94, when much of the area south of Paris was devastated by military campaigns, subsistence crises and murderous epidemics.[10] For England and Scandinavia too the final years of the sixteenth century have been viewed by historians as times of crisis and disaster.[11] According to Henry Kamen, 'the conditions of the 1590s were catastrophic' in much of Europe; 'probably never before in European history had so many popular rebellions coincided in time'.[12]

For some commentators the last years of the century may have marked a turning point in European economic and political development. Wilhelm

Abel has noted for this time the collapse of the long-term agrarian boom of the sixteenth century, and Ruggiero Romano points to the decisive deterioration in the agricultural situation at the end of the sixteenth and start of the seventeenth century. Kriedte suggests that the price revolution finally came to an end in the 1590s in an important part of Europe. For Trevor-Roper that decade saw 'the cracks . . . beginning to appear' in the governmental façade of the Renaissance State, which were to end in the political explosions of the mid-seventeenth century.[13]

If historical interest in the crisis of the 1590s is well established, it has received little sustained or comparative discussion. There are many questions outstanding. How widespread geographically was the crisis? Is it possible to identify common causes of difficulty? What were the immediate effects in terms of population, agriculture, living standards, and so on? To what extent is it possible to accept the suggestions of some historians that these climactic years at the close of the sixteenth century triggered long-term structural realignments in the European economy and society, heralding the General Crisis of the seventeenth century? The purpose of this book is to investigate at least some of these issues in depth – in Part One by way of regional case studies covering the principal countries in western Europe, in Part Two through more general thematic investigations considering in a European context the vital topics for the 1590s of crisis mortality, war, popular disorder and the role of the authorities. Finally, John Elliott concludes with some general thoughts on the possible significance of this traumatic decade.

It must be said at once that there has been no attempt to impose an artificial corset of consensus on the contributors. As we shall see, they often have quite different perceptions of the nature of the problems and also of their impact. This reflects in part the uneven quality of the evidence available for our various countries – as for example with the demographic data.[14] But such differences of interpretation also clearly mirror real differences on the ground between countries, towns and villages, and regional or local communities. One theme which emerges as we try and understand the variegated pattern of the crisis is not just the differing make-up of the crisis in particular areas – with war, for instance, having a directly devastating effect in some places and not in others – but also the crucial importance of the way an area's economic, social and other structures responded to the problems, tempering or sometimes exacerbating their effects. Thus our study of the 1590s may help us to explore both the commensal and divergent trends in the economic, social and institutional development of the major European countries during the late sixteenth and early seventeenth centuries.

II

Certainly there is a great deal of *prima facie* evidence to confirm that the last years of the sixteenth century were an era of acute distress, dislocation and disorder across much of Europe. In Northern France Philip Benedict describes in Chapter 5 a concatenation of catastrophes from the mid-1580s until the later 1590s: harvest failures and famines, scourging epidemics and fierce religious warfare. In the Île de France south of Paris villages were abandoned, agriculture nearly collapsed, and mortality rates soared. To the east in Lorraine, less badly affected by warfare, there was still growing pauperism, heavy rural indebtedness and a sharp fall in land values.[15] Further south, M. Greengrass shows how the years of the 1590s came as a desperate coda to several decades of mounting despoilment and distress as a result of long-running religious wars. In 1597 people were dying of hunger in the countryside of the Lyonnais; in Languedoc widespread famine led to concerted opposition to taxes and bloody popular risings.[16]

England, secure from civil strife, was less severely affected, but the period saw a disastrous sequence of harvest failures (1593–7) with economic depression, widespread poverty and high mortality from plague and starvation. Famine was particularly serious in the north but may also have seeped into the towns.[17] Scotland was afflicted by 'a great dearth' in 1594 and acute food shortages up to 1598; severe outbreaks of plague occurred in central and southern Scotland from 1597 until the end of the century.[18] Across the Irish Sea bad weather from 1594, poor harvests, and English military operations after Tyrone's Rebellion plunged the country close to ruin with a major fall of population in Ulster. During the great famine of 1601 there are credible reports of cannibalism.[19]

In the Low Countries the south experienced widespread destruction and turmoil with the Spanish army's successful advance against the rebels in the mid-1580s. 1585–6 saw famine in Liège and Antwerp and the latter's population fell from 80,000 in 1584 to 42,000 five years later. There was depopulation too in the countryside with many migrating from Brabant and Flanders to the United Provinces. By comparison conditions in the 1590s were less harsh, but it was none the less a time of renewed harvest failure (1594–6), the sporadic bombardment and pillaging of cities, and continuing social distress and disorder.[20] In the Dutch Republic, usually regarded as a paragon of economic growth and affluence, the last years of the century, as Leo Noordegraaf reveals (Chapter 4), were characterised by high prices, unemployment and social unrest, with local difficulties exacerbated by the massive influx of refugees from the southern Netherlands.[21]

Turning to Scandinavia we hear of crop failures in Sweden (1596–1603) with great scarcity and starvation in the west and south, and beggars roaming the countryside. Famine affected south-west Norway in 1596–8, while Finland had its 'Club War' in 1596.[22] Heinz Schilling suggests in Chapter 7 that short-term economic and social problems may have been less acute in much of Germany during the last years of the century, but in Austria there were large-scale peasant uprisings between 1594 and 1597, precipitated by higher food prices and the heavy exactions caused by the outbreak of war with the Turks in 1593.[23]

Whereas much of northern Europe suffered the main brunt of the crisis in the mid- and late 1590s (prefaced by major difficulties in the mid-1580s), the problems were often acute in the south in the early part of the decade. Terrible *crises de subsistences* occurred in Sicily and Naples in 1590–2 and severe food shortages in northern Italy as well. The great cities like Rome and Naples were overwhelmed with poor, mostly immigrants, and the Papal States were infested with bandits.[24] In Spain the bad harvests of the early 1590s led to a doubling or trebling of mortality levels in the Castiles; in parts of Galicia there was very high mortality from 1588 to 1591. Demographic disaster returned later in the decade: northern Spain lost perhaps half a million inhabitants between 1596 and 1602 due to dearth and plague; there was also heavy mortality in Seville, but not Valencia. In northern Portugal the inland town of Coimbra was also affected by high mortality in the 1590s, with famine in 1596. Two years later it was said there was 'a great multitude of poor' begging in the streets; the plague epidemic of 1598–9 set off a landslide of fatalities.[25]

As for Eastern Europe, Russia was still suffering in the 1590s from the disastrous war with Sweden over Livonia, which had caused a serious loss of agricultural production, food shortages, and high prices. The situation may have been improving in the late 1590s, but 1601–3 witnessed the resurgence of famine: 'so terrible and so great was the disaster over the whole country [that] mothers ate their children'; there were risings by villeins and peasants in the Moscow area. Famine likewise erupted in Poland in 1602.[26] In the Balkans and Romania, C. S. L. Davies reports how the outbreak of war between Austria and the Ottoman Empire provoked extensive nationalist risings against the Turkish oppressors, fired by heavy war levies and crop failures. The Turkish mainland was also hit: Istanbul, probably the largest European city, suffered from famine in the mid- and late 1590s, and there were the 'Celali' risings in Anatolia after 1596.[27]

III

The pathology of the crisis, then, is reasonably clear, with symptoms of distress and discontent visible across the European continent, particularly if we stretch the time-frame to embrace the late 1580s and first years of the seventeenth century. At the same time, the rhythms of suffering were by no means synchronised in all countries. As the following chapters make clear, there are also problems in the diagnosis, when we try and identify common causes for the disasters of these years.

The most obvious general source of difficulty was bad weather. There are reports of unrelentingly wet summers in England, Ireland and the Netherlands; of prolonged rains and heavy frosts around Paris and further south in the Midi; of alternating drought and torrential rain in Sicily; of flooding in northern Italy. Valencia and Murcia, James Casey observes (Chapter 11), had an exceptional run of wet years from 1589 to 1598 and rains were heavy in Galicia in 1589–91 and 1597. We learn of late springs and cold wet summers in Scandinavia and (unusually) of sea-ice off the northern coast of Iceland, bringing colder temperatures.[28] Switzerland and France broadly confirm the picture. Pfister's study of weather patterns in Switzerland indicates that the 1590s was one of the most severe decades in terms of winter temperatures in the early modern period. Work by Le Roy Ladurie and Baulant on the dating of the grape harvests in France, Switzerland and the Rhineland points to eight consecutively cool summers between 1591 and 1598, a terrible sequence which was only surpassed in the period by the years 1695–1703 and 1765–73. Other evidence suggests that 1595 may have been one of the six coldest winters between 1550 and 1700.[29]

The adverse climatic conditions of the 1590s can be viewed as part of a general deterioration in the European weather which may have begun in the mid-sixteenth century: the so-called 'Little Ice Age'. Indicative of this, low-reaching Alpine glaciers began to advance in the 1580s and a succession of glacier catastrophes occurred in the 1590s. Unfortunately the precise dating of the 'Little Ice Age' is uncertain, while the question of the repercussions of climatic deterioration is subject to continuing debate. In the long term, at least, farmers may adjust to bad wet weather by sowing different crops or abandoning low-lying land; improvements in food distribution or poor relief may moderate the full force of climatic and harvest disaster. In the short run a succession of bad summers may seriously affect agricultural production, but the severity of the impact on economic and social activity will depend very much on the resilience and response of the community.[30]

Even so there can be little doubt that harvest failure and agricultural shortage were important elements in the crisis of the 1590s in much of Europe. In many countries food prices rose with tremendous speed. In England corn prices doubled or trebled between 1590 and 1596–7; in France corn prices at Aix were higher in 1591–2 than at any time between 1570 and 1700; wheat prices at Rome during the 1590s were twice the average for the 1570s. Timothy Davies shows in Chapter 10 that after the famines of 1591–2 Sicily, one of the principal granaries of the Mediterranean, was no longer exporting corn on any scale.[31] Cities competed fiercely for supplies to feed their undernourished inhabitants. Certainly the late springs and wet summers contributed heavily to the disasters, but other factors aggravated the position. In France and parts of the Low Countries harvests were badly disrupted by warfare.[32] Moreover, throughout western Europe agricultural resources were already overstrained during the later sixteenth century, barely able to meet the demand of an increasing population. In the uplands such as northern England increased agricultural production may have relied on excessive use of marginal land, which may have suffered worst from continuous poor weather. In Spain, Casey emphasises how declining animal herds and the spread of a shifting type of arable farming reduced agricultural yields in certain areas before the bad harvests of the 1590s.[33]

In this time of natural disaster, the Baltic grain trade appeared as an angel of mercy to many European consumers. In the early 1590s hundreds of northern ships, mainly Dutch, unloaded great quantities of Baltic corn in Italian and other Mediterranean ports and imports continued for the rest of the decade. In the mid-1590s Baltic grain succoured the Netherlands, England, Scotland and parts of France. While the Polish commonwealth was the principal supplier, as agricultural commercialisation increased there, the scale of Polish exports must not be overstated. Denmark and northern Germany also exported grain at this time, and in the case of England and other countries Baltic supplies met only a small portion of total demand. But even this marginal rate of supply was vital in maintaining a measure of stability in the international grain markets, preventing prices and shortages getting completely out of control.[34]

Along with famine, another horseman of the apocalypse – war – was very much at large in Europe in the 1590s, with only Germany, Italy and Russia generally free from direct or indirect involvement in military conflict. Most were not new wars but, as I. A. A. Thompson stresses in Chapter 14, the often lethal paroxysms of older struggles – the Netherlands Revolt, the French Religious Wars, the Anglo–Spanish conflict. None the less, by the 1590s the Atlantic seaboard states were polarised on an international scale, Catholics versus Protestants, to an unprecedented degree, while the engines of war were absorbing exceptionally large amounts of men and money. But if war was a European phenomenon the impact was selective. Of those countries directly affected by military campaigning France clearly suffered grievously. In the Midi, fighting in the late 1580s and 1590s came as the culmination of decades of brutal conflict; in the north it was a relatively new and shocking experience. In both regions warfare gave a terrible extra dimension to other critical problems of the last decade and a half of the century. Military operations had a similar devastating effect in the southern Netherlands during the 1580s (though the situation was less serious in the following decade), and in Ireland in the late 1590s.[35] However, outside the cockpit of fighting the repercussions were more limited and mixed. For countries like Spain and England the demographic drain on manpower was small; the financial burden, though severe as R. B. Outhwaite documents for the Elizabethan Exchequer, not insupportable; the disruption of trade patchy. In the short run certain social groups (nobles, captains, financiers) and certain economic sectors (such as the iron industry) might actually benefit from war.[36] Compared with climatic and agricultural disaster, the wars of the end of the sixteenth century chanted a smaller part in the threnody of crisis.

Military activity in the 1590s may have contributed to the international incidence of epidemics in that decade, as marauding armies and fleeing peasants helped spread disease. There was a notable clustering of epidemics, especially plague, in most countries. Whether there was a direct connection between outbreaks of epidemic disease and agricultural failure and malnutrition is a matter of contention. Whereas several contributors see epidemics often following in the wake of harvest failure, battening on the weakened physical defences of their victims, David Souden (Chapter 12) urges scepticism in seeing any close link between epidemiological and economic and social phenomena.[37] It is likely, however, that one factor in the wide spread of disease in this period was the high level of migration which developed at this time. Another factor may have been the large-scale movement of grain (much of it not of good quality) from one region or country to another. Whatever the cause, the impact of the host of epidemics on mortality rates was dramatic – more immediately devastating than anything else in the 1590s. The disruption to trade and communications was no less severe. But in general the effects were short-term and geographically restricted, and demographic and economic recuperation followed apace.[38]

There were other problems and pressures of a more localised nature contributing to the upheavals of the 1590s. In France, Spain and parts of Italy rising taxation severely aggravated the plight of the peasantry and ordinary townspeople and depressed economic activity. In Ireland there was a damaging uncertainty over the coinage, in France a surfeit of inferior coins.[39] But the fundamental causes of the crisis had a European dimension, though the mix of difficulties might vary from one area to another, as might the intensity of their impact. One final point. In 1602 a Bologna cleric, Gian Battista Segni, commented:

> God sends three scourges to punish men for their sins: famine, war and pestilence. But of them all famine, so severe as it is, is less terrible.

> For while war and pestilence strike all men without distinction, famine spares the priests, one can thus confess before one dies; it spares the notaries, so it is still possible to make a will; it spares finally the princes who oversee the safety of the state.

One may not agree with Segni's ranking of the elements of the crisis, but he is surely right to remind us of the importance of elite institutions in dealing (or failing to deal) with the difficulties and distress created by the crisis.[40] In France the disputed royal succession and associated strife led to a near-paralysis of effective governmental mechanisms to combat the natural disasters. In Russia the harvest and other disasters at the turn of the century more or less coincided with the onset of the Time of Troubles.

IV

The most visible, immediate results of the crisis were fourfold: high mortality, extensive social distress, popular disorder, and severe strains on government. As the following chapters indicate, there is evidence for sharply higher levels of mortality due to famine and epidemics in most European countries during the last years of the century: in Italy and southern France during the early 1590s; in the north during the mid-1590s; and in Spain both at the start and end of the decade. As Souden argues, however, major problems arise in assessing and comparing these outbreaks of crisis mortality, either between countries or with other times of demographic upheaval. Documentation is uneven or incomplete. Prior experience of demographic disaster may well affect the level of mortality at a particular time, while the impact of disease may have a delayed effect. Conditions of crisis mortality probably have only limited consequences for fertility. In normal circumstances the population has its own built-in stabilising mechanism to mitigate the trauma of high mortality: a surge of burials may be followed (though not automatically) by a greater number of marriages (often earlier ones) and an upturn in the birth-rate. Demographic recovery is often surprisingly fast – at least in the short term.[41]

Where crisis mortality does seem to have done more permanent demographic damage is in areas such as northern Spain, the southern Netherlands and possibly northern England, where its impact may have been compounded by large-scale migration. Almost certainly migration was a growing phenomenon in the last part of the sixteenth century: movement from Castile to the cities of southern Spain; the exodus from Flanders and Brabant to the Dutch Republic; tramping from northern and western England to London and other major urban centres; religious migration in Germany; peasant movement away from marauding armies in France;

subsistence migration in Italy.[42] Big cities were often the principal, if unwilling, beneficiaries. The population of Paris fell by over a third to 200,000 after the siege of the early 1590s but had climbed back to 300,000 inhabitants by 1600. London, Naples, Palermo and Rome, also grew substantially during the 1590s.[43]

Subsistence migrants swelled the great armies of poor which were a striking manifestation of the social misery of the 1590s. Complaints of growing poverty are found in almost all European countries at this time.[44] Precise figures about poverty are, however, more difficult to obtain and interpret. At Cremona in Italy the number of poor inmates in the hospital of Santo Alessio nearly trebled between 1587 and 1593; in certain north Kent parishes in 1596 a high proportion of households were classed as destitute of corn; at Lyons in 1596–7 up to 20 per cent of the city's inhabitants were reportedly impoverished.[45] However, official definitions of poverty are notoriously slippery, while statistics generally relate to those receiving relief rather than the larger number in need. Only rarely do we have a series of data allowing us to plot the changing incidence of poverty. This makes it difficult to distinguish precisely between the casualties of the crisis proper with its harvest failures and trade disruption, and those suffering from structural changes in the economy, such as agrarian improvement or the decline of urban industries.

More useful perhaps is evidence for the standard of living of the lower classes. For Lyons an index of the purchasing power of craftsmen shows a steady decline throughout the sixteenth century, but with the 1590s registering the lowest decennial average between 1500 and 1629. In Paris there was a precipitate fall in the real income of building workers even after the siege: the cost of consumables was 40 per cent higher in 1594–8 than in 1571–5, and wages were only marginally greater. In Antwerp real wages sustained a serious deterioration in the mid-1590s; at Florence wages in 1592–6 were less than half in real terms what they had been in 1520–6. Harvest failure and soaring food prices were clearly a prime factor.[46]

In Chapter 2 Outhwaite argues persuasively that the elasticity of consumption patterns may have moderated the worst effects of the crisis on living standards. People ate cheaper grains and more fish; they cut back drastically on non-food items. At Antwerp in 1596–1600 78 per cent of a working-class family's expenditure was on food, a high proportion on bread.[47] None the less, the recessionary consequences of the decline in disposable income for the industrial and service sectors of the economy were undoubtedly profound. In the Netherlands the textile industry was seriously depressed in 1595 and 1597, times of high food prices; thereafter, it was unusual for unemployment to coincide with subsistence difficulties. In Italy and Spain the failure of domestic demand may have done more lasting damage to industry.[48] Falling industrial production and increased unemployment and underemployment added a further twist to declining living standards.

This sharp deterioration in living standards, after several decades of reverses, undoubtedly helped fuel the numerous if varied outbreaks of disorder which occurred during the last part of the century. However, C. S. L. Davies shows that there was no great upsurge of rebellions of the belly in the 1590s. Such revolts as did occur invariably had a mixed causation. The spectacular rising of the League in Paris in 1588–94 under the increasingly radical and violent leadership of the Sixteen was partly a reaction to royal intervention in civic affairs, partly a religious rising, and partly a social protest movement. The peasant revolts in France and Austria were triggered off by the fiscal and other burdens of war, though anti-seigneurial grievances were a powerful ingredient as well.[49] War also spawned the succession of mutinies which afflicted England and the Low Countries in particular. The Spanish Army of Flanders, for instance, mutinied nearly thirty times between 1590 and 1601.[50] Localised communal riots may have been more closely linked with food shortages and social distress; this seems to have been the case in England (Chapter 3). But less is known about these minor disorders on a European scale, though it is unlikely they were an exclusively English problem.[51]

If the starving peasantry was reluctant to take to the streets *en masse* to demonstrate their distress, there were other strategies of protest and survival. In the early 1590s, according to Nicholas Davidson (Chapter 8), there were great forces of bandits operating in Tuscany, the Veneto and the Papal States. Banditry is also found in the Midi, in Brabant (up to 1594–5), and further east in the Ottoman Empire.[52] We may also speculate that the incidence of crime was on the increase, though the little hard evidence we have, for Italy and England, possibly reflects increased official vigilance as well as a higher level of offending.[53] One type of crime which does seem to have come before the courts in greater numbers during the 1590s was witchcraft. Towards the end of the century there was a spate of witchcraft prosecutions in Scotland, England, Germany, the Catholic Low Countries and France. Social tension and polarisation may well have been a factor in this development, but it is also clear that official measures against witchcraft (for instance, Philip II's orders of 1592 in the Spanish Netherlands) spurred on the wave of trials on the continent and in Scotland.[54]

Social distress and discontent posed a medley of problems for central and local government. Princes and town authorities had to try and feed their starving peoples, relieve the impoverished and plague-stricken, give them work, control vagrancy, and quell disorders. All this imposed great strains on the rudimentary mechanisms of bureaucracy and was very expensive.[55] War was if anything more burdensome. Though in volume terms the financial cost of warfare was not enormous, in historic terms total expenditure on military activity, as in the case of the Anglo-Spanish conflict, was unprecedented and placed great strains on the financial imagination of rulers. As we have noted already, heavy taxes in France and Spain, linked with war, may have further depressed economic activity and so aggravated the already acute social malaise. Military levies caused bitter political and administrative conflict at the regional and local level and became an explosive popular grievance.[56] Even so the balance sheet was not completely negative. Effective official measures to alleviate suffering and maintain public order might help justify and buttress the power of the ruling classes.[57]

Assessing the scale of the immediate impact of the 1590s is clearly a complicated question. The most dramatic repercussions were not necessarily the most disruptive or damaging. As we shall see, in some countries or areas the upheavals of the 1590s, intense though they were, may have been surpassed in severity by other critical decades, for instance the 1620s and 1630s. None the less, the prolonged and extensive nature of the shock wave of problems affecting most countries confirm the last years of the sixteenth century as one of the most exceptionally difficult periods in early modern Europe.

V

If the contributors to this volume are generally agreed that the last years of the sixteenth century were a time of major demographic, economic and social difficulty (though with regional variations in their critical intensity), there is much less agreement on whether the period had a more wide-ranging permanent significance in European or national development. The spectrum of opinion ranges from Peter Burke, on the one hand, who contends (Chapter 7) that long-term repercussions are hard to discern for southern Italy, to Schilling on the other hand who sees the 1590s as marking the start of a general crisis in the German urban system.[58] We can none the less identify some major themes in the debate about the lasting impact of the crisis. One theme which recurs in several contributions is the emergence of a deep-seated social perception of failure as a result of the reverses of the 1590s. In Spain it leads to disillusionment, a sense of hopelessness about the country's underlying problems which makes the resolution of them much more difficult. In Germany privileged traditional cities and their rulers suffered a collective loss of nerve confronted with the apparently inexorable rise of the territorial states.[59] By contrast Noordegraaf in his study of the Netherlands argues that the difficulties of the 1590s are played down in order to emphasise the triumph of the rebel north compared with the ruined south. In England disillusionment with Elizabeth in her waning years was soon forgotten in the later haste to make favourable comparisons between the Virgin Queen and her early Stuart successors.[60]

The agrarian response to the setbacks at the end of the sixteenth century was highly complex and fragmented. In the northern Netherlands and England the crisis may well have given an important boost to agricultural specialisation: within a generation England itself was to become a large exporter of grain. Agricultural improvement is also visible in the Midi, as Greengrass notes.[61] In northern France, however, the picture is one of declining or stagnant productivity. In the Spanish Netherlands the beginning of the devastation of the last decades of the sixteenth century led to a retreat towards agricultural autarky with productivity failing to recover to earlier levels. According to Timothy Davies, Sicilian corn production was also geared now mainly for the home market; aristocratic control over agriculture was strengthened by the planting of new villages. Whether one can speak of a general aristocratic reaction or 'refeudalisation' in southern Italy is questionable, as Burke contends. In Poland the rise of the corn export trade in the later sixteenth century was only one factor in the growing power of the great landowners; political pressures were also important.[62] More general, perhaps, was the accelerated polarisation of rural society, in part at least the result of the heavy indebtedness of the peasantry incurred during the 1590s. In France, Spain, Italy and the Spanish Netherlands there was a large-scale invasion of outsiders, often of the bourgeoisie, into rural landownership.[63]

The available evidence would suggest that the 1590s were not an obvious turning point in the population history of western Europe. In Spain and the southern Netherlands the retreat from sustained demographic growth may have started earlier. In England, Italy and Germany expansion was renewed and continued into the first third or more of the seventeenth century. Only perhaps in parts of France, as we can see from Benedict's analysis, did the 1590s inaugurate demographic decline. At the same time speculation of this sort is fraught with difficulty. Assuming that population structures have inbuilt mechanisms to correct for crisis mortality, then periods of demographic recovery may actually disguise significant structural changes.[64]

Although it is difficult to establish a direct causal link between the crisis mortality of the 1590s and the demographic recession of the seventeenth century, the contribution of large-scale migration is more evident. The exodus from the countryside to the major towns does seem to have accelerated during the 1590s and remained at a high level thereafter, partly perhaps because the growth of poor relief and other civic agencies to deal with the immigrant problem encouraged a continuing influx, partly because of the agricultural changes just described. In consequence large towns with their endemic diseases and near-perpetual demographic deficits drained away a growing proportion of Europe's surplus population, particularly younger people, and thus served as a powerful damper on population increase.[65]

The rise of big cities was in fact one of the most striking phenomena in early seventeenth-century Europe. The total population of places with 50,000 inhabitants or more rose by over 50 per cent between 1600 and 1650. Many of these big cities expanding from the close of the sixteenth century were metropolitan centres, seats of government for new centralist states. London had 200,000 inhabitants about 1600 and 400,000 in 1660; Paris 300,000 in 1600 and up to 450,000 a half-century later; Madrid 65,000 in 1597 and about 180,000 by 1630. Amsterdam, combining commercial and political (but not government) functions, nearly trebled its population in the early seventeenth century.[66] This was a time of the extensive rebuilding of great cities.[67] Yet in other respects the end of the sixteenth century inaugurated a period of urban malaise. Medium and smaller-size towns with less than 50,000 people experienced a stagnation or decline in their population. Urban communities lost their traditional economic and political autonomy. Crafts were confronted with the growing threat of rural industries, exploiting underemployment, cheap labour and the lack of regulation in the countryside. Civic treasuries were burdened with heavy debts. There was mounting political interference by princes and landed magnates in town government. As in Germany, many of these problems predated the 1590s, but in numerous respects the situation became worse from the last years of the sixteenth century. In Provence urban indebtedness, as for instance at Marseilles, where it stemmed from the high cost of corn imports and plague relief during the 1590s, led to serious communal tensions and conflict into the early seventeenth century. In Lombardy high food prices in towns during the crisis years were an important factor precipitating the major transfer of industrial production to the countryside with deleterious consequences for the major urban centres.[68]

For states the 1590s were often a cathartic experience. In the case of Spain and England, ruled by two elderly regimes, the economic and military pressures dealt severe blows at their long-term political stability. They were increasingly dogged by apparently insoluble financial problems which were alleviated only by resorting to ultimately disastrous expedients such as the sale of honours and office. Thompson makes a strong case for a crisis of empires during the last years of the sixteenth century, with the threatened disintegration of much of the Spanish hegemony in Europe and the decay of the Ottoman Empire. One might also add the eclipse of the old consensus-style Holy Roman Empire under

Rudolph II.[69] Whether these political systems would have disintegrated without the crisis of the 1590s is an arguable point, but the acute and manifold strains at the end of the century undoubtedly accelerated the process.

On the other hand, certain states benefited from the crisis situation. The Dutch Republic used the famines in the Mediterranean and on the Atlantic seaboard and its dominance of the Baltic corn trade to establish the foundations of a powerful commercial and political presence in western Europe. In upper Austria, the Habsburgs seized the opportunity of the revolts of the 1590s and the interim Resolution of 1597, which supposedly dealt with peasant grievances, to extend royal control over the economic and social life of the rural population. In northern Italy too, as Davidson indicates, governments expanded their range of influence over the private activities of their subjects. In France the social and political upheavals of the later sixteenth century, with their bitter legacy of continuing divisions in local communities, generated a widespread thirst for strong government, which enabled the growth of an increasingly powerful centralist state.[70]

As for the development of administrative institutions, the impact of the 1590s was more uniform. One can see this in the field of poor relief, now one of the principal concerns of government. Throughout western Europe, in both the north and south, there was a striking similarity in the action taken to relieve the needy through public granaries and hospitals, and to control begging and vagrancy. But Brian Pullan concludes (Chapter 15) that there was no breakthrough in ideas or strategy. Most measures had well established precedents, especially in towns, reaching back to the early sixteenth century. Only with the extension of poor relief to the rural population was there an important advance. None the less, there is the suggestion in several contributions that the end of the sixteenth century witnessed a consolidation of administrative institutions, accompanied by some improvements in their effectiveness.[71]

VI

One conclusion of this collective inquiry into the European crisis of the 1590s is that the conventional concept of a crisis with massive, closely related economic, social and political upheavals leading to fundamental changes in the structures of society hardly seems applicable to the final years of the sixteenth century. Acute, short-term economic and social dislocations there certainly were, but only sporadically did these contribute to political *bouleversements*. There was no year of revolutions in the 1590s comparable to 1648. A number of contributors argue that the direct connection between short-run reverses and structural transformation – the onset of the General Crisis of the seventeenth century – was tenuous; crisis did not precipitate recession but recovery. This raises important questions about the nature of the short-term crises which beset Europe from time to time in the sixteenth and seventeenth centuries. There is the implication that crisis was in some ways a self-regulating phenomenon with its own technical correcting mechanisms. As population falls, pressure on resources declines, real wages rise, people marry earlier and demand revives: recovery and stability have arrived. John Elliott in Chapter 16 makes the valuable point that the concept of 'crisis' has its limits as an analytical device for an age when instability was a constant.[72] Certainly a study of 'stability' in the Europe of the sixteenth and seventeenth centuries might well reveal that this too had its own technical limitations as renewed population growth leads in many instances to declining disposable income and inevitable recession. Without being a demographic determinist, the picture is one of a tightrope artiste, slipping on the economic wire, only to recover, only to slip again. 'Crisis' and 'stability' are inextricably interlinked in Europe for much of the sixteenth and seventeenth centuries, rather as one once liked to think were the booms and slumps of the modern trade cycle. Only with the major changes in agricultural productivity and the rise of extra-European trade from the late seventeenth century onwards was there a general unravelling of the relationship.

Yet, as most of the contributors appear to agree, the 1590s cannot be dismissed simply as one of the periodic mini-crises of the period. The Netherlands and possibly England used the opportunities created by the late-sixteenth century crisis to start to loosen the Malthusian constraints on their economies. Pullan suggests that there was a growing divergence between countries (many of them in the Mediterranean) which put religious orthodoxy above economic performance and those more open societies (mostly of the Atlantic seaboard) which tolerated outsiders and minorities of differing persuasions in the cause of economic growth.[73] In spite of all the complex and often confusing differences between countries and regions, cities and countryside, one has a strong sense that the end of the sixteenth century saw the turning of a crucial page in European history, from an old world to the new.

Notes: Chapter 1

1 T. Aston (ed.), *Crisis in Europe 1560–1660* (London, 1965), esp. chs 2–4.
2 cf. R. Hilton (ed.), *The Transition from Feudalism to Capitalism* (London, 1976).
3 G. Parker and L. M. Smith (eds), *The General Crisis of the Seventeenth Century* (London, 1978).

4 M. Roberts's review of Parker and Smith, *General Crisis*, in *English Historical Review*, vol. 95 (1980), p. 150.
5 I. Schöffer, 'Did Holland's Golden Age Coincide with a Period of Crisis?', in Parker and Smith, *General Crisis*, ch. 4; see also J. de Vries, *The Dutch Rural Economy in the Golden Age, 1500–1700* (London, 1974), p. 242; J. Thirsk, *Economic Policy and Projects* (Oxford, 1978), ch. 7.
6 For the 1560s see J. Elliott, 'Revolution and Continuity in early modern Europe', in Parker and Smith, *General Crisis*, p. 112; for the 1620s, R. Romano, 'Between the sixteenth and seventeenth centuries: the economic crisis of 1619–22', in Parker and Smith, op. cit., ch. 7; for the 1640s, Aston, *Crisis in Europe*, p. 59 and *passim*; R. B. Merriman, *Six Contemporaneous Revolutions* (Glasgow, 1937).
7 See below, pp. 44, 93–5, 157; Fr Mario Antonio de Camos, *Microcosmia o Gobierno universal del hombre cristiano* (Barcelona, 1592), cited in M. Herrero Garcia, *Ideas de los españoles del siglo XVII* (Madrid, 1966), p. 29 (I am grateful to Tony Thompson for this and some of the following references).
8 For example, *List and Analysis of State Papers, Foreign*, 1590–1, p. 371; T. Campanella, *A Discourse touching the Spanish Monarchy* (London, 1654), p. 9.
9 J. H. Elliott, *Imperial Spain 1469–1716* (London, 1963), pp. 279–95; B. Bennassar, *Valladolid au siècle d'or* (Paris, 1967), pp. 199–207.
10 J. Jacquart, *La Crise rurale en Île-de-France 1550–1670* (Paris, 1974), pp. 179–84.
11 E. P. Cheyney, *A History of England from the defeat of the Armada to the death of Elizabeth* (London, 1914–26), Vol. 2, chs 25–6; P. Clark, *English Provincial Society from the Reformation to the Revolution* (Hassocks, 1977), chs 7–8; G. Utterström 'Climatic fluctuations and population problems in early modern history', *Scandinavian Economic History Review*, vol. 3 (1955), pp. 26–32 and *passim*.
12 H. Kamen, *The Iron Century: Social Change in Europe 1550–1660* (London, 1971), pp. 335–6.
13 W. Abel, *Agricultural Fluctuations in Europe* (London, 1980), p. 147; Parker and Smith, *General Crisis*, pp. 196 ff.; P. Kriedte, *Peasants, Landlords and Merchant Capitalists* (Leamington, 1983), pp. 52, 61; Aston, *Crisis in Europe*, p. 78.
14 Discussed by D. Souden below, chapter 12.
15 Below, pp. 84 ff; Jacquart, *Crise rurale*, p. 182 and *passim*; G. Cabourdin, *Terre et Hommes en Lorraine 1550–1635: Toulois et Comté de Vaudémont* (Nancy, 1977), pp. 360, 384–8, 392–7.
16 Below, pp. 106 ff; E. le Roy Ladurie, *Les Paysans de Languedoc* (Paris, 1966), pp. 440 ff.
17 See below, B. Outhwaite and P. Clark, pp. 28–35 and 46–7; A. Appleby, *Famine in Tudor and Stuart England* (Liverpool, 1978), esp. chs 7–8.
18 *Register of the Privy Council of Scotland*, 1592–9, p. 163 and *passim*; M. Flinn (ed.), *Scottish Population History from the 17th century to the 1930s* (Cambridge, 1977), p. 117.
19 Below, pp. 31–2; also D. B. Quinn, *The Elizabethans and the Irish* (Ithaca, NY, 1966), pp. 134–40).
20 M. L. Fanchamps, *Recherches statistiques sur le problème annoires dans la principauté de Liège* (Liège, 1970), pp. 6, 36–9; H. van der Wee, *The Growth of the Antwerp Market and the European Economy* (Louvain, 1963), Vol. 2, pp. 249–50, 258–62.
21 Below, pp. 67–78.
22 Utterström, 'Climatic Fluctuations', pp. 26–30; see below, pp. 244–5.
23 Below, pp. 136 ff; see the discussion of these revolts by C. S. L. Davies below, pp. 249–50; also J. Berenger, 'La Révolte paysanne de Basse-Autriche de 1597', *Revue d'Histoire Économique et Sociale*, vol. 53 (1975), pp. 465–92.
24 Below, p. 197 (Sicily); p. 180 (Naples); pp. 158–9 (northern Italy). See also *List and Analysis of State Papers, Foreign*, 1591–2, pp. 437–8; J. Delumeau, *Vie économique et sociale de Rome dans la seconde moitié du XVIe siècle* (Paris, 1957–9), Vol. 1, pp. 405 ff.; Vol. 2, pp. 529 ff., 616 ff.
25 Below, p. 211; J. E. Gelabert Gonzalez, *Santiago y la tierra de Santiago de 1500 a 1640* (Corunna, 1982), pp. 20–1, 38 199–200; B. Bennassar, *Recherches sur les grandes épidémies dans le nord de l'Espagne à la fin du XVIe siècle* (Paris, 1969), pp. 62 ff.; R. Pike, *Aristocrats and Traders: Sevillian Society in the Sixteenth Century* (London, 1972), p. 20; J. Casey, *The*

Kingdom of Valencia in the Seventeenth Century (Cambridge, 1979), p. 14; A. de Oliveira, *A Vida economica e social de Coimbra de 1537 a 1640* (Coimbra, 1971–2), pp. 269–78.

26 A. G. Mankov, *Le Mouvement des prix dans l'état russe du XVIe siècle* (Paris, 1957), pp. 36–8; R. E. F. Smith, *Peasant Farming in Muscovy* (Cambridge, 1977), pp. 108, 144–8; J. T. Alexander, *Bubonic Plague in Early Modern Russia* (London, 1980), p. 17; J.–N. Biraben, *Les Hommes et la Peste en France et dans les pays européens et méditerranéens: I* (Paris, 1975), p. 149.

27 Below, pp. 248–9; also S. Olteanu, *Les Pays roumains à l'époque de Michel le Brave* (Bucharest, 1975); Utterström, 'Climatic Fluctuations', p. 40; M. A. Cook, *Population Pressure in Rural Anatolia 1450–1600* (London, 1972), pp. 30–44.

28 I am grateful for advice on climatic conditions in the late sixteenth century to Dr. T. Wigley and Dr A. Ogilvie of the Climatic Research Unit, University of East Anglia. See below, p. 45 (England); p. 31 (Ireland); pp. 74–5 (Netherlands); pp. 126–7 (Midi); p. 199 (Sicily); p. 214 (Spain). Gelabert Gonzalez, *Santiago*, pp. 20–1; Utterström, 'Climatic Fluctuations', pp. 25 ff.; A. E. J. Ogilvie, 'Two descriptions of sea-ice off Iceland from the 1590s', *Climate Monitor*, Vol. 9 (1979–80), pp. 5–10.

29 C. Pfister, 'An analysis of the Little Ice Age climate in Switzerland and its consequences for agricultural production', in T. M. L. Wigley *et al.* (eds), *Climate and History* (Cambridge, 1981), p. 238; E. Le Roy Ladurie and M. Baulant, 'Grape Harvests from the fifteenth through the nineteenth centuries', *Journal of Interdisciplinary History*, Vol. 10 (1979–80), pp. 839–49; C. Easton, *Les Hivers dans l'Europe occidentale* (Leyden, 1928), pp. 204–7).

30 E. Le Roy Ladurie, *Times of Feast, Times of Famine* (London, 1972), ch. 4; for differing views about the consequences of climatic adversity see J. de Vries, 'Measuring the impact of climate on history: the search for appropriate methodologies', *Journal of Interdisciplinary History*, vol. 10 (1979–80), pp. 618–30; and the articles by A. Appleby and J. D. Post, op. cit., pp. 645–63, 719–23.

31 See below, pp. 28–9: R. Baehrel, *Une Croissance: La Basse- Provence rurale* (Paris, 1961), p. 535; Delumeau, *Rome*, vol. 2, pp. 694–5; also pp. 616 ff. Below, pp. 199–200; exacerbating the problem in the Mediterranean was the famine in North Africa in 1592: Biraben, *Les Hommes et la Peste*, p. 150.

32 See Clark below, p. 48; P. Benedict, below, p. 92.

33 Abel, *Agricultural Fluctuations*, ch. 4; Appleby, *Famine*, chs 2–4; J. Thirsk (ed), *Agrarian History of England and Wales: IV* (Cambridge, 1967), pp. 19 ff.; below, pp. 212–13.

34 M. Aymard, *Venise, Raguse et le Commerce du Blé pendant la seconde moitié du XVIe siècle* (Paris, 1966), pp. 155–61; see below, pp. 58, 79; S. G. E. Lythe, 'Scottish Trade with the Baltic', in J. K. Eastham (ed.), *Economic Essays* (Dundee, 1955), pp. 72–3; below, p. 90; J. Topolski, 'Sixteenth-century Poland and the turning point in European economic development', in J. K. Fedorowicz (ed.), *A Republic of Nobles* (Cambridge, 1982), pp. 82–4; see below, pp. 58–9.

35 Below, p. 261; for the Midi, below, pp. 106–7; for northern France, p. 84; H. van der Wee, 'Typologie des crises et changements de structures aux Pays-Bas (XVe–XVIe siècles)', *Annales, Économies, Sociétés, Civilisations* (hereafter *Annales ESC*), vol. 18 (1963), pp. 222–3; for the recovery: E. Thoen, 'Warfare and the countryside: social and economic aspects of the military destruction in Flanders during the late Middle Ages and the early modern period', *The Low Countries History Yearbook*, vol. 13 (1980), pp. 28–36. Quinn, *Elizabethans and the Irish*, pp. 134–40; C. Falls, *Elizabeth's Irish Wars* (London, 1950), ch. 13 ff.

36 See the wide-ranging discussion by I. A. A. Thompson, below, p. 261. Below, pp. 26–7.

37 Biraben, *Les Hommes et la Peste*, Vol. 1, pp. 141, 147, 377 ff. For Souden's argument, see p. 237; for the contrary view see pp. 33–4 (Outhwaite) and p. 181 (P. Burke).

38 See pp. 137, 160, 170.

39 For taxes see below, pp. 109 ff (France); pp. 219–20 (Spain); pp. 161–2 (Italy). For the coin problem in Ireland: *Calendar of State Papers Irish*, 1601–3, p. 228 and *passim*; in the Midi, below, pp. 111–12.

40 Quoted in D. Zanetti, 'L'approvisionnement de Pavie au XVIe siècle', *Annales ESC*, vol. 18 (1963), p. 62.
41 Below, ch. 12.
42 Pike, *Aristocrats and Traders*, pp. 17 ff. (Spain); van der Wee, *Antwerp*, Vol. 2, pp. 249, 262; also L. Noordegraaf, below, pp. 76–7 (Low Countries); below, p. 50 (England); p. 52 (Germany); pp. 140–1 (France); p. 166 (Italy).
43 J. Jacquart, 'Le Poids démographique de Paris et de l'Île-de-France au XVIe siècle', *Annales de démographie historique* (1980), p. 95; R. Finlay, *Population and Metropolis: the Demography of London* (Cambridge, 1981), pp. 51, 60–1; for Naples and Rome, see below, pp. 180–1; for Palermo, pp. 200–1.
44 For instance, in England, below, pp. 44 ff; France, pp. 96 ff; Italy, pp. 165 ff. See also Abel, *Agricultural Fluctuations*, p. 134.
45 See below, p. 293; Clark, *English Provincial Society* pp. 239–40; R. Gascon, 'Économie et pauvreté au XVIe et XVIIe siècles: Lyon, ville exemplaire et prophétique', in M. Mollat (ed.), *Études sur l'histoire de la pauvreté (Moyen Âge–XVIe siècle)* (Paris, 1974), Vol. 2, p. 755.
46 Gascon, 'Économie et pauvreté', p. 752; M. Baulant, 'Prix et salaires à Paris au XVIe siècle', *Annales ESC*, vol. 31 (1976), pp. 981 ff; van der Wee, *Antwerp*, Vol. 3, p. 94; G. Vigo, 'Real wages of the working class in Italy: building workers' wages (14th to 18th century)', *Journal of European Economic History*, vol. 3 (1974), p. 388. See also, for the Netherlands, Noordegraaf, below, pp. 69 ff.
47 See below, pp. 38–9; see also Schilling, below, pp. 142–3. Abel, *Agricultural Fluctuations*, p. 142.
48 Noordegraaf, below, p. 75; also J. A. Faber, 'Times of dearth and famines in pre-industrial Netherlands', *The Low Countries History Yearbook*, vol. 13 (1980), p. 56; N. Davidson, below, p. 162; D. Sella, *Crisis and Continuity: the Economy of Spanish Lombardy in the Seventeenth Century* (London, 1979), pp. 36 ff.; Casey, p. 217; but see D. Ringrose, 'The impact of a new capital city: Madrid, Toledo and New Castile, 1560–1660', *Journal of Economic History*, vol. 33 (1973), pp. 784 ff.
49 Below, pp. 245 ff. For the League in Paris and the rather acrimonious debate over the extent of its revolutionary character see J. H. M. Salmon, 'The Paris Sixteen 1584–94', *Journal of Modern History*, vol. 44 (1972), pp. 545–73; D. Richet, 'Aspects socio-culturels de conflits religieux à Paris dans la seconde moitié du XVIe siècle', *Annales ESC*, vol. 32 (1977), pp. 764–83; E. Bar-Navi, 'La Ligue parisienne (1585–94)', *French Historical Studies*, vol. 11 (1979–80), pp. 29–57; R. Descimon, 'La Ligue à Paris (1585–1594): une révision', *Annales ESC*, vol. 37 (1982), pp. 72–111. For French and Austrian peasant risings see below, pp. 119 ff, 249–50.
50 The mutinies in England are discussed below, p. 55; G. Parker, *The Army of Flanders and the Spanish Road 1567–1659* (Cambridge, 1972), pp. 290–2.
51 See below, pp. 52 ff, for England; for references to riots in the Dutch Republic and Germany see Noordegraaf, p. 75; and Schilling, p. 150.
52 See below, p. 167; for the Midi, below, p. 120; van der Wee, *Antwerp*, Vol. 2, p. 277 (Brabant); H. Inalcik, *The Ottoman Empire: The Classical Age 1300–1600* (London, 1973), pp. 50–1 (Anatolia).
53 See below, p. 167, for Italy; for England, J. S. Cockburn, 'The nature and incidence of crime in England 1559–1625: a preliminary survey', in J. S. Cockburn (ed.), *Crime in England 1550–1800* (London, 1977), p. 53; see also C. S. L. Davies, below, p. 245.
54 C. Larner, *Enemies of God: The Witch-hunt in Scotland* (London, 1981), pp. 60–2, 70–2; A. Macfarlane, *Witchcraft in Tudor and Stuart England* (London, 1970), p. 28; H. C. E. Midelfort, *Witchhunting in Southwestern Germany 1562–1684* (Stanford, Calif., 1972), pp. 72–3, 86–7, 91 ff.; also Schilling, below, p. 151; M.-S. Dupont-Bouchat *et al.*, *Prophètes et Sorciers dans les Pays-Bas XVIe–XVIIIe siècles* (Paris, 1978), pp. 172, 177; Le Roy Ladurie, *Paysans de Languedoc*, pp. 407–11; see also the discussion by C. S. L. Davies, below, p. 245.
55 For the response of the authorities to social problems see in particular the essays by Clark, pp. 56–61; Noordegraaf, pp. 77–8; Davidson, pp. 168–70; and Casey, pp. 221–4; also generally Pullan, pp. 290 ff.

56 The costs of war are discussed by Thompson, pp. 266 ff; for the political reverberations see, for instance, Clark, *English Provincial Society*, pp. 249 ff.
57 J. Walter and K. Wrightson, 'Dearth and the social order in early modern England', *P&P*, no. 71 (1976), pp. 31 ff.
58 Below, Burke, pp. 185 ff; Schilling, pp. 149–51.
59 Below, Thompson, p. 276; Schilling, p. 151.
60 Below, p. 80; J. E. Neale, *Essays in Elizabethan History* (London, 1958), pp. 14–15.
61 For the growth of Dutch agricultural specialisation see de Vries, *Dutch Rural Economy*, ch. 4; Thirsk, *Economic Policy and Projects*, p. 161; for the Midi, see below, p. 119.
62 Benedict, below, pp. 96–7; H. van der Wee and E. van Cauwenberghe (eds), *Productivity of Land and Agricultural Innovation in the Low Countries* (Louvain, 1978), pp. 14, 47; T. Davies, below, p. 200; Burke, pp. 185–8; Fedorowicz, *Republic of Nobles*, chs 4, 6.
63 Benedict, below, p. 97; see also Cabourdin, *Terre et hommes*, pp. 387 ff.; Casey, below, pp. 214 ff; Davidson, p. 165; T. Davies, p. 195; van der Wee and Cauwenberghe, *Productivity of Land*, p. 47.
64 Casey, below, pp. 209–11; P. M. M. Klep, 'Regional disparities in Brabantine urbanisation before and after the Industrial Revolution (1374–1970)', in P. Bairoch and M. Levy-Leboyer (eds), *Disparities in Economic Development since the Industrial Revolution* (London, 1981), pp. 260 ff.; E. A. Wrigley and R. S. Schofield, *The Population History of England 1541–1871* (London, 1981), p. 528; for Italy see Davidson, below, p. 159; for Germany, Schilling, p. 138. Benedict, below, pp. 95–6. See the discussion by Souden, pp. 234 ff.
65 For the negative impact of London's growth on the English population see E. A. Wrigley, 'A simple model of London's importance in changing English society and economy, 1650–1750', *P & P*, no. 37 (1967), pp. 46–8.
66 J. de Vries, 'Patterns of urbanization in pre-industrial Europe 1500–1800', in H. Schmal (ed.), *Patterns of European Urbanisation since 1500* (London, 1981), pp. 87 ff.; Jacquart, 'Le poids demographique', pp. 91 ff.; Ringrose, 'The impact of a new capital city', p. 765; de Vries, *Dutch Rural Economy*, pp. 89–90.
67 P. Francastel (ed.), *L'urbanisme de Paris et l'Europe 1600–1680* (Paris, 1969), pp. 29–30, 47 ff.; G. L. Burke, *The Making of Dutch Towns* (London, 1956), pp. 147–53 (Amsterdam).
68 De Vries, 'Patterns of urbanization', pp. 87 ff.; in the Spanish Netherlands the period from the late sixteenth century into the early seventeenth century was a time of de-urbanisation (with the notable exception of Brussels): van der Wee and Cauwenberghe, *Productivity of Land*, p. 14. For the problems of German towns see Schilling, below, pp. 143 ff; see also Davidson, pp. 162 ff (Italy); Benedict, pp. 98–9 (N. France). R. Pillorget, *Les Mouvements insurrectionels de Provence entre 1596 et 1715* (Paris, 1975), pp. 207 ff., 243; Sella, *Crisis and Continuity*, p. 36 and *passim*.
69 See Thompson, below, pp. 271–2, R. J. W. Evans, *Rudolf II and his World* (Oxford, 1973), p. 41 and *passim*.
70 Below, Noordegraaf, pp. 78–9; also R. T. Rapp, 'The unmaking of the Mediterranean trade hegemony: international trade rivalry and the commercial revolution', *Journal of Economic History*, vol. 35 (1975), pp. 500–1. H. Rebel, *Peasant Classes: The Bureaucratization of Property and Family Relations under Early Habsburg Absolutism 1511–1636* (Princeton, NJ, 1983), pp. 126–7, 167. Below, Davidson, pp. 170–1; Benedict, p. 99.
71 Below, Pullan, pp. 289 ff; Clark, pp. 56 ff; Davidson, p. 162 and *passim*.
72 Below, p. 304.
73 Below, pp. 296–7.

2 *Dearth, the English Crown and the 'Crisis of the 1590s'*

R. B. OUTHWAITE

While the idea of the 'crisis of the 1590s' has been in circulation for some time, there can be no denying that for historians of England Peter Clark's vivid and searching account of the many problems afflicting Kentish society in the late sixteenth century must be the starting point for discussion.[1] The impact of that 'succession of military, fiscal, economic and demographic problems' was there discussed in a particular local context; therein, indeed, lay much of the novelty of his treatment. The primary object of this chapter, however, is to view the experience from the centre, and to offer some reflections on how central government – the Crown and its ministers – saw, and reacted to, the events of these years. In doing so it is hard to avoid the force of one of Clark's observations: that whilst the great dearth of the mid-1590s may have been the most dramatic economic event of the period, it was only one of a succession of problems, and the duration of this whole period of difficulty coincided generally with the years in which England was in open conflict with Spain. Although the great dearth of the mid-1590s presented acute problems to government, it was not the sole problem that confronted the Crown. Nor, it will be argued, were its general consequences as serious as they might have been, and a discussion of why this should be concludes this chapter.

I

In one respect at least English government underwent a striking change. Age and illness wreaked havoc amongst the leading political figures of the day. In 1590 Elizabeth reached her fifty-seventh birthday and as that decade advanced her advisers had to think more and more, but always covertly, about the matter of the succession. Speculation was rife. Thomas Wilson wrote at the end of the decade: 'this crown is not like to fall to the ground for want of heads that claim to wear it, but upon whose head it will fall is by many doubted'.[2] The succession was always likely to be influenced by those closest to the monarch and this gave added point to that struggle for power and riches which was influenced also by demographic chance in late Elizabethan England. Of the fifteen Privy Councillors alive at the end of the Armada year, no fewer than eleven were dead by the end of 1596 and twelve of them by August 1598. Chancellor of the Exchequer Mildmay died in 1589; Secretary Walsingham, Comptroller Croft, Lord Marshal Shrewsbury, and Warwick of the Ordnance all went in 1590; Lord Chancellor Hatton succumbed in 1591 and Derby, the Lord Steward, in 1593; Treasurer of the Household Knollys, Lord Chamberlain Hunsdon, Cobham of the Cinque Ports, and the Latin Secretary Wolley all died in the devastating year of 1596; and Burghley, the Queen's oldest and most faithful adviser, followed in 1598. What is more, many of the post-1588 additions to the Privy Council failed to outlive the Queen: the soldierly Perrot died in 1592, Vice-Chamberlain Heneage in 1595, Lord Keeper Puckering in 1596, Lord North in 1600, and Essex, her greatest hope and disappointment, in 1601.[3] It is an extraordinary succession of deaths. Not only did the filling of these vacancies absorb a great deal of the time and political energies of those who survived, and especially those of the venerable Burghley, already seventy when the decade opened, but the untried and inexperienced nature of some of the newcomers added to the uncertainties and anxieties which are so characteristic of the closing years of Elizabeth's reign. In the event many of the burdens of policy-making imposed by events were shouldered by the ageing Lord Treasurer and it is perhaps not surprising that there is little novelty in the Crown's reaction to this succession of crises. He had seen much of it before, as his successors were to see much of it again.

II

The feelings of relief engendered by the defeat of the Armada in 1588 soon passed and were indeed replaced by repeated fears of further Spanish invasions. As a result English foreign policy in these years was persistently shaped by the desire to support anti-Spanish factions in France and the Low Countries, to control those Channel and Atlantic ports from which invasion forces might depart, and to quell unrest on English soil and possessions that could conceivably be exploited by the Spaniards. War and diplomacy, possible invasions and English military expeditions, are ever-present events in these years. The energy of administrators was continually absorbed by military matters: how and where to mobilise soldiers and sailors, how to provision them with food and munitions, how to pay for these supplies, how long such actions could safely be proceeded with. Strategy and economics constantly fought each other.

Almost every year after 1588 produced fears of invasion. The English raid on Portugal in 1589 was partly intended to head off such an event; in

1590 there were anti-invasion musters in southern England; troop movements from Spain to the Low Countries, Brittany and Normandy from 1590 to 1598 produced successive rumours that these movements were the prelude to invasions of England; such rumours were especially rife in 1592 and 1594; in 1595 a Spanish raid on Cornwall produced fresh alarms; in June and July 1596 the maritime counties were again put in a state of defence, whilst the English fleet ventured to Cadiz, and in fact an Armada did set out for England in October of that year, only to be savaged by gales after four days out at sea; in 1596 the sounds of Spanish cannon besieging Calais were actually heard in Greenwich; in July 1597 another attempt was made, under Essex, to destroy the Spanish fleet in its own harbours before it destroyed England; this attempt failed to engage the enemy, which in turn sent a further Armada against England in October 1597, once again to be thwarted by the weather. As Cheyney rightly said, 'the defeat of the Armada in 1588 was the beginning not the close of the great duel between England and Spain'.[4]

These threats, both imagined and real, produced a succession of expensive counter-strategies. England continually supported the Dutch rebels; five expeditions were sent also to Normandy and Brittany from 1589 to 1595; three punitive fleets were sent to Portugal, Spain and the Azores; from 1594 onwards reinforcements were sent to crush rebellion in Ireland, a rebellion which took serious root in 1597–8, leading to Essex's expensive failure to crush O'Neill in 1599. Such actions produced a succession of logistical problems and, more important, put the Crown's finances under very great pressure.

It is difficult to cost these measures precisely, partly because the Crown tried by various means – 'coat and conduct money' and 'ship money' – to throw some of the cost on to others. But even so it has been estimated that resisting the first Armada cost the Crown £161,000; that between 1585 and 1603 £1,420,000 was sent to prosecute the war in the Low Countries; that a further £424,000 went for operations in France over the same years; that prize-hunting, naval expeditions and other extraordinary disbursements on the fleet cost at least £575,000; that closing the back door by means of the pension given to James VI of Scotland accounted for £51,000 up to 1596; and on top of all this there was Ireland, upon which Elizabeth expended £1,924,000 from 1593 to her death. Altogether these various operations may have cost £4,555,000, and they were by no means the only items of extraordinary expenditure incurred by the Crown in these years.[5]

Parliamentary taxation brought some relief, but, as is well known, it was insufficient to foot the entire bill. Taxes were granted in 1585, 1587, 1589, 1593, 1597 and 1601, but only about a half of the last grant was collected before Elizabeth's death. Bearing this in mind, the entire yield of lay and clerical taxes in the era of conflict with Spain may be put at

£1,986,000,[6] or some 44 per cent of the extraordinary expenditure itemised above. The remainder had to be provided by other means, among which we should first consider the surplus on the ordinary account.

At the time that Burghley became Lord Treasurer in 1572 the gross ordinary revenue of the Crown was around £260,000 and its annual ordinary expenditure around £186,000, leaving an ordinary surplus of £74,000 per year. In the years immediately after Burghley's death in 1598 the gross ordinary revenue stood at about £360,000, out of which was ordinarily disbursed about £260,000, leaving a surplus of about £100,000 per year.[7] Even if an annual surplus of £100,000 was available throughout the period 1585–1603, its gross yield at £1,800,000 would have been marginally lower than that of the parliamentary taxes, still leaving some 17 per cent of that itemised extraordinary expenditure unprovided for.

Acute financial stringency thus characterised these years, though within the period it bit with varying force. Deficit financial situations produced a host of expedients: calls to Parliament for taxation, attempts to get revenue officials to turn balances in their possession into the Exchequer, leaving bills unpaid where this could be done with safety, borrowing to anticipate revenues and bridge deficits, further borrowing to manage these loans, and, frequently the last resort, the sale of royal land and other capital assets to reduce the debt. Borrowing in these years was not entered into lightly[8] and was strictly confined to the years 1588–93 and 1597–1603. The selling of Crown land, very much a last resort device, was undertaken by commissions set up for this purpose in 1589, 1599 and 1601. Robert Freake, the Teller appointed to receive the proceeds of the 1589 sale, was eventually charged with the receipt of £131,842,[9] whilst the proceeds of the two later sales entered into the normal course of receipt in the Exchequer and realised over £405,000 before Elizabeth's death.[10] It was insufficient to clear even the formal debt – £180,000 was still owing on privy seals and on mortgage when James came to the throne.

The best single measure of royal financial stringency that we have available, however, is the nominal balance remaining in the hands of the four Tellers of the Exchequer at the two accounting days of Michaelmas and Lady Day each year. Although there are gaps in the relevant record series, enough remains to give a good impression of what might be called the 'cash-flow problem' in the late Elizabethan Exchequer. Table 2.1[11] gives the balance at Michaelmas each year from 1584 onwards.

These figures must be assessed in the light of the information previously given about the timing of borrowing and land selling, devices which were strictly confined to the years 1588–93 and 1597–1603. The generally low balances of these particular years thus incorporate the benefits of these financial devices and indeed explain why they were so necessary. The situation became particularly acute from 1598 onwards as Irish

Table 2.1 *Balances Remaining in the Hands of the Tellers of the Exchequer*

Mich	£	Mich	£
1584	298,954	1594	74,554
1585	287,362	1595	131,250
1586	274,454	1596	101,940
1587	154,597	1597	26,003
1588	55,094	1598	17,045
1589	29,950	1599	9,206
1590	33,272	1600	11,112
1591	25,368	1601	10,559
1592	25,159	1602	15,882
1593	28,187	At Elizabeth's death	60,663

expenditure mounted greatly. Whereas Exchequer issues for Ireland in the year 1597–8 had totalled £108,000, a figure greatly in excess of previous years, in 1598–9 they climbed to £336,000 and never dropped below £263,000 in any whole year thereafter.[12] Thus in the two years from Michaelmas 1597 to Michaelmas 1599 Elizabeth consumed very nearly the whole of the multiple lay and clerical taxes granted in 1597, grants which eventually realised £451,000. It was expenditure upon this scale that lay behind the privy seal loans of 1597 and 1601, the loans from the Corporation of London in 1598–9 and from a London syndicate in 1601, and behind the desperate land sales of 1599 and 1601, during which the Crown was forced to let prices slip to stimulate business.[13] Even so, as Table 2.1 reveals, the balance was frequently perilously small and resort was made to a good many dubious devices to make ends meet. In 1599, for example, 'in respect the Remaines were so low at that time', the Crown made use of £3,000 which had been left by Burghley privately *in deposito* with Exchequer Teller Robert Taylor, and in 1600 it seized for its own use certain plate and money which had also been left with Taylor by Sir Francis Knollys. In October of that year it made plans to sell off its own old and unfashionable plate.[14] In the closing months of the reign Lord Treasurer Buckhurst had occasion to write to the Lord Mayor of London about the repayment of the loan from the city. 'I heare that there is a brute amongst you', he wrote, 'that her Majestie purposeth present to repaie the 60,000*l*. I wold to God there were meanes to do it but he that began that rumor noe doubt did apprehend it in his dreame, for in veritate there is noe possible meanes at this present to performe it.'[15]

III

The worst periods of financial stringency were clearly the years from 1588 to 1593 and from 1597 to the end of the reign. The respite between 1593 and 1597 coincided with the worst of the great dearth years of that decade. The wheat price series that we have available, shown in Table 2.2, tell some of this story. The poor harvest of 1594 caused wheat prices to leap everywhere. In some places, such as Cambridge, Oxford and Nottingham, the average was more or less double that of the preceding year. In the harvest year 1595–6 they rose still further in many places and then peaked almost everywhere in the terrible year 1596–7. In 1597–8 they fell almost everywhere, but the level was still uniformly higher than it had been even in 1594–5. It was not until the year 1598–9 that prices descended to near pre-1594 levels, though not apparently in London.

Table 2.2 *Average Wheat Prices: Shillings per Quarter*[16]

	Harvest year beginning at Michaelmas									
Place	*1590*	*1591*	*1592*	*1593*	*1594*	*1595*	*1596*	*1597*	*1598*	*1599*
Cambridge	18·76	17·10	15·83	18·32	35·40	35·85	41·07	39·67	22·87	23·89
Norwich	–	–	18·00	24·00	–	42·50	–	–	28·00	24·00
London	25·56	18·56	17·61	25·62	36·56	40·34	47·61	44·40	42·40	25·80
Oxford	–	16·33	14·95	19·86	37·03	33·81	55·59	44·69	25·07	21·23
Exeter	20·88	17·76	22·41	28·63	38·88	32·00	62·94	39·92	19·76	20·55
Nottingham	–	17·12	12·88	16·00	33·68	33·33	44·00	47·44	24·00	24·00
Worksop	31·11	18·00	18·44	22·67	26·70	33·73	46·30	55·14	–	32·00
York	26·00	24·00	20·00	28·90	36·00	44·00	64·00	42·86	28·00	31·00
Beveridge English average	23·75	18·41	17·52	23·00	34·87	37·09	50·07	46·18	28·03	25·39

That the 'national average' wheat price does not tell the whole story is evident in several respects. Literary evidence, for example, suggests strongly that complaints about dearth began a year earlier than is suggested by the Beveridge 'English average wheat price' series and Professor Hoskins's harvest classifications which drew on that series. Hoskins had classified the overall English wheat harvest of 1593 as 'good' whilst noting that it was below average in the west.[17] There was, however, talk by Lord Cobham of 'the present dearth of corn' in November 1593, whilst in the following January the Aldermen of London ordered that a letter should be sent to Burghley asking for a ban on exports of grain.[18] There were complaints of 'dearth and scarcity' from Berwick in July 1594 and at the same time from London where it was reported that 'the poorer sorte . . . are cheefely pinched with the dearthe'.[19]

Table 2.3 reproduces some rather slenderly based evidence about the movement of grain prices other than wheat, though an alternative wheat average is included to impart perspective. Clearly some of the clamour which occurred in 1593–4 may have been induced by the 33 per cent increase in barley prices which took place then, though London alarms probably owed more to the 45 per cent increase which took place in metropolitan wheat prices over the same period (see Table 2.2). What Table 2.3 also reveals, however, is how in the worst years the prices of the cheaper grains (barley, oats and rye) rose more steeply than wheat, as demands shifted from expensive to less expensive cereals. Clearly 1596–7 was a terrible year, with the prices of the lesser grains rising dramatically.

Table 2.3 *Average Indexed Prices of Particular Grains (1450–99 = 100)*[20]

Harvest year	*Wheat*	*Barley*	*Oats*	*Rye*
1590–1	394	720	757	–
1591–2	304	451	573	–
1592–3	295	287	392	210
1593–4	388	379	417	216
1594–5	578	520	765	–
1595–6	607	740	574	801
1596–7	811	971	1148	1227
1597–8	746	779	718	869
1598–9	462	545	535	531
1599–1600	407	617	498	706

To argue, however, that the Crown's financial problems were fewer in the years of dearth from 1593 to 1598 than in the years immediately before or after is not to argue that this lessening of financial pressure was primarily due to the dearth. The dearth did not, for example, produce any significant increase in the flow to the Exchequer of the two principal components of the ordinary revenue – the customs and land revenues. Whilst it is true that proceeds from these two sources were higher in the five dearth years than in the five years which immediately followed (from Michaelmas 1598 to Michaelmas 1603), this was mostly due to the heavy land sales which took place from 1599 and to the collapse of customs receipts in the Exchequer year ending in 1603.[21] The revenue system was inflexible: rentals were not adjusted to take account of short-term shifts in land values, and customs duties went unchanged for long periods. Some of these duties were also farmed.

Changes in prices probably had greater repercussions on the Crown's spending, though purchasing arrangements were designed to cushion it from the full effects of sudden price rises. It is hard to deny though that the dearth of the years 1593–8 created a whole series of perplexing problems for government, especially for one attempting to fight enemies abroad and keep the peace at home. Two such problems merit further discussion: both provoked a great stream of complaints to the Crown's principal officers, and to Burghley especially.

IV

A minor but extremely persistent and irritating problem was presented by the provisioning needs of the town and military garrison of Berwick. Its plight, advertised in a flood of complaints to the Lord Treasurer, was for it to be situated at the most northerly point on the east coast of England, in a generally grain-deficient region so that it had to be victualled by sea, and also to be subjected to bitter disputes between its officers. Its predicament became severe in the dearth years, and its acting governor, John Carey, tended to blame the official victualler, Robert Vernon, who in turn tended to pass on the blame to local magistrates, who held up supplies he had purchased elsewhere, or on to the Queen's financial officers, who would not make prompt payment or allow him realistic sums with which to purchase provisions in these difficult times. The garrison was a sizeable one, consisting of about 1,000 men, their wives and children, and those horses which were very necessary for effective policing of the borders.[22] These horses also required provisioning, as Carey complained to Burghley in December 1594. The garrison had been to see him, he reported, and the soldiers were asserting that they would either have to sell their horses or let them starve, such was the shortage of provender for them.[23] As often occurred, the situation eased somewhat in the summer months as ships were able to reach them with supplies, but then it tended to deteriorate sharply in the autumn and winter months as the weather made communications difficult. Thus in September 1596 Carey reported to Burghley that there was 'alredie a great death growen by reason of darthe and scarsetie in this countrey'. By the following March he was reporting that the dearth had 'bred a verey great deathe amongest us, in so much as we dey vii or viii a weke, ye and summe tymes ii and iii a daye, wiche is thoughte to be onley bey ouer scarstey and the illnes of that wiche is ouer bred, beinge as ill as horse bred and moer unholsome'.[24] In December 1597 the garrison was again threatening to sell its horses to the Scots, and asserting that the soldiers must either stay and die of famine or leave the town and go begging.[25] The victuallers were inclined to report a more comfortable state of affairs, but Carey's tale of mounting deaths in 1596 and 1597 is borne out by the Berwick burial register.[26]

If things were bad in Berwick, however, they were far, far worse in Ireland, where as we have seen English soldiers and money were being sent from 1594 to strengthen increasingly beleaguered garrisons as the Irish revolt spread. The English fought there under grave disadvantages.

Their troops were mostly conscripts – volunteers preferred the richer pickings of continental warfare – but they were led by seasoned officers. These officers had learned to fight, however, in the Low Countries and in France, where campaigning was relatively static and dominated by siege warfare. In Ireland they faced a mobile and, under O'Neill, a well trained soldiery, who were skilful, elusive, and frequently indistinguishable from the native peasantry. Moreover, whilst English garrisons totalling a few thousand had good prospects of living off locally purchased and pillaged supplies, forces many times larger such as that army eventually assembled under Essex, nominally comprising 16,000 foot and 1,300 horsemen, required to be provisioned from England. Winds were often contrary, however, for ships waiting to cross to Ireland and victuals could spoil in long transit. The terrain in Ireland and lines of communication were generally difficult, involving the traverse of bog, mountains and woods, and the English had to combat an enemy skilled in the art of ambushing. Artillery and heavy horses were positive disadvantages in this sort of country, liable to sink and slow down the columns.

All this is well known and vividly related in the standard accounts of these Irish wars, but what is not fully appreciated in these otherwise admirable accounts is the abnormality of the climatic experience of the years preceding 1598 and also perhaps that the policy of mutual devastation of the Irish countryside began well before the era of Mountjoy, with whose campaigns such policies are usually associated.[27] Together these two forces, the one natural and the other human, combined to wreak havoc and cause endless problems for the Crown's administrators.

There were complaints about the backwardness of the Irish harvest in late September 1594 and more or less continuous rain through the succeeding winter brought sickness and death to the English forces there.[28] The need to provision these troops from England necessitated the imposition of controls over marketing there, as well as bringing a succession of complaints from provisioning areas such as Cheshire.[29] The rain in the summer of 1595 made even summer campaigning difficult, as Sir Henry Wallop reported in August.[30] Beer was particularly difficult to supply to troops in the field so that the soldiers were driven to drinking water 'which doth breed in them many diseases' and much rancour.[31] From October 1595 the complaints of scarcity issuing from the garrisons reach a new pitch of intensity: we are at our wits' end, Sir John Norris reported. The harvest there was spoiled and the rains apparently unrelenting.[32] The summer and autumn of 1596 were equally inhospitable,[33] and by October there was talk of appalling dearth, produced partly by the spoiling activities of the Irish.[34] 'The ground', reported Maurice Kiffin in November 1596, 'is laid waste, and in a manner desolate, yielding neither food for man nor forage for beast. The dearth and scarcity of all things is incredible.'[35] 'The Pale', reported Sir Conyers Clifford in the January following, 'is miserably poor, and the people of it desperate by the famine they fear to endure' – a tale Maurice Kiffin was to support in February when he wrote, 'Whole countries, even within the English Pale, be left waste without habitation or tillage . . . Between the rebels on the one side, and our own soldiers . . . all is devoured and destroyed.' In March he reported of the hunger-starved soldiers that 'they die wretchedly and woefully in the streets and highways, far less regarded than any beasts', and the same was true of the populace in the Pale, as Sir Geoffrey Fenton and others related in April and May.[36] Kiffin restrained his own men from their customary 'cess and spoil', a thing difficult to perform in 'this most miserable time of extreme penury and famine, when so many dead hungerstarven carcases of men and women lie spread up and down the fields and ways, and when both the soldiers and himself did eat horseflesh'. The land was left untilled, so no harvest could be expected to relieve the situation.[37]

This, as far as the professional soldiers were concerned, was the most hated war of their era: England's Vietnam. The country, the elements, the general populace and adversaries skilled in the arts of guerilla warfare were all pitted against them. No wonder the upright Lord Burgh complained of Tyrone that 'for as he is the dishonestest rebel of the world so is he the most cowardly, never making good any fight, but bogring with his shot, and flying from bush to bush', and Sir Calisthenes Brooke could plead and entreat with Robert Cecil to put him in some other war than this, 'the dullest and obscurest war our nation serves in'.[38]

Complaints of dearth in Ireland continued through 1597 into 1598, when by the summer and autumn the provisioning situation improved.[39] This coincided with improvement in England and begs the thought that Essex's large-scale invasion early in 1599 could hardly have occurred before it did, and though the size of that army meant that complaints about provisioning persisted, its progress was not hampered by shortages to anything like the extent that previous campaigns there had been.

Dearth, therefore, severely hampered English military operations from 1593 to 1598, and it is tempting also to argue that these military operations made matters worse rather than better for the English population at large. That temptation ought to be resisted, however, for although there are reasonably clear adverse effects – such as the severe local shortages created in the provisioning and embarkation areas, and the disease and chaos that accompanied returning soldiers – possible benefits were derived from the imposition in England of those measures of internal and external control of marketing associated with the Book of Orders.[40] This was issued by the Privy Council in November 1594, reissued in October 1595 with some additional instructions attached, and the Orders thereafter remained effectively in force throughout the whole duration of the grain crisis.[41] Benefits there no doubt were: some communities would profit through more assured supplies and lower prices but at what cost to consumers elsewhere is impossible to decide; the complexities of the interrelationships between Conciliar policy, its patchy local implementation, and its more general consequences are awesome and will not be pursued here. Instead this chapter concludes with some general observations about the relationships of dearth and death and the relative severity of the mortality experience in late Elizabethan England.

V

A number of things might lead one to expect a close relationship between dearth and death in these years. One such thing might be the Hoskins view of the social and economic structure of early Tudor English society:

> In a country in which between one-half and two-thirds of the population were wage-earners, and a considerable proportion of the remainder subsistence farmers; in which about one-third lived below the poverty-line and another third lived on or barely above it; in which the working-class spent fully 80 to 90 per cent of their incomes upon food and drink; in such a country the harvest was the fundamental fact of economic life.[42]

Another might be the view of Adam Smith, as elaborated by T. S. Ashton for an eighteenth-century England where labourers were perhaps more comfortably situated, that harvest failures would either reduce wage rates or, more likely, reduce the amount of work available at a given rate, and so cause the disposable income of many wage-earners to fluctuate inversely (or perversely as Smith said) with prices.[43] A third line of argument might take account of some developments in the sixteenth-century economy. It is possible that in many areas population advanced more rapidly than agricultural productivity, so that rising agricultural prices severely curbed real wages; that there were growing problems of unemployment and underemployment for labourers; that small farmers, whose numbers in many areas may well have been increasing, not declining, were precariously placed to survive dearth years; that not a few towns grew substantially in size; and that some agricultural regions were pulled out of grain self-sufficiency by specialisation in animal farming or in industry. Such groups and populations might withstand an occasional dearth year but not an unbroken succession of them such as occurred in the mid-1590s. Finally we ought perhaps to note that the most authoritative scientific survey that we have of the complex interrelationships between starvation and disease insists, quite unambiguously, 'that nutritional deficiencies generally reduce the capacity of the host to resist the consequences of infection. An aggravation of disease, or synergism, is the expected result in man whenever nutritional deficiency is sufficiently severe.'[44] It is possible also that the links between nutritional deficiency and death may not be entirely one-way or entirely physiological – running from deficiency to disease and being the result of waning defence mechanisms or of people succumbing to enteric diseases as they were driven to eat disregarded, perhaps even discarded, foodstuffs. It is in the nature of such synergistic relationships that 'infectious disease nearly always makes co-existing malnutrition worse',[45] and economic and social historians would add that if epidemics arose in dearth situations they were likely to exacerbate the situation in a variety of ways. At the family level the death or incapacity of a breadwinner could precipitate acute poverty, and at a wider social level epidemics could disrupt the organisation of trade and industry. Thus in August 1597, poor Berwick, already fearing that it was ill provided to meet the coming winter, reported that plague had broken out in the surrounding country areas 'so as we nether dare soffer aney of the conterey to come unto us, nether dare we not kepe aney markett wherbey to have aney susteynans out of the conterey'.[46] Finally, with migration swelling in years of dearth and epidemics, it is little wonder that contemporaries became alarmed about vagrants and *inter multa alia* their role as possible agents of contagion.[47]

Two historians have recently argued strongly that large parts of England did suffer in these years real subsistence crises and that the growth of population was set back by soaring mortality. One is the late Professor Appleby, who demonstrated vividly the great suffering undoubtedly experienced in Cumberland and Westmorland in the years 1596–8, but who was convinced also that the dearth produced 'extreme hardship to most – perhaps all – of England' and that even London suffered rising deaths.[48] The other is Dr Slack, whose interesting general survey of mortality crises and epidemics in the sixteenth century argued 'that every bad harvest appears to have been followed by a period of high mortality', and that 'the crisis of 1597 . . . was undoubtedly a national rather than a purely localized phenomenon'.[49]

Some further evidence is assembled in Table 2.4. Column 1 lists Bowden's index numbers for the prices of 'all grains' for 'harvest years' from Michaelmas 1585 onwards; Column 2 the total 'corrected' number of burials in each calendar year in those parishes that entered into Wrigley and Schofield's recent, massive and complex reconstruction of the course of English population change from 1541 to 1871; and Column 3 the Wrigley-Schofield estimates of the Crude Death Rate in each of these calendar years.[50] The food crisis of the 1590s began, we have argued, late in 1593 or early in 1594 and prices did not subside until late 1598. Table 2.4 shows that the total of deaths and the Crude Death Rate rose to high levels in 1593, and although both fell back sharply in the two succeeding years the relentless nature of the famine brought the return of high mortality in the two years 1597 and 1598. From that point, however, the death total subsided as prices fell.

Table 2.4 *Grain Prices and Mortality 1585–99*

	1 *Index no. of 'all grains' in harvest year (1450–99 = 100)*		2 *Total no. of burials in Cambridge sample in calendar year*	3 *Crude Death Rate*
1585–6	556	1586	83,183	21·9
1586–7	684	1587	107,981	28·2
1587–8	365	1588	109,101	28·6
1588–9	407	1589	89,635	23·3
1589–90	531	1590	91,266	23·4
1590–1	624	1591	110,688	28·4
1591–2	443	1592	110,606	28·3
1592–3	296	1593	121,259	31·1
1593–4	350	1594	81,960	20·8
1594–5	621	1595	83,956	21·1
1595–6	681	1596	96,575	24·1
1596–7	1039	1597	133,155	33·2
1597–8	778	1598	105,307	26·4
1598–9	518	1599	91,825	22·8

In Table 2.5 the burial information, now gathered in years running from 1 July to the following 30 June, is processed to reveal the percentages of observed parishes experiencing within one of these years increases in burials of 50 per cent or more, and 100 per cent or more, than the average number as determined by an eleven-year moving average.[51]

Several features are noteworthy. One is the sharp rise in the proportion of those parishes experiencing an increase of burials of 50 per cent or more: from 4 per cent in 1595–6 to 18 per cent and then 33 per cent in the two succeeding years. It was not until 1599–1600 that the percentage dropped to single figures again. This crisis of 1596–8 was indeed fairly widespread, though some areas naturally escaped relatively lightly.[52] The second thing to note, however, is that few communities appear to have been hit as hard as those in Cumbria studied by Professor Appleby, where burials rose fourfold in places. It is noticeable that in only one of these

Table 2.5 *Mortality Rates 1585–99*

Year starting 1 July	*No. of parishes under observation*	*% of parishes experiencing 50% increase in burials*	*% of parishes experiencing 100% increase in burials*
1585	291	8	2
1586	292	12	3
1587	292	25	10
1588	295	17	4
1589	297	5	2
1590	297	15	3
1591	299	14	6
1592	300	20	4
1593	300	11	4
1594	302	8	2
1595	302	4	3
1596	302	18	6
1597	302	33	13
1598	302	13	3
1599	302	4	4

years of extreme dearth (1597–8), for example, did the percentage of parishes suffering a doubling of mortality above the trend rise into double figures.

One is tempted to ask, therefore, why these communities did not suffer more. Given the social structure and economic developments outlined earlier, and the undoubtedly prolonged nature of the dearth, why did more of them not succumb to soaring death rates? Why, even in the worst year, did two-thirds of all these parishes suffer increases in burials of much less than 50 per cent?

Several possible reasons suggest themselves. Two are technical and are connected with the nature of the measurements employed. If 'crisis' in a particular period is to be measured as a percentage deviation of deaths from normal, measurement of the norm assumes a crucial importance. In Table 2.5, for example, annual deaths are measured as a percentage deviation from an eleven-year moving average, a norm which unfortunately subsumes the crisis itself (and perhaps past and future mortality crises as well). The second failing derives from the fact that the event is sought for in specific twelve-monthly time-periods. The timing of the onset thus assumes importance: a crisis, and especially a harvest-induced one, could be spread over two years, thus lessening its statistical impact in any one of them. This apart, there is also a distinct possibility that the impact of dearth upon public health resulted not simply in concurrent deaths but also in future ones; that there were 'lags' producing higher than normal deaths in future periods when dearth had ceased to be a problem.[53] Some dearth-sensitive diseases may have been particularly prone to this process – tuberculosis, for example, a wasting disease which takes time to show itself in mortality figures.[54]

Some of these theoretical arguments take on point when we remember that the English population had already suffered a series of major mortality checks before the great dearth began. Death rates were extremely high, for example, in the three calendar years 1591–3, with plague apparently chiefly to blame. This, in turn, had followed hard on the heels of the major mortality crisis, perhaps dearth-induced, of the years 1587 and 1588. The Cambridge Group have ranked the mortality crises of 1592–3 and 1587–8 as the twelfth and thirteenth worst experiences of the whole long period 1541–1871.[55] Thus not only would population pressure have been relieved to some extent by these events, but they are partially subsumed in the measures of normal mortality against which crisis is estimated in Table 2.5.

A third reason for the seemingly modest nature of the mortality response may be that the Tudor population was well accustomed to the probability of harvest failure. Although severe 'dearths' were relatively infrequent – Hoskins finds only five from 1480 to 1590 – 'bad' harvests were much more common. There were some twenty years in the same period when wheat prices rose by 25 per cent or more above the trend price: about one in five or six harvests could therefore be serious failures. One would expect that when people live with such probabilities they would try to contend with them, although the arrangements they make to try to avert such disasters are not always easy for us to recognise.

Some forms of such 'life insurance' are, of course, easy to discern: the encouragement given to charity in time of severe need, the extolling of 'hospitality', the development of the poor law, public granaries, municipally organised grain imports, even Books of Orders. Some of these responses are well known; others, however, have been too lightly investigated and problems emerge. Why, for example, were there not more granaries, private and public, carrying over the surpluses of good years into bad ones? On the private front many farmers were probably too small to have surpluses to store. The larger farmer had the potential for it, but he probably had also a target income set by his rent, poor rates and taxes, tithes, etc., which, with the tendency for yields and prices to move inversely with each other, might lead him to market nearly all his output in an abundant year. It might be tempting to hold back for a higher price, but then it was difficult to safeguard stocks against the depredations of damp and heat, of fungi, mites and rodents, and of human beings. Robert Loder suffered all these and reasoned in 1612, 'soe that reckoning the losse a man is at in shrinking of his wheat, and in the spoile by mice, it was best soulde this yeare at the first; even presently after harvest.'[56] There was also, of course, the possibility that the next harvest might be even more abundant, in which case the old grain might be virtually unsellable. Storage by middlemen grain-dealers initiated fears of engrossing. Municipalities, often chronically insolvent, faced similar storage risks and had the additional problem of finding the capital to acquire a grain stock in the first place. Financial pressures plus the risk of monetary loss seemed to militate against such developments.

The public arrangements are easier to perceive as 'life insurance' than many private ones, which are frequently difficult to discern, partly because risk avoidance may be only a partial or even a subconscious motive. There might, for example, be preferences on the part of some wage earners for particular forms of payment. The unmarried might prefer wages 'with food and drink'.[57] Country labourers frequently took payments in kind – grazing rights for their livestock, for example. There might also be preferences for particular types of employment. Historians are rediscovering the fact that a large proportion of the population consisted of servants and apprentices. The attractions of such states did not include the actual pay, which was frequently modest, but most certainly included the fact that by living in the household of a master, and sharing his table, they were sheltered from adverse fluctuations to a much greater degree than they would have been as independent labourers. Some fortunate wage earners also had smallholdings and perhaps common rights to fall back on. But when one reads of the farmers, not the land-holding labourers, that 'the great majority of agricultural producers were subsistence farmers with little to spare for the market; indeed, in times of harvest failure many small cultivators were turned into buyers of grain',[58] one must be careful not to exaggerate the immunity this conferred. It raises interesting questions about all small cultivators. One would expect them to be risk-avoiders. 'The fourth and last abuse', said Walter Blith of the small farmer, 'is a calumniating and depraving every new Invention; of this most culpable are your mouldy old leavened husbandmen, who themselves and their forefathers have been accustomed to such a course of husbandry as they will practise, and no other.'[59] Such behaviour is not irrational, as Professor McCloskey had clearly indicated for the open-field farmer, hanging on to his 'inefficient' scattered strips as a form of 'risk insurance'.[60] What other forms were there – sowing mixtures of grain, concentrating on high-yield but not necessarily remunerative crops, concentrating also on flexible-usage crops, such as barley? The subject is rich in speculative possibilities.

Another reason for large-scale survival is that consumers were ready to shift their food purchases, if not their preferences. The greater fluctuations of the prices of the inferior grains clearly attest to this. People turned from first to second and from second to third class wheat; from wheat to rye, barley or oats. For the unfortunates at the bottom there was William Harrison's dearth diet of 'beans, peason, otes, tares, and lintels'. It was a common proverb, he reminded us, that 'hunger setteth his first foot into the horsse manger'.[61] A tract of 1596 advised ways of making 'Beanes, Pease, Beechnuts, Chestnuttes, Acornes, Veches, and such like' palatable.[62] England, with its strongly rural culture and extremely varied topography, was perhaps fortunate in producing a wide variety of both cultivated crops and 'hedge fruits'. In these respects those inhabitants of Kent studied by Peter Clark may have been especially, but not peculiarly, well blessed. Although, as he has shown, there were many reasons why 'the Kentish poor survived the trauma of the 1590s without a major demographic disaster',[63] this flexibility growing out of diversity may well have been an important one.

VI

Although it is difficult to make such comparisons, because historians have employed different concepts and measures, the extent of English misery in the period under discussion appears to have been less than that experienced in some other countries, not only in Ireland but also perhaps in northern France, the southern Netherlands and in parts of the Rhineland. If this is true, and the hypothesis ideally needs to be tested by looking comparatively and systematically at the volatility of prices and mortality, then what else could have lain behind it? One very obvious explanation of the comparative mildness of the English experience is the absence of any direct experience of warfare. Even the indirect effects, stemming from the mobilisation and demobilisation of soldiers and sailors, are traceable and make one realise how fortunate we were that war was never fought on English soil. Moreover, our limited military commitments and careful financial management helped to keep down the levels of government taxation and borrowing. Although they were heavier in England in the 1590s than they had been for perhaps half a century, those in the lower income categories may have been more lightly taxed than some of their continental counterparts. England appears also to have benefited from comparative internal stability. Tensions there undoubtedly were, as Peter Clark makes clear, but the divisions between Protestant and Catholic, between town and country, between landlord and tenant, and between landlord and merchant never erupted in widespread violence as in some other parts of Europe. Central government was not only better established but also much more powerful in this country than in those areas that suffered badly, and although the Crown and its ministers are not above criticism it must also be acknowledged that they did much that was correct. They kept the localities under close scrutiny, attempted to regulate marketing and relieve extreme distress, slapped down troublemakers high and low, and above all waged war within the limits of their purse. Nothing, even indebtedness, got totally out of hand, though O'Neil's rebellion brought matters very near to that state.

Was there, therefore, a crisis? There can be no doubt that the seventeen years from 1586 to 1603 saw much hardship and misery in England; perhaps very much more than had been experienced for generations. But was it a crisis? Definitions of the term are bound to differ but necessarily embodied in it is the notion of a turning point. Was the crisis of the 1590s a transforming experience? Did it promote fundamental structural changes within economic and social life or in governmental reactions to them?

Obviously this is too large a programme to be considered here and attention will be confined to exploring briefly several themes considered earlier in the chapter. James I's succession to the throne was followed by peace and eventual relief from the burdens of war expenditure. However, the replacement of one elderly queen who found it difficult to say yes, by another who found it equally difficult to say no, simply brought a different sort of financial pressure. By 1606 the Crown's debts had climbed to over £735,000,[64] an amount far greater than was ever reached in the 'crisis of the 1590s'; indebtedness and 'cash-flow problems' continued to plague James throughout his reign.

Nor, of course, did bad harvests disappear. Hoskins identified the wheat harvests of 1608–9, 1622–3 and 1630–1 as 'bad'. The latter two events saw a significant increase in mortality rates, though they never reached the sort of levels experienced in 1597–8. This is not surprising in that isolated years presumably were easier to withstand than a bunching of bad harvests.

What is also significant is that each of these episodes provoked that familiar central government response, embodied in an issue of the Book of Orders. The experience of the 1590s, if nothing else, perpetuated this governmental response. If turning points are to be found in this particular area they would certainly be placed some time after 1630–1.[65]

Whilst there may be turning points in central government responses not touched upon here, all in all the record would seem to support those who are impressed by continuities and who have seen the whole long period from about 1580 to the 1630s as a period of acute pressure and difficulty. Close investigation of local communities may confirm the 1590s as some sort of cathartic decade, but given the great number of such communities, their varied economic and social structures, and the differing experiences of the very few that have so far been closely investigated, one must urge a degree of caution before the 1590s are hailed as yet another 'general crisis'.

Notes: Chapter 2

I am grateful for the help and advice offered by a number of colleagues and especially Prof. D. C. Coleman, Dr R. S. Schofield, Mr P. A. Clark, Dr D. C. Souden and Dr B. I. Bradshaw. They are absolved from responsibility for the defects that remain.

1 P. Clark, *English Provincial Society from the Reformation to the Revolution: Religion, Politics and Society in Kent, 1500–1640* (Hassocks, 1977), pp. 221–68.
2 Cited in Joel Hurstfield, 'The succession struggle in late Elizabethan England', in S. T. Bindoff *et al.* (eds), *Elizabethan Government and Society* (London, 1961), p. 373.
3 See Tables II–VI of the helpful Chapter XIII ('Who ruled?') of Penry Williams, *The Tudor Regime* (Oxford, 1979), pp. 421–56.
4 E. P. Cheyney, *A History of England from the Defeat of the Armada to the Death of Elizabeth* (London, 1914–26), Vol. 2, p. 214. Cheyney's work has not been surpassed as a vivid chronological account of the difficulties of these years.
5 W. R. Scott, *The Constitution and Finance of English, Scottish and Irish Joint-Stock Companies to 1720* (Cambridge, 1910–12), Vol. 3, pp. 503–27.
6 BL, Add. MS 48,168, fos 10–11, gives the following totals for the lay and clerical taxes granted by the parliaments of

A° 27 Eliz.	£190,330
A° 28–9 Eliz.	£188,344
A° 31 Eliz.	£374,225
A° 35 Eliz.	£483,405
A° 39 Eliz.	£451,529
A° 43 Eliz.	£597,226

7 Support for these estimates and a detailed discussion of Elizabeth's financial situation in these years is to be found in the author's unpublished PhD thesis, 'Studies in Elizabethan government finance: royal borrowing and the sales of Crown lands, 1572–1603', University of Nottingham, 1964.
8 R. B. Outhwaite, 'Royal borrowing in the reign of Elizabeth I: the aftermath of Antwerp', *English Historical Review*, vol. 86 (1971), pp. 251–63.
9 PRO, A.O.I. 593/2.
10 Outhwaite, thesis, app. 2.
11 These figures are taken from PRO, E405/430–42, and where this source (the Tellers' Views of Accounts) is not available from E405/243, 245 (the Declaration Books, Pells'). Not all of these balances may have been available for immediate use. Although the practice was illegal, Tellers frequently loaned the queen's money at interest. In 1586, for example, Richard Stonely, the senior Teller at that time, was unable to make up his account by £16,000, part of which he represented as bad debts. See PRO, SP 12/192/9.
12 F. C. Dietz, 'The Exchequer in Elizabeth's reign', *Smith College Studies in History*, vol. 8, no. 2 (1923), pp. 103–4.
13 R. B. Outhwaite, 'The price of Crown land at the turn of the sixteenth century', *Economic History Review*, 2nd ser., vol. 20 (1967), pp. 229–40.
14 PRO, E405/243, fo. 210; BL, Sloane MS, 2251/4; *Calendar of State Papers, Domestic* (hereafter *CSPD*) 1598–1601, p. 476.
15 Corporation of London Record Office (hereafter CLRO), Remembrancia, II, no. 196.
16 These prices were extracted from the Beveridge price history collection in the Library of the London School of Economics. Owing to the differing nature of the original source

materials, regional differences are probably less significant than the annual variations in any one series.

17 W. G. Hoskins, 'Harvest fluctuations and English economic history, 1480–1619', *Agricultural History Review*, vol. 12 (1964), pp. 28–46. See also C. J. Harrison, 'Grain price analysis and harvest qualities, 1465–1634', ibid., vol. 19 (1971), pp. 135–55, where, using the Bowden material instead of the Beveridge figures, Harrison classifies the wheat harvest of 1593 as 'good', and the oats harvest similarly. The Harrison figures, however, should be approached carefully in view of the warning about possible computer errors imparted in A. B. Appleby, 'Nutrition and disease: the case of London, 1550–1750', *Journal of Interdisciplinary History*, vol. 6 (1975), p. 4, n. 10.

18 *CSPD*, 1591–4, p. 382; CLRO, Repertories, 23 f. 150b.

19 *Calendar of Border Papers* (hereafter *CBP*), 1560–94, p. 541; CLRO, Remembrancia, II, no. 31.

20 P. Bowden, 'Statistical appendix' to J. Thirsk (ed.), *Agrarian History of England and Wales*, Vol. 4, *1500–1640* (Cambridge, 1967), pp. 819–20.

21 Dietz's tabulations suggest the following annual averages for (*a*) 'Total customs revenues' and (*b*) the 'Receiver General of Crown lands' ('The Exchequer . . .', pp. 86–9) in these five-year periods:

	Mich. 1588–Mich. 1593	*Mich. 1593–Mich. 1598*	*Mich. 1598–Mich. 1603*
(*a*)	£100,198	£103,531	£86,849
(*b*)	£68,081	£68,420	£56,305

22 *CBP*, 1595–1603, pp. 27, 530.

23 ibid., 1560–94, pp. 554–5; see also ibid., 1595–1603, pp. 30–1.

24 ibid., 1595–1603, pp. 186, 191, 285.

25 ibid., p. 487.

26 The annual average for the ten years from 1586 to 1595 was 94 deaths; for the two years 1596 and 1597, 176 deaths; for the two succeeding years, 72 deaths. Source: Aggregate file, Berwick-on-Tweed, at Cambridge Group for the History of Population and Social Structure.

27 See, in particular, G. A. Hayes-McCoy, 'Strategy and tactics in Irish warfare, 1593–1601', *Irish Historical Studies*, vol. 2 (1940–1), pp. 255–79; Cyril Falls, *Elizabeth's Irish Wars* (London, 1950).

28 *Calendar of State Papers, Ireland* (hereafter *CSPI*), 1592–6, pp. 274, 304.

29 ibid., pp. 313, 314, 318, 373, 397.

30 ibid., pp. 333, 365–7.

31 ibid., pp. 397–8.

32 ibid., pp. 414–16, 420, 428–30, 437.

33 *CSPI*, 1596–7, pp. 62, 99, 101, 116.

34 ibid., p. 136.

35 ibid., p. 157.

36 ibid., pp. 216, 231–3, 250, 255, 262, 277, 282–5, 288.

37 ibid., pp. 291, 299, 378.

38 ibid., pp. 364, 381–2.

39 *CSPI*, 1598–9, pp. 60–5, 201–3, 222, 234, 267–8, 290–2.

40 Discussions of the origins and development of these Books of Orders are to be found in N. S. B. Gras, *The Evolution of the English Corn Market* (Cambridge, 1915), and E. Lipson, *The Economic History of England* (London, 1915–31), Vol. 3, ch. 6; and, more recently, Paul Slack, 'Books of Orders: the making of English social policy, 1577–1631', *Transactions of the Royal Historical Society*, 5th ser., vol. 30 (1980), pp. 1–22.

41 An earlier, brief discussion of the Privy Council response is to be found in the author's 'Food crises in early modern England: patterns of public response', *Proceedings of the Seventh International Economic History Congress* (Edinburgh, 1978).

42 Hoskins, 'Harvest fluctuations', p. 29; and for a reiteration of these views more recently, *The Age of Plunder: The England of Henry VIII, 1500–1547* (London, 1976).

43 T. S. Ashton, *An Economic History of England: The 18th Century* (London, 1955), pp. 60–2; *Economic Fluctuations in England, 1700–1800* (Oxford, 1959), chs 1 and 2.

44 N. S. Scrimshaw, C. E. Taylor and J. E. Gordon, *Interactions of Nutrition and Infection* (Geneva: World Health Organisation, 1968), p. 13. The authors are also careful to note the exceptions to this general rule.
45 ibid., p. 16.
46 *CBP*, 1595–1603, p. 374.
47 P. Slack, 'Poverty and politics in Salisbury, 1597–1666', in P. Clark and P. Slack (eds), *Crisis and Order in English Towns* (London, 1972), pp. 164–203, provides excellent illustrations of these economic and social links.
48 A. B. Appleby, *Famine in Tudor and Stuart England* (Liverpool, 1978), esp. ch. 9.
49 P. Slack, 'Mortality crises and epidemic disease in England, 1485–1610', in C. Webster (ed.), *Health, Medicine and Mortality in the Sixteenth Century* (Cambridge, 1979), pp. 17, 34.
50 I am grateful to Drs E. A. Wrigley and R. S. Schofield for supplying me with some of these figures and for innumerable other kindnesses. All of the figures can now be found in their great work *The Population History of England, 1541–1871* (London, 1981), where their derivation is also explained.
51 From data earlier compiled and kindly supplied by Dr Schofield of the Cambridge Group. More sophisticated measures were ultimately adopted in the *Population History*, but the information presented there is less suited to the purposes of this chapter. Even so, the severity of the crisis of 1597–8 is attested: it is ranked as the seventeenth worst mortality crisis year in the whole long period of that study, whilst the year 1596–7 was ranked the twenty-second worst (p. 653).
52 Wrigley and Schofield, *Population History*, fig. A10.3, p. 672.
53 ibid.: 'There can be no doubt that variations in prices were indeed followed by variations in mortality . . . the major effect occurs not in the year of high prices, but in the subsequent years' (p. 372); 'Following a price variation, mortality responded positively over the following two or three years' (p. 399).
54 This may explain why Appleby found little short-run correlation of bread prices and tuberculosis in London: 'Nutrition and disease', pp. 15–18.
55 Wrigley and Schofield, *Population History*, p. 653.
56 G. E. Fussell (ed.), *Robert Loder's Farm Accounts, 1610–1620*, Camden Society, 3rd ser., Vol. 53 (1936), pp. 28–9.
57 Hoskins, *Age of Plunder*, pp. 112–13, 223–6.
58 P. J. Bowden, in Thirsk, *Agrarian History*, p. 608.
59 Cited in Lord Ernle, *English Farming Past and Present*, 6th edn (London, 1961), pp. 110–11.
60 D. N. McCloskey, 'The persistence of English common fields', in W. N. Parker and E. L. Jones (eds), *European Peasants and Their Markets* (Princeton, NJ, 1975), pp. 73–119.
61 F. J. Furnivall (ed.), *Harrison's Description of England* (London, 1877), p. 153.
62 *Sundrie new and Artificiall remedies against Famine*, by H. P. Esq. [Hugh Platt] (London, 1596).
63 Clark, *English Provincial Society*, p. 244.
64 R. Ashton, 'Deficit finance in the reign of James I', *Economic History Review*, 2nd ser., vol. 10 (1957), p. 21.
65 R. B. Outhwaite, 'Dearth and government intervention in English grain markets, 1590–1700', *Economic History Review*, 2nd ser., vol. 34 (1981), pp. 389–406, explores further these themes of continuity and discontinuity.

3 *A Crisis Contained? The Condition of English Towns in the 1590s*

PETER CLARK

'Behold! What a famine God has brought upon our land,' Dr John King cried in a sermon at York in the mid-1590s. 'One year there has been hunger. The second there was a dearth. And the third there was great cleanness of teeth'; plague stalks our cities and the course of nature is turned upside down. Ordinary townsmen put the blame less on the deity than on the extortion of the upper classes. A popular libel at Norwich about 1595 denounced how 'for seven years space they [the rich] have fed on our flesh, on our wives and children . . . ; oh, who is the better for all the dearth? The rich.' The unnatural times bred chiliastic visions, as in 1599 at Cockermouth in Cumberland, an area of recent famine, where the inhabitants saw 'wonderful sights in the air . . . so rare and strange . . . two great circles of blood . . . two huge and great armies all in complete armour . . . then . . . a wonderful great troop of horsemen . . . who fought . . . till there appeared a river of blood . . . to the great terror . . . of all the beholders'.[1] With the country afflicted with famine, plague and war, historians since E. P. Cheyney (1926) have commonly referred to the last years of Elizabeth's reign as a time of crisis in England.[2]

The purpose of this chapter is to examine the nature of the crisis, focusing attention on the experience of urban communities. We shall need to examine the background to the crisis, its impact on towns, and the scale and success of the communal response. In the process it may be possible to assess not only the short-term course of the crisis but the wider significance. How far is it right to see the difficulties of the 1590s as just one of the periodic crises, serious but short-term, which affected England in the early modern period? And how far did the late Elizabethan troubles reflect and compound major structural problems in the economy and society during the sixteenth and early seventeenth centuries? More precisely, what light does the evidence of the 1590s shed on the controversial fortunes of English towns in the period before the Civil War?

By continental standards England, of course, was a land of small towns. Of 700 urban communities three-quarters had less than 2,000 people in

1600 and were primarily concerned with marketing the produce of their hinterlands. The larger, second-tier, county towns had more complex economies and greater corporate autonomy, but only a handful of English cities, regional capitals like Norwich, York and Bristol, had as many as 10,000–15,000 inhabitants. The mighty exception to the Lilliputian rule was London, whose population soared from 60,000 in 1520 to 200,000 by the 1590s, putting it in the front rank of European cities.[3] Documentation for the crisis years varies across the urban spectrum: it is generally best for the medium-sized towns, less complete for the smaller centres and surprisingly, perhaps, for London. In general, however, as we shall see, many of the difficulties of the 1590s pervaded all levels of the urban hierarchy.

I

English towns in the 1590s suffered from three principal, if interacting pressures: harvest failure, plague and overseas war. Following the dearth of 1586 the subsequent harvest years were tolerably good and those of the early 1590s attained near-glut proportions. But after 1593 there was a succession of climatic and agricultural disasters. As one observer noted: 'every man complains against the dearth of this time'. In the West Midlands the Shrewsbury town chronicle recorded for 1594: 'this year and most part of the summer and part of the harvest time continually for the most part was great wet . . . that where rye was at 18d or 20d the bushel and wheat 8 groats, now it is risen to 3s 2d rye and 5s 4d wheat'. There was a similar grim complaint at Coventry: it began to rain in May and 'rained every day or night till 28th July and in September great rains again'. 1595 was worse. Philip Wyot wrote at Barnstaple, 'By reason of rain and foul weather wheat is 9s a bushel.' The next year Wyot wrote, 'all this May has not been a dry day and night' . . . 'small quantity of corn brought to market [so] townsmen cannot have corn for money'; 'there is but little comes to the market and such snatching and catching for that little and such a cry that the like was never heard'. At Shrewsbury after another winter of storms and rain, corn reached 18s the bushel in May 1597; further downpours in July pushed it even higher at Barnstaple to 20s. Only in 1598 did the sun appear and the harvest improve. Even so there were renewed shortages in 1600. Though the west may have suffered worst from the weather, the sharp rises in corn prices in towns across the kingdom suggest that all felt the harsh pressures of harvest failure.[4]

Plague epidemics were increasingly localised to towns in sixteenth-century England. During the last part of Elizabeth's reign such communities were ravaged by two main outbreaks. The first began in London in 1592, the bacillus probably imported from the continent, perhaps by returning troops, and killed about 13 per cent of the city's population. Thereafter it fanned out to many provincial cities, including Leicester, Canterbury, Coventry, and Nottingham. The second plague epidemic appeared in the metropolis in 1603, killing about 33,000 people, and celebrated the accession of James I by a grim progress through the provincial capitals and county towns between 1603 and 1605. In addition to the assaults of plague, towns faced outbreaks of influenza, typhus, dysentery and smallpox, their impact frequently aggravated by malnutrition.[5]

English towns fortunately escaped the worst consequences of the civil and international wars which assailed the continent in the 1590s. However, Elizabeth's repeated naval expeditions against Spain, together with her military involvement in the Netherlands (from 1585), France (from 1589) and Ireland (mainly from 1595 to suppress Tyrone's rebellion), generated a complex of problems for towns and their rulers. Parliamentary taxes had to be levied and so-called loans extorted to cover part of the military costs; the main ports had to pay ship-money (in 1596). The fleet and overseas armies required replenishment with a constant stream of recruits, usually equipped at civic expense; roughly 700 men a year were conscripted in London in the early 1590s.[6] City trained bands were almost incessantly mustered, diverting respectable men from their trade and work. Foreign expeditions imposed severe difficulties at ports like Dover, Chester and Bristol where several thousand troops were often encamped for weeks on end waiting for shipment. Last, but not least, overseas war hindered trade, with the dislocation of north European markets for English exports and Mediterranean commerce disrupted by privateering.[7]

II

The most obvious impact of the crisis years was on urban mortality. Although the parish register data for larger cities is often incomplete and distorted by under-registration in the worst mortality years, the main demographic contours stand out. In London in 1593 the levels of mortality in city parishes like St Vedast or All Hallows, London Wall, was running at five times normal, while in outer parishes such as St Botolph, Bishopsgate, the ratio was over seven times. The scale of the mortality problem in the greater metropolis in 1592–3 and again in 1597 is evident from Table 3.1.[8]

Table 3.1 *Demographic Trends in Eight Parishes in London and the Greater Metropolitan Area, 1590–1600*

	1590	*1591*	*1592*	*1593*	*1594*	*1595*	*1596*	*1597*	*1598*	*1599*	*1600*
Total baptisms	328	315	358	313	327	335	360	313	365	396	408
Total burials	342	398	640	1163	378	353	340	661	379	391	345

At York nearly half the parishes analysed by David Palliser experienced demographic deficits during the 1590s and an overall excess of burials over baptisms is also recorded in parishes in other larger centres. Small towns were also victims. Mortality was especially high in the north: in Kendal town burials jumped from an average of about 67 in 1578–87 to 94 in 1591–2, 104 in 1592–3, 120 in 1593–4, 136 in 1595–6, and 268 in 1596–7.[9]

In the past much of this high mortality has been ascribed to plague outbreaks and these were undoubtedly decisive in the early 1590s and early 1600s. But recent research has revealed the likelihood of a major subsistence crisis in 1596–8. For the north Andrew Appleby has shown how in a number of places, including the towns of Kendal and Penrith, the pattern of burials during 1596–7 was determined to a considerable extent by starvation and related infections. At Newcastle and elsewhere we find references to people dying from hunger. People tramped from Carlisle to Durham to buy bread and country areas were deserted of inhabitants. Sixty years later an old woman at Bury in Lancashire recalled how during the 'grievous famine' her family were almost starved, so much so that on one of her children 'down began to grow on her cheeks for hunger'.[10] But the pall of famine extended across the country, particularly to the west Midlands and the south-west. The Shrewsbury chronicler recorded in late 1596 that without the supply of imported corn the town's poor were like to 'perish . . . as many in all counties in England die'. At Nantwich at the same time we hear how 'the scarcity was so great that many poor people were 'afamished'; mortality in the town was double the usual average. Death from famine also probably occurred at Stafford, Warwick and Tamworth, and in the West Country at Crediton, Barnstaple and Exeter. Towns in the south and east may have fared better, although famine mortality seems to have affected Reading and some of the Hampshire market towns. In London the seasonal pattern of deaths in 1597 also points to starvation as an important causal factor of the high mortality.[11]

The crisis made food provisioning a prime preoccupation of town magistrates. Generally speaking, English agricultural output was sufficient to meet demand in most years during the late sixteenth century. There had been severe shortages following the bad harvest of 1586, but by the early 1590s grain was being exported to the continent. None the less, shortages rapidly became acute in the middle of the decade with the problems caused by harvest failure compounded by a variety of other factors. One was London. Already buying grain from east Kent and other areas of the Home Counties before the 1590s, during the crisis years London merchants were driven to search further afield for supplies, encroaching on the established marketing spheres and hinterlands of other towns. Higher prices in London not only diverted corn from other communities but drove up rates in provincial markets. The provincial capitals caused similar, if more limited, difficulties: York's attempts to extend its catchment area into the east Midlands provoked considerable local opposition, while Bristol's demands had ripple effects right up the Severn valley, adversely affecting Gloucester and other places.[12] Another disruptive force was military provisioning, with grain transported for the navy, the Berwick garrison, and later the Irish army at the expense of the local needy. Whether the situation was aggravated by sales of grain to the continent is problematical. In 1595–6 there are reports of shipments from Kent and in 1600 the renewed high prices were blamed on the 'private avarice of some' exporting 'great quantities into foreign countries', probably into the Mediterranean.[13] But more crucial perhaps in the mid-1590s was the movement of cereals northwards, particularly to hard-pressed Scotland. In August 1596 the mayor of London voiced concern that Baltic grain ships bound for the Thames might be diverted towards 'Scotland and the north parts of this realm'. About the same time, boatloads of corn were being shipped under cover from Chester to Cumberland and so perhaps into the western lowlands.[14]

Food shortages and their inevitable corollary, high prices, had a powerful influence on the upsurge of poverty which was such a striking feature of the urban crisis in England. In the parish of St Mary's, Warwick, in 1587 those needing relief made up about one in four of all families; similarly at St Peter's, Sandwich, roughly a quarter of the parish were on relief in 1598; at Shrewsbury in the 1590s one in eight were in that category; at Kendal about 1595–9 40 per cent of the town's households were listed as poor.[15] The physiognomy of urban poverty defies precise evaluation. We can only speculate on the vital monthly oscillations of prices and wages; on the incidence of unemployment and underemployment; and conversely on the invisible helping hand of wages in kind and secondary employments. But it is clear that in addition to those traditional groups of urban poor, the elderly, the sick and orphaned, there were by the 1590s large tribes of labouring folk, unskilled and semi-skilled workers, on the breadline, and these were joined in the worst years of the decade by modestly respectable craftsmen and tradesmen. At Leicester in 1593 we are told that 'divers of the inferior sort (which were wont to live well) grow so poor for want of traffic . . . [that] they have more need to be relieved' than to help the poor. In 1596 at the height of the food shortages the Coventry annalist commented that 'many that had been good housekeepers begged'. Soon after, the mayor of Canterbury declared that the 'scarcity is such as the poorest folk and a great part of the people being of some small wealth are like to starve . . . having long time very hardly procured means for their sustenance by pawning and selling such small goods as they had'. As one sign of the deteriorating social position of the lower classes and the necessity for deferred marriages, there was a high level of illegitimacy in towns (as in the countryside) during the 1590s.[16]

Needless to say, high prices, for all their importance, formed only one piece in the jigsaw of urban impoverishment. Harvest failure spelt contraction across the economy as a whole, with a substantial reduction in demand for the non-food commodities and services provided by townsmen. Plague outbreaks disrupted communications, caused the closure of town markets, and frightened away rural customers; worse, they caused an exodus of wealthier people from town, further damping demand and thrusting much of the burden of relieving the infected on the smaller men who stayed behind.[17]

Economic activity in towns may also have suffered from the burden of national taxes, together with local assessments for mobilising troops, plague relief, and grain stocks, and, most important by the late 1590s, parochial rates for the poor. About 1599 Leicester's civic leaders blamed the town's decay on 'the long and extreme famine' and on 'these provisions for soldiers, fifteenths and subsidies [and] the relieving of the poor'. It is impossible to quantify the scale of the fiscal drain on the urban economy, but given the small size of many towns it was probably quite deflationary, generating increased unemployment and poverty.[18]

Not that the recession was entirely home-induced. Textile towns faced considerable difficulty in their overseas markets as a result of the military and economic crisis on the continent. In 1586–7 there was a sharp fall in cloth exports, partly as a result of Spanish military successes on the Rhine, while the 'Hallage' receipts of the London cloth markets suggest persistent problems for the urban cloth industry until the late 1590s. Shrewsbury, which was predominant in the finishing and sale of Welsh cloth, suffered an acute slump in the 1590s, leading to mass unemployment and distress.[19] Gloucestershire production, mostly centred in the market towns of the Stroudwater valley, was also badly affected, with cloth prices falling by up to 40 per cent between 1594 and 1598. Some of the ports were caught up in the backwash of continental dislocation, with Bristol, Exeter and Yarmouth complaining of the disruption of their Mediterranean trade.[20]

The anonymous author of the tract 'A Proffitable Discourse' deplored about this time the decay of 'towns that stood thereby sometimes in great wealth and prosperity'. However, the economic malaise of numerous established towns was not just the result of the short-term problems associated with the crisis. The difficulties of the 1590s were exaggerated by the structural instability of urban economies in the late sixteenth century, especially those of middle-rank towns. Admittedly, the first part of Elizabeth's reign had witnessed a recovery from the reverses of the early Tudor period, but the revival was fragile: the urban service sector was expanding only slowly; the marketing activity of county towns experienced tough competition from open market towns; and industry was often in the doldrums, outflanked by cheaper rural production.[21]

All these factors, then, played an important part in producing the massive wave of poverty among townspeople in the 1590s; but the urban poverty problem was also imported from outside, with large numbers of near destitute labourers and smallholders flocking to town from the villages. There is no space here to examine the crisis in the countryside, but there can be little question that many areas, especially in the highland zone, were increasingly beset in the late sixteenth century by overpopulation and land and housing shortages. During the 1590s labourers out of work and smallholders unable to pay their rent were forced to take to the road. In certain districts agricultural improvement accelerated the movement, while the decline of rural industries in depressed years may also have provided some of the impetus propelling poor migrants to town.[22]

Whatever the reason, the stream of country people arriving in English towns during the late sixteenth century turned into a flood. London was inundated. In 1593 the Queen herself rasped: 'there came more vagrant people and masterless men in at the gates of London and were within the city than within four score miles round about the same'. Indicative of the trend, London's Bridewell court dealt with 209 vagrants in 1578–9 and nearly three times that number in 1600–1. While the court's records are missing for the peak years of distress, those for the period 1597–1602 give us some idea of the great surges of poor migrants coming to the capital (see Figure 3.1). The numbers of cases dealt with by the court were particularly high during the difficult winter months, though the monthly fluctuations also reflect magisterial preoccupations with public order (for instance, after Essex's revolt in February 1601). As one might expect, there was large-scale subdivision of tenements and cottages in the suburbs and on the south bank of the Thames to house the impoverished newcomers.[23] Provincial towns faced a proportionate influx. Coventry magistrates complained in 1598 of 'the great number of strangers that do daily resort unto this city to inhabit and dwell'. At Bristol we hear of many who 'daily resort to this city to make their abode', whereby it is 'greatly charged with poor people'; at Carlisle the townspeople lamented how they were 'great[ly] molested with the poor that is strangers'.[24] Even small towns felt the swelling tide of immigration. At Faversham in Kent roughly 20 per cent of the householders were listed as recent incomers in 1596, mostly

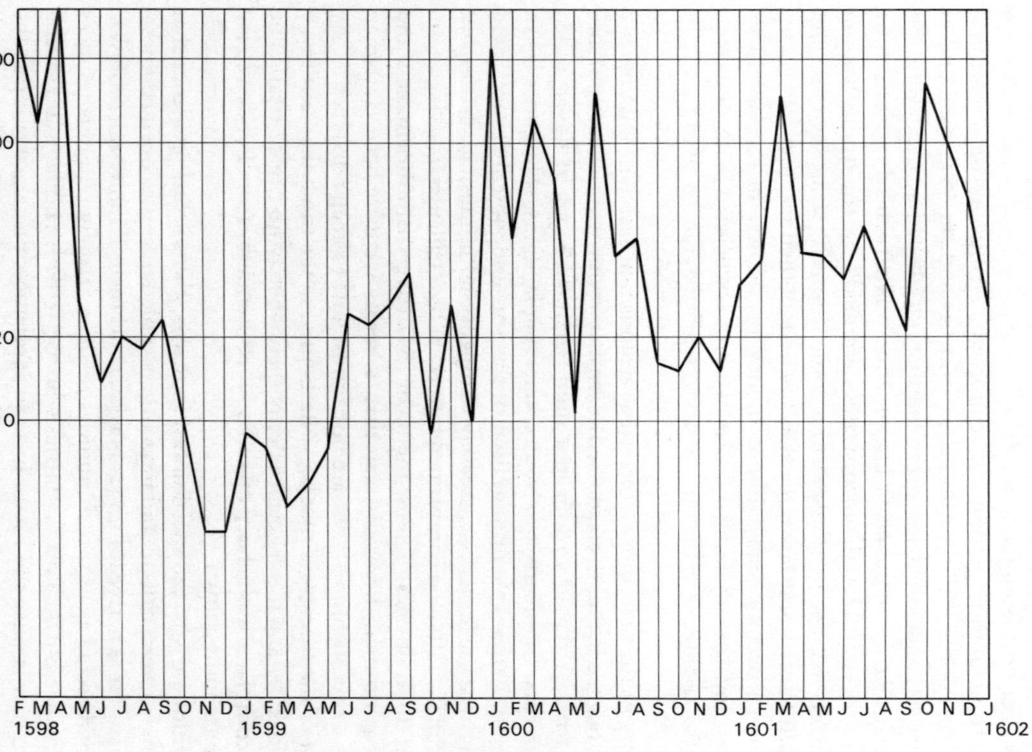

Figure 3.1 *Vagrants before the London Bridewell Court, 1598–1602.*

poor persons. A substantial portion of those tramping to town had travelled long distances. Of approximately eighty vagrants arrested in the capital by special commissioners in July–August 1595 and whose previous place of residence is known, the largest contingent, nearly a quarter, came from the west Midlands (particularly the upland Marcher counties) and over 12 per cent from the north.[25]

The surge of immigration was reinforced by gangs of troops returning from the continental expeditions or from Ireland. In 1593 the London authorities condemned the great numbers of alleged soldiers who 'do swarm in all parts of this city'. The situation was particularly serious at the ports. At Rye in 1590 the magistrates described how the troops landing there were 'in most miserable sort . . . some wounded, some their toes and feet rotting off, some lame, the skin and flesh of their feet torn away with continual marching', all without money or clothes. In the late 1590s Chester and the adjoining villages were overwhelmed with deserters, notwithstanding, it was said 'all devices that have been used to terrify them'.[26]

Many of the newcomers loitered at alehouses in search of lodging and work, begged in the streets, dossed down on pavements, in church porches and barns, or rented a room in a slum tenement – one of the so-called penny-rents, frequently run by a racketeering landlord, sometimes by an alderman. Large-scale immigration of this sort undoubtedly exacerbated the plight of the local poor, creating competition for housing, charity and jobs. Small craftsmen complained bitterly at the challenge from incomers setting up in business against them. In 1597 Faversham shoemakers and others petitioned the magistracy that 'whereas we have been craftsmen here . . . this 30 years . . . we are not almost able to keep ourselves . . . by reason of the foreigners that is . . . harboured in the town that take away our work . . . and if our science decay then we may go beg or steal'. The same complaint was echoed up and down the country from London to the smallest country town.[27]

Turning now to the social unrest in towns, there is little evidence that friction between citizens and newcomers spilled over into open conflict – at least as far as native immigrants were concerned. Popular agitation was mostly directed against communities of aliens, largely religious refugees from France and the Low Countries who had settled in London and several eastern towns since the 1560s. In 1586 apprentices planned a rising in the capital against the French and Dutch; the next year there was unrest at Canterbury over the strangers. In 1592 protests were made that the foreigners were robbing Londoners of work, and the following year discontent erupted into a spate of libels in the capital urging attacks on aliens. One proclaimed: 'Doth not the world see that you beastly brutes the Belgians, or rather drunken drones . . . [and] fraudulent . . .

Frenchmen' have departed their lands through cowardice, and ended with the warning that unless they left by July 'there shall be many a sore stripe. Apprentices will rise to the number of 2,336. And all the apprentices and journeymen will down with the Flemings and strangers.' The attacks had wide support. In June 1595 a pamphlet against alien silk weavers in and about London was being circulated with the backing of members of the Weavers' Company. There was also a more muted campaign against foreigners at Colchester. In the capital the ruling classes were clearly fearful of a repetition of the notorious 1517 rising against aliens; agitators were harshly punished and surveys drawn up to establish the true size of the stranger communities.[28]

Anti-alien protests were only one aspect of the mounting social disorder in English towns during the 1590s. Despite the absence of sessions records for the city of London, their paucity for Middlesex, and the intractability of Star Chamber records at this time, it is evident there was a spate of protest and disturbance in the capital, fuelled by the deteriorating economic climate. Certainly it would be naive to be complacent about the order problem in the metropolis during the 1590s.[29] In October 1590 a crowd of apprentices attacked the upper-class members of Lincoln's Inn; earlier that year a London baker was indicted for declaring he would kill the Queen and drink blood. Two years afterwards in June 1592 'great multitudes of people', led by a number of feltmakers' servants and including 'a great number of loose and masterless men', gathered in Blackfriars and engaged in a pitched battle with officials of the Marshalsea prison over the arrest of a feltworker; several people were killed. Later that month we hear talk of a proposed further rising at midsummer.[30] One man declared about this time that if only the apprentices had a leader all the commons would rise for they all disliked the state and government. In August 1592 enclosure riots broke out in the west of the metropolis, in St Martin's. In October a riot occurred at Holborn at the execution of a man who had killed a city officer. In December two or three hundred discontented sailors plotted to meet at St Paul's and march on the Court with their grievances. The Privy Council protested angrily to the mayor, 'how many of these disorders have of late been committed in divers places of the city'.[31]

The next two years saw something of a lull, apart from the occasional shouts of Londoners in favour of the Spaniards; but 1595 was dominated by disorder. The trouble began during June in Southwark, crowded with the poor and unemployed. According to Stow, 'some apprentices and other young people . . . being pinched of their victuals . . . took from the market people' a quantity of butter which was being sold at excessive prices. About the same time a gang of apprentices mobbed a crowd of Southwark fishwives who had been trying to monopolise supplies. The

Southwark rioters acted in a responsible, customary way, eschewing violence and offering money for the goods they took,[32] but the situation was explosive. The Southwark disorders coincided with renewed agitation against aliens, the circulation of seditious libels, probably against city leaders, and the forcible rescue of a prisoner by a throng of apprentices.[33] The government determined on a tough response. The Southwark rioters were tried in Star Chamber and sentenced to be flogged and set in the pillory on 27 June. None the less, two days later a major riot broke out on Tower Hill when a large force of young people, led by a former soldier, assaulted ward officials.[34] Thomas Earl, the minister of St Mildred, Breadstreet, noted in his commonplace book 'a foolish commotion of youths', but the details are unclear. The government was badly shaken by the incident. On 4 July a proclamation was issued excoriating 'sundry great disorders committed in and about the city of London by unlawful great assemblies of multitudes of a popular sort of base condition'. A provost-marshal was appointed to enforce martial law, and five of the Tower Hill rioters were charged with high treason and condemned to be hanged, drawn and quartered – virtually the only occasion in the century before 1640 when such a ferocious punishment was meted out to ordinary rioters. Vigorous police action and a concerted official drive to improve food supplies seem to have kept the cauldron from boiling over, but discontent continued to seethe.[35] In October 1595 there was a minor disorder near Cheapside; in July 1596 the mayor reported the arrest of Thomas Delony for publishing a ballad containing 'a complaint of the great want and scarcity of corn', and in September another outbreak of seditious libelling took place. Finally in the summer of 1598 there was a recurrence of apprentice agitation, with calls for a meeting in Islington Fields to be 'revenged' upon the Lord Mayor.[36]

The disorders of 1592 and 1595–6 were among the most serious to menace the metropolis in the decades up to the Civil War. News of them spread quickly to the provinces. A seditious tract at Norwich about 1595 spoke of 60,000 craftsmen in London and elsewhere ready to rise; the Oxfordshire rebels of 1596 talked of marching on London in anticipation of the support of the apprentices there.[37] In practice, however, there seems to have been no liaison between metropolitan and provincial discontent. Outside London lower-class disorders in urban centres tended to be self-contained, sporadic affairs, though their incidence at this time was probably greater than in any other decade between 1558 and 1640. In 1586 there were conspiracies at Sandwich and about Portsmouth, as well as food riots at Shrewsbury and Gloucester. In 1595 women attacked grain carts at the market town of Wye (Kent), while there were disturbances by clothworkers at Cranbrook in the Weald.[38] Further corn riots erupted at Canterbury in 1596, near Lynn in 1597, and at Bishop's Stortford in

Hertfordshire in 1598. Anger was particularly strong against prosperous corn dealers who were thought to be getting rich from the misery of the poor, but most of the protests were relatively small-scale and customary.[39]

A serious problem at this time was the disorders and mutinies by troops. Numerous 'great outrages and insolencies' were reportedly committed in London and other southern towns following the return of soldiers from the Counter-Armada of 1589. In London a mob of several hundred threatened to loot Batholomew Fair and others besieged the Court demanding their pay. Seven soldiers were subsequently executed. Three years later there was the demonstration by sailors in London.[40] In 1594 at Chester 1,500 soldiers en route for Ireland 'daily fought and quarrelled' and on one occasion, when the city was in uproar, the mayor set up a gibbet to execute martial law and three ringleaders were sentenced to death. Further disorders occurred there in 1595 and 1596.[41] In 1595 the pressed men of Norfolk, Suffolk and Essex refused to embark at Ipswich and threatened to march on London. In 1598, 300 Londoners marching up the Watling Street for service in Ireland mutinied at the market town of Towcester and elected their own leader. Meantime there were clashes between soldiers and townspeople at Plymouth and an agitation over pay at Canterbury.[42]

Probably the worst military disturbances occurred in 1600 in the western ports where large forces were massed for the suppression of the Irish rebellion. Substantial numbers of troops mutinied at both Chester and Bristol – at Bristol there was a repeat performance in 1602.[43] Mutinies were only part of the story. Bands of marauding troops also contributed to the general growth of crime and banditry in and about English towns in the 1590s.[44]

So far we have examined the demographic, economic and social dimensions of the crisis in English towns. How did the stresses of the 1590s affect urban politics? One apparent consequence was the heightening of intra-communal tension with a near epidemic of conflicts between civic rulers and commons. Among those towns embroiled in acrimonious disputes were Newcastle, New Romney, Stamford, Dartmouth, Canterbury, Gloucester, Nottingham, St Albans, Lincoln, Preston, Doncaster, Coventry, and Sandwich.[45] Internal divisions were hardly new to English towns, indeed the signs are they were on the increase throughout the sixteenth century, but the clustering of conflicts during the 1590s is notable. There were hard-fought mayoral and parliamentary elections, street demonstrations, allegations of oligarchic gerrymandering, and purges from the bench. Quite often the Privy Council was forced to intervene, almost invariably on the side of the urban elite. Fuelling the flames was general economic and social distress; the sharp deterioration of civic finances due to higher prices and extra expenditure on poor relief and military activity; the opportunities the crisis offered for oligarchic profiteering and abuse; and the heavy national and local taxation which magistrates had to impose. There was a powerful groundswell of urban opposition to these levies in the last years of Elizabeth's reign.[46]

Political relations with the Crown and county governments were hardly any more harmonious. The Privy Council constantly criticised the way that towns endeavoured to evade their share of financial and military burdens by taking refuge behind the smoke screen of corporate privileges. Town leaders resented the manner in which county justices exploited the various emergencies of the period to muscle in on civic jurisdiction, and there were clashes with local gentry at Gloucester, Lincoln, Coventry and elsewhere.[47]

In sum the crisis of the 1590s had severe repercussions for English towns. At certain times, as in London in 1595, it seemed as if the whole fabric of the urban community might be about to disintegrate. Yet what is also remarkable is that the urban crisis never careered out of control. There was no enormous landslide of fatalities from starvation (except perhaps in the north); no urban Jacquerie of the type which seized power in Paris after 1588. In 1600 Robert Devereux, Earl of Essex, hoped to overthrow Elizabeth by appealing to disaffected Londoners, but his frantic ride through the city in search of popular and middle-class support was in vain.[48] By then the worst of the economic crisis was over and the city authorities, like those elsewhere, were busy consolidating their political power and tightening the administrative reins.

III

How do we explain the relative success of English towns in weathering the storm? Two points must be made at once, self-evident though they are. First, while England was heavily committed to military adventures abroad she never suffered fighting on her own soil. Second, and related to this, Elizabeth's government, despite the distractions of party factionalism, remained fairly effective and interventionist in domestic politics, providing the framework of public order. In this situation English towns had a head start over many of their continental cousins in the struggle to overcome the crisis.

Looking now at the urban response to the problems of the 1590s, it seems likely that civic action against the spread of plague had only marginal value. The *cordons sanitaires* set up to prevent contact with stricken centres were ineffective against animal or insect vectors, while the strategy of shutting up complete households, both the diseased and the healthy, may actually have raised rather than reduced the level of mortality.[49] More fruitful were the measures adopted by civic fathers to try and maintain a reasonable supply of food to their inhabitants in dearth years.

Towns did their best to encourage farmers and others to bring corn and bread to their markets for sale. At Chester the city amended the usual corn tolls; at Shrewsbury there was a scheme by which the bailiffs would advance ready money to country farmers on their undertaking to deliver an agreed amount of grain after the harvest; in both towns the bakers' company monopoly was suspended during bad harvest years and village bakers allowed to come in and sell.[50] The Crown's Book of Orders (first issued in 1587, reissued in 1594, 1595) authorised local justices to direct supplies of grain from country districts to local market towns. Although the regulations were implemented in some areas, it is far from clear how effective they were generally. In the mid-1590s there was widespread evasion, with corn dealers, primarily from London, buying directly from farmers at their barn doors. The much higher prices offered by the metropolitan market produced serious problems for provincial towns, especially if their hinterland had river or coastal communication with the capital. In the mid-1590s there was a crescendo of complaints from the provinces that they were being deprived of sorely needed corn in order to feed the maw of the metropolis. Town and county justices imposed bans on the transportation of grain to London, and the government was obliged to intervene. In general the Crown, fearful of insurrection on its own doorstep, sided with the capital.[51] Civic leaders were left in a quandary. If they tried to beat off the London challenge by fixing high prices for the sale of grain in their own markets they were liable to provoke a riot. If the rates were too low the markets might be deserted by farmers and dealers.

The problem was that many ordinary townspeople could not afford even relatively modest market prices. To cushion the burden on these inhabitants most corporations, large and small, organised corn stocks which sold grain, flour or bread at below market prices. Stocks had been established intermittently in many southern towns since the early Tudor period; London had a municipal granary in the fifteenth century, but the 1590s saw the corn stock become an important agency of civic administration. In the capital the principal granary at the Bridgehouse was run from the late 1570s by the city companies who were responsible for purchasing and storing the grain; ancillary granaries were kept in Leadenhall and the Bridewell. In 1595 and 1597 the companies were charged with providing 10,000 quarters of grain for the city store, though the total stock may have been somewhat higher.[52] Corn stocks in provincial centres were smaller ventures, usually amounting to a few hundred quarters of wheat or rye, but they were important none the less in succouring poorer inhabitants. Records of the Coventry corn stock show that it served over 600 customers (generally different people) per week in the spring of 1597; in the summer the figure fell to just over 500, but rose again steadily after the poor harvest reaching an average of 725 a week in 1598. Assuming most customers were heads of households, up to 40 per cent of the city's inhabitants obtained food from this source.[53] Despite their advantages, grain stocks caused plenty of headaches for town rulers. To provision them large sums of money had to be raised by borrowing or local taxes; if market prices suddenly fell there was a good chance of a loss on sales; and supplies might be difficult to secure.[54]

In theory municipal stocks should have been filled with English corn bought during years of surplus. In reality they were often run down during the good years and had to be resurrected quickly at the worst possible time, when dearth was already looming. In the 1590s this often entailed buying imported grain. During the most difficult years there was in fact a significant influx of continental grain to English towns: in 1596 the Crown suspended customs duties on imports. The registers of vessels sailing through the Sound indicate sharp rises in 1586–7 and 1595–8 in the shipment of grain in English boats. Most of this was Polish rye bought at Danzig and Elbing; by the late sixteenth century the Polish commonwealth increasingly concentrated on the grain export trade. In 1595–8 approximately 72,520 quarters of rye and wheat were shipped through the Sound. Almost certainly this was only part of the picture: sizeable quantities of Polish grain were imported in Dutch or German vessels or were purchased on the Amsterdam corn market. Nor was the Baltic the only source of supply. In 1597, for instance, Chester was importing grain from France.[55]

Inevitably London, with its important position in European trade and its insatiable demand for food, was the principal destination for grain imports. During the first three weeks of November 1596 nearly half the ships entering the port were laden with corn. From October 1596 to March 1597 about 110,000 quarters of grain were imported into the port of London, though at least some of this was re-exported to provincial ports.[56] City fathers negotiated purchases with English and foreign merchants trading to the Baltic, as well as buying on the Amsterdam market. Importers were encouraged by the promise that if London prices fell before their corn arrived they would be at liberty to ship it elsewhere. In addition, Danzig grain ships sailing to Spain were repeatedly seized by the English fleet. In 1594 Lord Howard, the Lord Admiral, stopped three grain ships in the Channel and compelled them to change course for the Thames.[57]

The total flow of imported grain was clearly large. Putting the 1596–7 figures on an annual basis, foreign imports were running at four times the level of coastwise imports in 1585–6, though as we have said there was doubtless some leakage of foreign grain to provincial ports. The imports had a significant effect in moderating market prices, discouraging hoarding by home producers, and preventing panic. In the worst harvest years all eyes were on the Baltic. In April 1597 a Chester official sent to London to buy grain wrote back that the merchants there refused to fix prices 'till they hear what the prices be in Danzig'.[58]

London grain was shipped not only to Chester, but to Gloucester, Shrewsbury, Bristol and elsewhere. Provincial towns also pursued alternative channels of purchase. In 1586 Chester sent two of its magistrates to Hull to buy a boat-load of Danzig rye and there were large direct imports to Hull from the Baltic during the 1590s.[59] King's Lynn, Exeter and Plymouth may also have bought directly from Danzig. The scale of imports to provincial towns is difficult to calculate. In 1597 above a dozen ships came to Bristol with rye, and at Plymouth the previous year four boat-loads of Polish corn were landed, but some of the foreign grain was sold in the urban hinterlands.[60] In general, however, the imports helped provincial towns, as well as London, to ride out the worst of the crisis. In 1595 the corporation at King's Lynn avowed that 'if this realm had not been relieved [in the last year] from foreign parts, the misery of time had fallen out to be very great'. In 1597, after two more dearths, Roger Wilbraham of Nantwich declared that 'if great store of wheat and rye especially had not been brought to London and other haven towns from Denmark and Holland etc. . . . it is like we had felt and had a great mortality'.[61]

This is not to say that town inhabitants were totally dependent on cereals for sustenance. Coarse bread was made from a mixture of oats and beans; vegetables were increasingly popular and market gardens were starting to appear on the outskirts of cities. In London in 1593 we learn of 'a number of poor people living by roots, turnips, herbs and such like' grown upon the dungfields near to the capital.[62] Particularly nutritious was that old stand-by, fish. It can be no coincidence that London was swarming with fishwives in the 1590s or that one of the riots in 1595 was directed against abuses in the fish trade. At Canterbury there was a 20 per cent increase in the number of fish stalls open on market days in the late 1590s. Fish prices tended to advance in difficult harvest years, but the rise was always much less than for cereal products. In the mid-1590s sizeable quantities of foreign fish were imported. In November 1596, for instance, twenty-one Flemish ships landed ling, cod and eels at London.[63]

As well as taking steps to maintain food supplies, towns acted directly to relieve their poor. There was a flurry of private philanthropy in the worst years of hardship. At the same time attempts were made to put traditional almsgiving on a more regular footing. In London special funds were established to collect voluntary donations from householders with the proceeds used to distribute 4,000 loaves a week to the poor. (These were forerunners of the subscription funds which were to become an important element in urban poor relief in the seventeenth and eighteenth centuries). At Bristol the corporation appointed that every burgess should provide a meal a day for at least one poor person.[64] At the same time, desperate efforts were made to set the needy on work. In London they had to repair the city's ditches or make pins. Elsewhere, as at Lincoln, the poor were engaged in knitting and spinning wool; but few of the urban workhouses were very successful, often ending in insolvency. More positive were the coal and wood stocks which cities organised to help the poor to cook and keep warm in the inclement weather.[65]

Finally, a growing share of aid for the poor was channelled through parochial relief. Parish rates had been levied in a number of towns since the early part of Elizabeth's reign, if not before, but the amount of money actually expended was small and the beneficiaries almost exclusively the sick and elderly. However, by the late 1590s parish relief was increasingly important – encouraged by the 1598 Act. In St Martin's in the Fields, in the western suburbs of the capital, total parish expenditure on poor relief rose from about £36 in 1578–9 to £59 in 1594–5 and £109 in 1598–9, with most of the increase raised by parish rates; the number of parish pensioners more than doubled during this period. Nearby in St Margaret's, Westminster, poor relief payments increased from an average of about £36 a year in the 1560s to £223 per annum in the 1590s, with £457 paid out during the plague time of 1593–4. Outside London at the small Kent town of Lydd expenditure on the poor advanced from £38 in 1590–1 to £61 in 1594–5 and £72 in 1599–1600. Even so, the achievement of statutory relief must not be exaggerated. In St Martin's, Westminster, those receiving regular parish doles comprised only about 12 per cent of the needy in the parish; the situation was similar elsewhere.[66] A major difficulty in larger towns was the small size of parishes and their uneven social composition: parishes with many poor often had insufficient wealthy householders to support them, and vice versa. Attempts to redistribute income from rates to assist poorer parishes started to be effective only after 1598. Another difficulty stemmed from the widespread reluctance of many middling inhabitants to pay their rates, some no doubt regarding this as the last financial straw threatening to push them into bankruptcy.[67]

Given the problems of mobilising new forms of relief, it is not surprising that much of the action which the authorities took to deal with the plight of the lower orders was essentially negative and punitive. The immigrant poor were singled out for harassment. In January 1597 Shrewsbury town magistrates extended quarter sessions for three days because they had 'much ado with inmates and idle persons pestering the town, in examining of them and so driven out of the town'. At Lincoln after 1586 no poor incomer was allowed to settle without the mayor's consent; any newcomer to Coventry who married a city inhabitant was required to leave for home within a month; fines were imposed on persons lodging or employing immigrants.[68] Special beadles arrested vagrants at the gates or in the streets; parish constables and overseers organised weekly searches of tenements and alehouses to discover illicit inmates.[69] Those arrested were liable to be incarcerated in the houses of correction or bridewells which most towns had acquired by the late 1590s and then shipped back to their place of origin. Several score of Irish beggars were shipped home from Bristol in 1598.[70]

There were also various attempts to strengthen social control. For most of the 1590s London had two civic provost-marshals to keep order within the city. Despite their title their powers seem to have been fairly limited. In the critical situation of 1595, however, the Privy Council appointed the veteran soldier Sir Thomas Wilsford to act as provost-marshal in the city and the adjoining suburbs, backed up by a force of thirty cavalry. Wilsford was authorised to execute offenders under martial law. In addition, special commissioners were appointed to proceed against vagrants, soldiers and others brought before them. The commissioners' jurisdiction covered both the city and Middlesex, suggesting perhaps a government initiative to overcome the administrative confusion caused by metropolitan expansion outside the old city limits. But the commissioners functioned only for a short time and the innovation lapsed.[71]

More lasting were other measures to enforce public order and buttress urban administration. As we know, alehouses were popular meeting places for urban immigrants and the poor, often located in back alleys or cellars. Regulation up to now had been sporadic and ineffectual, but from the 1590s town magistrates, prodded by the Privy Council, did their best to tighten up the licensing system to suppress disorderly or illicit premises. In London special licensing sessions were held from this decade.[72] At the parish level vestries began to meet more regularly, once a month in the city of London, and their authority was extended by the various poor laws. Nottingham's constables were reorganised and their vigilance improved. The same years saw the emergence of standing committees of town magnates, who in their capacity as JPs met several times a week and administered an extensive summary justice.[73]

IV

To conclude, one can see that the crisis facing English towns during the 1590s was often severe, with short-term difficulties (due to war, harvest failure and epidemic disease) aggravated both by structural problems within urban society (especially the underlying economic instability of many of the established towns) and by long-term national pressures, including rapid population growth and large-scale pauper migration. There were other crises, of course, in Tudor England, as in the 1520s and 1550s, once again with harvest failure, disease and war among the causal factors. Unfortunately the evidence for these earlier periods is uneven and it is difficult to make detailed comparisons with the problems of the 1590s. It is arguable, however, that those times of difficulty, while they precipitated high mortality rates (possibly higher than in the 1590s), were not so prolonged and may have been less wide-ranging than in the 1590s. If towns were badly hit in the 1520s by economic depression, the countryside was more resilient, not as yet overwhelmed by population pressure and land shortages. In the 1590s the dearth, according to one writer, was 'greater than usually has been in any former age'.[74] By then heavy population increase, the rising tide of poverty (particularly in towns), the greater scale of military activity (and attendant disruptive demands), and the unprecedented and spectacular ascent of London creating a host of problems, gave an important new dimension to the late Elizabethan crisis.

And yet what is also striking about the 1590s is that, despite all the stress and strain in urban communities (most notably in London, the north and the west), there was no breakdown of urban government. Measures to ensure adequate food supplies, the consolidation and extension of poor relief, strong police action against migrants and the disorderly poor, and the strengthening of civic administration all helped to keep the situation in check. Here there may have been an important advance over the position during earlier crisis. To some extent the 1590s can be seen as a turning point in the development of English towns during the early modern period. Towns continued to suffer recurrent, sometimes critical, difficulties in the seventeenth century, not least in the 1620s and 1640s, but the impact tended to be more selective. This may be because the external pressures on urban communities began to diminish with slackening population growth and possibly lower levels of pauper immigration. At the same time town authorities began to show a great ability to cope, quite often building on the progress in poor relief and police control achieved during the 1590s. But it would be perverse to end a discussion of crisis on an optimistic note. The consolidation of oligarchic government during the 1590s and the souring of relations with the county gentry were two important ingredients in the increasingly unstable chemistry of urban politics in early Stuart England.

Notes: Chapter 3

1 J. Strype, *Annals of the Reformation* (London, 1725–31), Vol. 4, pp. 210–11; *Historical Manuscripts Commission* (hereafter *HMC*), Salisbury MSS, Vol. 13, pp. 168–9; the

microfilm of the original document is BL, Microfilms 485/49/129; *Acts of the Privy Council* (hereafter *APC*), 1595–6, pp. 88–9; Huntington Library, Calif., Ellesmere MS 6174.

2 E. P. Cheyney, *A History of England from the Defeat of the Armada to the Death of Elizabeth*, Vol. 2 (London, 1926), chs 25–6; J. B. Black, *The Reign of Elizabeth, 1558–1603* (Oxford, 1936), pp. 355–6; B. Darivas, 'Étude sur la crise économique de 1593–1597 en Angleterre . . .', *Revue d'histoire économique et sociale*, vol. 30 (1952), pp. 382–98; A. B. Appleby, *Famine in Tudor and Stuart England* (Liverpool, 1978), esp. chs 8–9.

3 For the urban hierarchy, see P. Clark and P. Slack, *English Towns in Transition, 1500–1700* (London, 1976); also J. Patten, *English Towns, 1500–1700* (Folkestone, 1978).

4 For the broad chronology, see J. Thirsk (ed.), *The Agrarian History of England and Wales*, Vol. 4 (Cambridge, 1967), p. 854; Huntington Library, Ellesmere MS 2242, fo. 1 (almost certainly datable to the 1590s); W. A. Leighton, 'Early chronicles of Shrewsbury, 1372–1606', *Transactions of the Shropshire Archaeological and Natural History Society*, vol. 3 (1880), pp. 331, 337; Coventry Record Office, Accession 535, Mayoral List, fo. 16; J. R. Chanter, *Sketches of the Literary History of Barnstaple* (Barnstaple, 1895), pp. 100, 102–3, 105.

5 C. Creighton, *A History of Epidemics in Britain*, new edn (London, 1965), Vol. 1, p. 351 and *passim*; P. Slack, 'Mortality crises and epidemic disease in England, 1485–1610', in C. Webster (ed.), *Health, Medicine and Mortality in the Sixteenth Century* (Cambridge, 1979), p. 43.

6 J. E. Neale, *Queen Elizabeth I* (London, 1934), esp. ch 17 ff.; P. Clark, *English Provincial Society from the Reformation to the Revolution* (Hassocks, 1977), pp. 221–8; Corporation of London Record Office (hereafter CLRO), Journals, 23, fo. 11 and *passim*; J. Stow, *The Annales of England* (London, 1631), p. 796.

7 *APC*, 1590s, *passim*; R. Davis, *English Overseas Trade, 1500–1700* (London, 1973).

8 R. Finlay, *Population and Metropolis: The Demography of London, 1580–1650* (Cambridge, 1981), pp. 120–1. The data for Table 3.1 were generously provided by Beatrice Shearer.

9 D. Palliser, *Tudor York* (Oxford, 1980), p. 126; Gloucestershire Record Office, Gloucester Parish Registers (originals and microfilms); A. Dyer, *The City of Worcester in the Sixteenth Century* (Leicester, 1973), p. 22; Kendal figures kindly supplied by Dr C. Phillips; see also the Hampshire market towns in J. R. Taylor, 'Population, disease, and family structure in early modern Hampshire with special reference to the towns', unpublished PhD thesis, University of Southampton, 1980, pp. 348–57. According to E. A. Wrigley and R. S. Schofield, *The Population History of England, 1541–1871* (London, 1981), pp. 332 ff., the 1590s saw a cluster of crisis years, but mortality rates were not as spectacular in some other periods (albeit with regional variations); however, this picture may well reflect the heavy rural bias of their evidence.

10 Appleby, *Famine*, pp. 109–19; E. M. Leonard, *The Early History of English Poor Relief* (Cambridge, 1900), pp. 124–5, J. D. Leader, *The Records of the Burgery of Sheffield* (Sheffield, 1897), p. 65; *CSPD*, 1595–7, pp. 347–8; R. Parkinson (ed.), *The Autobiography of Henry Newcome*, Vol. 1, Chetham Society, 1st ser., Vol. 26 (1852), pp. 82–3.

11 Leighton, 'Shrewsbury', pp. 335–6; J. Hall, *A History of the Town and Parish of Nantwich* (reprinted Menston, Yorks., 1972), p. 112 and n.; K. R. Adey, 'Seventeenth-century Stafford: a county town in decline', *Midland History*, vol. 2 (1973–4), p. 161; A. L. Beier, 'The social problems of an Elizabethan country town: Warwick, 1580–90', in P. Clark (ed.), *Country Towns in Pre-Industrial England* (Leicester, 1981), p. 55; D. Palliser, 'Dearth and disease in Staffordshire, 1540–1670', in C. W. Chalklin and M. A. Havinden (eds), *Rural Change and Urban Growth, 1500–1800* (London, 1974), pp. 70–1; Slack, 'Mortality crises', pp. 35–8; Taylor, 'Population', pp. 354 ff.; ex inform. B. Shearer.

12 N. S. B. Gras, *The Evolution of the English Corn Market* (Cambridge, Mass., 1926), pp. 105 ff.; York City Archives, E 40, items 85–7; *APC*, 1596–7, pp. 226–7; BL, Lansdowne MS 76, fo. 101.

13 See Chapter 2, by Brian Outhwaite, above; also CLRO, Repertories, 23, fo. 222; Remembrancia, II, 79; Staffordshire Record Office, D.593 S/4/39/8; BL, Lansdowne MS 78, fo. 153*v*; W. Camden, *The History of the Most Renowned and Victorious Princess Elizabeth* (London, 1688), p. 597.

14 For Scotland, see Appleby, *Famine*, p. 134; CLRO, Remembrancia, II, 164, also 162; Chester City Record Office, M/MB 30/190–1, M/MP 8/144.

15 Clark, *Country Towns*, pp. 58–60; *idem*, *English Provincial Society*, p. 239; J. Hill, 'A study of poverty and poor relief in Shropshire, 1550–1685', unpublished MA thesis, University of Liverpool, 1973, p. 162; ex inform. C. Phillips.

16 Leicestershire Record Office, Borough Hall Papers, II/18/4/15; Coventry Record Office, Accession 535, fo. 16*v*; Canterbury Cathedral Library (hereafter CCL), City MSS, Misc. Correspond.; P. Laslett, K. Oosterveen and R. M. Smith (eds), *Bastardy and Its Comparative History* (London, 1980), pp. 18, 95–7, 164–6.

17 cf. J. Hughes, 'The plague in Carlisle, 1597/8', *Transactions of the Cumberland and Westmorland Antiquarian and Archaeological Society*, n.s., vol. 71 (1971), pp. 52–62.

18 Leciestershire Record Office, II/18/5/33; also BL, Lansdowne MS 80, fo. 107.

19 J. D. Gould, 'The crisis in the export trade, 1586–7', *English Historical Review*, vol. 71 (1956), pp. 213–22; D. W. Jones, 'The "Hallage" receipts of the London cloth markets', *Economic History Review*, 2nd ser., vol. 25 (1972), p. 586; J. Hill, 'Poverty', pp. 161 ff.

20 Huntington Library, Ellesmere MS 2333; J. Vanes, 'The overseas trade of Bristol in the sixteenth century', unpublished PhD thesis, University of London, 1975, pp. 18, 22; BL, Lansdowne MS 80, fos 101*v*, 107; A. R. Michell, 'The port and town of Great Yarmouth', unpublished PhD thesis, University of Cambridge, 1978, p. 40.

21 Huntington Library, Ellesmere MS 2242, fo. 3. For a general account of these problems, see Clark and Slack, *English Towns*, pp. 103 ff.

22 Appleby, *Famine*, pp. 36 ff.; P. Clark and P. Slack (eds), *Crisis and Order in English Towns, 1500–1700* (London, 1972), pp. 142–4; M. Spufford, *Contrasting Communities* (Cambridge, 1974), pp. 77–8; J. Goodacre, 'Lutterworth in the 16th and 17th centuries', unpublished PhD thesis, University of Leicester, 1977, p. 42 and *passim*.

23 BL, Lansdowne MS 74, fos 71–*v*; A. L. Beier, 'Social problems in Elizabethan London', *Journal of Interdisciplinary History*, vol. 9 (1978–9), p. 204; court book, Bridewell Hospital, 1597–1604 (I am grateful to the Governors of Bridewell Royal Hospital for permission to refer to this court book, and to Dr Lee Beier for kindly letting me use his microfilm of the volume). Westminster Public Libraries (Victoria Library), St Martin's in the Fields records, F.6039; Greater London Record Office, P92/SAV/1316.

24 Coventry Record Office, A 3(b), pp. 21–2; Bristol Record Office, Ordinances of the Common Council, fo. 64; R. S. Ferguson and W. Nanson (eds), *Some Municipal Records . . . of Carlisle*, Cumberland and Westmorland Antiquarian and Archaeological Society, extra ser., Vol. 4 (1887), p. 272.

25 Kent Archives Office, Fa/JV 44; BL, Lansdowne MS 78, fos 126 ff.

26 CLRO, Journals, 23, fo, 214; HMC, 13th Report, app. IV, Rye MSS, p. 92; Chester Record Office, M/MP 8/51 and *passim*; QSF 49 *passim*; Huntington Library, Ellesmere MS 86.

27 Clark and Slack, *Crisis and Order*, pp. 138–40; CLRO, Remembrancia, II, 102; Kent Archives Office, Fa/JV 48, also JV 42; CLRO, Repertories, 24, fos 379, 382*v* ff.

28 BL, Lansdowne MS 49, fo. 22; *APC*: 1586–7, pp. 322–3; 1591–2, p. 507; 1592–3, pp. 187, 200–1, 222; Strype, *Annals*, pp. 167–8; CLRO, Remembrancia, II, 98; Repertories, 23, fo. 406*v*; *CSPD*, 1591–4, p. 153; *APC*, 1591–2, pp. 507–8.

29 For the claim that the capital was more orderly in the sixteenth and early seventeenth centuries than later, see V. Pearl, 'Change and stability in seventeenth-century London', *London Journal*, vol. 5 (1979), p. 5. For evidence of widespread disorder after 1600 see, K. J. Lindley, 'Riot prevention and control in Early Stuart London', *Transactions of the Royal Historical Society*, 5th series, vol. 33 (1983), pp. 109–16.

30 *APC*, 1590–1, pp. 634–5; J. S. Cockburn (ed.), *Calendar of Assize Records: Surrey Indictments Elizabeth I* (London, 1980), p. 345; BL, Lansdowne MS 71, fo. 28, 32; CLRO, Remembrancia, I, 662; *APC*, 1591–2, pp. 549–51.

31 *CSPD*, 1591–4, p. 282; BL, Lansdowne MS 71, fos 34 ff.; *APC*, 1592, pp. 242, 342.

32 e.g., Cockburn, *Assize Records*, p. 416; Stow, *Annales*, p. 769; CLRO, Remembrancia, II, 97.

33 BL, Lansdowne MS 78, fos 159, 161; CLRO, Remembrancia, II, 98.

34 Stow, *Annales*, p. 769; CLRO, Journals, 24, fo. 22*v*.

35 Cambridge University Library, MS Mm.1.29, fos 33–*v*; CLRO, Journals, 24, fos 25*v* ff.; Stow, *Annales*, pp. 769–70.
36 W. H. Overall and H. C. Overall (eds), *Analytical Index to the . . . Remembrancia* (London, 1878), p. 451; BL, Lansdowne MS 81, fos 76, 86; J. P. Collier (ed.), *Trevelyan Papers: Part II*, Camden Society, 1st ser., Vol. 84 (1863), p. 101 and n.
37 HMC, Salisbury MSS, vol. 13, pp. 168–9; *CSPD*, 1595–7, p. 343.
38 P. Clark, 'Popular protest and disturbance in Kent, 1558–1640, *Economic History Review*, 2nd ser., vol. 29 (1976), pp. 367 ff.; BL, Lansdowne MS 50, fos 44*v* ff.; Shropshire Record Office, SBR 2624: PRO, SP 12/188/47.
39 Clark, 'Popular protest', pp. 373 ff.; PRO, SP 12/262/151; Hertfordshire Record Office, HAT/SR 10/52. See also generally B. Sharp, *In Contempt of All Authority* (London, 1980), pp. 17–21.
40 *APC*, 1589–90, pp. 14, 47–8, 54–5; A. V. Judges, *The Elizabethan Underworld* (London, 1930), pp. xvii–xviii; Stow, *Annales*, p. 757; see above, p. 53.
41 Chester Record Office, Mayors List, Cowper MS, p. 210; M/MP 8/51; R. H. Morris, *Chester in the Plantagenet and Tudor Reigns* (Chester, n.d.), pp. 89–90; *APC*, 1595–6, pp. 331–3.
42 Cheyney, *History*, p. 28; Chester Record Office, M/L/1/165; *APC*, 1598–9, pp. 214–15; 1597–8, pp. 391–2; CCL, City MSS, Misc. Correspond.
43 *APC*, 1599–1600, pp. 137, 155, 163–5, 533–4; 1600–1, p. 52; *HMC*, Salisbury MSS, vol. 14, p. 136; *Adams's Chronicle of Bristol* (Bristol, 1910), p. 159.
44 e.g., Chester Record Office, M/MP 10/17–18; QSE 5/145; QSF 49/27 and *passim*; Shropshire Record Office, SBR 2621/9.
45 *APC*, 1597, pp. 311–13 (Newcastle); *APC*, 1590, p. 5 and *passim* (New Romney); *APC*, 1591–2, p. 447; 1592, p. 98 (Stamford); *APC*, 1598–9, pp. 297–8 (Dartmouth); Clark, *English Provincial Society*, pp. 253–5 (Canterbury and Sandwich); *Victoria County History, Gloucestershire*, Vol. 4 (Gloucester), forthcoming; W. H. Stevenson (ed.), *Nottingham Records*, Vol. IV (Nottingham, 1889), pp. 245–8 (Nottingham); A. E. Gibbs (ed.), *The Corporation Records of St Albans* (St Albans, 1890), pp. 50 ff.; *HMC*, 14th Report, app. VIII, Lincoln MSS, pp. 77–8 (Lincoln); H. W. Clemesha, *A History of Preston in Amounderness* (Preston, 1912), p. 114 (Preston); *APC*, 1591, p. 128 and *passim* (Doncaster).
46 *APC*, 1598–9, p. 401; 1597–8, p. 72; Shropshire Record Office, SBR 2621/8; Gloucestershire Record Office, GBR 1376/1451, fos 146*v* and *passim*.
47 J. W. F. Hill, *Tudor and Stuart Lincoln* (Cambridge, 1956), pp. 75–7; Gloucestershire Record Office, GBR 1376/1451, fo. 152 and *passim*; *APC*, 1601–4, p. 191.
48 Camden, *History*, pp. 602–10.
49 P. Slack *et al.*, *The Traditional Community under Stress* (Milton Keynes: Open University Urban History course, 1977), p. 98.
50 Chester Record Office, A/B/1, fos 207, 246; Shropshire Record Office, SBR 2624–5.
51 Clark, *English Provincial Society*, pp. 232–3; Gras, *Corn Market*, pp. 236–41; Overall and Overall, *Analytical Index*, pp. 378–80; BL, Lansdowne MS 78, fo. 153*v*; *APC*, 1595–6, pp. 8, 19–20; 1596–7, pp. 534–5, 558–9.
52 Gras, *Corn Market*, pp. 77–85; CLRO, Repertories, 23, fo. 458*v*; Journals, 24, 249*v*–50.
53 Clark, *English Provincial Society*, p. 233; Coventry Record Office, A 27.
54 Kent Archives Office: Madistone Burghmote Book A, fo. 58; NR/AC 1, fo. 98*v*; W. T. MacCaffrey, *Exeter, 1540–1640*, 2nd edn (Cambridge, Mass., 1975), pp. 157–8; CLRO, Repertories, 24, fo. 142.
55 Camden, *History*, p. 506; H. Zins, *England and the Baltic in the Elizabethan Era* (Manchester, 1972), pp. 258 ff.; also J. K. Fedorowicz, *England's Baltic Trade in the Early Seventeenth Century* (Cambridge, 1980), pp. 111–12; CLRO, Journals, 24, fo. 161; Cheyney, *History*, pp. 17–19; Chester Record Office, M/MP 8/136–7; other imports came from Denmark.
56 BL, Lansdowne MS 81, fo. 119; Cheyney, *History*, p. 19.
57 Overall and Overall, *Analytical Index*, pp. 378, 380; CLRO, Repertories, 23, fos 573*v*–4*v*; Journals, 24, fo. 161; Remembrancia, II, 31, 95.
58 For coastwise imports, see F. J. Fisher, 'The development of the London food market', in E. M. Carus-Wilson (ed.), *Essays in Economic History*, Vol. 1 (London, 1954), p. 136; Chester Record Office, M/MP 8/92.

59 Gloucestershire Record Office, GBR 1376/1451, fos 165*v*–7; Shropshire Record Office, SBR 2706; S. Seyer, *Memoirs Historical and Topographical of Bristol* (Bristol, 1821–3), Vol. 2, pp. 254–5; Chester Record Office, A/B/1, fos 203*v*, 207; R. Davis, *The Trade and Shipping of Hull* (York, 1964), p. 11.

60 BL, Add. Ms 8937, fo. 6; MacCaffrey, *Exeter*, pp. 157–8; R. N. Worth (ed.), *Calendar of the Plymouth Municipal Records* (Plymouth, 1893), p. 21; Seyer, *Bristol*, Vol. 2, p. 255.

61 BL, Lansdowne MS 78, fo. 191; Hall, *Nantwich*, p. 112.

62 CLRO, Remembrancia, II, 162; BL, Lansdowne MS 74, fos 75*v*–6.

63 CLRO, Journals, 24, fos 91*v*, 98*v*; Remembrancia, II, 97; CCL, F/A 19, 20; J. E. T. Rogers, *A History of Agriculture and Prices in England*, Vol. V (Oxford, 1887), p. 427; BL, Lansdowne MS 81, fo. 119*v*.

64 CLRO, Journals, 24, fos 148*v*, 152, 179; Seyer, *Bristol*, Vol. 2, pp. 255–6.

65 CLRO, Repertories, 22, fos 258*v*–9, 268*v*–9; 23, fo. 87; Lincolnshire Record Office, City MSS, L 1/1/1/3, fos 201 ff., 182; Clark, *English Provincial Society*, p. 239; CLRO, Repertories, 22, fo. 351*v*.

66 Westminster Public Libraries (Victoria Library): St Martin's, F.304 ff., F.6039; St Margaret's, E.144 ff.; Lydd, Z/P 4/2.

67 J. Hill, 'Poverty', p. 173.

68 Leighton, 'Shrewsbury', p. 336; Lincolnshire Record Office, L 1/1/1/3, fo. 161*v*; Coventry Record Office, A 3(b), pp. 21–2; Bristol Record Office, Ordinances, fo. 63; Stratford-upon-Avon, Shakespeare Birthplace Trust, BRU 2/2, p. 37; Dorset Record Office, Bridport MSS, B3/E5.

69 Bristol Record Office, Ordinances, fo. 64; Gloucestershire Record Office, GBR 1376/1451, fo. 164*v*; CLRO, Journals, 23, fo. 158 and *passim*.

70 J. Latimer, *Sixteenth-Century Bristol* (Bristol, 1908), p. 113.

71 CLRO, Repertories, 22, fo. 197*v* and *passim*; 23, fo. 503; BL, Lansdowne MS 66, fos 242 ff.; Stow, *Annales,* pp. 769–70.

72 CLRO, Journals, 23, fos 91*v*, 158 and *passim*; 24, fo. 209*v*; P. Clark, *The English Alehouse: A Social History, 1200–1830* (London, 1983), p. 172.

73 CLRO, Journals, 23, fo. 254*v*; E. Freshfield, *The Vestry Minute Books of the Parish of St Bartholomew Exchange* (London, 1890), pp. 37 ff.; Stevenson, *Nottingham*, pp. 256–7; Gloucestershire Record Office, GBR 1376/1451, fo. 188.

74 For towns in the 1520s, see C. Phythian-Adams, *Desolation of a City* (Cambridge, 1979), pp. 51–67, 187 and *passim*; also *idem*, 'Urban decay in late medieval England', in P. Abrams and E. A. Wrigley (eds), *Towns in Societies* (Cambridge, 1978), pp. 178, 180–2. For the 1550s, see F. J. Fisher, 'Influenza and inflation in Tudor England', *Economic History Review*, 2nd ser., vol. 18 (1965), pp. 120–9; J. Loach and R. Tittler (eds), *The Mid-Tudor Polity, c. 1540–1560* (London, 1980), esp. chs 5 and 7. Huntington Library, Ellesmere MS 2242, fo. 1.

4 *Dearth, Famine and Social Policy in the Dutch Republic at the End of the Sixteenth Century*

LEO NOORDEGRAAF

If we define the concept of 'crisis' as a complex of interrelated phenomena embracing severe dearth, a sharp decline in the standard of living, growing unemployment, widespread poverty and beggary, and the occurrence of epidemics and high mortality, then the question whether this term can be applied to the situation in the Dutch Republic during the last decades of the sixteenth century is certainly an open one. For the published work on the northern Netherlands during the pre-industrial period contains very little data on such a crisis and special studies, such as those made of similar crises in 1556–7, 1565–6, 1572–4, 1623–4, 1629–31, 1662 and 1698–9 are lacking for the last years of the sixteenth century.[1] The purpose of this chapter is to ask: was there a crisis according to our definition in the Republic at the end of the sixteenth century, and, if so, what was its nature, extent and intensity? The answer to the first part of the question will be, in part, affirmative and against this backdrop I would like to pose a second question: did this short-term crisis affect economic and social development in the northern Netherlands in the seventeenth century?

Since the war between the Republic and Spain extended over a good part of the Netherlands, it has proved difficult to determine the geographical limits for this study. Military operations caused continually shifting boundaries. Ultimately, I chose the area that fell under the official jurisdiction of the Republic when peace was concluded in 1648: the seven United Provinces including the region of Drente and the so-called 'Generaliteitslanden'. Venlo, in the south, was also included because very useful quantitative data were available. As shown in the map, the research area covers most of what is now the Netherlands.[2] The research material was drawn from the archives of a number of cities and villages and from the archives and printed resolutions of the Provincial States and the States General. This material was supplemented by data from parish records, diaries and correspondence, printed sources on international trade,

The Dutch Republic in the 1590s

seventeenth- and eighteenth-century chronicles and some modern studies.[3] The map shows those places and provinces for which there is information on social and economic disruption. This does not mean that the crisis was confined to those areas. In many places the necessary sources were missing or had been lost, while certain archives could not be consulted owing to their size or inaccessibility. The resolutions and ordinances issued by the central governments of both the north and the south show, however, that the problems occurred throughout the region covered by this research.

I

What leads us to believe there was a crisis in the Republic at the end of the sixteenth century? The first indications can be found by analysing purchasing power. The purchasing power of wages earned by 'opperlieden' (representative of the lowest income group) in some eastern Dutch cities and the city of Utrecht in the second half of the sixteenth century, and in the northern city of Alkmaar[4] from 1596, was examined in relation to rye and rye-bread prices. The analysis shows that incomes were greatly impaired in the years 1586–8, to a lesser extent in 1590–1, and to a greater degree in 1594–9 (see Figures 4.1–4.3). If we trace the decrease in purchasing power from 1550 until 1600 we find that in Nijmegen, Zutphen and, as far as we know, in Venlo, it was in fact at its lowest in 1587. Arnhem and Utrecht were rather more successful in maintaining purchasing power than in previous periods of dearth. The decrease in the period 1594–9 was both absolutely and relatively less marked but, on the other hand, it lasted comparatively longer. Generally speaking, if we compare the situation at the end of the sixteenth century with similar periods in the seventeenth and eighteenth, we find that the dearth was of relatively long duration, although in both intensity and duration the years 1624–32 and 1694–1700 were equally hard. In other years after 1600 purchasing power was at a considerably lower ebb than shortly before the end of the sixteenth century, but the duration was appreciably shorter. All in all we can conclude that both the periods 1586–8 and 1594–9 can be added to the list of crises in the northern Netherlands.

The cause of the decrease in purchasing power lay in price trends. Prices rose steeply within a short period. The increases not only affected rye (*the* staple), but also other grains, peas, and dairy produce.[5] How great these increases could be is shown by prices current in Nijmegen. The average annual price of rye per 'malder' (166·88 litres) rose from 6·19 Brabant guilders in 1585 to 28·23 in 1587. In the summer months of that year prices of 36 guilders and higher are recorded. The increase in the price of rye bread was lower, probably because city governments kept prices down by subsidies. But the rise was still 300 per cent. Elsewhere the increases were less marked, but they were still large enough to cause alarm. The same applies to the last decade of the sixteenth century. Prices doubled within a short space of time (see Figure 4.4: weekly rye prices fixed by Eindhoven's city government).[6] Countless contemporary complaints of extreme price increases and dearth support the conclusion that rising prices caused great anxiety. For example, the secretary to the law courts at Oirschot recorded in 1587 that bread was so dear that ordinary people were forced to eat bean soup instead. There was no bread at all in the August of that year. He further stated that bread was so expensive that people were offering a pound of good veal in exchange for a pound of bread.

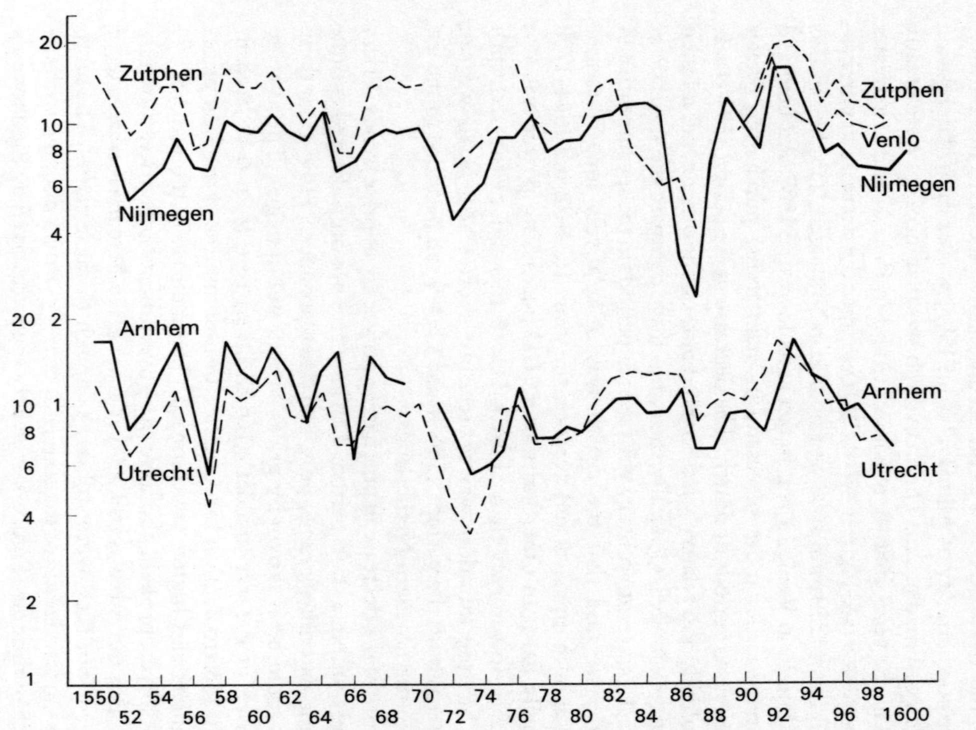

Figure 4.1 *Purchasing power of day wages of* opperlieden *(bricklayers' labourers) in litres of rye in Nijmegen, Arnhem, Venlo, Zutphen and Utrecht, 1550–1600.*

Source: P. H. M. G. Offermans, *Arbeid en levensstandaard in Nijmegen* . . . (Zutphen, 1972), pp. 119, 120, 147, 197–203.

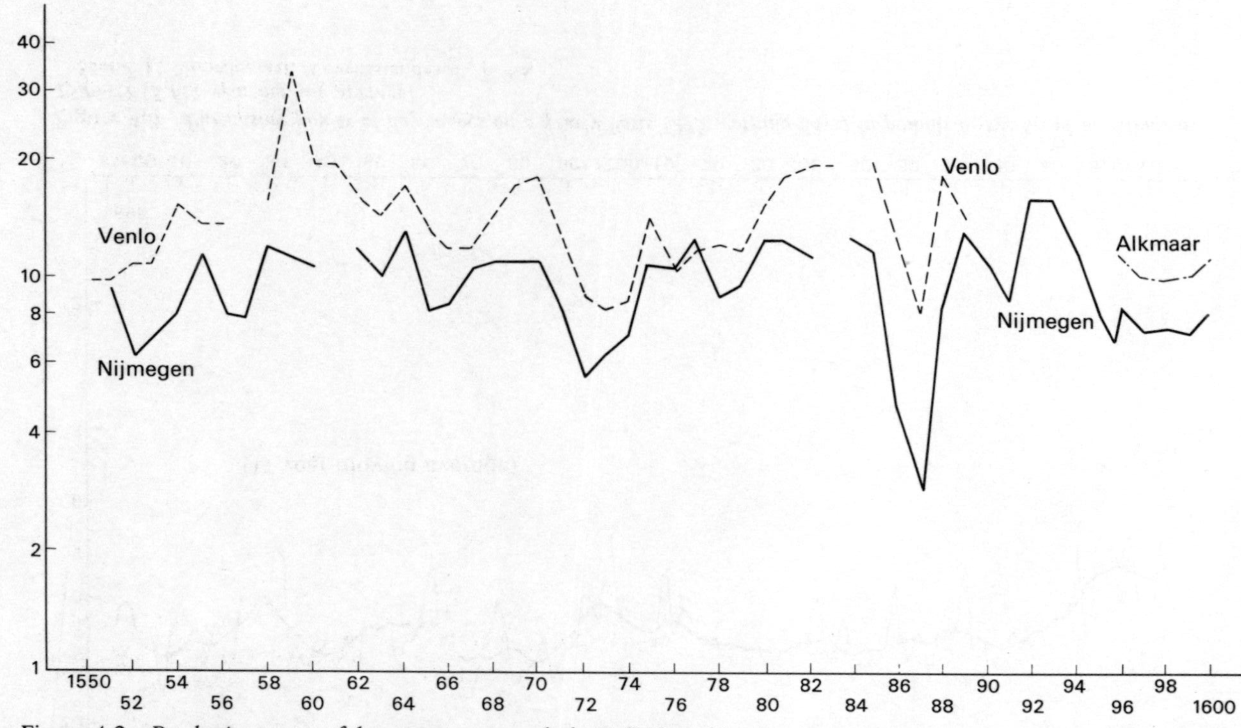

Figure 4.2 *Purchasing power of day wages on a yearly basis (250 working days) in pounds of rye bread in Nijmegen and Venlo, 1550–1600, and in Alkmaar (275 working days), 1596–1600.*

Sources: Offermans, *Arbeid en levensstandaard*, pp. 121, 147, 200–2; L. Noordegraaf, 'Levensstandaard . . . in Alkmaar', *Alkmaarse Historische Reeks*, vol. 4 (1980), p. 63.

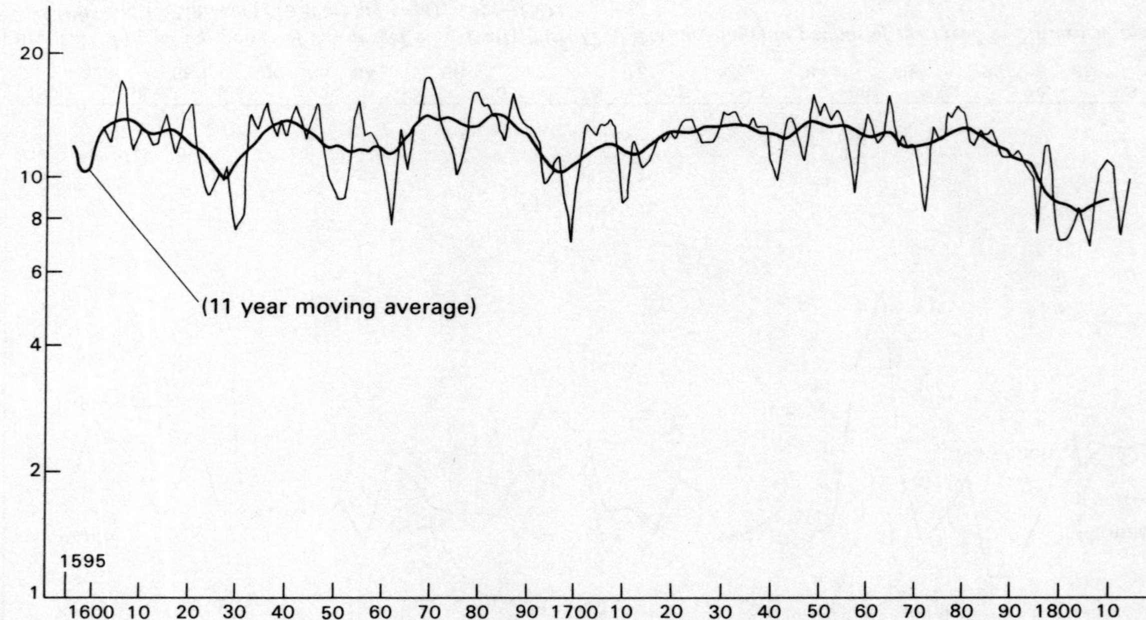

Figure 4.3 *Purchasing power of day wages on a yearly basis (275 working days) in pounds in rye bread in Alkmaar, 1596–1815 (11 year moving average).*

Source: L. Noordegraaf, 'Levensstandaard', p. 63.

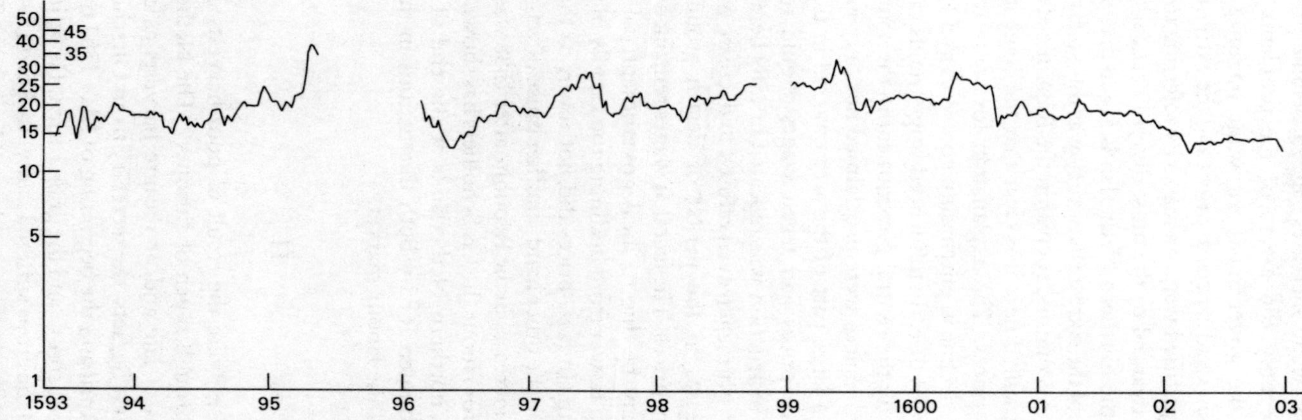

Figure 4.4 *Rye prices in* stuivers *(probably per barrel), fixed weekly by the city government of* Eindhoven, *20 April 1593–23 May 1595; 5 March 1596–13 October 1598; 1 January 1599–31 December 1603.*

Source: GA, Eindhoven, CGB 50/41, graanprijzen 1593–1623.

Due to rising prices, the decrease in purchasing power and subsequent reductions in demand, wage increases lagged behind price increases.[7] Contemporaries were only too aware of the problems. There were frequent requests to the government for wage increases. The reason always given was the sharp advances in prices and the extreme dearth. The government likewise justified wage increases by referring to rising prices. Wage increases were awarded to the most diverse occupational groups.[8]

Most historians of the northern Netherlands argue that the increase in basic wages at the end of the sixteenth century was due solely to scarcity of labour as a result of the economic revival in the Republic after 1580.[9] But from the evidence presented here it is clear that the wage increases were connected with high prices. The explanation for some wage increases appears to have been a decline in purchasing power. A good illustration of the way that rising prices directly influenced wage trends can be found in the ordinances issued by the central government in the southern Netherlands in 1588. The ordinances were proclaimed not only in what is now Belgium, but also in a large part of the area covered in this paper. The order stated that since prices had fallen wages should revert to their pre-dearth level. The instruction was repeated in 1589 because it had not been complied with.[10] Nijmegen even refused to decrease wages.[11] So we find that wage increases in the period of dearth around 1587 were prompted by the rise in prices. The fact that wages remained constant after prices fell in 1588 may be due to local government policies aimed at preventing purchasing power from declining too rapidly in relation to the years before the slump. In fact, prices did not revert to their pre-dearth level by any means. On the other hand, another cause of wage stabilisation and certainly of wage increases in the Republic after 1588 was undoubtedly the growing demand for labour. Just as Scholliers has shown for Antwerp, wage patterns in the northern Netherlands at the end of the sixteenth century must be accounted for by both fluctuations in the standard of living and the state of the labour market.

II

Increases in food prices were the result of poor harvests caused by bad climatic conditions through much of Europe.[12] The Netherlands had to contend with a series of late and/or meagre harvests as a result of the inclement weather. Aert Sgraets, the secretary from Oirschot, tells us that about the middle of April and the beginning of May 1587 the frost was so severe that crops did not sprout and the grain rotted. He writes that in 1590 very little rain fell and the crops suffered badly. In April 1594 the frost was again severe and a lot of barley, vegetables and fruit froze. That same year it rained from July to September, so there was no harvest at all. 1596 brought a plague of mice to the whole country.[13]

The connection between the dearth and the reduced supply of both home-grown and foreign grain was abundantly clear and the government became alarmed.[14] The shortages were not slow in making themselves felt. Countless sources report growing poverty, beggary and vagabondage throughout the country. In Nijmegen, and possibly in Alkmaar too, hunger riots threatened in 1597–8, and in a number of other cities disturbances were feared. There was unrest in Flushing in Zeeland when goods were to be exported from Holland to the southern Netherlands. The garrison at Bergen op Zoom became mutinous in 1597 because of food shortages and there were problems with the soldiers at Grave due to the lack of victuals.

It is possible that the considerable rise in the death rate in Nijmegen during 1587 can be attributed to famine. A highly placed official recorded both extensive dearth and high mortality. The same year the secretary from Oirschot was more explicit. He wrote that 'the famine was so wide-spread many died of hunger'. It was also feared that the dearth would cause unemployment. The idea that the high price of provisions was prejudicial to industry, because a larger part of disposable income had to be spent on food, was not altogether unknown. In 1597 the States of Holland declared grain shortages to be undesirable; they not only took the bread out of the mouths of the work force, they also led to unemployment. In 1595 the merchant de la Faille de Jonge saw a connection between the poor state of industry and the scarcity of food, observing that these are blows the poor endure only with difficulty. Indeed, there are various indications that the Leyden cloth industry experienced a slump in the 1590s. In 1594–5 the price of some textiles went down by about 25 per cent. Problems with sales and the dearness of provisions caused a sharp increase in the number of Leyden people on poor relief. In 1598 87 per cent of the population applied to the city for subsidised bread. Because of the high cost, Leyden's cloth companies were no longer able to provide free food for members. At Haarlem the city fathers spoke of inflation and the drop in trade in the same breath.[15] Whether there was a causal link between the dearness of provisions and the slump in industry cannot be determined with certainty, but it is clear that food shortages had a disruptive effect.

III

During the late 1580s and 1590s the country was beset by numerous other difficulties. In the first place, the shortage of provisions was increased by the war in the regions outside Friesland, Holland and Utrecht. The threat of war, siege, plundering and arson, and the resulting drop in production – farmers left their fields unsown – aggravated the food problem and forced prices up even further. Thus the comparatively sharp decrease in purchasing power in Nijmegen in 1590 can be attributed to the siege of that city. How deeply the war affected life in these already difficult years is again apparent from Aert Sgraets's observations. His village was plundered by soldiers in 1587. They carried off household goods, livestock and grain. His notes on other years are vivid, eyewitness accounts of the horrors of war. Numerous other sources report the harassment of inhabitants by wandering bands of soldiers.

Secondly, many of the dikes in Holland and Utrecht broke in 1595 and 1597, putting large areas of these provinces under water. The distress among the inhabitants was so great that special collections for their relief were organised throughout the region. Dikes burst in Groningen in 1597, causing equal distress.[16]

Thirdly, the plight of the lowest-paid workers in particular was worsened by long, hard winters, such as those of 1586–7 and 1594–5. As already stated, hard winters had a detrimental effect on the growth of spring crops, but they caused other problems as well. When it froze for long periods more fuel was needed. Peat became scarce and rose in price considerably. The peat reserves diminished so quickly in 1596 that the States General placed a total embargo on exports.[17] A few examples show how exceedingly cold it could be: at Oirschot the Easter of 1587 was so cold the congregation could not bear to stay in church; the minister of Nijkerk in the province of Gelderland had to postpone Holy Communion at Christmas 1594 because it was so frosty his parishioners took fright and fled.[18]

Fourthly, at various times during the dearth, plague broke out in a number of places, including Rotterdam, Delft and Utrecht. Whether this was closely connected to the food crisis need not be discussed here.[19] It is clear, however, that the economic disruption was intensified by the epidemics.

Not least of the problems was the rapid growth in population, especially in the west of the Republic.[20] This was due not only to natural increase, but also to extensive immigration from the surrounding territories, and in particular from the southern Netherlands as a result of economic and religious problems there. Movement was influenced not only by the relatively favourable economic situation and the success of Protestantism in the north, but also by the food shortages in the south. As the grain supply to the Republic was comparatively good (the Dutch controlled the international grain market to an increasing extent), conditions in the north were more tolerable than in neighbouring countries. Gravitation to the granary of Europe was, for many, the obvious solution, although this exacerbated the crisis in the north.[21] For this reason, in an attempt to combat the beggary produced by the crisis various cities in the province of Holland distinguished between indigenous and foreign beggars. During the crisis years the city governments saw themselves swamped by needy outsiders for whom they felt little responsibility. Foreign beggars were either excluded or afforded fewer facilities for the practice of their 'trade' than the townspeople. Obviously, some of the outsiders originated from the country areas of the Republic, but it is certain that a number of foreigners were among the needy. Dordrecht banished a woman from Bruges in the southern Netherlands in 1586 because, it was said, she gathered beggars and thieves to her. And an ordinance against beggary issued in 1587 mentions beggars from Liège by name. In the same year the States of Zeeland decided to expel poor people who were natives of enemy territory in Flanders. In 1595 the States General pointed to a direct link between immigration and price rises, declaring that in order to prevent increases in corn prices beggars and the like from enemy territory should be excluded from the Republic.[22] The assumption that the extent and intensity of the crisis outside the Republic stimulated migration to the north is also supported by our knowledge of the appalling conditions in the south. Contemporary writers may have exaggerated their descriptions somewhat, but it is equally apparent from the work of recent economic and social historians, particularly on the standard of living, that the crisis in the south was of an exceptional nature, especially in 1586–8.[23]

IV

The seriousness of the situation in the north can be judged not only from trends in living standards and complaints of dearness and the scarcity of provisions, but also from the reactions of the authorities. Many measures to alleviate the crisis were taken by local and provincial rulers as well as by the central government. There is indirect evidence of a crisis situation in places and areas where no illustrative wage and price indexes are available. We can conclude that dearth, shortage of food and the resulting poverty prevailed throughout the northern Netherlands. The measures taken to combat the crisis did not differ greatly from place to place. It is possible, therefore, to describe the methods in general terms. When prices rose and the grain reserves diminished, various attempts were made to control prices and ensure adequate provisioning. Supply and export and buying and selling were placed under restrictions in order to prevent inflation and hoarding. Maximum prices were fixed. Blackmarketing and tampering with weights and measures both carried severe penalties. If the supply of grain decreased and shortages threatened, or if prices rose steeply, city governments bought in the grain themselves. Bread was then distributed to the needy at a reduced price. The city fathers tried to keep the reserves level by reducing or prohibiting the export of grain, peas and beans. This measure led to conflicts between the towns and the country regions as both city and provincial authorities resorted to it. At various times the central government placed an embargo on the export of grain. The municipal authorities tried to organise a fair distribution by taking inventories of the grain already in the city and requisitioning it when necessary. In other cases rich citizens were obliged to buy in quantities of grain or provide the funds to enable the authorities to do so. The production of starch, certain kinds of cake and bread, beer and malt were limited or forbidden altogether. Government intervention in poor relief expanded. Overall the large number of government measures to ensure provisioning strongly suggests that the northern Netherlands was hit by a serious crisis at the end of the sixteenth century, and in 1587 and 1595–7 in particular. A comparison of social policies in other periods of dearth in the sixteenth and seventeenth centuries only serves to emphasise this conclusion.[24]

V

What about the impact of the crisis on the long-term economic and social development of the Republic? This was considerable. The effects of food shortages in the northern Netherlands itself were of a temporary nature and had only a limited effect. However, permanent and positive changes were brought about by bad harvests and grain shortages elsewhere in Europe, and particularly in the Mediterranean countries. When, around 1590, the demand for grain from the Baltic regions increased considerably, Dutch merchants, who until then had only touched on the Mediterranean occasionally, were able to corner the markets there. After the first commercial sallies, the market was consolidated and extended. In fact, grain shortages in certain parts of southern Europe were not confined to the last decade of the sixteenth century. For a variety of reasons grain was in short supply there until well into the seventeenth century.

This commercial activity, which was also directed at other European countries, also means that the food shortages in the Republic at the end of the sixteenth century cannot be considered as the first symptoms of the so-called crisis of the seventeenth century. On the contrary, the opening up of new markets was an enormous stimulus to the economy of the northern Netherlands and, as a result, obviously in combination with other factors, the symptoms of this 'structural' crisis were not apparent until 1660. The food shortages, which heralded a general and prolonged economic depression in southern Europe, brought about a shift in international trade which the Dutch used to full advantage. The food shortages elsewhere constituted an important contribution to the prosperity of the Republic in the first half of the seventeenth century.[25]

When grain became scarce in the Republic at the end of the sixteenth century the government was confronted with the problem of whether grain should be freely exported to other countries. A total embargo could lead to the removal of the grain merchants to free ports,[26] whereby supplies to the northern Netherlands from the Baltic would be threatened. On the other hand, free trade could strip the Republic bare of provisions or lead to excessive price increases. Which was the lesser evil? Discussions in and among municipal councils, the provincial states and the States General were heated, as was the case in other years of dearth in the pre-industrial period. The merchants themselves were often in doubt as to which policy was the right one; they constituted a large part of the governing bodies, or at least influenced them considerably. Their decisions could also have far-reaching political consequences. Should an embargo be placed on the Spanish enemy alone, or should exports be prohibited altogether? If the latter course was chosen the Republic's allies, if they appealed to the Dutch grain suppliers, would also suffer. In difficult years a lot of tact was required when dealing with requests for large quantities of grain from dearth-stricken England and France.[27]

At various times during periods of scarcity embargoes were placed on export to other countries. In general, however, these embargoes usually applied only to home-grown grain. Sometimes peas, beans, butter and cheese were also subject to embargo. Foreign grain, however, in transit through the staple market, was less liable to control. Generally, the embargoes applied to trade with the enemy only. As we can see from the number of evasions and frauds, however, the restrictions were not as effective as they should have been. This was largely due to the lax attitude of the authorities. They were only too aware of the advantages and disadvantages of export stoppages.[28] On occasion they came into conflict with their foreign allies who favoured a harder line on trade with the enemy.[29]

Free trade remained the point of departure for the Republic's policies. One total embargo on the export of grain was in force for six months during 1595–6. The exceptional length of the embargo shows how serious the situation must have been. In spite of the grain shortages and dearth in the Republic at the end of the sixteenth century, little attention has been paid to crisis phenomena in the 1580s and 1590s. Why?

VI

In answering this question various hypotheses can be put forward. First, especially in the eastern and southern provinces of the north, famine and war were interrelated. Because of this interrelation historians may have failed to appreciate that the crisis was caused not only by war, but mainly by climatic and economic developments. Secondly, the scale of the crisis at the end of the sixteenth century may have seemed comparatively small. This is certainly true if we contrast the experience of the Republic with other parts of Europe. Compared with some areas in southern and central Europe the standard of living in the seaward provinces of the Republic remained reasonably stable. The crisis was less obvious due to the relatively large supplies of grain from the Baltic. As a result prices remained comparatively stable.[30] Even though grain was sometimes scarce, there can be no question of real famine. There was no total lack of food causing high mortality. This situation occurred in 1587 only and was confined to the east and south of the Republic. In comparison, however, with other subsistence crises in the northern Netherlands at various times during the pre-industrial period, the years 1586–8 by reason of intensity and 1594–9 for duration must have been very critical indeed. Seen thus, one would have expected more attention to have been paid to the crisis during the last decades of the sixteenth century.

The explanation of this lack of attention can thus be ascribed to the Republic's comparatively favourable position during the years of dearth from 1586 onwards. On the other hand, other relatively minor crises in the northern Netherlands have attracted attention from historians. It is striking that contemporary historians, such as Hooft (1647) and van Meteren (1612), give detailed accounts of the appalling conditions resulting from war, bad harvests and dearth in the south during 1587.[31] They report at length how sharply prices rose and describe the effects of the famine and the Dutch blockades on what is now the Belgian coast. Famine, epidemics, high mortality, depopulation, beggary, usury, hordes of starving wolves and wild dogs, and all the other plagues of Egypt are recorded, vividly painted and exaggerated by fantastic examples. They hardly mention food shortages in the north although, as we have seen, they clearly occurred. In fact, the relatively favourable situation in the Republic is used as a comparison. Obviously, it cannot be denied that conditions in the south were worse. But this black-and-white picture would seem to suggest that war-inspired nationalism, or chauvinism, in so far as they existed at that time, led to an understatement of the seriousness of the situation in the north – an impression that may have caused later researchers to 'miss' this crisis.

Broadly speaking, I suspect that the idea of an economic revival in the north from around 1590 onwards has driven the less prosperous side of social and economic development into the shade. In this respect, I believe modern research to have been greatly influenced by the nineteenth-century historian Fruin. His book, which has been reprinted several times since its publication in 1857, portrays an enriched and prosperous Republic in the very midst of an economic revival at the end of the sixteenth century.[32] Fruin does mention the dearth in this period, but it becomes insignificant when compared with the information illustrating the growing prosperity of the northern Netherlands as a result of international trade. Like Hooft and van Meteren, he dwells on the appalling conditions in the south, describing them at length. His sketch undoubtedly influenced later historians with the result that the extent and significance of the crisis in the period 1586–1600 has not been recognised. The aim of this chapter has been to present a less one-sided view of development in the northern Netherlands at the end of the sixteenth century.

Notes: Chapter 4

1 A. Th. van Deursen, *Het kopergeld van de Gouden Eeuw*, Vol. 1, *Het dagelijks brood* (Assen, 1978), p. 91, notes the critical situation in the years from 1594 to 1597, but he is primarily concerned with other problems and does not discuss the extent of the crisis in any detail. More evidence for a crisis at the end of the sixteenth century can be found in L. Noordegraaf, 'Levensstandaard en levensmiddelenpolitiek in Alkmaar vanaf het eind van de 16de tot in het begin van de 19de eeuw', *Alkmaarse Historische Reeks*, vol. 4 (1980), pp. 55–100; P. H. M. G. Offermans, *Arbeid en levensstandaard in Nijmegen omstreeks de Reductie (1550–1600)* (Zutphen, 1972); and in N. W. Posthumus, *De geschiedenis van de Leidsche lakenindustrie*, Vol. 2 (The Hague, 1939). For a bibliography of other crises in the Dutch Republic in the pre-industrial period, see Noordegraaf, 'Levensstandaard'. For work on the area of the southern Netherlands which comprises present-day Belgium, see below, nn. 10 and 23.

2 So my use of the terms Dutch Republic and northern Netherlands is not strictly correct.

3 For a list of sources, see L. Noordegraaf, 'Crisis? Wat voor Crisis? . . . ', *Economisch-en Sociaal-Historisch Jaarboek*, vol. 45 (1982), pp. 39–57.

4 The Zutphen prices are not always correctly calculated by Offermans (see R. van Schaïk, 'Prijs- en levensmiddelenpolitiek in de Noordelijke Nederlanden van de 14e tot de 17e eeuw: bronnen en problemen', *Tijdschrift voor Geschiedenis*, vol. 91 (1978), pp. 241–2). The trend in wages and prices in Alkmaar is representative of the greater part of Holland (see L. Noordegraaf, *Daglonen in Alkmaar, 1500–1850* (n.p., 1980), pp. 73–80, and 'Levensstandaard', p. 96). The considerable reduction of purchasing power after 1780 was partly compensated for by people starting to eat potatoes instead of rye bread: L. Noordegraaf, 'Sociale verhoudingen en structuren. De Noordelijke Nederlanden, 1770–1813', *Algemene Geschiedenis der Nederlanden*, vol. 10 (1981), p. 381.

5 A. Heringa, 'Overzicht van marktprijzen van granen te Arnhem in de jaren 1544–1901', *Bijdragen tot de statistiek van Nederland*, n.s., vol. 26 (1903); J. C. G. M. Jansen, *Landbouw en economische golfbeweging in Zuid-Limburg, 1250–1800: Een analyse van de opbrengst van tienden* (Assen, 1979), app. IV; Offermans, *Arbeid en levensstandaard*; N. W. Posthumus, *Nederlands(ch)e prijsgeschiedenis*, Vols 1 and 2 (Leyden, 1943–64); J. A. Sillem, 'Tabellen van marktprijzen van granen te Utrecht in de jaren 1393 tot 1644', *Verhandelingen van de Koninklijke Academie van Wetenschappen to Amsterdam, afd. Letterkunde*, vol. 3, no. 4 (Amsterdam, 1901); W. Tijms, 'Prijzen van granen en peulvruchten te Arnhem, Breda, Deventer, 's-Hertogenbosch, Kampen, Koevorden, Maastricht, Nijmegen', *Historia Agriculturae*, vol. 10, no. 1 (1977).

6 During those weeks in 1595–6 for which data are lacking prices may have risen even more. We know that the provision of grain in the winter of 1595–6 was very difficult.

7 In comparison with our price data only a few wage series have been published. The available data are listed in Posthumus, *Leidsche lakenindustrie*, Offermans, *Arbeid en levensstandaard*, and in Noordegraaf, *Daglonen*.

8 As well as the publications mentioned in note 7, see 'Resoluties Staten van Holland, 1592–1598' (index *ad* 'tractementen' and professions); 'Notulen Staten van Zeeland' 18.4.1595; GA, Alkmaar 94–268 (1595); GA, Amsterdam, vroedschapsresoluties 8–102, 123/4, 142, 182, 298 (1595–6) (see also J. G. van Dillen (ed.), *Bronnen tot de geschiedenis van het bedrijfsleven en het gildewezen van Amsterdam*, Vol. 1, *1512–1609*, RGP Grote Serie 69 (The Hague, 1929), no. 865/6/8,870/3,890); GA, Delfshaven (not on the map, near Rotterdam), vroedschapsresoluties 1–194 v, 225 (1592–6); GA, Edam, vroedschapsresoluties 65–19–77 v (1594), 99 v (1597); GA, Haarlem, vroedschapsresoluties 3/4–7–207; 3/4–8–96, 106; archief Brouwersgilde 22 (1594); for Rotterdam, H. C. H. Moquette, 'Pestepidemieën in Rotterdam', *Rotterdams Jaarboekje* (1925), p. 14; GA, Utrecht, vroedschapsresoluties, II, 121 (9.2.1597); GA, Venlo, 1778–368 (25.6.1587). The municipalities objected most to wage increases in the food trades because such increases boosted prices even more.

9 P. W. Klein, 'De zeventiende eeuw (1585–1700)', in *De economische geschiedenis van Nederland*, ed. J. H. van Stuijvenberg (Groningen, 1977), pp. 88–9; Noordegraaf, *Daglonen*, pp. 84–6; Jan de Vries, 'An inquiry into the behaviour of wages in the Dutch Republic and the Southern Netherlands, 1580–1800', *Acta Historiae Neerlandicae*, vol. 10 (1978), pp. 87–9.

10 E. Scholliers, 'De levensstandaard der arbeiders op het einde der 16e eeuw te Antwerpen', *Tijdschrift voor Geschiedenis*, vol. 68 (1955), pp. 83–4, and *De levensstandaard in de XVe en XVIe eeuw te Antwerpen* (Antwerp, 1960), pp. 144–5. For the text of the placards, see C. Verlinden and J. Craeybeckx (eds), *Prijzen- en lonenpolitiek in de Nederlanden in 1561 en 1588–1589: Onuitgegeven adviezen, ontwerpen en ordonnanties* (Brussels, 1962).

11 Offermans, *Arbeid en levensstandaard*, pp. 139, 177.

12 See, for instance, F. Braudel, *La Méditerranée et le monde méditerranéen à l'époque de Philippe II* (Paris, 1966), Vol. 1, pp. 245–52.

13 See J. Santegoeds, 'Jaarkronicken uit de schepenprotocollen van Oirschot-Best, 1587–1591', *Campinia*, vols 5–10 (1975–80), and N. Japikse (ed.), *Resolutiën der Staten Generaal* (The Hague, 1921–30), RGP Grote Serie 55–490, 57–624; archief kerkvoogdij Dordrecht 575 (October 1597); Pieter (Christiaensz.) Bor, *Oorsprongk, begin, en vervolgh der Nederlandsche Oorlogen, ber oerten en borgerlijke oneenigheden*, Vol. 4 (Amsterdam, 1679), p. 267; A. Matthaeus and Th. Verhoeven, *Rerum Amorfortiarum scriptores duo inediti . . .* (Leyden, 1693), p. 402; G. Brom and L. A. van Langeraad (eds), *Diarium van Arend van Buchell* (Amsterdam, 1907), pp. 427, 430, 438 (for damage by birds, p. 218); H. O. Feith, *Register op het archief van Groningen* (Groningen, 1853–77), *ad* 1590, no. 53.

14 See, for instance, the placard of the government of the Spanish Netherlands of 26.1.1586 (GA, Breda H–8–197).

15 Van Deursen, *Het kopergeld*, Vol. 3, *Volk en overheid* (Assen, 1979), p. 50; Posthumus, *Leidsche lakenindustrie*, Vol. 2, pp. 134–5; R. C. J. van Maanen, 'De vermogensopbouw van de Leidse bevolking in het laatste kwart van de zestiende eeuw', *Bijdragen en mededelingen betreffende de geschiedenis der Nederlanden*, vol. 93 (1978), pp. 11, 36; GA, Leyden, secretarie-archief 9252 (4.1.1598); GA, Haarlem, vroedschapsresoluties 3/4–7 (1.7.1595).

16 'Resoluties Staten van Holland', index *ad* 'inundatiën' and 'Alblasserwaard'; Th. Velius, *Chronyk van Hoorn* (Hoorn, 1740), p. 499; 'Stukken voor de geschiedenis van het jaar 1595', *Kronijk Historisch Genootschap*, vol. 21 (1865), pp. 146–9, 159–63; 'Resoluties Staten van Groningen', Statenarchief no. 1, I (19.10.1597); for a survey of all floods in 1587–1600, see M. K. Elisabeth Gottschalk, *Stormvloeden en rivier-overstromingen in Nederland*, Vol. 2 (Assen, 1975), pp. 771–816.

17 Japikse, *Resolutiën*, 2.10.1596 (RGP 62–330); prices of peat in Posthumus, *Prijsgeschiedenis*, Vol. 2, pp. 58–9, 290–1, 503.

18 G. B(eernink) (ed.), 'Groote koude in 1594', *Bijdragen en mededeelingen Gelre*, vol. 6

(1903), p. 248. For the winter of 1586–7, see also GA, Dordrecht, Klepboek 14–155 (December 1586).

19 The argument against a close connection between food shortages and the occurrence of plague is supported by the fact that it was some time after the period of dearth that major epidemics broke out (esp. 1602–5).

20 Jan de Vries, *The Dutch Rural Economy in the Golden Age, 1500–1700* (New Haven, Conn., 1974), graphs 3.2–3.6; A. M. van der Woude, 'Demografische ontwikkeling van de Noordelijke Nederlanden, 1500–1800', *Algemene Geschiedenis der Nederlanden*, vol. 5 (1980), graph 5.

21 J. Briel's opinion that 'growing prosperity in the Dutch Republic was first of all caused by immigration from the Southern Netherlands' seems rather exaggerated, the more so since he fails to take into account the way that migration to the northern Netherlands exacerbated the critical problems there (J. Briels, *De Zuidnederlandse immigratie, 1572–1630* (Haarlem, 1978), p. 37).

22 GA, Dordrecht, Klepboek 14 (21.10.1586; 11.4.1587); 'Notulen Staten van Zeeland' 27.5.1587, 9.11.1595 (mentioning the letter of the States General).

23 For the opinions of contemporary historians, see below; for recent publications, see n. 10. As regards the south, see especially A. Cosemans, 'Het uitzicht van Brabant op het einde der XVIde eeuw', *Bijdragen tot de Geschiedenis*, vol. 27 (1936), pp. 285–351.

24 For literature on government strategies in other years of crisis, see n. 1.

25 J. G. van Dillen, *Van rijkdom en regenten* (The Hague, 1970), p. 17; F. Snapper, *Oorlogsinvloeden op de overzeese handel van Holland, 1551–1719* (Amsterdam, 1959), p. 47. For the factors behind this structural shortage of grain, see Jan de Vries, *The Economy of Europe in an Age of Crisis, 1600–1750* (Cambridge, 1976), pp. 48–55. For the most important publications about Dutch trade in the Mediterranean, see S. Hart, 'De Italie-vaart, 1590–1620', *Jaarboek Amstelodamum*, vol. 70 (1978), pp. 42–60; also printed sources in K. Heeringa (ed.), *Bronnen tot de geschiedenis van den Levantschen handel*, I, RGP Grote Serie 9 (The Hague, 1910).

26 For a good example of this, see Velius, *Chronyk*, p. 470.

27 Japikse, *Resolutiën*, 7, 9, 11, 14, 18, 20, 28.2, 27.3, 13.6.1587 (RGP 47–758–762, 764/5/8/9); 6, 12.11.1595 (RGP 57–438–440), 31.1.1596 (RGP 62–64). 'Notulen Staten van Zeeland' 28.5, 14.6.1590. These requests illustrate how important the Dutch grain staple was considered to be.

28 For conflicts between towns and provinces over free trade or protectionism, see J. H. Kernkamp, *De handel op den vijand, 1572–1609*, Vols 1–2 (Utrecht, 1931–4), and Noordegraaf, 'Levensstandaard', pp. 79, 80–6.

29 Kernkamp, *Handel op den vijand*, Vol. 2, pp. 74–84, 149, 150.

30 For a more detailed comparison of the standard of living in the Dutch Republic and in the rest of Europe during the seventeenth and eighteenth centuries, see J. A. Faber, *Dure tijden en hongersnoden in preïndustriëel Nederland* (Amsterdam, 1976).

31 P. C. Hooft, *Nederlandsche Historien*, Vol. 2 (Amsterdam, 1703), pp. 1159, 1160; Emanuel van Meteren, *Histoire der Nederlandscher ende haerer na-buren oorlogen ende geschiedenissen tot den jare 1612* (The Hague, 1623), pp. 264–5, 269, 270.

32 R. Fruin, *Tien jaren uit den tachtigjarigen oorlog, 1588–1598* (The Hague, n.d.), pp. 188–245.

5 *Civil War and Natural Disaster in Northern France*

PHILIP BENEDICT

While famine, plague, and periods of acute economic distress were recurrent phenomena in sixteenth- and seventeenth-century France, the last decades of the sixteenth century witnessed so closely spaced and devastating a series of catastrophes throughout the northern half of the kingdom as to mark these years off as ones of truly exceptional hardship. The backdrop was one of political conflict and disintegration. France's apparently interminable civil wars moved in a crescendo from 1585 onwards, as the emergence of the Protestant Henry of Navarre as heir apparent to the throne led to the revival of the militant Catholic League and renewed fighting against the Huguenots. In May 1588, the *ligueurs* of Paris rose up and drove Henry III from the capital. Seven months later, the assassination of the duke and cardinal of Guise at Blois prompted much of the rest of France to follow in revolt. The country soon plunged into the longest, bitterest, and most geographically all-encompassing conflict of the wars of Religion, a conflict which lasted until 1594 in most parts of the country but was not everywhere extinguished until 1598. These years stand out as particularly terrible ones in northern France, since, unlike the Midi, the region had been only lightly touched or even bypassed altogether by campaigning prior to 1588, while now it became the centre of the conflict. But the wars of the League were just part of a larger cycle of calamities here that also included catastrophic harvest failures over much of the region in 1586–7 and 1594–7 and serious outbreaks of plague between 1580 and 1586 and again between 1596 and 1598. Marauding bands of wolves were even terrifying the inhabitants of several areas by the middle 1590s. All four outriders of the apocalypse were at large.

That this series of closely spaced shocks had exceptionally serious consequences for northern France's economy and demography is clear from all the available evidence. Strong regional contrasts had marked northern France's economic history over the decades prior to the 1580s, with some areas enjoying a continuation of the demographic and commercial expansion of the earlier sixteenth century, others suffering from the fighting in the 1560s but then recovering markedly in the 1570s and early 1580s, and still others enduring a steady dose of hardship and decline, not

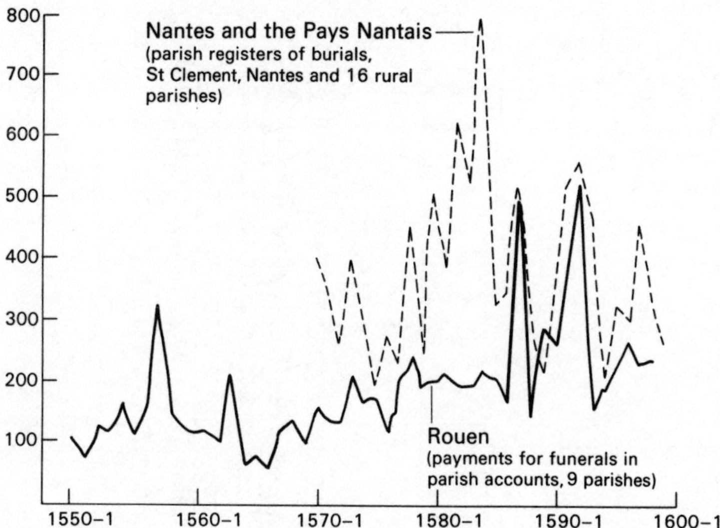

Figure 5.1 *Mortality.*

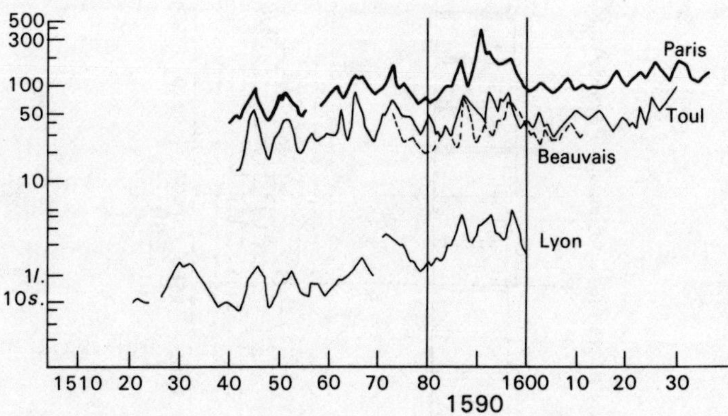

Figure 5.2 *Grain prices.*

always caused simply by the political events of the earlier Wars of Religion.[1] From the 1580s on, the evidence points unambiguously in a single direction. The only two sets of mortality figures available reveal sharp peaks in the 1580s and 1590s (see Figure 5.1), Price curves attain their highest levels of the entire period 1500–1625 at this time (see Figure 5.2). Sharp valleys appear in all detailed curves of industrial and agricultural

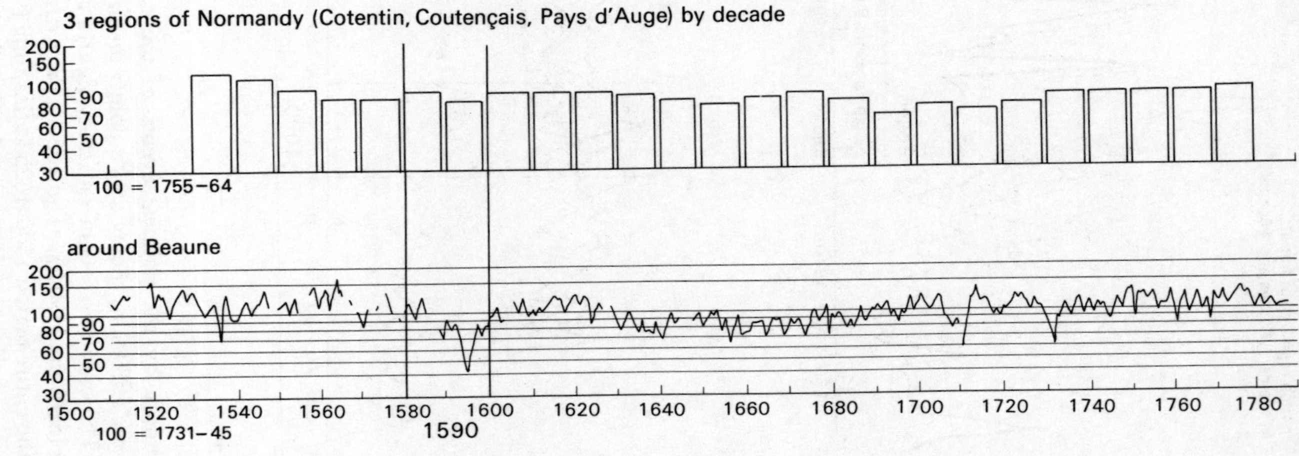

Figure 5.3 *Tithe yields.*

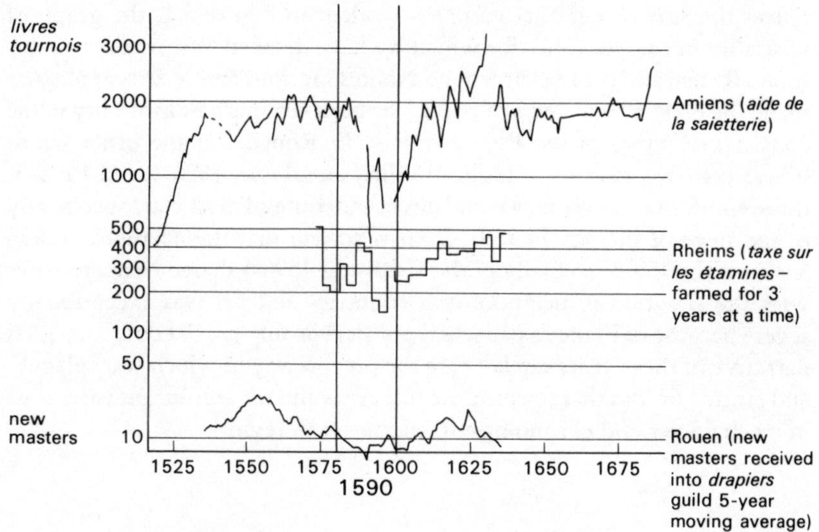

Figure 5.4 *Cloth production.*

production (see Figures 5.3 and 5.4). Those historians who have written about this period employ tragic superlatives to describe these last decades of the century. 'Les années terribles' is Jean Jacquart's label for the period 1589–94.[2] Henri Drouot concludes: 'La verité . . . est que la Bourgogne, depuis le haut moyen âge, n'a jamais autant souffert qu'a la fin du XVIe siècle.'[3]

While agreeing that these were years of exceptional suffering, recent scholars have at the same time differed somewhat over the precise nature and causes of the hardships. Some, like Jacquart, present the 'crisis' essentially as a consequence of the civil wars. Others, like Pierre Goubert and Alain Croix, have called attention to the role of disease and famines unrelated to the political upheavals, thereby suggesting, if only by implication, that France's crisis might also be linked to larger meteorological and epidemiological problems affecting all of Europe's Atlantic seaboard.[4] Some of the difference in emphasis here stems from the different phenomena examined. Those writing about the period's demography are particularly prone to stress non-war-related factors, since indeed the periods of peak mortality did not always coincide with the years of civil war. Conversely, those historians who have explored the volume of trade or the evolution of rural society tend to emphasise the impact of the fighting, since it disrupted the normal circuits of production and exchange more thoroughly and enduringly than did simple plagues or famines, even when it did not kill as many people outright. But the different emphases also reflect the sort of regional variation evident in Figure 5.1, the graph of mortality in two localities for which we have detailed information on this topic, Rouen and the region around Nantes. Serious and recurrent plagues made the early 1580s, years of peace, the period of highest mortality in the consistently crisis-prone Pays Nantais. In Rouen, on the other hand, where just two periods of high mortality stand out, 1586–7 and 1592–3, the second, greater crisis was the direct outcome of civil war, specifically of the siege of the city in 1591–2.[5] It is certain that the northern French 'crisis of the 1590s' (actually of the 1580s and 1590s) shared characteristics with the situation in neighbouring countries and yet was exceptionally severe because of France's particular political problems, but only a detailed narrative of these years can lay bare the precise way in which war, plague, and famine fit together to compose this crisis and the significant variations in its character and chronology from region to region.

I

In an account of France's recent 'maulx' written some time after 1595, Jacques Carorguy, a scribe of Bar-sur-Seine, began his litany of woe with the year 1582. His reason for choosing this year as his starting point was rather idiosyncratic; it was, he recorded, the year in which Pope Gregory XIII eliminated ten days from the year, a 'nouveaulté . . . estrange et d'ung synistre presage'.[6] But Carorguy was not the only chronicler to date France's troubles back to the early 1580s, and with good reason. The plague, which had been largely absent from France since the mid-1560s (see Figure 5.5), returned to many areas with a vengeance from 1580 to 1586, affecting localities scattered throughout northern France.[7] The example of the Pays Nantais shows just how severe this plague was in those areas most seriously touched. Not only did burials attain easily their highest levels of the entire troubled period from 1575 to 1600; the decline in the number of births registered in the years 1580–4 was also the sharpest of any five-year period between 1550 and 1600.[8] As was typical with plagues in this era, however, the incidence of the disease was very uneven. Many localities were spared entirely, and others, such as Rouen, were only lightly touched. Plague was reported in Normandy's capital in 1580 and 1581, but no significant increase is visible in the number of burials.[9]

On the heels of the plague came the terrible *crise de subsistences* of 1586–7 which affected so much of north-western Europe. From Lorraine and the Lyonnais to Normandy, the harvest was poor in 1585 and worse the next year. 'No one could remember a comparable *disette de vivres* since time immemorial', wrote Carorguy.[10] A mark of the severity of the crisis was

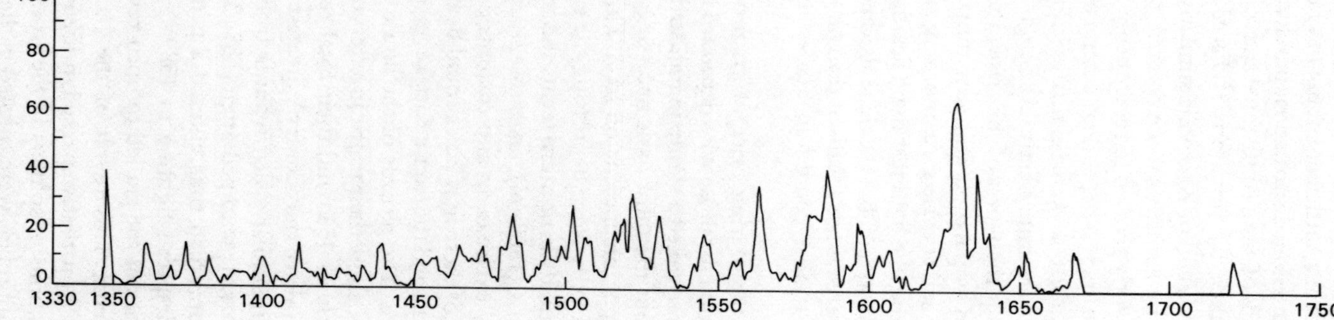

Figure 5.5 *Number of localities touched by plague, by year.*
Source: J.-N. Biraben, *Les Hommes et la Peste en France* . . . (Paris, 1975), Vol. 1, p. 120.

the virtual war waged by municipal authorities throughout northern France and beyond to obtain a sufficient supply of grain for their towns. Rouen's authorities commissioned substantial purchases from the Baltic, only to see several shiploads of grain confiscated and sold in Southampton, where they had been taken by privateers.[11] Faced by rioting in the markets, the mayor and *échevins* of Abbeville similarly stopped a convoy of Danzig rye purchased by Amiens's town council, commandeered half of the stock, and subsequently refused to recompense Amiens even in the face of royal orders to do so.[12] This sort of emergency procurement of grain, and the creation of *ateliers de charité* in many cities, could mitigate the effects of the famine only very imperfectly. Although 14,000 people were receiving relief in Rouen at the worst of the crisis, the ravages of disease among the malnourished population still sent mortality rates soaring. 'They dye in evrie streete and at evrie gate, morning and eveninge, by viii or xii in a place, so that the like hath not byne hearde of. And the poore doth not onely die so in the streete, but the riche also in their bedde by 10 or 12 in a daye.'[13] *Disettes* were far less localised than plagues in their effects, and we have reports of similar conditions across almost the whole of northern France.[14]

As always happened, the soaring price of grain not only occasioned hardship and even starvation for those who depended upon the market for their daily bread; it also provoked a slump in industrial production, since demand for everything but the most basic necessities of life collapsed as people spent all their disposable income on food. Furthermore, the high cost of bread was not the only force depressing the economy in the later 1580s. After rising only mildly in nominal terms and actually decreasing in real terms under Charles IX (1560–74), taxes rose sharply during the reign of Henry III, particularly excise taxes and customs duties.[15] Bitter complaints about the burden of these new taxes could be heard from the early years of the 1580s onwards, and the excise duties even provoked artisans in certain trades to emigrate. The records of the house of Bonvisi, Lyons's richest merchant bankers, show their traffic in letters of exchange entering a phase of decline as early as 1583 and their total receipts dropping off sharply from 1587 on. Amiens, the country's greatest weaving town, saw its cloth production turn similarly downwards from 1586. In France's leading seaport, Rouen, trade slumped after 1585. The leading poles of northern France's economy had thus entered a period of decline even before the onset of widespread fighting in 1589.[16] In the countryside, meanwhile, the difficulties of the era led to open revolt in the region of Normandy around Lisieux. This revolt of the Gautiers remains very imperfectly understood. Apparently sparked in 1586 by resentment over taxes and/or the depredations of soldiers in the area, it simmered on for two years until the peasant rebels were enlisted in the cause of the League by the Count of Harcourt, only to be abandoned at the moment of a decisive engagement with the royalist troops of the Duke of Montpensier and left to be slaughtered.[17]

By the time the Gautiers were crushed at Falaise, far more than their cause was being caught up in the conflict between royalists and *ligueurs*. From late 1588 onward, this conflict began to impinge on the lives of people throughout France far more directly than had previously been the case. In ordering the Duke of Guise killed at Blois in December 1588, Henry III wished to rid himself of the League's challenge to his authority. What he accomplished was to provoke full-scale rebellion. City after city renounced its allegiance to the 'tyrant', expelled all troops and officials loyal to him, and swore the Oath of the Union; in the words of one pro-League historian of the period, the king at Blois soon found the limits of his kingdom to be Tours and Beaugency.[18] But the strength of the League was not as great as it initially appeared. While most towns cast their lot against the king, certain major cities remained loyal: Rennes, Angers, Tours, Caen, Dieppe, Châlons-sur-Marne, and Saint-Quentin, to name only the most important royalist towns in northern France. Furthermore, there was enough of an air of urban radicalism about the League to awaken that great fear of the aristocracy – republicanism. This and the ties of interest and loyalty which bound many noblemen to the Crown led a substantial fraction of the nobility to oppose the League. Even in regions like Burgundy, the stronghold of the Duke of Mayenne and a province in which virtually all the major towns declared for the League, the nobility was about equally divided between royalists and *ligueurs*. Since many of the pro-League noblemen left the province to serve with Mayenne, the royalists actually controlled most of the countryside.[19] Every other province similarly divided into two rival camps.

The events of 1588–9 did not start a civil war; fighting had been under way since 1585. But the initial hostilities provoked by Henry III's reluctant crusade against the Huguenots had involved merely the sort of localised conflicts which had been the rule during the preceding civil wars. The region between Fontenay-le-Comte and Angers witnessed some campaigning late in 1585 and early in 1586. The German *reiters* intervened in 1587 with an ill fated expedition that saw them march – or, rather, loot – their way across a narrow band of Lorraine, Burgundy, and the Beauce, only to be routed by Guise at Auneau and sent quickly back again. Otherwise the campaigning was reassuringly confined to the Midi once more. That is what now changed. With the division of every province into two rival camps, a confused *petite guerre* of skirmishes, raids, and pillaging operations between each side's strongholds soon broke out. As one despairing merchant described the situation in 1589, 'No one can leave his house or send a letter from one place to another ... for the cities are fighting each other . . . and even within certain cities one man is fighting the next . . . No more courtesy or respect remains between father and son.'[20] With time, a few regions came to be entirely controlled by the troops of one side or the other. More commonly, the 'guerre des châteaux' simply became permanent, a means of survival for otherwise unpaid garrison soldiers. In a few areas, it degenerated into full-scale brigandage, most notoriously in the Basse-Bretagne of the dread Sieur de La Fontenelle.[21]

Meanwhile, alongside this *petite guerre* was the *grande guerre* between the Duke of Mayenne and his Spanish allies on one side and Henry III, Henry of Navarre, and their English reinforcements on the other. This large-scale fighting once more touched only relatively restricted areas, but now these were in the north. From 1589 to 1592, the cyclone moved up and down through a narrow corridor running from Tours and Orleans through the Beauce and around Paris, then down the lower Seine to Rouen and Dieppe. After 1592, Henry was in a sufficiently strong position to be able to dismiss many of his troops and rely less on arms than the internal paralysis of the League to bring people back into his camp, but 1594 saw La Capelle and Laon besieged and taken. The declaration of war against Spain in January 1595 led to campaigning in Burgundy and Brittany and a fitful war of sieges and surprises along the frontier of the Spanish Netherlands, a conflict that was only ended in 1598 by the utter financial exhaustion of both parties.

Such extensive fighting inevitably had considerable economic and demographic consequences. Unprotected by any walls, subject to the raiding parties of both sides, the countryside bore the most direct burdens. The local skirmishing alone posed so significant a threat to work in the fields that after 1589 troops had to be sent out into the countryside around many major cities to protect the peasants trying to get the harvest in. Around Dijon, for instance, the *vendange* became a complex military operation, with members of the city's harquebusiers accompanying cart-loads of *vignerons* from village to village and mounting guard as they gathered the grapes. Despite their protection, stray groups of *vignerons* were regularly picked off by royal raiding parties and held for ransom or forced labour; much of the 1591 vintage was captured by the troops; and the number of men available to work the fields gradually diminished as more and more villagers abandoned their homes for the safety of nearby cities or the adventure (and sustenance) offered by the bands of *mauvais garçons*.[22] The cumulative effect of the 'guerre des châteaux' on agricultural production is suggested by Albert Silbert's figures concerning grain production around Beaune, which shows tithe receipts in the years 1588–93 to have been 22 per cent lower than in 1581–6.[23] At the same time, the burden of taxes required to support the fighting rose in Burgundy from 313,305 *écus* in 1584–6 to 977,946 *écus* in 1590–2 – and in many areas the troops of both sides demanded payment.[24] The weight of the soldiers' 'vols, exactions, et pilleries' complained about in so many documents of the period must also be added to the balance sheet of the effects of the *petite guerre*.

Wherever major campaigns occurred and large armies passed for any length of time, the burden was heavier yet. The troops typically stripped the land of all provisions and seized whatever livestock they could find. They usually left behind only two things: famine and disease. The Paris *mercuriale* in 1590–1, the curve of mortality in Rouen in 1592, and the evolution of baptisms in Toucy and Darnétal, two *gros bourgs* sacked and occupied during the wars, all provide statistical evidence of the dramatic consequences of major campaigning in an area.[25] The most vivid pictures of war's effects come from contemporary accounts such as Antoine Richart's description of the aftermath of the siege of Laon in 1594. Following the siege, the surrounding area had been so denuded of grain that wheat cost ten times as much locally as it did in nearby Châlons-sur-Marne and Saint-Quentin, and the inhabitants of the region were reduced to carting their bedding and clothing to these towns to trade them for bread. Although the construction work which began immediately on Laon's fortifications provided employment for the urban poor and reduced their suffering, many peasants of the surrounding countryside were obliged to sell their land to obtain food. The poorer ones were driven to foraging, an all but hopeless quest since many of the villages of the region were now half deserted and much of the land lay uncultivated. Some died in the fields, the victims either of starvation or the epidemic raging in the region. This in turn engendered another scourge: the wolves. In the absence of livestock they began to attack men, their appetite for human flesh having been whetted by the unburied corpses scattered across the countryside.[26]

Sheltered behind their ramparts, the cities could offer a degree of asylum from the violence unleashed on the *plat pays*. The vacant lots and stables of many towns consequently filled up with men and cows from the surrounding countryside. While the rural population was declining, often drastically, in the early 1590s, most cities for which demographic statistics have been assembled show a striking increase in their population.[27] But asylum was all that most cities could offer the refugees from the countryside – certainly not employment, or even relief, for the urban economy suffered almost as badly as the rural one. With travel rendered insecure, trade fell nearly everywhere to a mere fraction of its normal volume, although one or two advantageously located and well fortified cities such as La Rochelle managed to skim off some of the trade diverted from other cities and enjoy a measure of prosperity.[28] Industrial production for anything other than purely local markets also collapsed, as the evidence for cloth production makes clear. (See Figure 5.4.) Even Paris' printers, to whom the League had initially been such a boon with its tracts and pamphlets, saw production in their industry fall to a small fraction of pre-1588 levels once the initial outpouring of propaganda subsided.[29] Although unemployment undoubtedly increased enormously, one is struck in reading through the activities of municipal governments in this period how little attention is given to providing relief for those out of work, even if special tax reductions were given to many guilds, 'vu la nécessité at calamité du temps', and house rents were ordered reduced in Paris. Migration was one response to this situation. Apprentices in Rouen broke their contracts to look for work in Flanders, while established merchants and artisans also left the city to seek better places to carry on their trade. The sharp rise in forest offences around Rouen and the arrest for theft of several Parisian printers suggest the more desperate measures to which others turned to meet the crisis.[30]

The desperation that could lead to crime could also lead to political action. In several cities, the *menu peuple* made its only appearance in the events of the League late in the movement's history with demonstrations or revolts against it. In the Burgundian cities, small incidents began early in 1594. Insults were uttered against *ligueur* mayors and militia captains, and stones were thrown through the windows of the ardently pro-League Jesuit house in Dijon. In February 1595 Beaune rose up and opened its gates to the King. Several months later Dijon and Autun followed.[31] The countryside meanwhile witnessed sporadic, small insurrections throughout the period 1589–94. Brittany was particularly unsettled. Scattered peasant risings continued as long as did the fighting, often taking on anti-seigneurial or anti-urban overtones.[32] Incidents also spread to Burgundy in the later years of this period. Châteaux were attacked around Beaune in 1592, soldiers were set upon and massacred by the *vignerons* of Meursault in 1594, and peasant bands took up arms for the King in several regions.[33] Though none of these movements could match the revolts of the Croquants and Tard-Avisés of the south-west in scale or organisation, northern France witnessed the same sort of militant, often anti-seigneurial, peace movement that marked the last years of the civil wars in the Midi.

Between January and August 1594, the groundswell of popular support for Henry IV combined with the richly rewarded defections of many wavering *ligueur* potentates to bring much of northern France back into the royal camp. Commerce resumed, *laboureurs* returned to their villages, and the work of reconstruction could begin. But the cycle of calamities was still incomplete, for both famine and plague each had one more visit to pay. The harvest had already failed in Lorraine in 1592, a failure unrelated to France's civil wars and which probably represents the extension northward of the grave Mediterranean *disette* of that year.[34] The cold, wet weather which made the years from 1594 to 1596 so dismal in England caused bad harvests over virtually all of northern France as well. Grain prices soared from Lyons and Toul to Beauvais, Saint-Brieuc and Poitiers.[35] The plague also flared up in many localities between 1596 and 1598. Neither the plague nor the *disette* seem to have been quite as serious as those, respectively, of 1580–6 and 1586–7. In Rouen, for instance, mortality was only slightly above normal between 1596 and 1599, while the movement of baptisms suggests a strong recuperation in the town's overall population. On the other hand, Anjou, the Beauvaisis, and the Île de France were all peaceful regions which seem to have experienced a significant mortality crisis in these years.[36] Meanwhile, those regions in which the fighting had not yet been extinguished, most notably Burgundy and Brittany, suffered a nightmarish combination of plague, famine, and warfare. In the words of one Burgundian chronicler: 'Sur les dernières années le pauvre monde estoit cy ruinée que les maisons estoient toute démeublé, tellement qu'il n'y avoit rien demeurée que les quatre muralle . . . Toute l'armée estoit ycy alentour, qui mangere tout les bled, lequel ont ne moyssonnoy rien.'[37] For three consecutive years the harvests yielded less than half their normal output; by 1597 some 864 houses in the *bailliage* of Auxerre were destroyed and another 1,144 had been abandoned.[38] The situation in Cornouaille depicted by the canon Moreau was more dramatic yet. In certain areas, for want of livestock the peasants had to hitch themselves to the plough in teams of three or four, ploughing at night to escape the attention of the soldier-brigands. Here again great packs of wolves were on the prowl.[39] Relief came only with the surrender of Mercoeur and La Fontenelle in 1598, the good harvests of 1597 and 1598, and the abatement of the plague. Not until after 1598 can it be said that the crisis of the League was fully over.

II

Assessing the longer-term consequences of this combination of natural and political disasters is no easy matter, particularly since the crisis varied so much in character and chronology from region to region. We still know dismayingly little about French social and economic history from the later sixteenth into the early seventeenth centuries, and much of what we do know is based on studies of a few regions – the Hurepoix, the Toulois, Brittany – whose typicality of the rest of northern France is uncertain. Some tentative evaluations can none the less be attempted.

To begin with, quite obviously, the population was smaller in 1600 than it had been two decades earlier. Just how much smaller is still uncertain, but the decline between the early 1580s and the late 1590s could have been as high as 20 per cent or more. That, at least, is the figure suggested by the evidence from the Pays Nantais. The rare information from other regions offers no reason to modify significantly such an estimate.[40]

More striking than this decline is the subsequent failure of the rural population to reattain its sixteenth-century peaks in many areas despite the demographic growth which occurred during the first third of the seventeenth century. This phenomenon has been observed in four different corners of the great open-field region surrounding Paris, although it emphatically did not occur in Brittany, whose rural economy rested on an unusually diversified base that included fishing and a growing linen industry as well as the production of cereal crops.[41] The restricted population growth can in turn be related to two other phenomena: the somewhat higher age at first marriage found in many areas in the seventeenth century by comparison with the sixteenth, and the slightly lower levels of agricultural output revealed by tithe records. All these symptoms point to a reduction in the productive capacity of rural society and in the opportunities for young men to establish households of their own.

Three effects of the late-sixteenth-century crisis could have contributed to this. First, the crisis reduced the supplemental resources available to all members of the village community. Both the unusually high tax demands of the period and the additional protection money often extorted by soldiers pushed many rural communities so deeply into debt that they had to alienate communal land.[42] With less common land, there was less opportunity for those makeshifts such as pasturing a few head of cattle or letting a pig or two loose in the forest on which so many members of the village community depended for bridging the gap between the output of their land and the needs of their families.

Second, the resources of individual villagers were also thoroughly depleted, so thoroughly that they could only be reconstructed at the expense of new forms of dependence. Livestock, always the favourite target of the foraging soldier, was in particularly short supply by 1598. In the short run, this meant less manure and hence lower agricultural productivity. In the long run herds could be replenished, but the only way in which many villagers could now afford a cow was to rent one. The frequently encountered practice of renting livestock is one of the most striking symptoms of the poverty of the old-regime peasantry, and it is precisely around the end of the sixteenth century that this practice seems to have begun to spread widely.[43] An even more notorious form of peasant dependence encountered in many parts of the countryside by the end of the old regime, *métayage*, or crop-sharing, also experienced its first significant expansion in certain regions, as a way of rebuilding from the crisis of the late sixteenth century.[44] This development was linked to the third and most significant change in rural society: the expropriation of many smallholders by outsiders to the village community and the consequent polarisation of rural society between an elite of *laboureurs* and *fermiers* and the mass of *journaliers, métayers, sossons,* and *haricotiers.*

This last development forms one of the great themes of French rural history from the reign of Francis I until that of Louis XIV. In every area where the evolution of property ownership has been followed over part or all of this period, small peasant holders lost ground while their richer neighbours and bourgeois or noble outsiders came to control more and more of the land. Such an ongoing process obviously cannot be linked to a single short period. It stemmed ultimately from demographic pressure which forced the subdivision of land-holdings into parcels smaller than the minimum needed to provide a family with the food it required, aggravated in the seventeenth century by the growing burden of taxation. None the less, the transfer of property was particularly likely to occur in periods of war or *cherté,* when high prices and extraordinary exactions forced many poorer peasants so deeply into debt that they could only extricate themselves by surrendering part of their land. By virtue of their exceptional severity, both the warfare and the *disette* of the end of the sixteenth century provoked a particularly rapid turnover in land.

Guy Cabourdin has used notarial records brilliantly to illuminate this process in the Toulois. Price fluctuations and the volume of certain kinds of notarial transactions, he shows, moved with a striking parallelism; as grain prices increased following a bad harvest, so too did the number of contracts in which villagers either sold land or borrowed the grain they needed to tide themselves over to the next harvest. The loans of grain, usually for six or seven months, peaked in April; a second peak of land sales then followed in December or January, as those peasants unable to pay off their loans now had to surrender some of their land. Not surprisingly, the volume of land transactions was particularly high throughout the period from 1586 to the end of the century. And Cabourdin shows who profited most from the smallholder's plight: prosperous peasants to some extent (they purchased 17·5 per cent of the land sold), but primarily nobles and *anoblis* (35 per cent of the land acquired), urban merchants, lawyers, and even artisans (29 per cent), and the First Estate (13·5 per cent).[45]

It is clear that other regions witnessed the same surge of peasant expropriation in the late 1580s and 1590s,[46] but it may be wondered whether the identity of those who profited was the same elsewhere as it was in Lorraine. While sharing France's climate and epidemics, Lorraine was an independent duchy and thus escaped the worst of the civil wars.

Unfortunately we have no other studies of land turnover in the period as detailed as Cabourdin's, but those areas harder hit by fighting and brigandage than Lorraine probably witnessed a slightly different pattern to such transactions. Richer peasants would have been less able to profit from their poorer neighbours' distress wherever warfare was significant, for they suffered the worst losses of all whenever soldiers passed their way. Certainly it was with good reason that they were always the first to flee at rumours of approaching troops. They owned the most livestock. They owned the silver goblets and well stocked chests looted so thoroughly by the *soldataille* in Moreau's Cornouaille.[47] Conversely, if anybody was in a position to profit from the disorder, it was those in the marauding armies, and particularly those at their head. Not that there was not a debit side to warfare for the nobility. Like all those dependent on land rents, the income of their *terres* fell sharply as the rural economy was disrupted.[48] Furthermore, war was a risky business, not only because one might not return from it at all, but also because one could return in the situation of Jérome de Luc, sieur de Fontenay-le-Comte, who had to excuse himself from the *ban* and *arrière-ban* in 1597 on the grounds that the ransom of 200 *écus* he had had to borrow several years previously had left him hopelessly in debt to a merchant of Orleans. His case was not unique.[49] But no other group had the nobility's opportunities for offsetting the losses of war. The *hobereau* with even the slightest military bent might fortify his château, revive or invent tolls, dues and exactions, and terrorise the peasantry – as many did. According to Moreau, 'Les casaniers, qui ne cherchaient que le petite guerre . . . faisaient bien leurs affaires.'[50] As for the great military commanders, while they often had to advance large sums to their troops during the fighting, the most important among them received a handsome return on these investments in the form of the huge pensions paid out by Henry IV to bring the *ligueur* commanders into the fold or to reward his faithful servants. A man like the Duke of Villars, granted an annual pension of 60,000 *livres* and the income of five fat abbeys, ended the Wars of Religion with his fortune made.[51] The complaint of the commoner in the famous *Dialogue d'entre le Maheustre et le Manant* deserves to be taken seriously: 'the nobles and soldiers enjoy war and we pay for all'.[52]

The consequences of the crisis for urban society are more problematic. Were there any significant shifts in urban social structure or wealth distribution? Did the poorer artisans have to sell their tools just as poorer peasants sold their land, thereby accelerating the polarisation evident within many trades between wealthy master-entrepreneurs and permanent journeymen? These questions simply have never been investigated. It does seem that the state of urban finances often deteriorated in the same way as those of the rural communities, a development with ominous future implications for municipal autonomy since the sorry state of a town's fiscal situation was often used later in the seventeenth century to justify increasing royal intervention.[53] A town's indebtedness could also have unfortunate immediate consequences for its town councillors, who frequently had to cover the debts out of their own pockets. In 1596 Orleans' entire *Corps de Ville* petitioned to be relieved of its duties for this reason.[54] Perhaps the clearest consequence of the crisis for France's urban communities is the permanent economic damage it inflicted on the country's leading commercial cities. Lyons's position as a leading European financial capital, already shaken by the events of the 1560s, ended for good between 1588 and 1595 when the great majority of the city's foreign merchant-bankers abandoned the town.[55] In a similar fashion, the unusual prosperity brought Rouen by Antwerp's decline was forfeited when warfare brought disruption to Normandy as well.[56]

In so far as the long-term effects of the economic disruption and recurring subsistence crises of the last decades of the sixteenth century can be ascertained, they thus seem to have depressed the productive capacity of the French economy and increased the polarisation of wealth, at least within rural society. This is not to imply, however, that they must have had a significant destabilising effect on French society, for that would be to overlook a final and particularly important consequence of the crisis. Later historians might pick apart the precise elements of political, meteorological, and epidemiological disaster which went into the *malheurs* of this harsh *fin de siècle*. Contemporaries almost uniformly perceived them as the interrelated fruits of the civil war. The lesson seemed to be how terribly dangerous theories of popular sovereignty and rebellion against the duly constituted sovereign could be. In the process whereby sixteenth-century ideas of the right of resistance to tyrants and of the place of the Estates General in the ancient constitution became discredited and gave way to the triumph of absolutist theories – a change of opinion symbolised by the third estate's famous request at the Estates General of 1614 that it be declared a fundamental law of France that the king holds his crown from God alone – the frightful economic crisis associated with the events of 1585–98 played a major role.

Appendix 5.1 Some Evidence on Population

Although parish registers from the sixteenth century are relatively scarce, figures are available on the number of baptisms in a few scattered areas. These offer the best measure of the evolution of the population over the late sixteenth century. This table lists the average number of annual baptisms in those communities for which figures have been published. The reader's attention is also called to the important graph in Jean-Marc Moriceau, 'Mariages et foyers paysans aux XVIe et XVIIe siècles: l'exemple des campagnes du sud de Paris', *Revue d'Histoire Moderne et Contemporaine*, vol. 28 (1981), p. 483.

1 RURAL AREAS AND BOURGS

18 rural parishes of the Pays Nantais		*Toucy (Burgundy)*	
1550–4	760	1549–84	140
1555–9	724	1585–99	92
1560–4	668	*Souvigny (Touraine)*	
1565–9	719	1580–9	37
1570–4	731	1590–9	30
1575–9	793	*Darnétal (Normandy) (one parish)*	
1580–4	708	1585–9	117
1585–9	676	1590–4	38
1590–4	616	1595–9	72
1595–9	563	*Saint-Lambert-des-Levées (Anjou)*	
		1564–89	127
		1590–9	120

2 FOUR CITIES

	Rouen (20 parishes and Protestant temple)	*Nantes (8 parishes)*	*Saint-Malo*	*Compiègne*
1550–4		616		
1555–9		594		
1560–4		608		
1565–9		652		
1570–4	2109	747	313	
1575–9	2229	866	345	337
1580–4	2302	701	303	349
1585–9	1900	733	335	333
1590–4	1676	836	384	446
1595–9	1995	901	435	339

3 FOUR SMALLER TOWNS

	Le Croisic	Chateaubriant	Meulan (one parish)	Coulommiers
1550–4	160	71		
1555–9	155	64		
1560–4	173	73		238
1565–9	167	67		244
1570–4	155	48		239
1575–9	167	69	21·4	229
1580–4	150	55	23·6	220
1585–9	174	52	22·6	213
1590–4	180	60	27	–
1595–9	184	82	15	162

Sources: Nantes, Saint-Malo, Le Croisic, Chateaubriant and the Pays Nantais – A. Croix, *Nantes et le Pays Nantais . . .* (Paris, 1974), p. 87 and tables 1–5, 7–8, 10–11, 13–14, 16–19, 21–2, 28, 31–40; Rouen – Benedict, 'Rouen during the Wars of Religion: popular disorder, public order, and the confessional struggle' (unpublished PhD. thesis, Princeton University, 1975), Appendix IV; Meulan – Marcel Lachiver, *La Population de Meulan du XVIIe au XIXe siècle (vers 1600–vers 1870): Étude de démographie historique* (Paris, 1969), p. 215; Darnétal – Archives Départmentales de la Seine-Maritime, E, St-Ouen-de-Longpaon; Toucy, Souvigny, and Saint-Lambert-des-Levées – Pierre Goubert, 'Recent theories and research in French population between 1500 and 1700', in D. V. Glass and D. E. C. Eversley (eds), *Population in History* (London, 1965), pp. 464–5; Coulommiers – J.-C. Polton, 'Coulommiers et Chailly-en-Brie (1557–1715),' *Annales de Démographie Historique* (1969), p. 29; and Compiègne – Carolus Barré, 'La Paroisse Saint-Jacques de Compiège sous Henri III et Henri IV d'après les Registres de Catholicité' and 'La Paroisse Saint-Antoine de Compiègne de 1554 à 1610 d'après les Registres de Catholicité, '*Société Historique de Compiègne: procès-verbaux, rapports et communications diverses*, vol. 34 (1931), pp. 77–8, and vol. 37 (1934–6), pp. 156–8. For Rouen, Nantes, and the 18 rural parishes of the Pays Nantais, gaps in the registers of individual parishes have been corrected for by assuming an evolution parallel to that of the other parishes for which records are available.

Notes: Chapter 5

1 The sharp regional contrasts in economic evolution emerge from: J. Jacquart, *La Crise rurale en Île-de-France, 1550–1670* (Paris, 1974), ch. 5; P. Goubert, 'Recent theories and research in French population between 1500 and 1700', in D. V. Glass and D. E. C. Eversley (eds), *Population in History: Essays in Historical Demography* (London, 1965), pp. 463–6; Goubert, 'Registres paroissiaux et démographie dans la France du XVIe siècle', *Annales de Démographie historique* (1965), pp. 43–8 (both reprinted with a few additional observations in Goubert, *Clio parmi les hommes* (Paris, 1976), pp. 171–94); F. Lebrun, 'Registres paroissiaux et démographie en Anjou au XVIe siècle', *Annales de démographie historique* (1965), pp. 49–50; A. Croix, *Nantes et le Pays Nantais au XVIe siècle: étude démographique* (Paris, 1974), ch. 5; J. Tanguy, *Le Commerce du port de Nantes au milieu de XVIe siècle* (Paris, 1956), pp. 78–9; P. Benedict, 'Catholics and Huguenots in sixteenth-century Rouen: the demographic effects of the religious wars', *French Historical Studies*, vol. 9 (1975), pp. 209–34; Benedict, 'Rouen's foreign trade in the age of the religious wars (1560–1600)', *Journal of European Economic History* (vol. 13 (1984),

pp. 29–74); J. Dewald, *The Formation of a Provincial Nobility: The Magistrates of the Parlement of Rouen, 1499–1610* (Princeton, NJ, 1980), pp. 201–20; B. Garnier, 'Pays herbagers, pays céréaliers et pays "ouverts" en Normandie (XVIe–début du XIXe siècle)', *Revue d'histoire économique et sociale*, vol. 53 (1975), p. 503; J. Goy and E. Le Roy Ladurie (eds), *Les Fluctuations du produit de la dîme: conjoncture décimale et domaniale de la fin du Moyen Age au XVIIIe siècle* (Paris, 1972), pp. 21, 44–57, 134–52; P. Deyon, 'Variations de la production textile aux XVIe et XVIIe siècles: sources et premiers résultats', *Annales, Economies, Sociétés, Civilisations* (hereafter *Annales ESC*), vol. 18 (1963), pp. 948–9; J.-L. Bourgeon, *Les Colbert avant Colbert: destin d'une famille marchande* (Paris, 1973), p. 166; R. Gascon, *Grand commerce et vie urbaine au XVIe siècle: Lyon et ses marchands (vers 1520–vers 1580)* (Paris, 1971), pt II; and F. Bayard, 'Les Bonvisi, marchands-banquiers à Lyon, 1575–1629', *Annales ESC*, Vol. 26 (1971), pp. 1234–69. These works represent the basic bibliography on the northern French economy in the later sixteenth century and will serve as the basis for much of what follows.

2 Jacquart, *Crise rurale*, ch. 5, pt 3.

3 H. Drouot, 'Vin, vignes, et vignerons de la Côte dijonnaise pendant la Ligue', *Revue de Bourgogne*, vol. 1 (1911), p. 361.

4 Goubert, 'Recent theories', pp. 464–5; Croix, *Nantes*, pp. 139–50.

5 The *mercuriales* in Figure 5.2 also demonstrate significant regional variations in the pattern of high prices between 1590 and 1595, a function of the varying intensity and chronology of the fighting of these years and of localised meteorological disasters.

6 *Mémoires de Jacques Carorguy, greffier de Bar-sur-Seine* (Paris, 1880), p. 2.

7 The fullest list of those areas touched by the plague is in J.-N. Biraben, *Les Hommes et la Peste en France et dans les pays européens et méditerranéens* (Paris, 1975), Vol. 1, pp. 377–88, which indicates forty-five towns in the northern half of the kingdom infected between 1580 and 1586.

8 See Appendix to this chapter. The plague was also serious in Anjou and much of Burgundy. See here F. Lebrun, *Les Hommes et la Mort en Anjou aux 17e et 18e siècles: essai de démographie et de psychologie historiques* (Paris, 1971), pp. 303–8; H. Drouot, *Mayenne et la Bourgogne: Étude sur la Ligue (1587–1596)* (Paris, 1937), Vol. 1, p. 26.

9 See Appendix to this chapter. The evolution of Compiègne and Coulommiers appears to have been similar.

10 Carorguy, *Mémoires*, p. 9.

11 P. Benedict, *Rouen during the Wars of Religion* (Cambridge, 1980), p. 173.

12 E. Prarond, *La Ligue à Abbeville, 1576–1594* (Paris, 1868–73), Vol. 1, pp. 277–86.

13 Benedict, *Rouen*, pp. 10, 173.

14 For evidence of the *disette* and its effects across Burgundy, Franche-Comté and the Lyonnais, see Drouot, *Mayenne*, p. 29; in Lorraine, G. Cabourdin, *Terre et Hommes en Lorraine (1550–1635): Toulois et Comté de Vaudémont* (Nancy, 1977), pp. 159–60; in Bar-sur-Seine, Carorguy, *Mémoires*, p. 8; around Laon, A. Richart, *Mémoires sur la Ligue dans le Laonnois* (Laon, 1869), p. 505; in Rheims, J. Pussot, 'Mémoires ou journalier', *Travaux de l'Académie Impériale de Reims*, vol. 23 (1856), pp. 172–4; in Abbeville, Prarond, *La Ligue à Abbeville*, Vol. 1, pp. 277–86; in Brittany, Figure 5.1 and Croix, *La Bretagne*, pp. 270–1, which indicates an attenuated crisis in Haute-Bretagne. Basse-Bretagne may have escaped the *disette* entirely. The *mercuriale* of Saint-Brieuc is absolutely level in these years. J. Meyer, *La Noblesse bretonne au 18e siècle* (Paris, 1966), p. 848.

15 Benedict, *Rouen*, pp. 156–9.

16 Ibid., p. 161, and 'Rouen's foreign trade' pp. 60–2; Deyon, 'Variations de la production textile', pp. 948–9; Bayard, 'Les Bonvisi', pp. 1255–8.

17 J. Davies, 'Popular revolts in Normandy', *History Today*, vol. 31 (December 1981), pp. 24–9, is now the best introduction to what is known about the Gautiers.

18 BN, MS Français 23295, 'Histoire de la Ligue', fo. 466. This is perhaps the fullest guide to the politics of this period. J.-H. Mariéjol, *La Réforme et la Ligue*, Vol. 6, pt 1 of E. Lavisse, *Histoire de France* (Paris, 1900–11), is a more easily accessible standard work.

19 Drouot, *Mayenne*, pt 1, ch. 4.

20 H. Lapeyre, *Une Famille de marchands, les Ruiz: Contribution à l'étude du commerce entre la France et l'Espagne au temps de Philippe II* (Paris, 1955), p. 431.

21 The constant local skirmishing emerges from virtually any local history of the League. On the particularly serious brigandage in Brittany, see J. Moreau, *Histoire de ce qui s'est passé en Bretagne durant les Guerres de la Ligue* (Brest, 1836), *passim*; and A. La Borderie and B. Pocquet, *Histoire de Bretagne* (Rennes, 1913), ch. 19.

22 Drouot, 'Vin, vignes, et vignerons', pp. 347–55. Troops were similarly raised to protect the villagers getting in the harvest around Paris and Amiens, while other towns sought to work out treaties with their enemies 'pour le repos des laboureurs'. A. Dubois, *La Ligue: Documents rélatifs à la Picardie d'après les registres de l'échevinage d'Amiens* (Amiens, 1859), p. 65; Prarond, *Ligue à Abbeville*, Vol. 2, pp. 217–18 and *passim*. Neither method seems ever to have been very successful.

23 Silbert, 'La production des céréales à Beaune d'après les dîmes, XVIe–XVIIIe siècles', in Goy and Le Roy Ladurie (eds), *Fluctuations de la dîme*, p. 151. Bernard Garnier's figures suggest a similar, although perhaps slightly less sharp, decline in agricultural output in three regions of Basse-Normandie. Garnier, 'Pays herbagers', p. 503. The precise decline during the war years unfortunately cannot be calculated since the author provides figures only on a decade-by-decade basis.

24 Drouot, *Mayenne*, Vol. 2, p. 104.

25 See Figure 5.1 and 5.2 and Appendix. Croix, *La Bretagne*, pp. 270–7, is also valuable here.

26 Richart, *Mémoires sur la Ligue dans le Laonnois*, pp. 485–7. Confirmation of the frightful mortality in this region may be found in Noël Valois (ed.), *Inventaire des arrêts du Conseil d'État (règne de Henri IV)* (Paris, 1886–93), entries 1790, 1873, 1914, 1924 and 2839. The numerous *arrêts* such as these granting tax relief for communities badly hit by the fighting provide at least a rough indication of the geography of the civil war's worst ravages. As one might expect, this corresponds fairly closely to the geography of campaigning indicated above. The greatest number of such *arrêts* concern villages located in a corridor stretching from the modern department of the Yonne through Paris and into the Eure (Yonne, ten communities; Seine-et-Oise, thirteen communities, Seine-et-Marne, seventeen communities and a general decree for the *élection* of Meaux; old department of the Seine, nineteen communities; Oise, eighteen communities; Eure, twelve communities). Many reductions were also granted to communities in the region of the Loire valley centring on Blois (Loir-et-Cher, eleven communities, Indre-et-Loire, nine communities and general decree for the *généralité* of Tours; Maine-et-Loire, five communities; Loiret, four communities). Finally, the fighting around Laon is reflected in *arrêts* concerning eighteen communities in the Aisne. The other regions of northern France are represented by a few *arrêts*, with the exception of Basse-Normandie and Maine, for which there are almost none. These areas were secured by Henry IV early on in the fighting and probably suffered less from this civil war than any other part of northern France. One also finds no *arrêts* concerning Brittany between 1594 and 1597, but this is because the province was outside Henry IV's control until 1598.

27 Such an increase can be observed in Nantes, Le Croisic, Chateaubriant, Saint-Malo, Meulan, Saint-Denis, Compiègne and Metz, although not Rouen. See, in addition to the Appendix, E. Lesgold and M. Richard, 'St Denis aux XVIe et XVIIe siècles (1560–1670)', *Bulletin de la Société de Démographie Historique*, vol. 2 (1971), pp. 15–19; Cabourdin, *Terre et Hommes*, p. 157.

28 La Rochelle enjoyed 'un trafic comme incroyable' between 1592 and 1594, largely as a result of trade that normally went to Nantes or Bordeaux. Lyons and Rouen, on the other hand, were both abandoned by most of the members of their large colonies of foreign merchants, and in the latter trade in wine and linen can be measured to have been just 20–33 per cent its pre-1588 volume during the early 1590s. Nantes, too, saw its wine trade suffer, and the commerce of many smaller inland cities seems to have been brought to an almost complete standstill. Saint-Malo may be a second town whose trade was not too seriously interrupted in these years. E. Trocmé and M. Delafosse, *Le Commerce rochelais de la fin de XVe au début du XVIIe siècle* (Paris, 1952), p. 198; Bayard, 'Les Bonvisi', pp. 1256–9; Gascon, *Grand commerce*, pp. 597–9, 607–10; Benedict, 'Rouen's foreign trade' pp. 64–5; Lapeyre, *Les Ruiz*, pp. 429–35; J. Delumeau, 'Le commerce extérieur français au XVIIe siècle', *XVIIe siècle*, 70–1 (1966), p. 82; Carorguy, *Mémoires*,

passim, esp. pp. 150–1; B. d'Houet, *Compiègne pendant les guerres de religion et la Ligue* (Compiègne, 1910), p. 94; C. Laronze, *Essai sur le régime municipal en Bretagne pendant les guerres de religion* (Paris, 1890), p. 231.

29 D. Pallier, *Recherches sur l'imprimerie à Paris pendant la Ligue (1585–1594)* (Geneva, 1975), p. 16.

30 Ibid., pp. 119–30; Benedict, *Rouen*, pp. 222–4, 226; Drouot, *Mayenne*, Vol. 2, p. 126 n.

31 Drouot, *Mayenne*, Vol. 2, pp. 286–8. Urban uprisings against the League also occurred in Amiens and Rheims. Dubois, *La Ligue*, pp. 89–90, 100; Pussot, 'Mémoires', *Travaux de l'Académie Impériale de Reims*, vol. 25 (1857), p. 22.

32 Moreau, *Histoire de ce qui s'est passé en Bretagne*, ch. 7; J. H. M. Salmon, *Society in Crisis: France in the Sixteenth Century* (New York, 1975), pp. 278–9.

33 Drouot, *Mayenne*, Vol. 2, pp. 395–6, 409–15, and 'Vin, vignes, et vignerons', pp. 359–60.

34 Cabourdin, *Terre et Hommes*, pp. 104–50, 347.

35 For prices in Poitiers, see Paul Raveau, 'La crise des prix au XVIe siècle en Poitou', *Revue historique*, vol. 162 (1929), p. 282.

36 Goubert, 'Registres paroissiaux et démographie dans la France', p. 45; Lebrun, 'Registres paroissiaux et démographie en Anjou', p. 50; Jacquart, *Crise rurale*, pp. 185–6.

37 M. C. Oursel (ed.), 'Deux livres de raison bourguignons', *Mémoires de la Société Bourguignonne de Géographie et d'Histoire*, vol. 24 (1908), p. 360.

38 Silbert, 'Production de céréales à Beaune', p. 151; Drouot, *Mayenne*, Vol. 2, p. 137.

39 Moreau, *Histoire de ce qui s'est passé en Bretagne*, pp. 335–7. See also H. Sée, *Les Classes rurales en Bretagne du XVIe siècle à la Révolution* (Paris, 1906), pp. 473–4. Most of the information on these years in Croix, *La Bretagne*, pp. 277–82, concerns Haute-Bretagne, which also experienced a major, albeit less dramatic, mortality crisis born of the combination of war, plague and famine.

40 In the Hurepoix the decline appears to have been closer to 30 per cent. J.-M. Moriceau, 'Mariages et foyers paysans aux XVIe et XVIIe siècles: l'exemple des campagnes du sud de Paris', *Revue d'histoire moderne et contemporaine*, vol. 28 (1981), p. 483.

41 Compare the examples cited by Le Roy Ladurie, 'Les masses profondes: la paysannerie', in F. Braudel and E. Labrousse (eds), *Histoire économique et sociale de la France* (Paris, 1970–), Vol. 1, pt 2, pp. 728–9; and J.-M. Constant, 'La propriété et la problème de la constitution des fermes sur les censives en Beauce aux XVIe et XVIIe siècles, *Revue historique*, vol. 249 (1973), p. 365; with Croix, *La Bretagne*, ch. 3.

42 Cabourdin, *Terre et Hommes*, pp. 304–14; Jacquart, *Crise rurale*, pp. 220–3; P. de Saint-Jacob, 'Mutations économiques et sociales dans les campagnes bourguignonnes à la fin du XVIe siècle', *Études rurales*, vol. 1 (1961), pp. 38–40.

43 Cabourdin, *Terre et Hommes*, pp. 609–10; Saint-Jacob, 'Mutations', p. 37.

44 L. Merle, *La Métairie et l'Évolution agraire de la Gâtine poitevine de la fin du Moyen Âge à la Révolution* (Paris, 1958), pp. 179–80; Saint-Jacob, 'Mutations', pp. 45–8.

45 Cabourdin, *Terre et Hommes*, pp. 377–424.

46 Jacquart, *Crise rurale*, pp. 214–20; Saint-Jacob, 'Mutations', pp. 40–3; E. Gruter, *La Naissance d'un grand vignoble: les seigneuries de Pizay et Tanay en Beaujolais au XVIe et XVIIe siècles* (Lyon, 1977), ch. 9.

47 Moreau, *Histoire de ce qui s'est passé en Bretagne*, p. 152.

48 For the decline in land rents, see J.-P. Desaive, 'A la recherche d'un indicateur de la conjoncture: Baux de Notre-Dame de Paris et de l'abbaye de Montmartre', in Goy and Le Roy Ladurie, *Fluctuations de la dîme*, pp. 50–5; Jacquart, 'La rente foncière, indice conjoncturel', *Revue historique*, vol. 253 (1975), pp. 364–5; Dewald, *Formation of a Provincial Nobility*, pp. 212–13; and Deyon, *Contribution à l'étude des revenus fonciers en Picardie: les fermages de l'Hôtel-Dieu d'Amiens et leurs variations de 1515 à 1789* (Lille, n.d.), p. 73.

49 Jacquart, *Crise rurale*, pp. 223–7; Drouot, *Mayenne*, Vol. 2, pp. 311–13.

50 Moreau, *Histoire de ce qui s'est passé en Bretagne*, p. 153. For varieties of the seigneurial reaction of these years, see Drouot, *Mayenne*, Vol. 1, pp. 348–52, Vol. 2, pp. 135–7, 316–23; Trocmé and Delafosse, *Commerce Rochelais*, p. 145 (new tolls); C. de Robillard de Beaurepaire (ed.), *Cahiers des états de Normandie sous la regne de Henri IV* (Rouen,

1880–2), Vol. 1, pp. 79–80, 85 (complaints about fortified châteaux and unauthorised *corvées*).

51 According to J. Russell Major, Henry IV's pensions to *ligueur* noblemen totalled 24,000,000 *livres*: 'Noble income, inflation, and the wars of religion in France', *American Historical Review*, vol. 86 (1981), p. 42. This article assembles a good deal of evidence of warfare proving profitable for leading military commanders.

52 F. Cromé, *Dialogue d'entre le maheustre et le manant*, ed. P. Ascoli (Geneva, 1977), p. 75.

53 Drouot, *Mayenne*, Vol. 2, pp. 108–12; d'Houet, *Compiègne*, pp. 76–7. This latter case is slightly ambiguous. The municipal deficit increased sharply to a level twice annual revenues in the years 1595–8; it is unclear if this rise is related to the crisis of the League.

54 F. Bonnardot, 'Essai historique sur le régime municipal à Orléans d'après les documents conservés aux archives de la ville (1389–1780)', *Mémoires de la Société Archéologique et Historique de l'Orléanais*, vol. 18 (1884), pp. 124–5.

55 Gascon, *Grand commerce*, Vol. 2, ch. 3.

56 Benedict, 'Rouen's foreign trade', pp. 63 ff.

6 *The Later Wars of Religion in the French Midi*

M. GREENGRASS

I

The complexity of the French civil wars demands a regional perspective. Even then, only a rapidly evolving kaleidoscope of images can capture the vivid reality of its effects. There is an abundance of evidence – regional representative assemblies (both Catholic and Protestant), town council deliberations and accounts, detailed reports from royal officials and diocesan administrative records – on which to assess the impact of the civil wars. But, in the Midi at least, it would be difficult to attempt to isolate the 1590s as a particularly critical or especially ferocious period of the civil wars. What the north of France was to experience for the first time in the 1590s was a repetition of earlier campaigns in the provinces of Gascony, Languedoc, Provence and Dauphiné. This appears particularly in the splendid private diary of Eustache Piémond, notary and secretary to the small Catholic *bastide* town of Saint-Antoine in Dauphiné.[1] Written in retrospect, although clearly from extensive contemporary notes, Piémond's diary was partly intended to present the necessity of the town's case for reassessment of tax in the wake of the civil wars. Despite his occasional prejudice and superstition, his vivid eye for detail has provided a magnificent first-hand testimony of the impact of the civil wars on one community in the Midi.

'C'estoient de terribles afflictions de famine, peste et guerre. Dieu aye pitié des poures affligez,' wrote Piémond, and famine, plague and war dominate his diary. He had been born in 1550 and the province of Dauphiné was first engulfed by major civil disturbances when he was eleven years old. The diary runs from 1572, the year of the St Bartholomew massacres and the beginning of the longest period of formal hostilities up to that moment in the civil wars. When a national peace was finally arrived at in Bergerac in 1577, Piémond mistrusted it, recording in his diary the rumours and fears of the Huguenot campaigns which disturbed it from 1577 to 1585. He despised the Huguenots' techniques of guerilla warfare – their use of woodland for cover, their living off the countryside, their capture of granaries and haystacks, their heavily

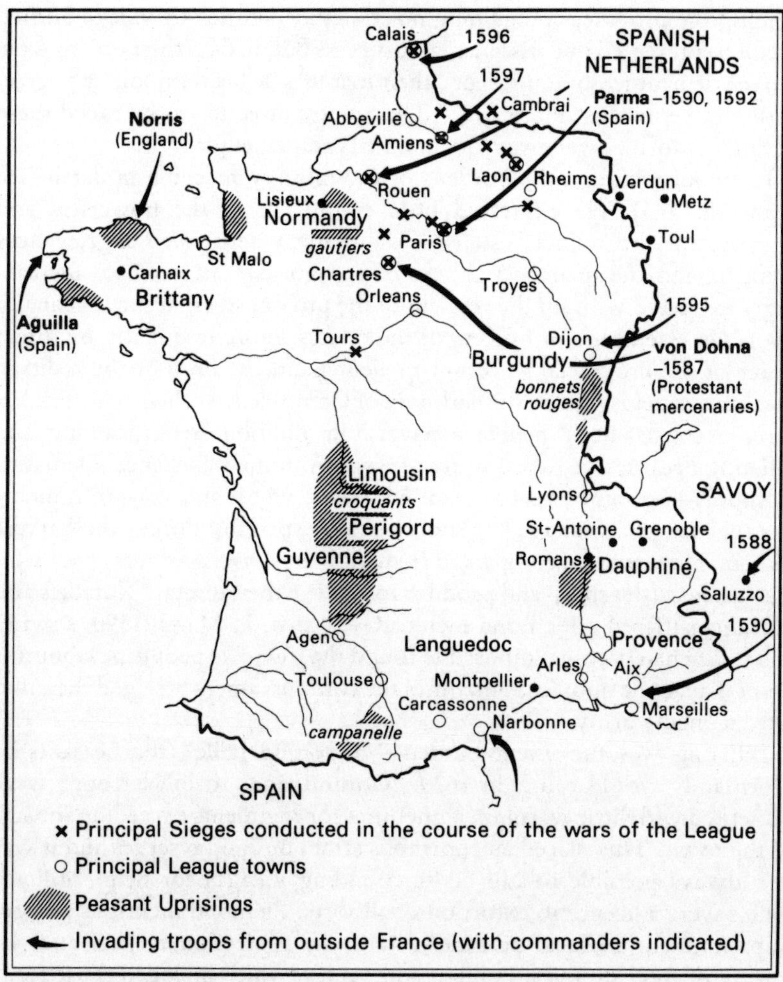

France in the 1590s

fortified garrisoned forts 'pour manger le peuple' – so widespread and successful in the geography of the Midi and so damaging to settled communities. They fought wars without the normal rules, attacked towns on feast days, robbed prisoners and used the new weapons, *pétards* (mortars), to settle old scores.[2] Huguenots became indistinguishable from the brigands who infested the roads, particularly in the wake of a pacification when unpaid troops from both sides became a widespread menace in the Midi. But the royal armies of the period, especially those of the wars of the League from 1586 to 1595, earned little more respect from the notary of Saint-Antoine. Their campaigns were 'que vraye mocquerie', ruining the province and gaining no strategic victories. A village burned could be presented in Paris as a major success but, in fact, their battles were 'un jeu de paume, joué au tricot', their marches 'le beau exploit de guerre, d'aller et venir sans se mordre'.[3] The 'guerre ouverte', as he called these periods of formal war, was 'que pour ruyner le peuple'.[4]

Piémond recorded the burdens of the military machine in detail (see Appendix 6.1). He expressed little confidence in the powerless and unsympathetic provincial estates of Dauphiné, where *cahiers* of grievances went unread and unanswered.[5] As he recognised, taxation was increasingly extracted without the consent of the provincial estates, occasionally by *ad hoc* assemblies of officers of the estates, more frequently by direct order of the provincial governor or lieutenant, the head of the military machine, as registered in the *parlement* of Grenoble.[6] As Piémond said, 'La force a constraint le peuple à payer.' In addition, requisitioning and billeting became a regular feature of Saint-Antoine's existence. Demands to supply large amounts of bread, hay, oats, wheat and wine to military reserves (*magasins*) arrived at short notice, especially during the harvest season. These were accompanied frequently by *commissaires des vivres* who distrained cattle, sheep and produce to achieve their quotas. Notables and peasants suffered – Piémond included – so that, in March 1590, sowing and tilling had become impossible round the town: 'le peuple ne labouroit point n'ayant de quoy'.[7] Sometimes the commissioners beseiged the town like an enemy army.[8]

Billeting was the worst burden – a 'second taille', the peasants of Normandy would call it in 1639.[9] Commissions to billet troops were presented with little warning, sometimes for regiments exceeding the size of the town. This placed an enormous strain on food reserves and it was not always possible to call on surrounding villages for help. Military billets were a licence to extortion of all sorts. Piémond mentions pillage, imprisonment of local peasantry, ransom, protection rackets and the seizure of food supplies. Foreign companies (which included those from northern France) were most to be feared and appeals to their captains fell on deaf ears because those in authority were frequently those most responsible for the abuses.[10] Occasionally, Saint-Antoine requested the protection of the provincial lieutenant or military commander, but such protection did not extend to their own companies.[11] Bribery of a regimental sergeant or captain (in one case, his secretary – 'notre compatriotte') could be effective in gaining temporary relief but it also advertised the town's willingness to be blackmailed.[12] To the army on the move, there was always another community ready to hold to ransom and to the community there was always another captain ready to stand before the gates and demand subsistence and lodgings. To close the gates of the town led to the ravaging of the surrounding villages and Piémond was clearly as concerned for the security of the *plat pays* around Saint-Antoine as for the town for which he was secretary.[13] Such refusals could lead to military revenge later for the collective memory of a military company was long and, by the 1590s it was quite easy to arrange to have a town's elected *consuls* imprisoned to encourage them to pay for a past wrong or indemnity.[14] As Piémond said, with that private sarcasm which is the last refuge of the impotent (the famous pamphlet of the League period, the *Satyre Ménippée* utilised the same tone), the military 'avaient la misér-icorde de Néron'.[15]

Compensation for these exceptional burdens was theoretically provided by assigning the costs on the provincial *taille* but this handed over the collection of taxation to the militia with unfortunate consequences. In 1591, for instance, Captain Briquemault was assigned 2,262 *écus* from the *taille* of Saint-Antoine for a billet and, in November 1591, he was still owed 966 *écus*. So, in December

> pour nous ayder à payer et non obstant nostre misère, nous envoya toutte sa compagnie en nombre de 60 chevaux . . . avec délibération de prendre les hommes prisonniers et ne partir qu'ils fussent payés.[16]

His company had difficulty in carrying out his orders because many inhabitants had 'débagagé'. Piémond also suspected that, since Briquemault was a Huguenot and his uncle, 'auquel il vouloit mal', was a Catholic and seigneur of Saint-Antoine, the town was the victim of more than its inability to meet its debts.[17] In the end, it borrowed 1,000 *écus* from one of its wealthy inhabitants, François de Frize, with whom the town was fighting a legal suit over his recently acquired letters of nobility. His gift became an out of court settlement to meet the town's claim that his tax exemption would be a burden to the other taxpayers. Briquemault died shortly afterwards, claiming that his debt was still unsettled, and the town had eventually to pay a considerable sum to his principal legatee, the consistory of Grenoble, in order to avoid an expensive law suit. By the 1590s there were more assignations issued in Dauphiné than there were taxes to pay for them.[18] Sometimes, companies were assigned on future revenues for which they demanded immediate payments.[19] In 1594, there were a 'grand nombre aux assignations' and, towards the close of 1596, there was a real possibility that the King might issue an amnesty for all wartime debts. The result was that the nobles to whom Saint-Antoine still owed money imprisoned its town councillors, threatened it with regiments of troops, and charged extortionate rates of expenses and interest to constrain them to a speedy settlement.[20]

In addition, communities like Saint-Antoine had their own mounting burden of debt. This was separate from the debts of the province of

Dauphiné which were owed to its own treasurer and the war treasurers (*trésoriers de l'extraordinaire des guerres*). Repayment of debts tended to be demanded in the immediate aftermath of the 'guerre ouverte' – in 1577–85 and in 1598–1602 – with inevitable resulting tensions at the meetings of the provincial estates.[21] Among the creditors of Saint-Antoine in 1579 was one Captain Cussinel, who arrived in the town with some armed men to collect by force the interest on his debt.[22] While he was there, another noble captain appeared at the gates, one Sébastien de Monteux, Seigneur de Mirebel. He came directly from suppressing the popular rising at Romans and accused Cussinel of leading the peasantry in an attack on his brother-in-law's landed estates near Saint-Antoine. The town councillors were in a difficult position. They stood surety for Cussinel but Mirebel promptly called on the provincial provost (*prévôt des maréchaux*) to arrest these councillors for their seditious tendencies. As Piémond recorded, there was a risk that Mirebel's men would massacre 'un poure peuple qui tousjours avoit esté et demouré soubs le joug et obeyssance du Roy et de ses magistrats'.[23] Debts, noble quarrels, peasant leagues, city uprisings, divided loyalties – such was the confusing interrelatedness of things during the wars of religion in the Midi. In 1591, Saint-Antoine was among 200 communities in Dauphiné which asked for its communal property to be mortgaged to free it from its debts.[24] In 1598, it estimated its personal indebtedness at 8,000 *écus* or perhaps as much as 10 *écus* per inhabitant.

The most permanent solution for a town in Saint-Antoine's unfortunate position was to gain a reduction in its *taille* assessment, based in Dauphiné on a community's number of *feux*. The *feux* had last been reassessed in 1453 when Saint-Antoine had been rated at 25 *feux*. With the town's loss of population during the wars it was imperative that it should gain a permanent reassessment. Unfortunately the town's archives were mislaid from 1586 until 1590.[25] In August 1590, a deputation was sent to the president of the royalist *parlement* sitting at Romans which sent a judge to receive a substantial dossier on the town's case in January 1591.[26] This inquiry cost the town 50 *écus* but achieved nothing so, a year later, deputies approached the provincial lieutenant, Alphonse d'Ornano. He was sympathetic to the town's plight (they took care to present him with a lavish gold cup and chain worth 20 *écus* and he had an eye to the living of the abbey in the town), 'disant qu'il deplorait nostre misère' – and sent their deputies to the provincial estates.[27] The estates were, as usual, unwilling to change tax assessments piecemeal and referred the deputies to the king. Then, Saint-Antoine approached d'Ornano's *intendant de l'armée* and he referred them to the treasurers at Vienne.[28] The treasurers refused to act without specific orders from the king but, despite having gained all the necessary letters of introduction from d'Ornano and others, Saint-Antoine could not afford the expenses of a delegation to northern France –

'Nous n'eûmes les moyens de pouvoir obtenir.'[29] Eventually, in 1593, they gained temporary relief of 10 *feux* against the opposition of the provincial treasurers and some *gens de guerre* who were worried about their assignations.[30] In 1597, Saint-Antoine finally presented its case for permanent derating. Its supplication was clear and its case overwhelming (see Appendix 6.2) and, with 120 other villages, it gained its tax relief.

The afflictions of famine and plague cannot be restricted either in breadth or severity to the 1590s. Piémond recorded 'cherté de vivres' leading to some loss of life several times in his diary, notably in the early summers of 1580, 1586, 1592 and 1597. The most serious of these was the 'grande famine' of 1586. He noticed deaths among starving people in April; in May, the town council established a relief fund to 'faire les fossez de plusieurs poures gens qui journellement mourroient'.[31] June and July were months 'si miserable de famine que le peuple estoit au desespoir' and when 'ne se trouvoit de pain pour argent en ladite ville'.[32] Towards the end of July, harvesting began, but it was a slow business because plague was already virulent in the villages and Saint-Antoine was near a state of siege. Similar conditions were recorded in the early summer of 1592 when the 'populat estoit en grande disette de vivres, plusieurs faisoient de pain de gland en ce païs' and again in 1597.[33] Troop movements were partly to blame for the grain shortages and high prices in times of open war (as, for instance, in November 1592 when a regiment encamped in Saint-Antoine increased the price of grain by 30 per cent). But, to Piémond, the climatic conditions were far more important. He was a keen meteorologist and his observations were quite precise (see Appendix 6.3). He recorded the late frosts of the 1580s and 1590s along with the accompanying cyclonic conditions which lasted sometimes well into July. He spoke of seven sterile years from 1584 to 1591, and, in fact, only recorded one harvest for the decade 1580–90 as 'honnestement fertile'.[34] The following decade was a little better in this respect, with good years in 1593, 1595 and 1599. With advancing glaciers in the Alps round Chamonix destroying villages at this period, it is difficult not to take Piémond's meteorological evidence as an illustration from a village only 80 miles from Chamonix of the effects of what has been termed the 'mini-ice age' of the later half of the sixteenth century.[35]

Another famine – that of coinage – also had an effect on prices during the Wars of Religion. Monetary instabilities had been serious and very disruptive in the period 1572–7; they were to be partially rectified by the royal edict of 1577 which established a temporary monetary stability in France, although the extent to which this was felt among coins of small denomination and the extent to which coinage circulated round the rural world of France is still a subject of great uncertainty.[36] Such stability as was achieved in 1577 was quickly eroded after 1589, especially by the minting of *pinatelles*. These were small silver coins worth at face value 2s 6d or 10 *liards*. As Piémond said, 'Plusieurs avoient faict fabriquer à chut-chut des pinatelles à leur mode au coin du Roy'.[37] Military commanders commissioned mints to pay for the wars and, to do so, they produced inferior coins.[38] In March 1593, the *pinatelles* of Valence were worth 1s 6d, those of Nyons, 9d, some from Grenoble only 4d. The result of 'l'affoiblissement de la monnoye' was, as Piémond recorded, a rapid appreciation of gold in relation to silver coins and a monetary inflation. During the winter of 1592–3, he recorded that foodstuffs appreciated more than 50 per cent in price, while quality products like cloth and imported luxuries like silk appreciated 60 per cent and 300 per cent respectively.[39] In January 1593 there began attempts to stabilise money, in their way as painful as the instabilities which they were trying to cure. Languedoc cried down its *pinatelles* before Dauphiné so that many merchants unloaded poor-quality coin in Dauphiné in exchange for merchandise. Some coins ceased to be legal tender and this resulted in a period of three months when coins disappeared from many villages, leaving them 'en désolation estant sans aulcune monnoye . . . et neantmoins travaillé au payement des tailles' (*taille* had to be paid in money).[40] Inevitably, such a revaluation led to monetary (and economic) deflation whose effects did not escape Piémond. It was a

> chose admirable que lorsque les marchandises estoient à l'haut prix durant le cours de la pinatelle, le peuple avoit moyen de l'achapter et lors qu'elle fust rabaissé de moitié, le peuple n'avoit moyen de l'achepter et plusieurs enduroient la faim en ce païs à cause du descry.[41]

This deflation would provide the basis for Sully's reordering of the coinage in 1601 and his important reorganisation of the mints in France.

Infectious diseases – smallpox, malaria (*fièbvre chaude*?) and plague – were still the worst enemies to southern communities. Plague – '*la contagion*' – was endemic in the Midi in the Wars of Religion, spreading from the towns in the aftermath of serious and widespread malnutrition, to become epidemic and sometimes pandemic in an area. Piémond noticed plague spreading towards Saint-Antoine from the south in 1581, from the north in 1584–5, from the south again in 1586 and from the east in 1597–8.[42] He believed soldiers to be the greatest carriers of infection although other mobile individuals or groups could be implicated.[43] Saint-Antoine was infected by the plague in 1582, 1586–7 and 1598, and the outbreaks in the 1580s appear to have been much worse than those of the 1590s. In 1582, 140 died in the town at a cost of 90 *écus* for the *désinfecteurs*, *cabannes* (temporary shelters for plague victims erected outside the city walls) and food, as well as for the town guards appointed to prevent further contamination. In 1586, the plague returned, apparently having been brought from Romans by a regiment of soldiers. According to Piémond, 160 people died between April and July 1586. A further 551 people succumbed from September 1586 to October 1587.[44] In the course of this sustained attack, the town lost perhaps half its population, something of a blessing in disguise, to the surviving who were more easily able to live on the frugal harvest of 1586.[45] In the 1590s, plague was not so commonly mentioned in his diary, and the only serious outbreak appeared in 1598, when about 25 people died from the infection.[46] Plague was still virulent in the Midi and perhaps Piémond was more inured to its incidence. More likely, Saint-Antoine found itself able to feed its reduced population better in the 1590s and was thus able to escape more effectively from the ravages of infectious disease.

Brigandage, fears of the 'loups garrous', were both to be found in the diary;[47] only the increased pressures on witches and cunning men and women which can be found in other Midi communities at the same moment appear to be absent in the area round Saint-Antoine. Underscoring Piémond's account, however, is the clear message of social tensions in Dauphiné. The notary of Saint-Antoine at heart detested noble exploitation. Nobles who exploited their position in the army, who ransomed, captured, peremptorily executed, and bankrupted the commoners, were his principal hatred. *Their* estates were never touched by the guerilla warfare waged by the Huguenot nobility.[48] Their garrisons were an opportunity to extend their political authority and 'canton themselves' illegally in an area at the expense of its inhabitants.[49] Sectarian disorders were a pretext for them to settle their own private quarrels. The *ban* and *arrière-ban* (the feudal military levy) was used by them as an excuse for political meetings to co-ordinate the noble estate in advance of meetings of the provincial estates.[50] When the king needed their services, as before Amiens in 1596, many of the nobles 'estoient contens demourer au païs où les assignations des tailles estoient plus proffitables que les coups de Picardie'.[51] The provincial governor was theirs to manipulate unless he was exceptionally strong-willed. For new nobles, Piémond reserved a special venom. There were twenty-six nobles in Saint-Antoine in 1598 when there had been only one in 1450, mostly creations of the period of the civil wars. Some of them were captains, Kentucky colonels, become 'riches et opulens'.[52] Others were office-holders or treasurers. M. Veyron, a treasurer of the province, had done nicely from the wars. A new noble, he was 'un des arpies qui a ruyné le peuple – fils d'un hoste et estre devenu par son estat riche de 5,000 écus au sac et sang du peuple'.[53] His clerk, M. le Blanc, had managed his own affairs well too; he eventually was able to afford to buy the treasurership of the province from M.

Thomasset, who had himself risen from being a button-maker. Le Blanc was able to retire as a wealthy nobleman through the profits of his office.

Piémond's views were shared by, and to some extent informed by, the third estate of the province. Changes in the administration of the *taille personnelle* of Dauphiné had been a major demand from 1539 onwards, when the province began to feel the burdens of taxation in the Italian wars.[54] Civil war taxation and the increased number of tax exemptions granted to new nobles made their demands more insistent and opened wider the social divisions of the province.[55] Catherine de Médici tried to mediate between the estates in 1579 but the nobility refused to accept her compromise. In October 1592, Piémond probably attended the estates of Dauphiné in Romans to hear the third estate's spokesman demand the enactment of the agreement of 1579, but the provincial lieutenant was surrounded by nobles who saw to it that there were no changes.[56] His relative, Claude Piémond, was sent to represent the town at a meeting with Henry IV in Lyons in September 1594 when a large series of specific charges were laid against the provincial nobility by sixty deputies from the *plat pays* – 'milles violences', 'impositions extraordinaries', 'maulvais usages' and many more. They particularly disliked the

> exemption d'un nombre effrené d'officiers principalement de finance tirés de la crasse de nostre lie, qu'ils souffrent ains voir ordonnent jouir de privilege de noblesse, mesme extensible à leur postérité.[57]

The privileges of the *parlement* of Grenoble created 'une telle pépinière de gentilshommes qui pullulent tous les jours par la vénalité des offices' and increased the tax burden on the commons.[58] As for the 'monstres indignes de commissaires et financiers', words failed to describe their iniquities. 'Ah! Malheureux province', he said, 'qui a engendré des vipres qui luy rongent ainsi les entrailles.'[59]

Social tensions reached beyond these carefully rehearsed speeches into the fabric of Dauphiné society and emerged with compelling force in the *Ligue des Villains* in 1579–80. This widespread peasant uprising spread beyond Dauphiné over a wide area of the Rhône valley and was more than an expression of peasant frustrations with the civil wars.[60] Its leadership lay in the smaller towns, especially Montélimar, Valence and Romans.[61] Captain Pomier was a draper from Romans who led the rising within the town; Michel Barbier, or Champlong, a recent arrival from the villages around, led the revolt *extra muros*.[62] They helped provide the sense of organisation, cohesion and purpose which impressed Piémond. He also recognised – as E. le Roy Ladurie has demonstrated – that the 'branles et masquerades' of a smaller town like Romans imitated social organisms in imagery and ritual and exposed social divisions where 'les riches de leur ville s'estoient enrichis aux despens des poures gens'.[63] Piémond readily believed that the odious judge Guérin and 'les gros de Romans' would institute a 'furie' and 'massacroient le peuple'.[64] He had done so in 1572 against the Protestants and, in the climate of the civil wars of the Rhône valley, it *was* easily imaginable. Piémond described the attacks on châteaux and noble estates. His testimony of the vengeance exacted by the nobility during the suppression of the rising is also clear. From Romans, the nobles 'faisoient des coursses aux villages tuant les païsans comme porceaux qui fust cause que plusieurs tindrent les bois attendant que la terreur fust passée'.[65] The remnants of the peasant army were massacred at Moyrens, where one noble '. . . y avoit tué d'une seule espié dix-sept (paysans), chose la plus desplorable et escandaleuse'.[66] A special legal tribunal established afterwards in Romans acted arbitrarily and 'certains de la noblesse et des soldats' seized wealth and massacred peasants and 'gens de bien' indiscriminately.[67] Piémond's attitude towards the *Ligue des Villains* was an ambiguous one. The uprising had been disgraceful and perhaps stimulated by the Protestants. But there *had* been exploitation, rapaciousness, betrayal of the province by its elected estates, incompetence on the part of the provincial lieutenant and abuses against the peasants, which together explained the fears of the third estate of the *plat pays* for the body politic of Dauphiné.

II

A variety of evidence suggests that Saint-Antoine was not unique in the military and fiscal burdens which it carried in the civil wars. Over 150 dossiers of military accounts for the civil wars in the neighbouring province of Languedoc are a testimony to the brutal efficiency with which the war machine of the Duke of Montmorency imposed and collected contributions and provisions capable of maintaining it on the southern Languedocian plain, on campaigns in the Gévaudan, outside Narbonne, or on expeditions to Provence or down the valley of the Aude.[68] The troops lived well, thanks to the commissioners' efforts, and the pressure on regional food supplies can be deduced to some extent from the price of mutton at Narbonne, the price of bread in Montpellier, and the price of wine at Arles.[69] Individual communities wrote begging letters to the commander to try and gain exemption from the burden or to evade the army commissioners.[70] Royal taxation records and registers of *décimes* (ecclesiastical taxation) reveal the extent of the depredations of warfare.[71] A survey of seventy-nine communities of the diocese of Toulouse – an important grain-producing region – for the years 1585–7 becomes a tragic litany.[72] At Montgiscard, the land had not been cultivated for three years, the village of Montesquieu was 'mis à bas et rasé', the land uncultivated. Round Pamiers, all the villages suffered from Huguenot attacks 'qui journellement font courses sur lesdits lieux ayant ravy le bestail du laborage, bruslé méteries et tiré les métayers en plusieurs endroictz d'iceulx lieux'. The deliberations of the estates of Languedoc, the best kept of the provincial estates' records in the Midi, are annually full of complaints against garrisons, illegal seizures, levies, ransoms and brigandage.[73]

Trèves de labourage, applicable to small regions, were a feature of the warfare of the Midi from 1585 until the national truce in 1595.[74] Although badly enforced, they give some evidence of recognition among provincial military commanders of a military and also economic stalemate, an awareness that if the harvest were not collected the army would not be fed. Town accounts present a pattern of the burden of fiscality similar to that of Saint-Antoine although larger towns had resources of their own to rent out at a profit and could borrow from individuals living within their walls more easily. For a town the size of Montpellier, for instance, the costs of the outbreak of plague in 1586–7 were still considerable, forcing the city to contract loans. The rising amount of unpaid taxation suggests an inability or unwillingness to continue shouldering the burden of high taxation.[75] In the *plat pays*, refusal to pay taxes became an annual feature of the estates of Languedoc, especially in the upland regions of the Velay, Vivarais, Gévaudan, Albigeois and parts of the diocese of Uzès.[76] In Gascony, dislike of high taxation was among the principal features of the support for the Catholic League in Agen, Moissac and Comminges and appeared prominently in the *cahiers* presented from the Midi to the Estates General of Blois in 1588.[77] Provincial military leaders ran some risk of being imprisoned or assassinated and relief at the departure of a governor was clearly expressed by provinces and towns in the 1590s after their vigorous campaigns for retrenchment of garrisons in their region.[78]

Famine was no stranger to the upland regions of the Midi but the intensity and frequency may have constituted a novelty in the 1580s and 1590s. There is evidence of dearth in 1579–80, 1585–7, 1590–3 and 1595–7. The spring of 1586 was the worst period in many different localities. Achille Gamon reported from Annonay in the Vivarais that grain had become 'sans prix' and that the peasants:

> furent obligés de se nourrir de glands de chêne, de racines sauvages, de fougere, du marc et des pépins des raisins séchés au four, qu'ils faisoient moudre pour en faire du pain, aussi bien que de l'écorce des pins et des autres arbres, de coquilles de noix et des amandes, de vieux tuilles et briques, mêlés avec quelque poignée de farine d'orge, d'avoine et du son, ce qui n'avoit jamais esté pratiqué dans le pays . . .

> il mourut un grand nombre de froid et de faim, tant dans les villes que dans les villages.[79]

On 5 May 1586, the English ambassador reported to Walsingham from Paris:

> Here have been with the King two deputies, one from Xaintonge and the other of Périgord, who, upon their knees have humbly desired the King to make a peace and to have pity upon his poor people, whose want was such as they were forced to eat bread made of ardoise and of nut-shells, which they brought and showed to the King. They told him also that the famine was so great as a woman in Périgord had already eaten two of her children and the like had been done in Xaintonge. The king at the hearing of this changed countenance.[80]

Two weeks later, he wrote that the news from the Auvergne was that there were 'many thousand there already dead for hunger, and, in that extremity . . . that they feed upon grass . . . like horses and die with grass in their mouths'.[81] Similar reports from more restricted geographical locations appear in 1597. There was 'si grande cherté de vivres que villages on vendait les cloches pour nourrir les pauvres' in the Lyonnais. 'L'on mourra de nécessité aux champs'.[82] Towns did what they could to control prices, purchasing grain stocks on the market in normal times in order to release them in times of scarcity, but civic indebtedness prevented this being done on a large scale. They all faced a considerable number of poor on the streets which the limited hospital provisions were inadequate to control. Towns therefore acted against grain hoarding and sometimes spent lavishly on outdoor relief (Lyons distributed 26,216 loaves in two months in 1597) but these efforts were merely a pale reflection of the true size of the welfare problem facing Midi cities in the 1580s and 1590s.[83]

The effect of contagious diseases is more difficult to assess. Each locality had its own rhythm of infection, determined by influences which cannot be precisely delineated but which included war, famine and exogenous (geographically speaking) contagion. In the course of the sixteenth century, the underlying trend was towards a greater intensity of plague and shorter periods of remission.[84] Every major town in the Midi had at least one serious attack of plague during the last quarter of the century although it was not necessarily the worst outbreak during the century as a whole.[85] The peak years were 1580–2, 1585–8, 1592–3 and 1596–8. That of 1585–8 rivalled in its recorded intensity the more notorious plague pandemic of 1628–32. Casualties were very high, proportionate to the estimated populations of the towns, and easily overwhelmed the public health provisions of cities.[86] In Die, Gaspard Gay reported that 100–120 people died on some days and that there was no one to bury that multitude.

> Le mal estoit si contagieux que d'aussitost qu'une personne en estoit atteinte elle mourroit. Il s'est veu des hommes, crainte de n'estre ensevilis, comme une infinité qui mourroit et demeuroit sans sépulture, fesoient leur fossés et se mettoient dedans.[87]

Villages did not remain immune. In the course of 1586, plague attacked villages in the Cévennes, Vivarais, Lyonnais, Forez and Dauphiné so that retreat to the countryside for the well-to-do provided no immunity from the contagion.[88] The harvest was seriously disrupted and larger market towns were 'sans commerce'. There were increased risks of sedition and Lyons recruited the cleansing services of the hermit of Aix-en-Provence to lessen the risk of insurrection as well as of plague.[89] He was later accused of sorcery in Aix.[90] The effect on population levels is impossible to quantify. There is, as yet, no serious study of parish registers before 1600 in the Midi. It would appear to be a reasonable hypothesis that the cumulative effects of famine and infectious disease may have temporarily wiped out the population increase of the century.

Cadastral evidence was used in 1966 by Le Roy Ladurie to demonstrate a serious structural impediment in the agricultural economy and a growing shortage of resources in the lower Languedoc region. Nothing written since that date for other regions in the Midi has done anything except reinforce his conclusions.[91] His demonstration of the progressive *morcellement* (subdivision) of peasant properties among poorer peasants during the sixteenth and seventeenth centuries is also confirmed by evidence from Provence.[92] The collapse of wages for labourers (not just eroded by inflation, but reduced in size as well) can be documented from many municipal accounts. His suggestion of dietetic changes has been supported from elsewhere.[93] Contracts for farming certainly became tougher (*métayage dur* – the sleeping partner taking half the gross produce *including* the seed-corn) and especially on ecclesiastical estates after the civil wars.[94] Contracts for transhumance pastoral farming (*mégerie*) also grew more rigorous.[95] Seigneurial dues were not insignificant and there is some evidence to suggest that seigneurs used first fruits, *cens, prélations* and *bans* of various kinds (quitrents and other seigneurial dues) to increase the yield from their estates. At the same time there were clearly pressures on other resources. At the *parlement* of Toulouse a large number of cases involving disputes over communal grazing rights, rights to woodland and tithe assessments were presented on appeal, more than in the first half of the century, even allowing for the increase in the court's business.[96] Of course, even marginal increases in land productivity might have made a considerable difference, for the yields from southern soils were generally low.[97] But the civil wars delayed and postponed many improvements. Expansion of viticulture to the Beaujolais and in Languedoc occurred mainly after the civil wars.[98] Elaborate irrigation projects in Provence and Dauphiné were halted during the civil wars and it was only in the 1590s that drainage schemes for the Mediterranean littoral in Languedoc and the Rhône valley began to appear again with the double benefit of releasing fertile land and draining the malaria-infested marshes which made these areas so unhealthy.[99] The development of a native silk industry in Nîmes, the Cévennes and Lyons also required the relative stability of conditions after the civil wars to make any headway. There were some cautious changes in ploughs with better ploughboards producing improved grain yields in areas where it was possible to use them and maize may have begun to appear as a crop, especially in the area round Toulouse where woad had previously been cultivated as a cash crop.[100] There is some suggestion that the economic crisis of the later sixteenth century itself produced fruitful agricultural changes, for some areas turned to increased pastoral cultivation after the loss of population and this encouraged the use of new crops such as sainfoin and alfalfa, whose introduction was enthusiastically advocated by Olivier de Serres.[101]

A sense of social conflict was certainly not restricted to the Dauphiné in the later period of the civil wars. In a sense, the 'branles et masquerades' at Romans, with their underlying social tensions, were taken up in the 'nuits aux falots . . . chantant en musique' of the penitents' processions associated with the popular front of the Catholic League in some towns.[102] In Toulouse, the collapse of the woad trade and the immediate effects of plague led to a populist movement in which the first president and senior judge of the *parlement* and the *avocat du roi* were both murdered, the seneschal excluded from the city walls and the provincial governor (the Viscount Joyeuse) threatened.[103] Similar tendencies may have been present elsewhere in municipalities which joined the League – Marseilles, Salon, Agen, Limoges – but the League in the Midi has yet to find its historian. In one or two Huguenot towns there were disputes over noble intrusions into their affairs.[104] In other areas of *taille personnelle*, there were serious peasant insurrections, most notably the revolt of the *Croquants* of 1594–5 in south-west France. In a comprehensive recent study of this affair, Y.-M. Bercé concluded that the *Croquants* were principally the 'parti du plat pays', that they were opposed to the towns, and that they did not consciously break the 'solidarité verticale' – the 'fidélité au seigneur du lieu qu'on voyait souvent prendre tête de ses tenanciers pour chasser . . . les ennemis'.[105] There was no 'antagonisme sociale de structure'.[106] His analysis of the revolt is not the only one possible from the evidence. It is important to remember that the rebels called themselves the *Tard-Avisés*, those last to be considered in the race for concessions and favours at the end of the League. As a counsellor of the *parlement* of Bordeaux told the consuls in Agen, the peasants feared that they would have to pay for the assignations granted to the League towns and nobles.[107] From the start of the insurrection, the weight of taxation and the oppression of the nobility were the two main grievances of the *Croquants*. Bercé fits the *Croquants* into a continuum of antifiscal agitation within Gascony and it is true that the revolt took place in areas which had refused taxation in the past and would continue to do so into the seventeenth century, but their two demands cannot be so easily separated. The taxation they were complaining about was the military *taille* imposed on them by League nobles, assigning their debts on communities as nobles were doing in Dauphiné. The problem of the 'brigans et perturbateurs du repos publique' went far beyond the problem of a few military commanders. Brigandage had become a way of life for many nobles and the *Croquants* specify their various exactions with some precision.[108] They were prominent, even distinguished, local figures, and some *Croquants* complained of their *own* seigneurs.[109] In Périgord, they protested in 1594 that the nobility had taken over royal taxes and imprisoned more than 200 peasants 'pour les tailles'. The Quercy *Croquants* claimed that they had royal permission to wage war on the nobility 'pour ce que toutz lesd [its] gentilshommes luy avoient esté traystres'.[110]

Initially the *Croquants* called on their social superiors to lead and direct them. Their manifesto of June 1594 hoped that they would be assisted by 'tous les seigneurs et gentilshommes sans reproches'.[111] Such co-operation was not unthinkable, for peasant armies had been raised in Gascony in the course of the League and one or two nobles had assisted in the *Ligue des Villains* in 1579–80.[112] It is significant that most of Bercé's evidence for 'solidarité verticale' comes from the period before the summer of 1594 and the first signs of suppression of the revolt by the Limousin and Saintonge nobles. Even in their initial meetings, however, enough was said to alarm the nobility and capital cities. One assembly called on peasants to take up arms and 'razer plusieurs maisons de gentilshommes qui ne faisoient autre chose que courrir sur le boeuf et la vache de leurs voisins'.[113] At another, they told the mayor of Périgueux that:

> ils estoient eslevés pour empescher les exactions et subsides, que les voleurs et gens de guerre leur faisoient paier, et qu'ils estoient résolus ne le souffrir plus; ne vouloient souffrir les exactions des gentilshommes.[114]

From another assembly in April 1594 appeared also their bitterness towards the capital towns of the province, which

> au lieu de les faire entretenir et tenir la main à la justice ne se soucient de la ruine de paouvre peuple parce que nostre ruine est leur richesse.[115]

Among the individuals they mentioned by name in this context were two *receveurs* of taxes for the Périgord and Ogier de Gourgues, formerly a merchant of Bordeaux, who had made immense profits from war contracts and tax-farming and had died one of the wealthiest men of the province.[116] They also demanded the right to elect their own syndic of the *plat pays* to the provincial estates. A similar demand had been presented by the smaller towns of the Périgord in 1583 and its reappearance in 1594 suggests that the organisation of the *Croquants* was influenced by the smaller towns.[117] What is known of their leaders reinforces this impression. A *procureur fiscal*, a notary from a Catholic *bastide*, an *avocat* from a Protestant *place de sûreté* and a physician – it is the world of Eustache Piémond and Captain Pomier with the same outlook and similar grievances.[118]

Bercé wrote of 'une subversion imaginée' but those in authority in Guyenne during the *Croquant* rising thought that it was very real. Bourdeille and Monluc, seneschals in the area, were prepared to take immediate military action against the rebellion but were deterred by their strength of numbers and contrary orders from the King. From Sarlat, the cathedral canon, Jean Tarde, wrote of the anti-noble inspirations and social antagonisms which he observed in the uprising.[119] From Périgueux, the *greffier* of the town heard:

> Aucuns parlaient tout hautement de détruire la noblesse, d'être francs de tout. Les métayers mêmes levaient la tête contre leurs maîtres . . . La brutalité du peuple fut telle qu'ils entreprirent plusieurs fois d'arrêter les grains et autres qu'on portoit en ville.[120]

From Limousin came the testimony:

> ils menacent la noblesse, la dédaignent et tiennent des langages hauts même contre les villes . . . jusqu'à se faire accroire que le roi ne seroit pas leur maître et qu'ils feroient des lois toutes nouvelles. Bref, ils donnaient terreur et épouvantement à plusieurs et sembloit que ce fut le monde renversé.[121]

What contemporaries tell us three times over should not be dismissed as an illusion, especially when the social antagonisms became active in the form of anti-peasant noble leagues (mainly round Sarlat) where League captains and Huguenot nobles buried their differences and joined forces against those who wished to establish 'une démocratie à l'exemple des suisses', whose insurrection was 'si folle . . . si pernicieuse . . . si dangereuse . . . et de si périlleux conséquence'.[122] The brutality with which the *Croquants* were defeated suggests an element of vengeance; only the strong-minded action of the royal lieutenant in Guyenne, Jacques de Matignon, and an amnesty granted by the King, prevented the vengeance from being as brutal as that in Dauphiné a decade previously. As in the Carnival, there were elements of ritual to the social antagonisms, but this did not make them less real. In the *Croquants'* demands, their anti-noble sentiments, in their suspicions of the provincial capital cities, in their dislike for the financiers and *commissaires des vivres*, they present many affinities with the *Ligue des Villains*. The *Croquants* were undoubtedly 'le parti du plat pays' but it was a countryside like the Dauphiné, bitterly resentful of 'le très malice dessein que les supérieurs avaient'.[123]

When the last phase of the wars of religion was over, who had gained and who lost? The answer is complicated and only some elements can be indicated by way of conclusion. Among those who might reflect on a 'bonne guerre' were military captains who had succeeded in acquiring noble status or managed to secure royal pensions, lands or assignations for their debts.[124] Provincial governors at the head of war machines in their provinces may have had to mortgage part of their private fortunes at the end of the civil wars, but they had also generally acquired landed wealth and were able to recoup their debts by gifts from the King. Some may even have taken the opportunity to rationalise their estates by selling the least profitable parts of their patrimony and shortening the leases on some farms.[125] War contractors, salt farmers, senior tax collectors and royal officials could do well, especially if they managed to spread their investments widely and to speculate in offices, debts (communal, provincial and royal), land (alienated royal domain and ecclesiastical property) and other rights.[126] The number of royal officers grew throughout the sixteenth century but never at so considerable a rate as in the last quarter. In Montpellier, the increase was reflected also in the salaries with which they were (theoretically) remunerated (see Table 6.1).[127]

Table 6.1 *Office-Holding at Montpellier 1500–1600*

	1500	*1550*	*1575*	*1600*
All royal officers in Montpellier	112	125	253	442
Total salaries (in livres tournois)	14,885	33,350	67,520	256,791
Salaries adjusted for inflation, taking the year 1575 as a base	59,540	66,700	67,520	184,890

Commercial and industrial ventures offered small percentage returns in comparison with these other forms of speculation. Fulling and grain mills were expensive to set up and maintain, they were taxed in Languedoc and Provence under the *taille réelle*, they required detailed regulation and were vulnerable in wartime conditions. There may have been overcapacity which may also have prevented a decent return on investment.[128] In comparison, land remained an excellent long-term prospect. From towns such as Montpellier, Carcassonne and Toulouse, the urban nobility spread to own the soil of nearby villages. The process had begun before the civil wars and accelerated during the years of disruption.[129] In the village of Clapiers, just outside Montpellier, the *cadastre* of 1520 indicates that about 80 per cent of the land was owned by its twenty inhabitants, each of whom had on average 6·1 hectares of land. No one owned more than 11 hectares and only one owned less than 2·7 hectares. All but two possessed at least a mule or an ass. By 1606, when the village took advantage of the Henrician calm to remake the *cadastre*, over 40 per cent of the village was in the hands of figures of wealth and respect from Montpellier. The average inhabitant's holding was reduced to 4.5 hectares with eighteen peasants owning less than 2·7 hectares. On the other hand, five peasants owned more than 11 hectares. It is clear that, at this lower level, some village entrepreneurs could do well for themselves by farming lands for others, lending at short term and acting as merchants in grain and salt.[130] So the *cadastres* of lower Languedoc reveal a minority of prosperous peasants increasing their landed portions, just as they also indicate the growth of a peasant proletariat. Among those who lost out were the village communities, burdened with debts and legal suits.[131] These burdens were due less to gross profligacy on the part of the consuls than to an ignorance of elementary book-keeping combined with the fact that after the wars declining rates of inflation reduced the possibilities of amortising debts as in the past. Those who were landless, with no rents to collect or with debts to pay, certainly suffered. Provincial representative institutions equally sacrificed some of their vigour and became more vulnerable.

The *cumulative* effects of the civil wars were therefore very serious in the Midi and felt most keenly during the later wars of the League. But, looked at in the medium term, the picture is one of half-tones and shades of grey. The military machine was dismantled by Henry IV's government and royal authority became associated with stability. This gave an opportunity for recuperation. The repopulation of the countryside took place speedily so that there were apparently few communities rendered so marginal or their age-structure so imbalanced as to imperil their replenishment. Pressure for skilled labour in the period of postwar reconstruction remedied some of the cuts in wages. Only in the longer term when viewed restrospectively from the experience of the Midi in the Thirty Years War do the Wars of Religion become something of a dress rehearsal for things to come.

Appendix 6.1

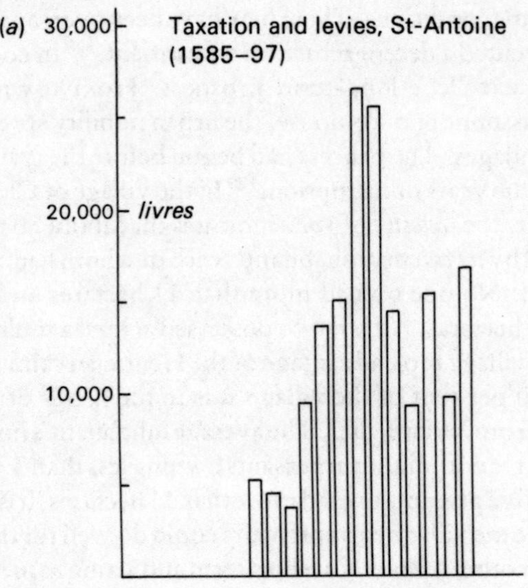
(a) 30,000
Taxation and levies, St-Antoine
(1585–97)
20,000
livres
10,000

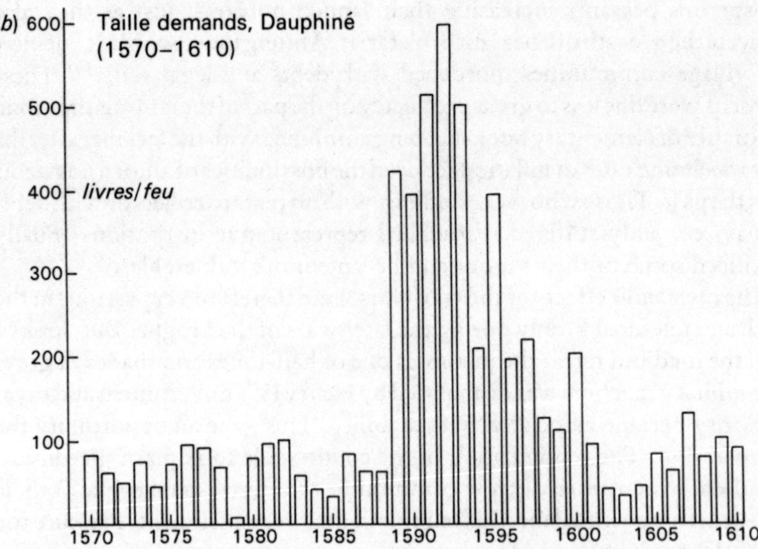
(b) 600
Taille demands, Dauphiné
(1570–1610)
500
400
livres/feu
300
200
100
1570
1575
1580
1585
1590
1595
1600
1605
1610

Appendix 6.2

A summary of Saint-Antoine's case for derating in 1598 (J. Brun-Durand (ed.), *Mémoires d'Eustache Piémond (1572–1608)*, pp. 468–9.)

Land newly acquired by nobles (and therefore derated)	2,037 *sesterées*
Waste land (uncultivated because of civil wars)	855 *sesterées*
Numbers of nobles now exempt from taxation in Saint-Antoine (number in 1450–1)	26 *nobles*
Costs of *tailles* (1585–98)	51,234 *écus*
Costs of military expenses (1585–98)	25,500 *écus*
Debts in the town's name	8,800 *écus*

(NB A *sesterée* in Dauphiné was approximately 0·25 hectares)

Appendix 6.3

The Meteorological Observations of Eustache Piémond 1579–1600

Year
January
February
March
April
May
June
July
August
September
October

1579
1580
1581
1582
1583
1584
1585
1586
1587
1588
1589
1590
1591
1592
1593
1594
1595
1596
1597
1598
1599

Diagram Key

//// Heavy frosts or damaging snow
XXXX Prolonged periods of rain
---- Satisfactory climate for sowing and growing
——— Excessively hot and dry summer.

Piémond's general summary of the harvest

1579 Mediocre
1580 Mediocre
1581 Mediocre
1582 Poor
1583 'honnestement fertile'
1584 Very poor
1585 'La plus tardive et la plus stérile que l'on eust veu de mémoire'
1586 'infertile de vin et la saison tardive . . . tellement qu'on se trouvoit toujours en grande charté'
1587 'la saison fust pauvre de bled, vin, vin et aultres fruits'
1588 Mediocre
1589 Chestnuts damaged. Other crops reasonably good
1590 Grain harvest a disaster. Frost and hail ruined the vines
1591 Poor
1592 Grain harvest failed. Vines and nuts damaged by frost
1593 Good for grain, oil and fruit 'car il y avoit plus de dix ans passez qu'il n'y avoit eu tant de bled ny de noix'
1594 –
1595 Summer drought ruined pasture and fruit. But grain good. Vines very fine, better than for ten years.
1596 Very poor 'guere de fruictz . . . peu de noix et chastaignes . . . les bledz estoient nyez de l'herbe'
1597 Chestnuts ruined. Vines poor. Grain very poor
1598 Mediocre
1599 Good. 'Par ce moyen de beau temps la saison fust la plus premoroye qu'elle n'avait esté depuis trente ans Dieu merci'

Appendix 6.4 Taxation in Montpellier (1578–1602)

(Based on the *Comptes de la Claverie*, AM, Montpellier, cols 762–88)
All the account is rendered in *écus* and *sols*. *Deniers* have been ignored.

Year	*Taille*	*Extra Impositions and Loans to the City*	*Extra Town Revenues* (rents and fines, etc.)	*Unpaid Taxes*
1578	2,121e	—	188e 39s	557e 37s
1579	1,144e		149e 17s	815e
1580	419e	—	104e 27s	1,381e
1581	1,163e	—	243e 35s	1,801e
1582	3,889e	552e (billet costs)	552e	?
1583	4,511e		674e	?
1584	4,958e	—	?	?
1585	—	—	—	—
1586	4,459e	700e (military costs)	716e	—
1587	6,426e	840e (military costs) 628e (plague expenses)	1,018e	732e
1588	6,602e	800e (military costs) 497e (plague expenses)	742e 16s	1,107e
1589	9,200e	1,919e (extra impost) 640e (plague expenses)	573e	1,235e
1590	7,481e	3,179e (*emprunt pour la peste*)	736e	?
1591	12,166e	—	821e 53s	1,451e
1592	14,860e	—	914e	1,985e
1593	15,047e		867e	1,461e
1594	13,612e	—	826e	2,713e
1595	9,369e	—	945e	2,429e
1596	12,955e	—	706e	2,195e
1597	6,634e	641e (*emprunt*)	894e	?
1598	7,440e	1,011e (*emprunt*)	1,011e	?
1599	9,295e	3,533e (*emprunt*)	?	?
1600	11,510e	323e (*emprunt*)	?	?
1601	6,603e	1,100e (*emprunt*)	1,277e	?
1602	11,383e	300e (*emprunt*)	1,210e	?

Notes: Chapter 6

1 *Mémoires d'Eustache Piémond (1572–1608)*, ed. J. Brun-Durand (Valence, 1885); hereafter referred to as Piémond. I have used the published version despite the reported inaccuracies contained therein in comparison with the manuscript: H. Hauser, *Sources de l'histoïre de France*, Vol. 3 (Paris, 1901), p. 93.

2 *Piémond*, pp. 77, 110, 112, 149, 166–7, 177, 204, 235, etc.

3 ibid., pp. 183, 185, 200; cf. the unsuccessful campaigns of the Duke of Joyeuse in the Gévaudan and that of the Duke of Mayenne in Gascony in 1586–7. Mayenne could not even manage to convince Parisians that his campaign had been a success. See *Discours du progress de l'armee du roy en Guienne, commandee par Charles de Lorraine, Duc de Mayne . . .* (Paris, 1586); cf. P. de L'Estoile, *Journal du règne de Henri III*, ed. J. Lefevre (Paris, 1943), pp. 444, 447–8, 458, etc.
4 *Piémond*, p. 165.
5 ibid., pp. 183, 202, etc.
6 ibid., pp. 202, 332, 339, etc.; cf. L. Scott Van Doren, 'The royal taille in Dauphiné, 1560–1610', *Proceedings of the Third Annual Meeting of the Western Society for French Historians* (Kansas, 1975–6), pp. 35–53, for a detailed analysis of the method of provincial tax-raising in Dauphiné. Only four levies were conducted without the consent of the estates in the period 1560–77. Sixteen were raised from 1577 to 1596.
7 *Piémond*, pp. 262–3.
8 ibid., pp. 131, 261, etc.
9 M. Foisil, *La Révolte des Nu-Pieds et les révoltes normandes de 1639* (Paris, 1970), p. 111.
10 *Piémond*, p. 181. Also J. Chevalier, *Mémoires des frères Gay de Die . . .* (Montbéliard, 1888), pp. 33, 82–3, etc.
11 *Piémond*, pp. 179, 187, 239–40, 246, 256, 266.
12 A table itemising the billets, requisitions, distraints of cattle and levies raised from the community of Saint-Antoine has been omitted here for reasons of space. It appears that there was nothing as organised as the *Kriegskontribution* system in Germany in the Thirty Years War.
13 *Piémond*, pp. 123, 179, 187 and 430.
14 ibid., pp. 187, 217, 435.
15 ibid., p. 187.
16 ibid., p. 286.
17 ibid. Piémond's evident disgust – 'Voillà une belle religion de ruyner les poures gens pour leur querelle particulière.'
18 ibid., pp. 287–8.
19 ibid., pp. 302 and 322.
20 ibid., pp. 328, 410, 435 and 438. For the problem nationally, see J. Russell Major, 'Bellièvre, Sully and the assembly of notables of 1596', *Transactions of the American Philosophical Society*, n.s., vol. 64 (1974), pp. 4–10. For Sully's battle against illegal assignations, see *Économies royales*, ed. J. Michaud and J. Poujoulat, Vol. 16 (1881), p. 298.
21 *Piémond*, pp. 73, 129, 329 and 408. For a general outline of the provincial estates of Dauphiné, see J. Russell Major, *Representative Government in Early Modern France* (New Haven, Conn., 1980), pp. 69–80 and 229–36. Also A. Dussert, 'Les états de Daupiné de la guerre de cent ans aux guerres de religion', *Bulletin de l'Académie Delphinale*, 5th ser., vol. 13 (1922), pp. 250–8 and 271–300. Also A. Lacroix, 'Claude Brosse et les tailles', *Bulletin de la Société Départementale d'Archéologie et de Statistique de la Drôme*, vol. 30 (1897), pp. 180–90, 289–99, 388–98; vol. 31 (1898), pp. 54–68, 142–60.
22 *Piémond*, pp. 96–7.
23 ibid.
24 ibid., p. 363.
25 ibid., p. 276. *Feux* means literally 'hearths'; in practice a fiscal unit for the repartition of the *taille* in Dauphiné.
26 ibid., p. 277.
27 ibid., pp. 282, 289, 307.
28 ibid., p. 289.
29 ibid.
30 ibid., pp. 289, 330, 439.
31 ibid., p. 188.
32 ibid., p. 193.
33 ibid., pp. 288 and 411.
34 See Appendix 6.3, above.

35 E. Le Roy Ladurie, *Times of Feast, Times of Famine* (London, 1971), ch. 4. There is a close correlation between Piémond's data on the timing of wine harvest each year and the series provided by Le Roy Ladurie on pp. 366–7.
36 For monetary history in the 1570s, see the contribution to *L'Amiral de Coligny et son temps (Actes du colloque l'Amiral de Coligny . . . Paris, 1972),* Société de l'Histoire du Protestantisme Français (Paris, 1974), pp. 672–734; cf. F. C. Spooner, *The International Economy and Monetary Movements in France* (Cambridge, Mass., 1972), pp. 157–97. The royal edict of 1577 caused hardship and was difficult to enforce in the Midi (*Piémond*, pp. 56–7. AD Haute-Garonne, B 76, fo. 216; 77, fos 103 and 396; and 79, fo. 248); cf. R. Gascon, *Grand commerce et vie urbaine au XVIe siècle* (Paris, 1971), Vol. 2, p. 572.
37 *Piémond*, pp. 310–11.
38 J. Bailhache, 'La monnaie de Montmorency pendant la ligue à Montpellier, Beaucaire, Béziers et Villeneuve d'Avignon', *Revue numismatique*, vol. 35 (1932), pp. 37–91. Also 'La monnaie de Toulouse pendant la Ligue', *Revue numismatique*, vol. 35 (1932), pp. 199–230. Also 'La monnaie de Narbonne pendant la Ligue', *Revue numismatique*, vol. 32 (1929), pp. 37–68.
39 *Piémond*, p. 310. These figures are in line with those discovered in Provence. See F. C. Spooner, 'Monetary disturbance and inflation, 1590–93: the case of Aix-en-Provence', *Mélanges en l'honneur de Fernand Braudel: Histoire économique du monde méditerranéen* (Toulouse, 1973), pp. 582–93.
40 *Piémond*, p. 311. This must have been a result of merchants anticipating a change because the Languedoc coinage was not officially altered before 28 April 1593 (J. Philippi, *Histoire des troubles de Languedoc*, ed. L. Guiraud (Montpellier, 1919), p. 201). The scarcity of coin was not novel (R. Gascon, *Grand commerce*, Vol. 2, p. 533). There were perpetual complaints about it in the estates of Languedoc (AN, H 748[19], fos 31, 128, 237, etc.). J. Meuvret, 'Monetary circulation and the use of coinage in sixteenth and seventeenth century France', in P. Earle (ed.), *Essays in European Economic History (1500–1800)* (Oxford, 1974), p. 93, doubts whether much circulation of coins occurred in rural France, but this is apparently contradicted by notarial records (P. Leclerq, *Garéoult, un village de Provence* (Paris, 1979), p. 66).
41 *Piémond*, p. 311.
42 ibid., pp. 128, 154, 174, 399.
43 ibid., p. 187.
44 ibid., p. 210.
45 ibid., p. 199.
46 ibid., pp. 461, 464.
47 ibid., pp. 418 and 437. Also A. Gamon, *Mémoires*, ed. J. Michaud and J. Poujoulat (Paris, 1881), p. 632. For witchcraft and sorcery cases, see E. Le Roy Ladurie, *Paysans de Languedoc* (Paris, 1966), pp. 407–14.
48 *Piémond*, pp. 235–6. For inter-confessional marriages among nobles to protect their patrimony, see 'Mémoires de Batailler sur les guerres civiles à Castres et dans le Languedoc', *Archives historiques de l'Albigeois*, vol. 3 (1894), pp. 41–2.
49 *Piémond*, p. 212 – 'Chascun vouloit avoir un canton pour en faire de petits royaumes.'
50 ibid., pp. 295, 401 and 408. For the *bans* and *arrière-ban*, see Vallentin du Cheylard, 'Les bans et arrière-ban de 1594', *Bulletin de la Société d'Archéologie et de Statistique de la Drôme*, vol. 307 (1960), pp. 273–84.
51 *Piémond*, p. 395.
52 ibid., p. 360.
53 ibid., p. 296. Also pp. 282 and 308.
54 L. Scott Van Doren, 'The royal taille in Dauphiné, 1494–1559', *Proceedings of the American Philosophical Society*, vol. 121 (1977), pp. 70–96.
55 E. Le Roy Ladurie, *Carnaval de Romans* (Paris, 1979), chs 2 and 3.
56 A. Dussert, 'Catherine de Médicis et les États de Dauphiné', *Bulletin de l'Académie Delphinale*, 6th ser., vol. 2 (1931), pp. 123–89. *Piémond*, pp. 300–3.
57 ibid., p. 361. The conflict over the *taille* in Dauphiné produced a considerable number of *factums* and memoranda, touched on in D. Bitton, *French Nobility in Crisis* (Stanford, Calif., 1969), and Le Roy Ladurie, *Carnaval*, ch. 14.

58 *Piémond*, p. 361.
59 ibid., p. 363.
60 J. Roman, 'La guerre des paysans en Dauphiné (1579–80)', *Bulletin de la Société d'Archéologie et de Statistique de la Drôme*, vol. 11 (1877), pp. 22–50 and 149–71. Also Le Roy Ladurie, *Carnaval*, ch. 8, and J. H. M. Salmon, 'Peasant revolt in the Vivarais, 1575–1580', *French Historical Studies*, vol. 11 (1979), pp. 1–28.
61 Le Roy Ladurie, *Carnaval*, ch. 4. Also L. Scott Van Doren, 'Revolt and reaction in the City of Romans, Dauphiné, 1579–80', *Sixteenth Century Journal*, vol. 5 (1974), p. 71.
62 Le Roy Ladurie, *Carnaval*, pp. 369–70.
63 *Piémond*, p. 88.
64 ibid., pp. 88–92.
65 ibid. Also Le Roy Ladurie, *Carnaval*, ch. 13.
66 ibid., pp. 96–7.
67 ibid.
68 AD, Hérault, B 22.383–546. Further analysed in M. Greengrass, 'War, politics and religion in Languedoc during the government of Henri de Montmorency-Damville (1574–1610)', unpublished DPhil thesis, University of Oxford, 1979, chs 8–9; cf. AN, AB Collection Coppet XIX (papers of Le Tour-Du Pin Gouvernet).
69 Rations were laid down by provincial governors: e.g. B22.414. For prices, see Le Roy Ladurie, *Paysans de Languedoc*, Vol. 2 (*Annexes*). No attempt is made here to correlate the various price series now available for this period in the Midi. These include series from Lyons (A. Latreille (ed.), *Histoire de Lyon et du Lyonnais* (Toulouse, 1975), p. 167); Grenoble (grain), Arles (oil), Aix (oil, grain and wine), in R. Baehrel, *Une Croissance: la Basse Provence rurale* (Paris, 1961), pp. 534–5, 554 and *graphiques*; Toulouse (grain, wine and vegetables) in G. and G. Frêche, *Les Prix des grains, des vins et des légumes à Toulouse* (Paris, 1967). No series of value has yet emerged for western or central southern France.
70 e.g. Castres (AD, Hérault, B22.390); Marvéjols (B 22.424), etc.
71 e.g. AD, Haute-Garonne, 1G 187 (26), a detailed investigation of depredations round Saint-Félix in the Lauragais in 1587.
72 AD, Hérault, B 22.433.
73 AN, H $748^{17–19}$. Also AD, Haute-Garonne, C 2284–2288.
74 *Trèves de labourage* were temporary truces for harvesting and ploughing. In Languedoc the following truces were signed in the course of the wars of the League until 1593:
   1 Harvest-time truce for Narbonne, Saint-Pons and Béziers dioceses, 20 December 1586 ('Délibérations de la ville de Carcassonne', *Mémoires de la Société des Arts et des Sciences de Carcassonne*, 1st ser., vol. 2 (1856), pp. 372–3).
   2 Harvest-time truce for the dioceses of Nîmes and Beaucaire for four months (L. Ménard, *Histoire des antiquités . . . Nîmes* (Nîmes, 1750–68), Vol. 4, p. 239).
   3 Truce for low Languedoc (Nîmes, Uzès and Agde, etc.), March 1588 (ibid., Vol. 4, p. 246). Extended for a year in March 1589 (ibid., *preuves*, p. 187).
   4 Truce for upper Languedoc (Rouergue and Albi, etc.), March 1591 (AM, Cordes, BB 16, *liasse*).
   5 Truce for commerce between Provence and Languedoc, March 1592 (Ménard, *Nîmes*, Vol. 4, p. 268).
   6 Full provincial truce for a year from January 1593 (ibid., Vol. 4, p. 274).
75 See Appendix 6.4, above.
76 e.g. AN, H 748^{19}, fos 42, 182, etc.
77 Various references in the correspondence of the royal lieutenant for Guyenne, Jacques de Matignon, cited in R. Tait, 'The king's lieutenants in Guyenne (1580–1610)', unpublished DPhil thesis, University of Oxford, 1977.
78 The governor of Provence, the king's half-brother, was assassinated in 1586. His successor, Épernon, narrowly escaped a similar fate in 1595 at Brignoles (L. Mouton, *Le Duc et le Roi* (Paris, 1924), pp. 45–6). Matignon was the object of a plot in Bordeaux in March 1589 (*Archives historiques du département de la Gironde*, Vol. 1, p. 105). Relief at the departure of military forces was frequently expressed. In Bordeaux the diarist Étienne Cruseau recorded that, on Matignon's departure from the province in 1593, 'on luy crioit par les rues qu'on prioit dieu qu'il se trouvast si bien en son voyage qu'il n'eust

envie de retourner' (*Chronique d'Étienne Cruseau* (Bordeaux, 1879–81), Vol. 1, p. 105). Similar sentiments were expressed in Montpellier towards Montmorency-Damville's departure, according to Jacque Gaches, *Mémoires*, ed. C. Pradel (Toulouse, 1886, p. 454).

79 *Mémoires d'Achille Gamon*, p. 621.

80 *Calendar of State Papers, Foreign*, Vol. 20, p. 603.

81 ibid., Vol. 21, p. 8 (7 June 1586).

82 A. Latreille, *Histoire de Lyon et du Lyonnais* (Toulouse, 1975), p. 170. Everywhere there are signs of what Braudel described as 'cette étonnante montée de misère du XVIe finissant'. See Leclercq, *Garéoult*, pp. 33–4. For Montpellier's purchase of grain, AM, Montpellier, CC 654, 658, etc. Marseilles consumed about 12,000 tons of grain by 1585 per year (E. Baratier (ed.), *Histoire de Marseille* (Paris, 1981), p. 153). For Aix's purchases of grain, see C. Y. Chandoreille, *Histoire d'Aix* (Paris, 1977), pp. 130–1.

83 Latreille, *Lyon*, p. 170.

84 J.-N. Biraben, *Les Hommes et la Peste en France et dans les pays européens et méditerranéens* (Paris, 1976), Vol. 1, annex 4 and p. 120.

85 In Lyons, for example, the worst plagues were in 1564 and 1628, although the city was infected in 1577, 1581, 1586 and 1597.

86 e.g., Bordeaux, 18,000 (May–autumn 1585: BN, MS Fr. 15570, fo. 261); Agen, 1,500–1,800 dead (June–autumn 1585 and again in 1586: Biraben, *Les Hommes et la Peste*, Vol. 1, p. 144); Rodez, 4,000 (September–December 1586), Saint-Côme, 2,400, Laissac, 3,000, etc. (H. Enjalbert (ed.), *Histoire du Rouergue* (Toulouse, 1979), p. 214). Romans lost 'la bonne moitié' of its inhabitants – 4,096 recorded as having died from the plague (Le Roy Ladurie, *Carnaval*, p. 12). Tournon, over 2,000 people (Baron de Coston, *Histoire de Montélimar* (Montélimar, 1878), Vol. 2, p. 451).

87 Chevalier (ed.), *Mémoires des frères Gay*, p. 287.

88 *Mémoires d'Achille Gamon*, p. 621. AD, Gard, suppl. 796, fo. 34 (Aramon). Ménard, *Nîmes*, Vol. 4, p. 233. 'Délibérations de la ville de Carcassonne', pp. 372–3, 384–5. Leclercq, *Garéoult*.

89 M. Péricaud, *Notes et Documents pour servir à l'histoire de Lyon* (Lyons, (1839–41)).

90 C. Y. Chantoreille, *Aix*, p. 131.

91 Le Roy Ladurie, *Paysans de Languedoc*.

92 Leclercq, *Garéoult*, pp. 34–75.

93 ibid., pp. 67–8.

94 ibid., pp. 53–5.

95 ibid., pp. 40–5; cf. P. Cayla, *Dictionnaire des institutions, des coutûmes, et de la langue . . . de Languedoc* (Montpellier, 1964), pp. 351–7.

96 e.g., Le Roy Ladurie, *Paysans de Languedoc*, Vol. 2, p. 763 (*annexe* 11). Compare AD, Haute Garonne, B 76, fos 225, 455–63; B 79, fos 103–4; B 83, fo. 325; B 84, fos 37–40 and 437; B 85, fos 522–3, etc. – all cases of disputed pasturage. The number of appeals on cases of woodland rights and tithe disputes appears to be greater.

97 Le Roy Ladurie, *Paysans de Languedoc*, Vol. 2, pp. 849–52.

98 G. Durand, *Vie, vigne et vignerons en lyonnais et beaujolais* (Paris, 1979), pp. 210–20. Le Roy Ladurie, *Paysans de Languedoc*, Vol. 2, p. 761.

99 ibid., Vol. 2 (*annexe* 12). E. Arnaud, *Histoire et description des antiquités de la ville de Crest* (Grenoble, 1903), pp. 125–31.

100 Cayla, *Dictionnaire*, pp. 491–2. G. and G. Frêche, *Les Prix*.

101 Olivier de Serres, *Théâtre de l'agriculture* (Paris, 1804), Vol. 2, p. 514. Le Roy Ladurie, *Paysans de Languedoc*, Vol. 2, pp. 68–9.

102 Piémond's journal, quoted in V. Chomel (ed.), *Histoire de Grenoble* (Toulouse, 1976), p. 118. See also the processions reported in Montélimar in de Coston, *Montélimar*, pp. 416–21.

103 See M. Greengrass, 'The *Sainte Union* in the Provinces: the case of Toulouse', *Sixteenth Century Journal* (Vol. 14 (1983), pp. 469–96).

104 A. H. Guggenheim, 'The Calvinist notables of Nîmes during the era of the religious wars', *Sixteenth Century Journal*, Vol. 3 (1972), pp. 91–6.

105 Y.-M. Bercé, *Histoire des Croquants* (Paris, 1974), Vol. 1, p. 292.

106 ibid., p. 291.
107 Cited in Tait, 'Guyenne', ch. 7. I am indebted to Dr Tait's analysis of events in 1594–5 in Guyenne for many of the following points.
108 The *Croquants* specified the exactions of the Baron de Gimel in the Limousin, the Sieur de Saint Chamont in the Haut-Auvergne, the Sieur de Tayac in the Dordogne valley and the Sieur de Penne in the Albigeois.
109 e.g., AD, Dordogne, IVE 66/3, fo. 313*v* (the complaints of the community of La Linde).
110 Archives communales de Périgueux, FF 174/8. L. Greil, *Le Livre de main des du Pouget* (Cahors, 1897), p. 132.
111 Bercé, *Croquants*, Vol. 1, p. 288.
112 The revolt of the peasantry of Comminges (the 'Campanelle') was partially sponsored by the League lieutenant for the locality (J. Lestrade, *Les Huguenots en Comminges* (Auch, 1900–10), p. 239. In the Velay, the governor excited the peasants against the League capital cities of Le Puy and Yssingeaux in 1595 (*Mémoires de Jean Burel* . . . , ed. A. Chassaing (Le Puy, 1875), pp. 424–30). Matignon also licensed the raising of some peasant militias in 1590 in the Gironde: AM, Bordeaux, EE 3 (1 March 1590).
113 Palma Cayet, *Chronologie novenaire*, ed. J. Michaud and J. Poujoulat, Vol. 12 (1881), pp. 574–5.
114 Archives communales de Périgueux, FF 174/87 (15 May 1594).
115 BN, MS Fr. 23194, fo. 373*v*.
116 Bercé, *Croquants*, Vol. 1, pp. 267–70.
117 Explored in Tait, 'Guyenne', ch. 7.
118 Bercé, *Croquants*, Vol. 1, pp. 267–70.
119 *Les Chroniques de Jean Tarde*, ed. G. de Gérard and G. Tarde (1887), p. 327.
120 Bercé, *Croquants*, Vol. 1, p. 285.
121 ibid., Vol. 1, p. 286.
122 ibid., Vol. 1, p. 287. *Mémoires authentiques de Iacques Nompar de Caumont duc de la Force*, ed. Marquis de la Grange (Paris, 1839), Vol. 1, p. 247.
123 AD, Dordogne, IV E 66/3, fo. 313*v*.
124 D. Hickey, 'Procès des tailles et blocage sociale dans le Dauphiné du XVIe siècle', *Cahiers d'histoire*, vol. 23 (1978), pp. 25–49. This is a valuable analysis of the social origins of those who lent money to Dauphiné communities during the civil wars. Also Le Roy Ladurie, *Carnaval*, pp. 363–6.
125 Lesdiguières acquired lands and wealth in Dauphiné: see C. Dufayard, *Le Connétable de Lesdiguières* (Paris, 1892), Ch. 13. Also Chomel, *Grenoble*, p. 122. J. Russell Major, 'Noble income, inflation and the wars of religion in France', *American Historical Review*, vol. 86, pp. 21–48, presents an optimistic assessment. R. R. Harding, *Anatomy of a Power Elite* (New Haven, Conn., 1978), is more cautious. His statistics for the Duke of Nevers's debts are modified in D. Crouzet, 'Recherches sur la crise de l'aristocratie en France au XVIe siècle: les dettes de la maison de Nevers', *Histoire économie et société*, Vol. 1 (Paris, 1982), pp. 7–50.
126 The purchasers of alienated ecclesiastical estates provide historians with a glimpse of those with the capacity to exploit opportunities created during the civil wars. Much more ecclesiastical property was alienated, and at an earlier stage, in the Midi than in the north of France. See I. Cloulas, 'Les aliénations du temporel ecclésiastique sous Charles IX et Henri III', *Revue d'histoire de l'église de France*, vol. 44 (1958), pp. 5–56. Also 'Les acquéreurs des biens ecclésiastiques vendus dans les diocèses de Limoges et de Bourges sous les règnes de Charles IX et Henri III', *Bulletin de la Société Archéologique et Historique du Limousin*, vol. 91 (1964), pp. 87–140. N. Becquet, 'Les aliénations du temporel ecclésiastique au diocèse de Périgueux de 1563 à 1585', *Annales du Midi*, vol. 86 (1974), pp. 325–41. L. Walter, 'Les aliénations du bien ecclésiastique en Auvergne au XVIe siècle', *Bulletin historique et scientifique de l'Auvergne*, vol. 66 (1946). There is no study of the farmers of expropriated church wealth in Huguenot areas; extensive documentation exists in, e.g., AD, Hérault, B 22 547–84.
127 F. Irvine, 'Social structure, social mobility and social change in sixteenth century Montpellier', unpublished PhD thesis, University of Toronto, 1979, pp. 47–8.

128 ibid., pp. 131–2, and also M. Lacave, 'Entreprises industrielles comtadines, 1450–1550', thesis, University of Montpellier, 1971, consulted in AD, Hérault.

129 E. Le Roy Ladurie, 'Sur Montpellier et sa campagne aux XVIe et XVIIe siècles', *Annales ESC*, vol. 12 (1957), pp. 223–30. A. Mahul, *Cartulaire des communes de l'ancien diocèse . . . de Carcassonne* (1857–61). J. Estèbe, 'La bourgeoisie marchande et la terre à Toulouse au 16e siècle', *Annales du Midi*, vol. 76 (1964), pp. 457–67.

130 e.g., the splendid example of the Grisolles family in Garéoult: Leclercq, *Garéoult*, pp. 56–7, 64–5 and 71–5. This is not to argue that the trend would not have occurred without the civil wars and the demographic and economic difficulties of the later sixteenth century, but to say that their resilience appeared more clearly and that their opportunities (and risks) were increased by such difficulties.

131 A good example from the Midi, too long to recount at length here, is of the small town of Gaillac-Toulza. Details are to be found in M. Barrière-Flavy, 'Un épisode des derniers troubles de la ligue dans une petite ville du Languedoc', *Mémoires de l'Académie des Sciences . . . Toulouse*, 10th ser., vol. 11 (1911), pp. 49–64.

7 *The European Crisis of the 1590s: the Situation in German Towns*

HEINZ SCHILLING

The idea that we should reconsider the 'General Crisis' of the seventeenth century through detailed research on the conditions of towns and countryside and by focusing attention on the 1590s is especially helpful in the context of central-European history. For it is very difficult to discuss within the framework of early modern German history long-term trends in demographic, economic and social development beyond the disruptive intervention of the Thirty Years War. At the same time, the long-standing controversy about the economic and demographic state of Germany on the eve of the war still remains to be resolved.[1] Thus it may be appropriate to concentrate our analysis of what was happening in Germany in the last decade of the sixteenth century which is sufficiently distant from the outbreak of the war and from the preceding decade of increasing political and religious tensions.

The purpose of this chapter is to provide a general survey of the condition of German towns during the period from about 1580 to about 1610. Besides my own archival research in the north-west region of the Holy Roman Empire, data has been obtained from the few monographs on the period, from the mass of detailed and specific research done by local historians, and especially from the ten volumes of Erich Keyser's *Deutsches Städtebuch*.[2] Everybody who is acquainted with early modern sources knows well that the information available for individual towns is extremely uneven and that it is difficult to make valid statements on urban society in general. Furthermore, we have to keep in mind that the legal framework of the imperial towns on the one hand and towns belonging to one of the territorial states (*Landstädte*) – or territorial towns – on the other hand differed widely and that urban conditions also varied with regard to the regions of the Empire. For example, we have to differentiate between the north and north-west region of Hanseatic towns, and the south and south-west region with its many imperial cities.

This chapter considers three main problems: population trends (section I); the economic position of towns (sections II–IV); and political and ecclesiastical developments (sections V–VII). The conclusion (section VIII) offers a general assessment of the state of German urban society in the wider context of the late sixteenth and seventeenth centuries.

I

In his brilliant pilot study of the demographic development of the south-German imperial town of Nördlingen, Christopher Friedrichs brought to light for the period between 1580 and 1625 a discrepancy between the rise in the number of households and the fall in the number of births and the levels of immigration from the countryside.[3] Friedrichs shows convincingly that the changing number of citizen households, which can be determined from tax registers, provides only a rough indication of overall demographic trends in early modern cities. During the first four decades after 1579, when the tax register gave a total of 1,541 citizen households, the number of citizen households remained essentially stable, showing even a slight increase – up to the number of 1,619 in 1627. As the community lost 793 citizen households in the period between 1627 and 1640, an evaluation of the population movement in Nördlingen concentrating on the number of citizen households alone would suggest that the Thirty Years War was the crucial event in the city's demographic history during the late sixteenth and early seventeenth centuries. But by turning to the data on marriages, baptisms, and burials available in the parish registers Friedrichs demonstrates that this is misleading, because the number of persons living together in one household varied considerably during this period. There was a striking fall in the number of births and baptisms between 1580 and 1620, from about 400 to about 300, using five-year averages. Thus it was evident that the demographic slump started in Nördlingen well before the Thirty Years War – namely during the 1580s. This development must have been associated with the city's increasingly restrictive policy towards immigration.

We have to examine whether it is possible to generalise from Friedrich's analysis of Nördlingen. Does there exist evidence for a Malthusian crisis on the eve of the Thirty Years War in other German towns too? In the light of Friedrich's findings we have to deal with data on total population and on birth and immigration rates separately. In addition, it is necessary to discuss the extent and the influence of epidemics, because many German towns had heavy losses through plague and other epidemic disease during the late sixteenth and early seventeenth centuries, whereas Nördlingen was only afflicted during the 1630s, simultaneously with the impact of war.

Two significant plague epidemics occurred in Germany in the second half of the sixteenth century: the first in the 1560s and the second mainly between 1575 and 1578 but going on into the first decade of the seventeenth century.[4] These plagues resulted in extreme losses for German towns. In Nuremberg, for example, with a total population of about 45,000 inhabitants, epidemics caused the deaths of more than 20,000 during the second half of the sixteenth century.[5] Heavy losses in nearly all north and middle German cities are indicated during the 1590s, particularly in the second half of this decade, covering an area from Bremen, Hamburg and Lübeck across the entire Baltic coast to Danzig, as well as the inland zone of the Lower Saxon and Westphalian towns up to Magdeburg and the Saxon and Hessian towns. The demographic consequences are described in a detailed case study of the small town of Uelzen in Lower Saxony situated in between Celle and Lüneburg.[6] The Rhenish and south German towns were hit severely too.

However, there appear to be notable exceptions where losses were small, as for instance at Nördlingen, Passau and Regensburg in the south, and Frankfurt, Düsseldorf and Duisburg in the west.[7] For a considerable number of towns, mainly in the north and central regions, we have evidence that there was, at the same time as or immediately after the plague, an epidemic of dysentery, which resulted in a particularly dangerous wave of losses. Finally it is worth mentioning that detailed work on the epidemic at Uelzen in 1597–9 shows an excessive proportion of women and children among the victims, which dealt a hard blow at the reproductive potential of these towns.[8] The data on epidemic losses are clearly impressive. Nevertheless, it is questionable whether the 1590s saw a Malthusian crisis with inevitable demographic contraction following from overpopulation. The data on epidemic losses are of limited value in this context for at least two reasons.

First, we know that plague is spread by particular plague fleas living on rats and not by interhuman infection. Consequently, a concentration of plague at a given time does not prove overpopulation. Dysentery is a different case, because it depends to a certain extent on interhuman infection, which correlates with density of population. With regard to the dysentery epidemic of the 1590s, we must take into account the special conditions of the years 1597–8. In the summer and autumn of 1597 a long spell of damp, warm weather encouraged a great increase of the flies which carried the disease.[9] We cannot argue then that dysentery losses were caused by overpopulation. The epidemics of the 1590s ran their natural, exogenous course, not closely linked with demographic and economic conditions.

Secondly, as far as the demographic effects of epidemics are concerned, it should be noted that early modern urban society was accustomed to replacing epidemic losses very quickly by a rise in birth-rates.[10] Paradoxical as it might seem, in urban areas at least, epidemics did not support the Malthusian mechanism of falling birth-rates and decreasing immigration. On the contrary, by stimulating the birth-rate and immigration, plague outbreaks prevented the operation of the Malthusian trap.

With regard to the total population of German towns, Friedrich's results for Nördlingen, which show the apogee of the demographic expansion at the end of the sixteenth century, are valid for most other towns too. From Bremen and Hamburg, Lower Saxony and Schleswig-Holstein across the Baltic coast to Stralsund and Danzig in the North, and from the Rhineland across Westphalia, Hesse, Thuringia and Saxony in the middle, to south German towns like Würzburg, Passau, Munich and Augsburg, the data available indicate that the end of the sixteenth century witnessed the highest level of inhabitants since the demographic expansion started at the end of the fifteenth century.[11] In some cases we even identify during the 1580s and 1590s a new phase of growth after previous decline or stagnation, as for instance at Trier, Augsburg and probably Cologne.[12] Some of these towns whose populations increased up to the end of the sixteenth century experienced a slight demographic decline during the first decades of the seventeenth century: thus Aix-la-Chapelle, Cologne and the Hanseatic towns of Stralsund, Rostock and Wismar. But it is difficult to decide whether, if peace had lasted longer, this decrease would have been a major demographic turning point. Evidence for population growth up to the beginning of the war and even beyond can be found for Hamburg, Hanover, Leipzig, Frankenthal, Kaiserslautern, Saarbrücken, Schweinfurt, Amberg, Weissenburg, Munich and even Augsburg.[13] As far as growth rates are concerned, that is to say the speed of growth, our information is sparse indeed. Calculations done on the basis of material from some districts of the Electorate of Saxony show falling rates throughout the sixteenth century from 7 per cent in the 1520s to 3·3 per cent in the 1590s, with an average of 5·5 per cent per decade throughout the whole century.[14]

It is important to note that demographic growth beyond the end of the sixteenth century was possible for all types of German town: for imperial and territorial towns, traditional and new, inland and coastal commercial centres, old industrial towns, capital cities, and both Protestant and Catholic towns – with the large southern and western cathedral cities amongst the latter. Of course there are also some towns with declining or clearly stagnating populations. In particular Lübeck and Goslar, some Saxon mining towns and certain towns in the west and the south like Dortmund, Neuss, on the lower Rhine, Dinkelsbühl, Rotenburg and Biberach. What is significant for these and similar towns is that the end of the sixteenth and the beginning of the seventeenth centuries rarely emerge as a decisive turning point, and that specific political and economic developments of local or regional significance can be seen as causing the decline – for instance, political and economic interference by the territorial ruler in the case of Goslar and Dortmund; technical and economic problems in the Saxon mining industry; or the shift of commerce and the main trading connections from the south to the north-west Atlantic zone in the case of the south German imperial cities.

Limited data make it difficult to say whether and to what extent the fall in Nördlingen's birth-rate after the 1580s, as documented by Friedrichs, was a general phenomenon. Rising or high birth-rates are normally found where there is evidence of large-scale immigration, for instance, in Hamburg and Frankfurt with their growing settlements of Dutch and Walloon refugees; also in Munich, Augsburg, and Schweinfurt, which experienced only normal streams of immigrants from the countryside.[15] Hamburg, a town with a complete series of church registers starting in 1614, experienced a continuously rising trend in the birth-rate, not only with regard to immigrants from the Netherlands but also in the case of the indigenous population. Frankfurt reached a peak in its birth-rate in 1608. Here the birth/death rates were more favourable amongst native Germans than amongst foreigners. Even Augsburg, the leading south German industrial and commercial centre during the early sixteenth century, which had some economic problems in the 1570s and 1580s, shows rising birth-rates at the beginning of the seventeenth century, and after a climax in 1618 the curve remained high until 1625; only in the mid-1630s did a clear contraction occur.[16]

In the Westphalian cathedral town of Münster at the end of the sixteenth century, the movement in the birth-rate was obviously similar to that at Nördlingen. Analysis of wills reveals a noticeable shortage of children.[17] We find an average of two children per married couple in a sample of all recorded cases, and 3·2 for couples with children. That is to say that among those couples making a will a remarkably high number did not mention their children, either because all their children had died or because none were born at all to these couples. On the whole, the birth-rate data fail to produce a general picture in accord with Friedrich's findings for Nördlingen. However, the patchy nature of the evidence means that Friedrichs's argument is by no means controverted.

To assess the scale and importance of migration, two phenomena must be dealt with separately: ordinary migration between countryside and town, and long-distance mass migration due to particular crises. As far as ordinary migration is concerned there is ample evidence that restrictions on immigration, such as those devised by the Nördlingen magistrates, were not the norm for urban society as a whole. Basle is similar to Nördlingen,[18] but in many other towns the registers of new citizens show notably high figures in the 1590s and in the first decade of the seventeenth century. We can see this for instance in the north and middle of the Empire, at Bremen, Hamburg, Stralsund, Hanover, Osnabrück, Paderborn, Coblenz and Coesfeld. At Coesfeld there were 140 new citizens in the 1550s; 207 in the 1580s; 257 in the 1590s, and 229 in the 1600s. The picture was similar at Amberg, Passau, Schweinfurt, Weissenburg and probably also at Nuremberg in the south. Even in Goslar and Münster, where the total number of inhabitants was starting to decline, the number of new citizens remained high – in Goslar it reached its peak in 1616 with 121 persons.[19] Admittedly it is difficult to estimate to what extent the figures for new citizens reflect total immigration. Not all immigrants achieved citizenship immediately, while long-standing inhabitants might also gain citizenship, particularly after the heavy losses caused by epidemics. To describe migration movement adequately we need to correlate the immigration figures with those for emigration, which are rare. Fortunately we have information on Münster: between 1600 and 1620 the town gained an average of 100 new citizens per annum; between 1607 and 1632 it lost 383 persons by emigration – 112 men, 97 women, 184 children.

Long-distance migration to German towns during the late sixteenth and early seventeenth centuries was caused by religious persecution primarily in the Spanish Netherlands and the Empire. This 'confessional migration', which became a special type of movement in the early modern period,[20] led to considerable shifts of population in German towns, sometimes combined with heavy social and political disturbances. The Dutch and Walloon refugees, predominantly Calvinists, settled mainly in regions bordering the eastern Netherlands, on the North-Sea coast at Emden, Bremen, and Hamburg; in the Rhineland at Wesel, Aix-la-Chapelle, Cologne and Frankfurt; and in several small towns in Lower Saxony and the Rhineland. More distant places were also affected, such as Danzig, Leipzig, Nuremberg, Augsburg and Basle in Switzerland. Whereas these latter settlements were small in size – one or two hundred people in general – the increase of new inhabitants in the north-western towns was considerable. In the case of Wesel and Emden, it ranged from 4,000 to 7,000 during the second half of the sixteenth century; at Frankfurt and Aix-la-Chapelle between 2,000 and 4,000; and at Cologne and Hamburg between 1,000 and 2,000. The proportion of immigrants in the total population varied from approximately 40–50 per cent in the case of Wesel and Emden to between 10 and 20 per cent at Aix-la-Chapelle and Frankfurt, down to 5 per cent at Hamburg and Cologne.[21]

To understand the precise nature of the crisis within the German towns, it is necessary to be aware of the socio-psychological, socio-cultural, economic and, to a certain extent, political problems of this mass immigration. The economic and social systems of the towns concerned were put on a completely new footing not only by the large proportion of foreigners but also because of the superior character of their enterprising activity, their technical know-how and skill, their modes of production and their commercial and financial methods. The immigrants contributed to the transformation of the medieval economic system based on guild regulations and the growth of more modern and liberal forms of economic activity.

At the end of the sixteenth century a similar wave of religious emigration was launched within the Holy Roman Empire itself by the Counter-Reformation. Protestants were persecuted and expelled mainly from the towns of the ecclesiastical territories in the south and west, such as Salzburg, Mainz, Würzburg, Bamberg, Trier and Cologne, and from the two Catholic imperial cities of Cologne and Aix-la-Chapelle.[22] The losses in population by confessional emigration were partly compensated by immigration from the Catholic countryside, encouraged by the ecclesiastical rulers (the bishops). The problem of integrating these newcomers was not so complicated compared with the influx of Netherlanders. But it existed nevertheless, because the immigrants were protégés of the rulers and an instrument in their fight against the traditional autonomy of German towns.[23]

The Protestant towns in the neighbourhood of Catholic states saw remarkable increases in population: for instance, Protestant 'islands' in Catholic Westphalia, like Burgsteinfurt and Bentheim, or the Protestant imperial towns in the south like Schweinfurt and Regensburg. Some small towns in the jurisdiction of tolerant Catholic rulers also benefited: thus the mining town of Stolberg in the Duchy of Jülich, where the Protestant immigrants of nearby Aix-la-Chapelle fostered impressive economic and demographic growth.[24]

II

From the excellent studies of Professor Wilhelm Abel we have detailed information on the increasing difficulties in corn supplies (owing to low agricultural yields) and on the parallel decline of the real value of wages in the second half of the sixteenth century.[25] Both developments led to a growth of poverty. This can be studied in almost every German town. But there is no evidence that the 1590s marked the climax of these problems. Particularly difficult years were the second half of the 1550s, the first half of the 1570s, when north and south Germany were affected by severe harvest shortages after heavy rainfall, and the middle of the 1580s.[26]

Evidence for the quantity and price of corn brought to market is extremely good for Cologne, where weekly fluctuations were recorded.[27] As this big Rhenish city was one of the most important commercial centres, these data are significant for general trends, at least in the north-west and the west of the German Empire. On the Cologne markets there were serious difficulties in grain supply during the first half of the 1590s, especially in 1592–3, when the turnover of rye – the grain normally used for bread – declined to 10,400 *malter* (Cologne dry measure of approximately 164 litres). But the crisis was not so severe as in the years 1551–2 (7,411 *malter*) and in the years 1585–6 and 1586–7 (6,347 and 3,886 *malter* respectively) or 1556–7 and 1570–1, when prices rose extremely high.[28] As far as sales of rye per decade are concerned, there was a remarkable collapse in the 1580s – from about 200,000 *malter* per decade between 1550 and the 1570s down to about 127,000 *malter*. But in the 1590s there was a new rise to 138,000 *malter*.[29] The Cologne evidence suggests a clear improvement in the subsistence situation: about 1595 the secular trend in rising corn prices was broken and reversed.[30]

It is not easy to evaluate the social consequences of this situation. In my opinion the connection between high prices and declining real wages on the one hand and hunger and starvation rates on the other is very complicated. In the first place, we have to keep in mind that many of the inhabitants of smaller towns in rural surroundings had the chance of breeding poultry, pigs or goats on common grounds and of cultivating vegetable patches. Only when common lands passed into the hands of the princes, or into the hands of town oligarchies,[31] were broad strata of urban inhabitants pushed into a real subsistence crisis. One consequence of this was that they were willing to participate in the predominantly political uprisings against territorial rulers and autocratic town magistrates (see below, p. 150). A second mechanism limiting starvation in times of bad harvests was the sophisticated system of corn stocks and of price controls introduced into many German towns during the sixteenth century. Town officials watched closely the quantity and prices of grain on the local and regional markets. They stocked up corn in public buildings and forced private householders to do the same in their own lofts or cellars. During corn shortages they tried to plug the gap in the market by selling from the public stocks at low prices. Corn exports were banned and imports of bread encouraged.[32]

Similar problems arise when we consider the social consequences of declining real wages. To understand the scale and nature of poverty within towns, we need to consider the state of the labour market. The amount of work available varied considerably according to region and time. There was high unemployment in Württemberg and the adjoining south German regions during the 1590s and the following decades.[33] On the other hand, evidence from north and west German towns points to sufficient work for craftsmen, especially in the building industries.

More detailed research is needed on the impact of the changes in food supply, prices, wages and the labour market on different social groups within towns. Nevertheless, we can give some data on the growth of poverty in urban society. In the second half of the sixteenth century there was a large proportion of people living on or below subsistence level: 20 per cent in Coesfeld, over 30 per cent in some Saxon towns, 35 per cent in Uelzen and up to 40 per cent in the Wendish Hanse towns. Whether this group grew particularly fast in the 1590s is difficult to say. In Stralsund there was a clear decline in the proportion of day labourers and workers amongst the new citizens – falling from 50 per cent in the 1580s to 39 per cent in the 1590s. But this evidence is ambiguous because the decline may have been connected with the fact that incoming workers – perhaps rising in number – were so poor that they could not afford to buy the citizenship. The same problem arises with Augsburg, where the proportion of 'have-nots' paying no tax at all declined from 47.4 per cent in 1558 to 43.9 per cent in 1590 and to 42.6 per cent in 1604, whereas the members of the lower tax classes (paying up to 10 gilders) rose from 46.5 per cent to 48.9 per cent and 49.4 per cent of the taxpayers. Was there really a general improvement in living standards or did a substantial group of 'have-nots' leave the city? We do not know. The data on the medium-sized town of Coesfeld in Westphalia are more precise. Here the lowest category of taxpayers, which included day workers, married boys (*Knechte*) and servants, rose between 1580 and 1594 from 29 to 39 per cent, while the next tax class of small independent craftsmen sank from 38.8 to 23.5 per cent.[34]

Irrespective of the exact proportion of poor there can be no doubt that the decline in harvest yields and in real wages made urban populations liable to subsistence crises and – in extreme cases – even to starvation. This is true of both the middle and the lower classes. Lack of work or more expensive corn after a bad harvest threatened the very existence of town inhabitants, particularly if they had no chance of supplementing their grain supplies by meat, milk or vegetables, by free use of the common lands or by tillage of allotments. Poor harvests and lack of work swelled the number of people who became dependent on civic or church handouts of corn and bread.

III

Historians have paid much attention to the increasing indebtedness of German towns on the eve of the Thirty Years War. Most of them argue that this indicates a deep crisis in the economic and social life of the towns concerned and in German urban society in general. The evidence is pretty clear. Financial accounts show that both the size of town budgets as well as urban borrowing to finance them grew rapidly. This applies to towns in the north and in the centre of Germany as well as to those in the south, to imperial as well as to territorial/country towns, to commercial as well as to industrial centres. It is true that we have to deflate the figures to take account of price inflation, but it remains undeniable that many town budgets in the late sixteenth and early seventeenth centuries reached a critical point where the proportion of capital repayments and interest on the debts became a major embarrassment.

Nevertheless, I am not convinced that these problems indicate a general crisis of the German urban economy. We have to examine the particular circumstances very carefully. We must distinguish at least two types of urban indebtedness at the end of the sixteenth century. First, the indebtedness of towns like Frankfurt, Goslar and Stralsund had started in the middle of the sixteenth century as a result of external political activity. In the case of Protestant Frankfurt, it stemmed from imperial involvement during the Schmalkaldic War between Emperor Charles V and the Protestants (1546–7). In the case of Goslar and Stralsund indebtedness was linked with political entanglements at the level of the territorial states: Goslar had been in conflict with the Guelfs, and Stralsund with the Dukes of Mecklenburg to defend their respective autonomy.[35] Here urban indebtedness was a result of political pressures and played a part in the decline of the old political power of the German towns, from the middle of the sixteenth century.

However, quite a different type of urban indebtedness was represented by towns like Hamburg, Essen and Munich. The increase in the size of their budgets and in the level of indebtedness was of recent origin, starting only at the end of the sixteenth century. It was the result of capital investment by the community to improve facilities for economic and social activities in the town. Treasury accounts show that Hamburg's budget increased parallel with the growth of its economy and its population. The total volume rose between 1596 and 1626 from around 252,000 to about 873,000 marks. In spite of some growth in regular income from indirect taxes and customs, borrowing increased as did interest repayments. A similar financial picture can be seen at Essen, which became a medium-sized centre of the metal and arms industry during the second-half of the sixteenth century. Expenditure on urban improvements led to a sharp rise in the budget, municipal borrowing and interest charges. At Munich high municipal expenditure was dictated by political pressures – the claim over the town by the Dukes of Bavaria and their expanding early modern state. Munich had to develop institutions befitting its new importance as a state capital. It had to provide accommodation and facilities for the Court and the state's expanding bureaucracy. Though heavily burdened by taxation to finance Duke Maximilian's 'great power policy' during the Thirty Years

War, in the long run the town took advantage of this development too.[36]

In conclusion it must be stressed that increasing debts do not necessarily mean a general crisis in a town's economy or even a decline in the economic prospects of its inhabitants.[37] Indebtedness has to be judged according to its background, the level of interest charges as a proportion of the total budget and – last but not least – according to the various types of creditors. These might be citizens, as at Hamburg; the local ruler, as in Munich; or institutions and persons, who had no interest at all in the fate of the town and its inhabitants, as in the case of some other towns which were indebted to church institutions or to the nobility. In each case the consequences for urban society and economy might be quite different.

IV

In the case of the urban economy proper, we need once again to make careful distinctions. The period under consideration was characterised by both recessive and expansionist tendencies, by innovation and reinforced traditionalism in economic life. Thus we should be cautious with generalisations. Nevertheless we can make some observations on the structural changes resulting from the shifts in the economic and political balance of power within Germany, as well as on the question of economic growth.

It is sometimes suggested that the well-known shift in the main commercial routes from the Mediterranean-Alpine-south-German region to the Atlantic and the North Sea coast caused the rapid decline in the sixteenth century of leading towns in south Germany – such as Augsburg, Nuremberg and Ulm. This is oversimplistic. Throughout the sixteenth century the middle-Rhine area (Aix-la-Chapelle, Cologne and Frankfurt) and the upper German region kept close ties with the new Atlantic zone of commerce via Antwerp. In the last decade of the century a completely new situation arose when this reorientation of the south German commercial centres towards the Atlantic seaboard was checked by the conquest of Antwerp by the Spanish army in 1585 and the blockade of the Schelde by the Dutch Republic. However, it is arguable that the south-German merchants and entrepreneurs might well have adapted to the transfer of the Atlantic and Baltic trades to Amsterdam had the Thirty Years War not intervened. It is not inconceivable since the emigration of merchants and entrepreneurs from Antwerp to the northern Netherlands and to Frankfurt and some of the south German towns provided a new personal network linking the new Dutch region of world commerce and central and south Germany.[38]

The widely held view that the north German region suffered economic decline in consequence of political and economic changes which ruined the traditional Hanseatic trade also needs reconsideration. Without doubt, Lübeck had suffered in the course of the sixteenth century because of these changes. But recent research on the Wendish Hanseatic towns – Wismar, Rostock and Stralsund – has shown that the last decades of the century were marked by commercial and industrial experiments. Such new economic initiatives were even stronger in the western Hanseatic region. This zone was influenced by more dynamic economic connections with England (through the Merchant Adventurers) and with the neighbouring Netherlands. Of special importance was the economic activity of Calvinist refugees who had migrated to Hamburg and Bremen. The medium to large Hanseatic towns in the Lower Saxony-Westphalian inland region also adjusted to the new economic world created by the rise of the Atlantic and colonial trades. They oriented their commerce towards the German harbour towns on the North-Sea coast or directly towards the Northern Netherlands.[39] Towns in Westphalia and Lower Saxony benefited from the high prices of agricultural products and from the new rural linen industry. A new type of businessman emerged, who not only distributed the final products (like the traditional Hanseatic merchants) but became involved as an entrepreneur in manufacturing. Similar developments can be observed in the Rhineland, in the Duchy of Berg and in the Sauerland in the textile and mining industries.[40]

The rise of the territorial state and the associated changes in the political framework put an end to the medieval autonomy of German towns. On the other hand it permitted forward-looking economic and social tendencies in urban development. This is obvious in the case of residence cities, mostly small or medium-sized centres so typical in seventeenth- and eighteenth-century Germany. As in Munich, referred to above, the 1590s and the first decades of the seventeenth century marked the starting point in the rise of many residence towns. Most of them were previously rather unimportant places that now grew at the expense of older urban centres: thus Wolfenbüttel, Aurich and Detmold outstripped Emden and Lemgo. Munich, Dresden, Berlin, Kassel, Celle, Heidelberg and Stuttgart are other examples of this class of expanding town. A special group comprised cathedral or episcopal towns like Paderborn, Bonn, Trier, Mainz, Würzburg, Bamberg and Passau, which experienced new growth from the end of the sixteenth century. This was a result of the religious, social, cultural and even economic dynamic that followed the re-establishment of their ecclesiastical rulers with the Counter-Reformation.[41]

Against these towns, where one cannot speak of an economic decline at all, there are some examples of definite economic slump as, for instance, the old Hanseatic centres of Lübeck, Lüneburg and Dortmund; the mining towns of the Harz – notably Goslar – and of the Saxony Thüringen region; and also many of the smaller imperial towns in the south, that could not stand the economic pressures of the rising territorial state. But there is no evidence that the decades before the outbreak of the war were of special significance for the economic contraction of these towns.

Information currently available indicates the general growth of the German urban economy up to the beginning of the war period. It is not quite clear, however, whether this means absolute growth or relative growth, that is, growth measured per head of the population. Research by Ingomar Bog on the upper German region and by Wolfgang von Hippel for Württemberg suggests that *per capita* income was already declining in the 1590s and that, in consequence, some social groups were faced with severe problems.[42] Professor Bog argues that, in the upper German region, there was pressure for structural and organisational changes because economic growth lagged behind demographic expansion. Once again the question arises whether, without the outbreak of war, the German economy would have successfully adapted to the high population level. Any answer must take account of regional differences. In Württemberg such adaptation was hardly possible. But, in my opinion, the chances were much better within the north-west region where the economic system in towns (especially the smaller ones) and countryside was more flexible.[43]

V

Because of the close relationship between Church and State during the Reformation era, especially with regard to the heavy political impact of the religious Peace of Augsburg, it is necessary to analyse political and ecclesiastical developments together. German towns – imperial as well as territorial and country towns – were under political and sometimes even military pressure from the princes and their rising early modern states from the beginning of the sixteenth century. In my view, these political confrontations and the profound changes in the legal and social framework imposed upon towns during the process of early modern state building, rather than economic problems, were responsible for the serious tensions and strains that can be observed within German urban society at the end of the sixteenth century and during the early decades of the seventeenth. I would argue that direct and permanent state interference in the political, social and religious life of the towns, hitherto accustomed to a nearly complete autonomy, led to a growing sense of urban decline among German citizens. This was the kernel of the psychological crisis within so many German towns. In this respect the decades at the turn of the sixteenth century were a crucial period.

The 1590s were characterised by increasing political and religious tension throughout the Empire, which eventually led to confrontation between the two religions and political and military factions, and to the Thirty Years War. But militancy started at the regional level much earlier than 1618; it was closely connected with political and military struggles outside the Empire and affected the towns to a considerable extent. The Baltic seaports were increasingly drawn into the struggles for the *dominium Maris Baltici*, with Lübeck in particular complaining about infringements by the Swedish fleet. The towns on the North Sea coast, especially Emden, but Bremen and Hamburg too, were affected by Spanish warfare in the Netherlands and the trading blockades enforced by the Dutch. Westphalia and the Lower Rhine region were involved even more severely in the Spanish–Dutch war. Many towns suffered occupation by one or other power or by both successively. Due to its geographical position and internal conflicts between Protestants and Catholics, the imperial town of Aix-la-Chapelle was at the centre of this field of military and political tension between 1592 and 1614.[44]

Some towns in the south, especially Passau, became embroiled in the 'Long Turkish War' between the Empire and the Ottomans (1593–1607) by troops marching east to the front. The upper Rhine area from Lake Constance to Alsace, Lorraine and the Rhine Palatinate was affected by the French religious wars and by Spanish troops, who marched up the 'Spanish Road', the main connecting artery between Spanish upper Italy and the battle area in the Netherlands. Damage in this zone was not as heavy as in the lower Rhine region, because the warring powers did not establish themselves in the German towns.[45] As well as the immediate effects of the war, the military and political crisis in these regions had further consequences since the rulers now started to build new types of urban fortifications. This led to heavy financial burdens on towns and to restrictions on the urban economy for strategic purposes.[46]

VI

To describe the impact of the expansion of the early modern state on German towns adequately, we have to be aware of the unique circumstances of German history in the sixteenth century. It saw the Reformation and the related formation of 'confessional churches' (*Konfessionskirchen*) coincide with state-building – state-building on regional and not on national lines, as in the other European countries. At this regional level many independent states, the *Territorialstaaten* (territorial states), appeared during the late fifteenth and sixteenth centuries – Saxony, Brandenburg, the Rhine Palatinate and Bavaria are only some of the best known. The power of these states and their rulers, the German territorial princes, was strengthened considerably by the Reformation or the Counter-Reformation. By assuming the position of *tutores religionis* and supreme heads of their respective territorial churches, they acquired the use of those mechanisms and instruments which were traditionally associated with the Church in order to establish their domestic sovereignty. In this way, they tamed the political estates – the nobility as well as the bigger territorial cities – and sought to integrate them into the new absolutist concept of the State.[47]

The states' pressure on the towns within their territories – and sometimes even on imperial cities – started at the end of the Middle Ages. It reached its first climax during the 1520s and 1530s in connection with the Lutheran Reformation. The second climax, in many cases the decisive one, came at the end of the sixteenth century. The legal position of the princes had been advanced by the famous *cuius regio eius religio* settlement of the Religious Peace of 1555. Under this the ruler decided the creed (Protestant or Catholic) and constitution of the territorial church (*Landeskirche*), and so enabled the German princes to make fundamental encroachments upon the traditional rights and privileges of their subjects. Central government and the will of the sovereign were now present in town and countryside in the persons of the local parson and the local bailiff.[48]

The state could use the clergy to give instructions to its subjects in the most remote corner of the territory. Conversely, the clerics reported information needed by the central government for effective planning and for its expanding administrative activities. All this had profound political, social and cultural effects, especially on the territorial towns (*Landstädte*). Many of them – notably the Hanseatic towns of the north – had been fairly independent during the Middle Ages. Their political power had often been much stronger than that of the medieval princes. Because the first period of the Lutheran Reformation in the 1520s and 1530s was, as Professor Dickens says, an 'urban event',[49] during the first half of the sixteenth century these towns had been able to enlarge their autonomy by building up independent Lutheran town churches. The position changed rapidly after the settlement of 1555.[50] Town churches had to conform to the territorial churches in regard both to their creed and their organisation. The Protestant clergy, up to now appointed by the citizens or by town councils, became part of the administration of the territorial states, appointed and controlled by the state bureaucracy – as much by the consistories as by the bailiffs and councillors of the princes.

In Catholic territories – for example, in Bavaria – there was a similar alliance between the church and the emergent early modern state.[51] The second half of the sixteenth century saw severe setbacks for those towns in Catholic territories which had joined the Protestant movement before

1555. Citizens had to abjure and conform or leave the town and the territory. Between 1580 and 1610 Protestant refugees emigrated in considerable numbers from country towns, especially in the ecclesiastical territories in Westphalia, the Rhineland and south Germany, as for instance from Münster, Paderborn, Trier, Würzburg, Bamberg, Passau and Salzburg.[52] Even imperial cities came under pressure. Most famous was the conquest of Donauwörth by the Duke of Bavaria on the pretext of religious conformity, which was an important step towards the Thirty Years War. The inhabitants of Aix-la-Chapelle were able to defend their political autonomy against the neighbouring Dukes of Jülich and the Spaniards in the southern Netherlands, but they had to abjure Protestantism.[53]

This enforcement of religious and ecclesiastical conformity together with political, economic and administrative pressures undermined traditional urban autonomy and burgher rights. There was considerble opposition in many towns and a wave of urban uprisings throughout Germany.

VII

At the same time as there was a growing conflict between towns and territorial states, German urban society was afflicted by serious internal tension. This was between the town councils and the oligarchies that dominated them and the ordinary citizens who demanded their traditional privileges and greater participation in town government. The situation was aggravated by the demographic pressure and difficulties in food supply described earlier. Town oligarchies tended to close their ranks increasingly and to hinder rising new families from entering the council. Furthermore, relations between town councils and the citizens changed profoundly with the spread of Roman Law and the new ideas of sovereignty. Under the traditional theory of urban corporatism the authority of the town council was based on the approval of the commonalty of citizens. Now it became authority *deo gratia* or *Obrigkeit*. The citizens became ordinary subjects who could not participate in town government at all. This change meant a grave deterioration in the political and social position of the citizenry. Consequently during the 1590s and the following decades in many towns the burghers rose against the town councils.[54] These politically and socially motivated uprisings were much more dangerous than mere starvation riots, for the citizens themselves were entitled by sacred tradition to oppose the magistrates and to remove them from office. These political uprisings were usually led by well-to-do members of the upper class who had been excluded from power by the old oligarchies.

VIII

In conclusion, we need to comment on the extend and character of the crisis in German towns. As a result of the changes already discussed, the inhabitants of many German towns saw themselves confronted by a variety of difficulties from the end of the sixteenth century – economic, social and political as well as religious and cultural ones. Notable exceptions notwithstanding, one can argue that during the 1590s urban life on the whole – especially that of territorial/country towns – was marked by a crisis. This crisis was not simply economic, demographic, religious or political. It was a deep crisis of the old traditional town system in Germany which was based on medieval privileges and wide-ranging independence and on ideas of the civic corporation or commonalty as the legitimate source of political authority within the town. The 'general crisis' in urban life was focused on political and constitutional questions closely related to confessional and ecclesiastical changes. For the growth of the early modern state posed a fundamental challenge to the old medieval town system in Europe in all its aspects.[55]

This challenge was particularly dramatic in Germany because the rise of small-scale regional or territorial states gave local rulers particularly direct and effective leverage over towns and powerful control of their subjects. At the same time the medieval tradition of autonomous and corporate towns was stronger in Germany than in any other European country. Thus one might well argue that the deep crisis of urban life, which broke out at the end of the sixteenth century and lasted well into the second half of the following century, was the special German version of the General European Crisis of the seventeenth century.

The socio-psychological character of the problem can be described by reference to the well-known theory of revolutions by James Davies. According to Davies, revolutions do not break out when economic and social conditions are worst, but at the time when optimistic expectations of the future are suddenly undercut by contrary developments in reality.[56] It was exactly such a swing, from an optimistic to a pessimistic expectation of the future, that took place in the minds of German citizens at the end of the sixteenth century, that is to say at the end of that century which is often called *das bürgerliche Jahrhundert.* For students of socio-psychological mass behaviour it is hardly surprising that we have extensive evidence of increasing hostility to foreigners and intolerance towards religious minorities: as with the expulsion of Jews from cities like Dortmund, Düsseldorf, Düren, Frankfurt, Worms and Speyer; and witch-hunting in Stadthagen, Rinteln, Osnabrück, Dortmund and several Bavarian towns, especially during the first decade of the seventeenth century.[57]

Notes: Chapter 7

This is an abridged version of my paper delivered at the Leicester conference in 1981. I read a draft of the present text at the Historical Institute, Boston University, in February 1982. I should like to thank Peter Clark for his general editorial advice.

1 F. Lütge, 'Die wirtschaftliche Lage Deutschlands vor dem Ausbruch des Dreissigjährigen Krieges', in F. Lütge, *Studien zur Sozial- und Wirtschaftsgeschichte* (Stuttgart, 1963), pp. 336–95; *idem*, 'Strukturelle und konjunkturelle Wandlungen in der Wirtschaft vor Ausbruch des Dreissigjährigen Krieges', in *Sitzungsberichte der Bayrischen Akademie der Wissenschaften, philosophisch-historische Klasse*, vol. 5 (1958); W. Abel, 'Zur Entwicklunge des Sozialproduktes in Deutschland im 16. Jahrhundert. Versuch eines Brückenschlags zwischen Wirtschaftstheorie und Wirtschaftsgeschichte', *Jahrbuch für Nationalökonomie und Statistik*, vol. 173 (1961), pp. 448–89; T. K. Rabb, 'The Effects of the Thirty Years War on the German Economy', *Journal of Modern History*, vol. 35 (1962), pp. 40–51; I. Bog, 'Wachstumsprobleme der oberdeutschen Wirtschaft 1540–1618' in F. Lütge (ed.), *Wirtschaftliche und soziale Probleme der gewerblichen Entwicklung im 15.–16. und 19. Jahrhundert* (Stuttgart, 1968), pp. 44–89.

2 If there is no specific reference in the notes the material in the text has been taken from E. and H. Stoob (eds), *Deutsches Städtebuch: Handbuch städtischer Geschichte* (Stuttgart, 1939–70). Important regional studies are R. Endres, 'Zur wirtschaftlichen und sozialen Lage Frankens vor dem Dreissigjährigen Krieg', *Handbuch für fränkische Landesforschung*, vol. 28 (1968), pp. 5–52; W. von Hippel, 'Bevölkerung und Wirtschaft im Zeitalter des Dreissigjährigen Krieges. Das Beispiel Württemberg', *Zeitschrift für Historische Forschung*, vol. 5 (1978), pp. 417–48.

3 C. R. Friedrichs, *Urban Society in an Age of War: Nördlingen 1580–1720* (Princeton, 1980).

4 W. Sticker, *Abhandlungen aus der Seuchengeschichte und der Seuchenlehre* (Leipzig, 1909–10).

5 R. Endres, 'Zu Einwohnerzahl und Bevölkerungsstruktur Nürnbergs im 16. und 17. Jahrhundert', *Mitteilungen des Vereins für Geschichte der Stadt Nürnberg*, vol. 57 (1970), pp. 242–71; W. Jungkunz, 'Die Sterblichkeit in Nürnberg (1714–1850)', *ibid.*, vol. 42 (1951), pp. 289–352.

6 E. Woehlkens, *Pest und Ruhr im 16. und 17. Jahrhundert in Uelzen* (Hanover, 1954); H. Schwarzwälder, *Geschichte der freien Hansestadt Bremen: I* (Bremen, 1975), p. 265.

7 Friedrichs, *Nördlingen*; A. Erhard, *Geschichte der Stadt Passau* (Passau, 1862–4); P. Gluth, *Dinkelsbühl. Die Entwicklung einer Reichsstadt* (Dinkelsbühl, 1958).

8 Woehlkens, *Uelzen*, p. 53, table V.

9 Woehlkens, *Uelzen, passim.*

10 cf. for instance the evidence for Amberg: H. Klinger, 'Die Bevölkerungsbewegung der Stadt Amberg bis zum ausgehenden 19. Jahrhundert', *Verhandlungen des Historischen Vereins von Oberpfalz und Regensburg*, vol. 109 (1969), pp. 145–68.

11 Schwarzwälder, *Bremen*, vol. 1, p. 289; H. Mauersberg, *Wirtschafts- und Sozialgeschichte zentraleuropäischer Städte in neuerer Zeit* (Göttingen, 1960) (on Hamburg, pp. 34, 40, 47, 73, 102; on Hanover, pp. 59 f., 74; on Frankfurt, p. 50 f., 73; on Munich, pp. 64 f., 102); H. Langer, 'Wirtschaft und Politik in Stralsund von 1600–1630' (unpublished PhD thesis, University of Greifswald, 1964), p. 21 f. (on Stralsund, Stettin and Rostock); H. Spannth, *Geschichte der Stadt Hameln* (Hamelin, 1955), vol. 2, p. 59; H. Ditt, 'Entwicklung und Raumbeziehungen der Stadt Paderborn', *Westfälische Forschungen*, vol. 28 (1976), p. 78, graph VII; H. Ditt and K. H. Kirchhoff, 'Struktur und Raumbeziehung der Stadt Coesfeld', *ibid*, vol. 25 (1973), p. 34; A. Schoop, *Quellen zur Rechts- und Wirtschaftsgeschichte der rheinischen Städte. Jülische Städte I, Düren* (Publikationen der Gesellschaft für rheinische Geschichteskunde, vol. 29, Bonn, 1920), p. 8; R. Blanck, 'Die Bevölkerungszahl der Stadt Köln in der 2. Hälfte des 16. Jahrhunderts', *Beiträge zur Geschichte Kölns* (Cologne, 1895), pp. 324 f.; W. Laufer, *Die Sozialstruktur der Stadt Trier in der frühen Neuzeit* (Bonn, 1973), p. 98 with diagrams; E. Christmann, 'Kaiserslauterns Bevölkerung vor und nach dem Dreissigjährigen Krieg', in O. Münch (ed.), *Kaiserslautern 1276–1951* (Kaiserslautern, 1951), pp. 67–106; E. Saffert, 'Die Reichsstadt Schweinfurt von 1554–1615' (unpublished PhD thesis, University of

Wüzburg, 1951), p. 285 f.; F. Seberich, 'Die Einwohnerzahl Würzburgs in alter und neuer Zeit', *Mainfränkisches Jahrbuch für Geschichte und Kunst*, vol. 12 (1960), p. 65 f.; A. Lechner, 'Die Pest in Würzburg im 16. Jahrhundert', *Archiv für Unterfranken*, vol. 68 (1929), pp. 247–341; F. Blendinger, *Die Bevölkerungsbewegung in der ehemaligen Reichsstadt Weissenburg am Nordgau von rund 1580–1780* (Leipzig, 1940), p. 46 f.; Klinger, 'Amberg', p. 165; A. Schreiber, 'Die Entwicklung der Augsburger Bevölkerung vom Ende des 14. bis zum Beginn des 19. Jahrhunderts' (unpublished PhD thesis, University of Erlangen, 1922); A. Buff, *Augsburg in der Renaissancezeit* (Bamberg, 1883).

12 Laufer, *Trier*, pp. 76, 98; Saffert, 'Schweinfurt', p. 285; Schreiber, 'Augsburg'; Blanck, 'Köln', pp. 312, 324; A. Dietz, *Frankfurter Handelsgeschichte: I* (Frankfurt on Main, 1910; new edition, Glashütten, 1970).

13 Mauersberg, *Zentraleuropäische Städte*, pp. 33, 47, 59 f., 74, 102; E. Ennen and F. Irsigler, 'Die frühneuzeitliche Stadt', *Westfälische Forschungen*, vol. 24 (1972), p. 27; Blendinger, *Weissenburg*, p. 46 f.; Klinger, 'Amberg', p. 165.

14 F. Koerner, 'Die Bevölkerungszahl und Bevölkerungsdichte in Mitteleuropa zu Beginn der Neuzeit', *Forschungen und Fortschritt*, vol. 33, part 9 (1959), pp. 325–31. There were high rates of growth at Württemberg up to the beginning of the Thirty Years War (6–7 per cent per decade): von Hippel, 'Wurttemberg', p. 417. Most parts of Germany followed the pattern of developments in Saxony rather than that in Württemberg.

15 Mauersberg, *Zentraleuropäische Städte*, p. 44 f.; F. Bothe, *Beiträge zur Wirtschafts- und Sozialgeschichte der Reichsstadt Frankfurt* (Alternburg, 1906), p. 145; Saffert, 'Schweinfurt'; Schreiber, 'Augsburg'.

16 Schreiber, 'Augsburg', p. 122 f.; for similar developments at Schweinfurt see Saffert, 'Schweinfurt', p. 285 f.

17 F. Lethmate, 'Die Bevölkerung Münsters in der 2. Hälfte des 16. Jahrhunderts', *Münstersche Beiträge zur Geschichtsforschung*, new series, vol. 29 (1912); H. Hövel, 'Zur Bevölkerungsgeschichte Münsters im 16. und 17. Jahrhunderts', in *Festgäbe für A. Fuchs* (Paderborn, 1950), pp. 471–83.

18 Mauersberg, *Zentraleuropäische Städte*, p. 102 f.

19 R. Prange, *Die Bremische Kaufmannschaft des 16. und 17. Jahrhunderts in sozialgeschichtlicher Betrachtung* (Bremen, 1963); Langer, 'Stralsund', p. 21 f.; Mauersberg, *Zentraleuropäische Städte* (on Hamburg and Hanover); Ditt, 'Paderborn', p. 62 f.; Ditt and Kirchhoff, 'Coesfeld', pp. 18 f., 48; Klinger, 'Amberg', p. 156 f.; Saffert, 'Schweinfurt', pp. 99, 285, appendix 7; Blendinger, *Weissenburg*, p. 45 f. (Hesse), p. 5 (Goslar); Hövel, 'Münster', pp. 471, 483.

20 This is discussed in more detail in H. Schilling, 'Innovation through migration: the settlements of Calvinistic Netherlanders in sixteenth- and seventeenth-century central and western Europe', *Social History–Histoire Sociale*, vol. 16 (1983), pp. 7–33.

21 H. Schilling, *Niederländische Exulanten im 16. Jahrhundert* (Gütersloh, 1972), appendix, pp. 175–9.

22 G. Florey, *Bischöfe, Kaiser, Emigranten. Der Protestantismus im Lande Salzburg* (Graz, 1967), pp. 57, 63 f.; H.-C. Rublack, *Gescheiterte Reformation. Frühreformatorische und protestantische Bewegungen in süd- und westdeutschen geistlichen Residenzen* (Stuttgart, 1978), esp. pp. 68, 74, 88 f., 104, 115, 118; Schilling, 'Migration'; F. Bothe, 'Erzbischof Johann Schweikart von Mainz', *Archiv für Frankfurts Geschichte und Kunst*, fifth series, vol. 1, part 3 (1951).

23 As for instance at Paderborn: R. Decker, *Bürgermeister und Ratsherren in Paderborn vom 13. bis 17. Jahrhundert. Untersuchungen zur Zusammensetzung einer städtischen Oberschicht* (Paderborn, 1977); K. Henselmann, 'Der Kampf um Paderborn 1604 und die Geschichtsschreibung', *Westfälische Zeitschrift*, vol. 118 (1968), pp. 229–338; K. Hengst, *Kirchliche Reformen im Fürstbistum Paderborn unter Dietrich von Fürstenberg (1585–1618)*, (Munich, 1974).

24 Schilling, 'Migration'.

25 W. Abel, *Agrarkrisen und Agrarkonjunktur* (Hamburg, 1978); *idem, Massenarmut und Hungerkrisen im vorindustriellen Europa* (Hamburg, 1974).

26 Abel, *Massenarmut*, p. 70 f.; Endres, 'Franken'; H. Mauersberg, *Beiträge zur Bevölkerungs- und Sozialgeschichte Niedersachsens* (Hanover, 1938); D. Saalfeld, 'Die

Wandlungen der Preis- und Lohnstruktur während des 16. Jahrhunderts in Deutschland', in W. Fischer (ed.), *Beiträge zu Wirtschaftswachstum und Wirtschaftsstruktur im 16. und 19. Jahrhundert* (Berlin, 1971); M. J. Elsass, *Umriss einer Geschichte der Löhneund Preise in Deutschland* (Leyden, 1936–49); D. Ebeling, 'Versorgungskrisen und Versorgungspolitik während der zweiten Hälfte des 16. Jahrhunderts in Köln', *Zeitschrift für Agrargeschichte und Agrarsoziologie*, vol. 27 (1979), pp. 34, 40 f., 47.

27 Published in D. Ebeling and F. Irsigler, *Getreideumsatz, Getreide- und Brotpreise in Köln, 1368–1797* (Mitteilungen aus dem Stadtarchiv von Köln, parts 65–6, Köln, 1976–7).

28 Ebeling, 'Versorgungskrisen'; Ebeling and Irsigler, *Getreideumsatz*, p. 672 f.

29 Ebeling and Irsigler, *Getreideumsatz*, p. 672 f. It is not possible to evaluate the subsequent trend because data on turnover is meagre from the beginning of the seventeenth century (*ibid.*, p. xlvi).

30 Ebeling and Irsigler, *Getreideumsatz*, p. xvii; diagrams III (2) and III (9) in the appendix to vol. 2.

31 See the examples in H. Schilling, *Konfessionskonflikt und Staatsbildung* (Gütersloh, 1981), pp. 65, 91 f., 111 f., 227 f., 272 f.

32 For an excellent case study see Ebeling, 'Versorgungskrisen'; this has bibliographical notes on the urban corn-stock system in Germany (p. 53, n. 8).

33 Bog, 'Oberdeutsche Wirtschaft'; von Hippel 'Württemberg', p. 430. For a general discussion of the correlation between the labour market and income trends see H. Freiberg, 'Agrarkonjunktur und Agrarstruktur in vorindustrieller Zeit . . .', *Vierteljahrsschrift für Sozial- und Wirtschaftsgeschichte*, vol. 64 (1977), pp. 289–327.

34 Abel, *Massenarmut*; Ditt and Kirchhoff, 'Coesfeld', pp. 23 f., 30 f.; Woehlkens, *Uelzen*; Langer, 'Stralsund', p. 22; J. Hartung, 'Die direkten Steuern und die Vermögensentwicklung in Augsburg von der Mitte des 16. bis zum 18. Jahrhundert', *Schmollers Jahrbuch für Gesetzgebung, Verwaltung und Volkswirtschaft im Deutschen Reich*, new series, vol. 22 (1898), pp. 1255–97.

35 Mauersberg, *Zentraleuropäische Städte*, p. 453; Bothe, *Frankfurt*, p. 104 f., table p. 115; W. Hesse, 'Der Haushalt der freien Reichsstadt Goslar im 17. Jahrhundert (1500–1682)' (Faculty of Law thesis, University of Halle, 1935), pp. 4, 75 f., 114 f., 155; Langer, 'Stralsund', p. 172 f. The situation was similar at Schweinfurt, Nuremberg, Würzburg and Bamberg after the so-called second Markgräfler-Krieg (1552–4): Saffert, 'Schweinfurt', pp. 118 f., 125 f., 137, 161.

36 Mauersberg, *Zentraleuropäische Städte*, p. 462 f.; P. Borchardt, 'Der Haushalt der Stadt Essen am Ende des 16. Jahrhunderts und Anfang des 17. Jahrhunderts', *Beiträge zur Geschichte von Stadt und Stift Essen*, vol. 24 (1903), esp. p. 113 f., 117 f., 120 f. Examples of towns with balanced budgets up to the beginning of the Thirty Years War are given in Saffert, 'Schweinfurt', pp. 137, 161; Friedrichs, *Nördlingen*, p. 146 f., table p. 160; Ditt and Kirchhoff, 'Coesfeld', p. 34.

37 cf. Lütge, 'Wirtschaftliche Lage', p. 360: 'Where we can find debtors, so there must have been creditors too.'

38 C. Bruckner, *Zur Wirtschaftsgeschichte des Regierungsbezirks Aachen* (Cologne, 1967); H. Kellenbenz (ed.), *Schwerpunkte der Kupferproduktion und des Kupferhandels in Europa 1500–1650* (Cologne, 1977); *idem, Zwei Jahrtausende Kölner Wirtschaft* (Cologne, 1976); Dietz, *Handelsgeschichte*; Endres, 'Einwohnerzahl Nürnbergs'; Hartung, 'Augsburg', esp. the tables on pp. 1276, 1284 f.; W. Zorn, *Augsburg. Geschichte einer Stadt* (2nd edn, Augsburg, 1978), p. 305.

39 Langer, 'Stralsund'; H. Kellenbenz, *Unternehmerkräfte im Hamburger Portugal- und Spanienhandel 1590–1625* (Hamburg, 1954); B. Hagedorn, *Ostfrieslands Handel und Schiffahrt im 16. Jahrhundert* (Berlin, 1910–12); G. D. Ramsay, *The Politics of a Tudor Merchant Adventurer. A Letter to the Earls of East Friesland* (Manchester, 1979). Even at Lübeck economic innovations occurred alongside the contraction: M. L. Pelus, 'Lübeck au milieu du 17e siècle: conflits politiques et sociaux, conjoncture économique', *Revue d'Histoire Diplomatique*, vol. 92 (1978), pp. 189–209; *idem, Wolter von Holsten marchand lubeckois dans la seconde moitié du seizième siècle* (Cologne, 1981); P. Jeannin, 'Contribution á l'étude du commerce de Lübeck aux environs de 1580' in *Hansische Studien* (Berlin, 1961), pp. 163–89.

40 B. Kuske, *Wirtschaftsgeschichte Westfalens in Leistung und Verpflechtung mit den Nachbarländern bis zum 18. Jahrhundert* (2nd edn, Münster, 1949); H. Aubin, 'Das westfälische Leinengewerbe im Rahmen der deutschen und europäischen Leinwanderzeugung bis zum Ausbruch des Industriezeitalters', *Vortragsreihe der Gesellschaft für westfälische Wirtschaftsgeschichte*, vol. 11 (1964); H. Hohls, 'Der Leinwandhandel in Norddeutschland vom Mittelalter bis zum 17. Jahrhundert', *Hansische Geschichtsblätter*, vol. 31 (1926), pp. 116–58; H. Rothert, *Westfälische Geschichte: II* (Gütersloh, 1962), p. 203, Ditt and Kirchhoff, 'Coesfeld', pp. 22, 32, f.; J. C. B. Stüve, *Geschichte des Hochstifts Osnabrück: II* (new edn, Osnabrück, 1970), pp. 33, 141; H. Wiemann, 'Die Osnabrücker Stadtlegge', *Osnabrücker Mitteilungen* vol. 35 (1910–11; E. Geiger, *Die soziale Elite der Hansestadt Lemgo und die Entstehung eines Exportgewerbes auf dem Lande in der Zeit von 1450–1650* (Detmold, 1976); A. Neukirch, *Hamelner Renaissance* (Hamelin, 1950), p. 52 f.; Schoop, *Düren*, esp. p. 112; Schilling, 'Migration'; *idem*, 'Wandlungs- und Differenzierungsprozesse innerhalb der bürgerlichen Oberschichten West- und Norddeutschlands im 16. und 17. Jahrhundert', in M. Biskup und K. Zernack, (eds), *Schichtung und Entwicklung der Gesellschaft in Polen und Deutschland (16. und 17. Jahrhundert*) (Wiesbaden, 1982), pp. 121–73. The articles by Schilling have bibliographical notes on the north-west and Rhine region.

41 E. Ennen und M. van Rey, 'Probleme der frühneuzeitlichen Stadt vorzüglich der Haupt- und Residenzstädte', *Westfälische Forschungen*, vol. 25 (1973), pp. 168–212; F. Petri (ed), *Bischofs- und Kathedralstädte des Mittelalters und der frühen Neuzeit* (Cologne, 1976) (see the contributions by H. Mauersberg, H. Kellenbenz, I. Maierhöfer); Rublack, *Gescheiterte Reformation*; for Paderborn see n. 23, above.

42 Bog, 'Wachstumsprobleme'; von Hippel, 'Württemberg'.

43 Schilling 'Migration'; *idem*, 'Wandlungs- und Differenzierungsprozesse' (both with bibliographical notes).

44 M. Ritter, *Deutsche Geschichte im Zeitalter der Gegenreformation und des Dreissigjährigen Krieges: I-II* (Stuttgart, 1889–95); H. Schmidt, *Politische Geschichte Ostfrieslands* (Leer, 1975); Rothert, *Westfälische Geschichte*, vol. 2, p. 92 f.; P. Casser, 'Der niederrheinisch–westfälische Reichskreis (1500 bis 1806)' in H. Aubin *et al.* (eds), *Der Raum Westfalen: II* (Berlin, 1934), esp. p. 46 f.; L. Keller, *Die Gegenreformation in Westfalen* (Leipzig, 1881–95), vol. 2, pp. 13, 265; W.-H. Wiedmann, 'Die Barmer Unternehmer. Ein Beitrag zur Soziologie des Unternehmertypus' (economics thesis, University of Cologne, 1952); F. Petri und G. Droege (eds), *Rheinische Geschichte: II* (Düsseldorf, 1976).

45 Erhard, *Passau*, W. M. Schmid, 'Passauer Waffenwesen', *Zeitschrift für Waffenkunde* (1905); G. Parker, *The Army of Flanders and the Spanish Road, 1567–1659* (Cambridge, 1972).

46 Examples: Neukirch, *Hamelner Renaissance*; H. P. Dorfs, *Wesel. Eine städtisch-geographische Monographie mit einem Vergleich zu anderen Festungsstädten* (Bonn, 1972); W. Maack, *Grafschaft Schaumburg. Die Geschichte eines kleinen Weserlandes* (Bückeburg, 1964); W. Kohl, *Christoph Bernhard von Galen. Politische Geschichte des Fürstbistums Münster 1650–1678* (Münster, 1964); V. U. Meinhardt, *Die Festung Minden. Gestalt, Struktur und Geschichte einer Stadtfestung* (Minden, 1958); C. Hanse, 'Die mittelalterliche Stadt als Festung', in C. Haase (ed.), *Die Stadt des Mittelalters: I* (Darmstadt, 1975), pp. 377–407; G. Eimer, *Die Stadtplanung im schwedischen Ostseereich 1600–1715* (Stockholm, 1961); Parker, *Spanish Road.*

47 For a case study with discussion of the general problem see Schilling, *Konfessionskonflikt*; for other examples in the north-west: H. Schilling, 'Die politische Elite nortwestdeutscher Städte in den religiösen Auseinandersetzungen des 16. Jahrhunderts', in W. J. Mommsen (ed.), *Stadtbürgertum und Adel in der Reformation* (Stuttgart, 1979), pp. 84–94.

48 See the detailed description in Schilling, *Konfessionskonflikt.*

49 A. G. Dickens, *The German Nation and Martin Luther* (London, 1974), p. 182.

50 The Hanseatic towns tried to get a *ius reformandi* like the imperial towns, but they had no success: G. Pfeiffer, 'Der Augsburger Religionsfriede und die Reichsstädte', *Zeitschrift des Historischen Vereins für Schwaben*, vol. 61 (1955), pp. 213–321. Some made a new attempt later: Stüve, *Hochstift Osnabrück*, vol. 2, pp. 488 f., 503, 522 f.

51 cf. M. Spindler (ed.), *Handbuch der bayrischen Geschichte* (Munich, 1967–74), vol. 2.

52 cf. n. 22, above.
53 Schilling, 'Migration'.
54 I first commented on the clustering of urban conflicts in 'Bürgerkämpfe in Aachen zu Beginn des 17. Jahrhunderts', *Zeitschrift für historische Forschung*, vol. 1 (1974), p. 176, n. (with an incomplete list of towns affected). Further research has been undertaken by C. R. Friedrichs, 'Citizens or Subjects? Urban Conflict in Early Modern Germany', in M. Usher Chrisman and O. Gründler (eds), *Social Groups and Religious Ideas in the Sixteenth Century* (Kalamazoo, 1978), pp. 46–58. An extended list of uprisings by Friedrichs can be found in 'German Town Revolts and the Seventeenth-Century Crisis' in *Renaissance and Modern Studies*, vol. 26 (1982), pp. 27–51.
55 For more detail, see Schilling, *Konfessionskonflikt*.
56 J. C. Davies, 'Eine Theorie der Revolution', in W. Zapf (ed.), *Theorien des sozialen Wandels* (Cologne, 1971), pp. 399–417.
57 cf. Keyser, *Städtebuch*; M. Meyn, *Die Reichsstadt Frankfurt vor dem Bürgeraufstand von 1612–1614. Struktur und Krise* (Frankfurt on Main, 1980); G. Schormann, 'Hexenprozesse in Schaumburg', *Niedersächsisches Jahrbuch*, vol. 45 (1973), pp. 145–69; G. Wilbertz, 'Hexenprozesse und Zauberglaube im Hochstift Osnabrück', *Osnabrücker Mitteilungen*, vol. 84, (1978), p. 40 f.; S. von Riezler, *Geschichte der Hexenprozesse in Bayern* (Stuttgart, 1896, reprinted Aalen, 1968); K. Rübel, 'Hexenaberglaube, Hexenprozesse und Zauberwahn in Dortmund', *Beiträge zur Geschichte Dortmunds und der Grafschaft Mark*, vol. 22 (1913), pp. 96–117.

8 *Northern Italy in the 1590s*

N. S. DAVIDSON

> Dio non è, son le persone
> Ch' ogn'hor fan la carestia . . .
> Dio ci manda l'abondanza
> Ma l'huom fa la carestia.[1]

In November 1595, Paolo Paruta, Venetian Ambassador in Rome, returned home to deliver a stylish report to the Senate in which he recorded his impression of the Papal States.

> The contentment that the populace used formerly to derive from living under the restrained government of the Church, neither burdened with taxes, nor trodden down by extortion and arbitrary power, was the main foundation on which that government could, whatever events or developments might occur in Italy, rest in security. Now these things have become so different that it hardly seems possible, in so short a time, that there could have been so great a change and deterioration.

Paruta doubtless exaggerated the satisfaction of earlier times, but his years in Rome between 1592 and 1595 had persuaded him that the problems had become serious:

> grave famine, and continued taxation that is increased and collected with all rigour; the most severe exercise of the law; unending harassment by bandits; and the other misfortunes that originate as a consequence of these developments; all these have given birth in the soul of the Church's temporal subjects to a deep dissatisfaction with their government, and a profound desire for change in the hope that whatever else happens, they might improve their present most tormented condition.[2]

Paruta neatly summarised the most obvious characteristics of the 'Crisis of the 1590s' in northern Italy: famine, high taxation, crime, harsh justice and a gnawing sense of political insecurity. These problems did not affect all regions to the same degree, but they all hastened developments that significantly altered the nature of government and society in the early modern period.

I

Some features of the 1590s affected everyone from the Alps to the Tiber. Certainly everyone noticed the bad weather: the decade was ushered in by floods in Tuscany, Rome and the Campagna during the autumn of 1589; heavy rain continued in 1590, in Rome until June. The Venetian Terraferma too was damaged by floods and storms. The summer, when it arrived, was cold and dry. The following two years were scarcely better, and, although the middle years of the decade were not so wet, the Tiber was flooded again in February, March and December 1598 – reaching at one stage nearly twelve feet up the façade of S. Maria sopra Minerva. The bad weather had a direct effect on agriculture: the rain damaged crops, the floods destroyed harvests.[3]

The bad weather of the 1590s deserves particular attention, because between 1550 and 1590 demand for food from the cities of northern Italy had increased. The population of Florence rose by about 35 per cent between 1551 and 1589; in Lucca the number of baptisms recorded at the city's two baptisteries rose by nearly 20 per cent between the early 1550s and the early 1580s. In Venice, where the plague of 1575–6 had been especially severe, the population rose (according to the regular censuses) by over 11 per cent in the first five years of the 1580s.[4] Even in good years, however, the food supply grown within Italy was unreliable, and evidence from some areas suggests that crop yields occasionally began to fall in the 1590s.[5] The wet winters and dry summers of the early 1590s therefore created serious food shortages in northern Italy. Nearly every city suffered between 1590 and 1593. In Rome, the hungry frequently took to the streets; queues formed outside bakeries, bakers were threatened, and even the Pope himself was mobbed in St Peter's.[6]

Growing demand had pushed grain prices higher throughout the second half of the sixteenth century and, in famine years, of course, prices were liable to jump suddenly: in Florence, wheat prices rose by over 140 per cent between 1560 and 1590, but could rise by as much as 33 per cent in one month during the famine year of 1588. The 1590s therefore mark a further stage in a long inflationary development. In Venice, average prices were about 90 per cent higher between 1589 and 1598 than between 1567 and 1576; in Modena the prices for 1590–9 were well over double the average price for the 1580s; in Florence they were nearly 70 per cent higher in the 1590s than in the 1580s. But such statistics disguise the real misery of the 1590s, for hidden within the averages are some violent fluctuations. In

Venice, for example, the average price of grain between 1589 and 1598 was about twenty-four lire a *staio*; but in February 1591, grain sold for 40 lire a *staio*, and the average price between 1590 and 1591 was three times higher than in 1580. In Padua, the average price in the 1580s was nearly five *lire piccoli*; after the 1590 harvest it reached over nine *lire piccoli*. Throughout northern Italy, in fact, it seems that grain prices in the early 1590s – when the weather was at its worst – were significantly higher than in the rest of the decade. In Bassano, for example, grain prices began to fall from 1593. In Modena they reached over 406 *soldi* after the 1590 harvest, and over 383 *soldi* after the 1592 harvest; but they fell to some 287 *soldi* in 1593 and rose above that figure only once again before 1600. In Venice, Modena and Florence too, the price rise slowed down before 1600. The link between poor weather, bad harvests and high grain prices was clearly recognised at the time: in July 1596, the papal nunzio in Venice in a letter to Cardinal Blandrata reported that grain prices were already rising in anticipation of a poor harvest after a period of unseasonable rain.[7] Clearly, the severe weather between 1589 and 1593 was a major cause of the high grain prices of those years; prices then moved down in better years, but could swiftly rise again. After the good harvest of 1597, for example, grain prices in Rome had sunk to almost the same level as in the 1580s; but after the rains and floods of 1598 the price rose again by 36 per cent in 1599.[8]

The bad weather and its consequences inevitably had a significant effect on the growing Italian population. The increase of the second half of the sixteenth century – interrupted though not obstructed by the plagues of the later 1570s – came to a genuine halt in the 1590s. In Venice the census records suggest a 7·3 per cent drop in population between 1586 and 1600. Some Italian towns, like Ferrara, actually had a smaller population in 1600 than in 1550, and the Venetian mainland Empire contained a significantly smaller population in 1607 than in 1590. The most striking evidence, perhaps, comes from Friuli. In 1599, Marc Antonio Memmo, proveditor general at Palma for the previous three years, estimated that the Friulan population had dropped by over 50 per cent from a figure of 196,000 in the middle of the century to only 97,000 in his own day; another contemporary estimated that in about 1590 the figure had been 110,000, thus suggesting a fall of nearly 12 per cent during the crisis decade of the 1590s. In some smaller towns, the decline was even greater: the population of Cividale, troubled by disease, fell from some 17,000 in 1587 to only 12,000 in 1599 – a drop of nearly 30 per cent in a dozen years. But nearly all the figures show a clear recovery after 1600: obviously the 1590s were unusual years of population decline in a long period of growth.[9]

Sometimes the bad weather was directly responsible for increased mortalities: one contemporary estimated, for example, that about 1,400 had been killed in the Roman floods of 1598, and the decaying corpses and unhealthy conditions left when the waters receded raised fears of an epidemic. Disease also frequently followed famine – though the precise link between them is not always easily identified. While not as severe as in the 1570s or 1520s, the plagues of the 1590s could still have a serious effect on the local population. In Cividale, the plague of 1598–9 touched a quarter of the city's inhabitants; some 12 per cent perished. The effect of the bad weather, food shortages and disease on the birth-rate is less easy to document, but where appropriate records survive they suggest that the number of births declined in the 1590s. In Lucca, for example, recorded baptisms show a drop of 9·3 per cent by the early 1590s from the early 1580s.[10]

When the Italian harvests failed, the only way to avoid famine was to import grain from abroad. Between June 1590 and May 1591, imports of grain through Livorno were over 470 per cent higher than in 1585; by May 1592 they had increased by a further 50 per cent, and there was another 16 per cent increase by May 1593. Between 1590 and 1591, over 52 per cent of these imports came from northern Europe; between 1591 and 1592, that figure increased to nearly 95 per cent. And this northern grain was transported in northern ships: only 31 English and North European arrivals were recorded at Livorno between 1582 and 1585; 227 arrived between 1590 and 1593, of which an ever-increasing proportion came from Amsterdam.[11]

This huge increase in grain imports in the 1590s inevitably affected the Italian states' balance of trade; but for some years before 1590 demand abroad for Italian manufactured exports had been declining, as the Turkish advance in the east Mediterranean, the civil wars in France and the Dutch Revolt all reduced commercial opportunities. And, even in Italy itself, local producers had for some years been forced to compete with rival manufacturers from northern Europe: a number of Venetian and Lombard industries had secured their European reputations by their specialist, and sometimes secret, techniques, and their competitors realised that only by adopting those techniques, and then pricing their goods more cheaply, could they hope to compete successfully. Long before the 1590s, Italian craftsmen had been tempted by lucrative contracts to leave Italy to develop rival industries abroad. In November 1568, for example, the Venetian authorities investigated rumours that two German gold beaters and a former Murano glass worker had travelled to Venice 'in order to lead skilled glass workers back to work' with them in Habsburg territory.[12]

The increased food prices and the fall in population that characterised the 1590s therefore further damaged domestic demand at a time when Italian industries were increasingly in trouble. The most striking examples of this process are the textile industries. The Florentine woollen industry was already in difficulty by the 1580s; in 1589, production was only half that of 1572, and the 1590s saw a further drop of over 60 per cent from the figures for 1585. The industries in Milan and Como also declined in the later sixteenth century; and, even though the Venetian industry maintained and even increased its production beyond 1600, the early 1590s at least were a period of contraction: production dropped more than 12 per cent between 1592 and 1593, and a further 24 per cent between 1593 and 1594.

But, while woollen production declined, the silk industry flourished. By the early seventeenth century, the Florentine industry produced some 10,000 pieces a year – the city's most valuable export – and employed about 20 per cent of the city's population. As early as 1580, Milanese silk production was worth 5 million lire a year in exports, and 15 per cent of the total value of all Spanish Lombardy's manufactured goods. In Venice, the number of active silk looms actually increased in the 1590s, and silk continued to dominate the Lucchese economy.

Neither the woollen nor the silk industry suffered in this period from serious supply problems, even though both depended on imports for their raw material; yet one declined and the other prospered. The most significant problem facing the woollen industry was a change in demand, as both at home and abroad lower quality northern goods were more popular than the Italian products; but the fashionable silk market continued to favour high-quality Italian goods. Changes in demand also damaged the silver-mining industry in Tuscany: as the volume of American silver in circulation increased, the value of silver declined against that of gold, and Duke Ferdinand was forced to close the mines of Pietrasanta in the mid-1590s.[13]

As demand fell at home and abroad, producers kept their prices as low as possible. Demand for food, especially bread, inevitably stayed high whatever the price; but prices for manufactured goods did not rise as much. In Rome, the average price for wax and lime was actually lower in the 1590s than the 1580s; prices for firewood and boxes rose by less than 7 per cent, glass flasks rose by 10.9 per cent. Foods like meat and eggs rose by over 12·2 per cent. Wheat rose by over 75 per cent.[14]

But the producers' attempts to limit their price rises were hampered by government taxation policies. In all parts of Italy, taxation rose in the sixteenth century – in the Papal States, for example, by as much as 300 per cent in the course of the century.[15] Much of this burden inevitably fell on the most productive sectors of industry and trade: by 1602, taxes on industry and trade accounted for 37 per cent of Venetian government income. It is not clear whether governments really recognised the long-term effects of such high taxation, which squeezed profits at a time of reduced demand. One contemporary estimated that as much as 42 per cent of the price of Venetian woollen cloths was taken by the State. And as foreign trade diminished, and the carrying trade was lost, so the demand for new ships declined too. Already, between 1567 and 1576, the Venetian merchant fleet had been reduced (in terms of volume) by over 70 per cent, and the decline continued beyond 1600; by the early seventeenth century a large proportion of the Genoese and Venetian fleets were built in Holland and England.[16]

On the other hand, arms manufacturers flourished at the end of the sixteenth century. Here again the supply of raw materials was not a problem; iron was mined in the southern Alps and in Elba, and Italian metallurgical techniques were unusually advanced. The production of weapons and armour in Gardone Val Trompia and Milan was stimulated by warfare elsewhere on the continent. And government policies boosted production further as defence spending increased. By the end of the sixteenth century, the Spanish government in Lombardy devoted up to 90 per cent of its expenditure to the military, and Venetian expenditure on the Arsenal and navy could absorb up to 30 per cent of the Republic's budget. Spending on fortifications also rose: by 1602 Venice disbursed more than five times as much as it had in the 1520s. Economic activity was also encouraged by garrisoned soldiers who spent their pay on local goods and services. By 1602, there were well over 7,000 troops in Spanish Lombardy.[17]

Apart from the arms and silk industries, then, Italian manufacturers were forced to reduce wages and overheads – or risk bankruptcy. To find cheaper labour, a number of industries – especially textiles – moved away from the large cities into smaller towns and the countryside, where the labour force could often rely on several sources of income, and was therefore willing to accept extra work at low wages. In Bergamo, for example, cloth production continued to increase into the later 1590s; and the village of Lissone north of Milan had 110 active looms in 1613.

But, as industry and trade declined in the 1590s, government revenues from taxation were reduced; the response of the authorities was to act whenever possible to protect local industries from competition. Local market conditions were strictly controlled, and laws passed to discourage emigration: as early as 1549, for example, a Venetian law threatened any glass workers from Murano known to be working abroad with four years in the galleys; in 1613, soap workers were given a three-month amnesty to return to the city without fear of punishment.[18] Sometimes governments intervened directly to increase production: in Rome, both Sixtus V and Clement VIII tried to introduce skilled metalworking to the city and to salvage the textile industry by importing foreign workers. In the last quarter of the century, Venice and Rome had fought to protect their printing industries in the profitable market for devotional literature; their most dramatic disagreement was over the imposition of the 1596 Index of Prohibited Books. Sometimes governments encouraged industries to become more self-sufficient: a number of laws were passed in Florence between 1576 and 1593 to encourage the planting of mulberry trees to increase the domestic supply of silk. The policy seemed to work – between 1595 and 1610, the industry doubled its local consumption. Governments could also stimulate the construction industry: Sixtus V spent over 1 million silver *scudi* on building in Rome between April 1585 and December 1589, and over 50 churches were built in Rome during the second half of the century; Michelangelo's dome on St Peter's was completed in 1590.

The most important achievement of government protectionism would have been to make Italy once again self-sufficient in grain; by the end of the century, perhaps only the Venetian government had approached this ideal. But, whether successful or not, government moves towards greater interference in the economy in the 1590s were of greater significance than is sometimes realised.[19]

II

The 1590s, then, were discouraging years for Italian industry. Its difficulties might have been less if it had been able to borrow cash to cover its current costs and boost its working capital. The Church's traditional prohibition on usury was no longer a major obstacle to investment: throughout the sixteenth century the Cardinal Chamberlain had sold licences to Jews to permit them to lend to Christians, and from 1542 the Papacy also began to authorise the payment of interest, normally at 5 per cent, to depositors who lent cash to the Christian loan banks, the Monti di Pietà, for redistribution to the poor.[20] But the Church's relaxed attitude did not necessarily help manufacturers: by the later sixteenth century, investors' confidence in industry had been too seriously reduced. The Turkish advance, financial uncertainties in Europe and economic difficulties in Italy discouraged investment in industry and trade in the 1580s and 1590s. From 1590 to 1596, for example, investment in Florentine industry seems to have been lower than at any time since 1561.[21]

Investors turned to a number of more secure activities. By the 1590s, the most important alternatives were the money market and land. Loans to governments could be particularly profitable: all governments had to borrow to cover deficits and finance particularly expensive projects. Venetian involvement in the Cyprus War, for example, had been financed by a public loan fund of 5·7 million ducats, on which the government paid interest totalling ½ million ducats a year at rates from 7½ to 14 per cent. But by setting interest rates at such attractively high levels governments were committing themselves to a major long-term expenditure; by 1592, interest payments on such loan funds were accounted the largest single item in the papal government's annual budget, some 29·4 per cent of the total, rising to 34·8 per cent by 1599. Lending to governments was therefore very much more attractive to investors than industry and manufacturing – as long as the governments could afford the interest payments. Before his election as Doge of Venice, Leonardo Donà received up to 16 per cent of his annual income from government loan funds, and even smaller investors found them a useful source of income: Aurelio Stichiano, a renegade religious and charlatan, had investments worth 48 ducats a year in the Venetian mint when he was arrested in 1549.[22]

But, here too, private investors seem to have been more cautious as the century closed. In Florence and Venice, private involvement in government finance had been reduced by 1600. The Venetian government's successful liquidation of its loan funds from 1596 reduced opportunities in one area, while Philip II's bankruptcies must have shaken the confidence of private investors at least in government reliability. Even the papacy, which rarely defaulted, recorded a drop in income from the sale of office and its loan funds after 1592.[23] Confidence in the money market was also put at risk by bank failures. Genoese bankers certainly profited from the increased availability of silver as Spanish bullion was diverted through Italy after the early 1570s, but elsewhere private banks were less fortunate. Between 1551 and 1584 five major banks failed in Venice, of which only one was able to pay its creditors in full; when the Pisani and Tiepolo bank finally collapsed in 1584, it left liabilities of over 1 million ducats. In the 1580s and 1590s, the Strozzi, Soldani and Ricci banks collapsed in Florence, and about half a dozen more in Rome. They were not really replaced: the state banks founded in the same period – like the Venetian Banco della Piazza di Rialto in 1587 – took deposits and effected transfers between customers, but gave no credit to individuals, or indeed to industries.[24]

One form of investment that did become more popular at the end of the sixteenth century was personal loans. Here the Monti di Pietà already played an important role, of course; in Venice, the Jews were obliged after 1573 to perform this important function at only 5 per cent interest per annum.[25] But Venetian borrowers could also resort to contractual agreements called *livelli*, in which the loan was disguised as a mortgage. Ownership of the borrower's property would be transferred to the lender in return for the loan; interest was then paid as if it were rent for the continued use of the property by the borrower. These *livelli* remained popular, even when repayments in kind were declared illegal in the 1580s, as the interest rates were always fixed at a healthy 6 per cent, and the contractual ownership of the property represented good security.[26]

But a more significant area for investors than the money market was land. By 1600, Venetian patricians had shifted a major portion of their investments to estates on the Terraferma. In a period when food prices were high, land was a good investment: landlords were assured of a good income, unaffected by inflation, and in famine years they had at least the comfort of knowing they had access to their own grain first. Profits on land might have been smaller than from other forms of investment, but the risks were small too, and the investment was therefore worth fostering. Leonardo Donà derived about 45 per cent of his income from his estates before 1606, and he prudently reinvested his profits annually in repairs, improvements and further purchases. After 1587, as the Medici enlarged the area under cultivation on their private estate at Altopascio, their income steadily increased. If properly managed, land could yield a guaranteed return. Investment in land had other advantages too, for it could be kept within the family. Venetian patricians often prohibited the alienation of inherited property in their wills, and limited the number of their sons who could marry to prevent the break-up of their holdings.

And so, in the later sixteenth century, landowning passed increasingly to the hands of urban investors. By 1600, the Venetian patriciate owned about 11 per cent of the Terraferma's cultivated land, producing almost one-third of Venetian grain imports. In 1585, residents of Padua owned four times as much of the Padovano as its inhabitants. By as early as the 1550s more than half the best farming land in the 'low plain' of Spanish Lombardy was owned by townspeople. A new ideal of nobility developed in the Italian towns, one in which land conveyed prestige. It could even be argued that in north-eastern Italy, at least, a new form of 'feudalism' had developed: in many areas, Terraferma land brought with it all the feudal obligations observed by previous owners; but now the estates were run by city investors with an eye on their profits.[27]

III

These changes on the land and in industry had serious implications for the labour force. Employment in export-related industries such as textiles was reduced as demand fell: membership of the Venetian wool guild dropped from over 3,300 in 1595 to only 770 in 1690.

The Venetian workforce adapted to these new conditions with surprising agility, moving swiftly into different areas of employment such as domestic service, construction, and the retail trades. In the big cities, there was rarely any shortage of labour. But alternative employment was not always available, and not always profitable: the abundance of labour held unskilled wages down, and in the 1590s, even skilled wages could not keep pace with inflation. In Modena, for example, a mason could buy six or seven kilograms of bread with a day's wages in the 1580s but only four in the 1590s. In Florence, his wage would provide between nine and twelve kilograms a day in the 1580s, but only five between 1592 and 1596. Evidence from Rome suggests that urban rents did not fall in the 1590s; if this is true in other Italian cities, then it is clear that an artisan's wages must frequently have been inadequate, and that borrowing from the Monti di Pietà or the professional lenders must have become more common.[28]

Agricultural workers often had to be adaptable too. As land was purchased by wealthy urban investors, peasant proprietors were squeezed off the market; tenants on fixed rents, in cash or kind, suffered from inflation but could gain little from rising grain prices; day labourers often found less work as pasturage or more profitable crops were introduced. Rural wages could not keep pace with inflation either, and many in the countryside became dependent on the lenders as well. According to contemporary observers in Friuli, the combined burden of rents, taxes, interest rates and prices could make whole families destitute. Such conditions were enough to stimulate a regular emigration from poorer regions. Mountain areas like the Apennines and the Garfagnana, the Lombard Alps and the Bergamasco, were dependent on the income sent home from local men and women employed elsewhere. In 1606, a census revealed that 35 per cent of the total population of Olmo worked in Milan, Venice or further afield. In times of particular difficulty – epidemic, flood or famine – the numbers on the move increased, mostly seeking in the cities for work or charity. They did not often find the former. It was rumoured in the later 1580s that as many as 4,000 peasants had entered Rome in one night in search of food, and during the famine years from 1590 to 1592 rural immigration reached crisis proportions, adding to the crowds of urban poor whose wages (if any) could not match prices. The migrants and the destitute lived rough, risking disease and turning to prostitution and crime. In 1599, there were over 800 prostitutes in Rome – 2·3 per cent of the city's female population; the figures were almost certainly higher in the early 1590s. Beggars interrogated in the city in the mid-1590s presented an alarming (and perhaps not wholly accurate) picture of life among a number of organised and disciplined bands of vagabonds, charlatans, and petty thieves, sexually promiscuous and without religion, taking seasonal work if they could get it, and relying on crime, fraud and charity when they could not.[29]

This sort of evidence seemed to confirm a number of the authorities' assumptions about the poor. In 1587, for example, Tommaso Garzoni described the peasants as 'uncivilised . . . and normally without any sense of duty, especially when they get a chance to steal their master's property'.[30] Governments were increasingly convinced that a barbarous 'anti-society' threatened public order in town and country. Subsequent events did not increase their sense of security. Violence erupted during bread shortages; the number of infanticide cases increased in some areas; public drunkenness became even more common in Venice. Most disturbing of all was the growth of crimes committed by organised gangs of outlaws: between 1575 and 1595, armed bands terrorised the Papal States, Tuscany and the Veneto. Initiated by the peasantry as an alternative to unemployment and hunger, they attracted migrants, beggars and even renegade priests to their colours. Between 1594 and 1595, for example, forty six Veronese artisans were tried in Padua for banding together and 'declaring themselves publicly as hired killers, willing to serve anyone with their weapons and committing crimes for money'.[31] Such groups flourished in border areas, and could often count on the support of the local rural populations, which welcomed their assault on the privileged rich in the cities. Frequently they were organised and sustained by the rural nobility, who resented government attempts to limit their effective local influence; sometimes they were financed by foreign governments. The Duke of Montemarciano, Alfonso Piccolomini, received money from the Grand Duke of Tuscany until his arrest in 1591, and Marco Sciarra's thousand followers may have been supported by Spanish money from Naples until he hired himself to the Venetian government in 1593. Rival gangs often fought against each other: in 1596, according to the papal nunzio in Venice, bandits supporting the aristocratic Martinenghi family openly attacked a castle belonging to the Marchese of Castiglione on the Brescian border.[32]

Evidence like this convinced the authorities that they had to deal with an unprecedented crime-wave in the 1590s. It is not easy now to decide whether they were right, but figures for both trials and convictions rose. In Perugia, for example, in the twenty years before 1580, 88 criminals were executed; in the twenty years after, 250 were executed, including 22 in 1593. Contemporaries became convinced that the methods available for dealing with crime were not appropriate to the new problems. The forces of law and order were badly organised, badly paid and badly disciplined; judicial procedures were slow and cumbersome; witnesses were often frightened into silence by threats of murder if they told the truth – as indeed happened in 1590 to some Brescian priests and their families; local government officials were sometimes corrupt, usually frightened and almost always ill prepared. The prisons were overcrowded and notoriously insecure.[33] Suspects found it all too easy to escape justice.

Clearly a new approach was required. Sixtus V and Clement VIII tried to deal with the bandits by financing a war against them. The Venetian and Tuscan governments, on the other hand, tried to hire or bribe criminals to join them in the fight against crime: as the Governor of the Maremma told his government in Florence in 1586 when discussing the bandit leader Sacripante di Toscanella, 'we cannot place any faith in the local police authorities and their troops; it now seems that the only remedy will be to use his enemies against him.'[34] Governments also gradually relaxed the procedural restrictions that prevented their officials from reaching swift and secret decisions. They encouraged secret denunciations, promised immunity to all who confessed, and offered rewards for information leading to convictions. Laws against carrying arms were revised – in 1596 Venice declared that carrying certain types of firearm would be treated as a capital offence. The harshest punishments of exile, the galleys and death were used more often. In 1595, the Venetian government even passed a law which encouraged the murder of bandits found within its territory. None of these measures was really effective, however – and many of them simply aggravated the problem. By using criminals to fight crime, and by ignoring the provisions of the law which gave protection to the innocent, some states had effectively allied themselves to the criminal community, and put themselves above the law.[35]

If crime did increase in the later sixteenth century, there seems little doubt that the economic problems of the 1590s contributed to it. One final solution attempted by the governments was to improve the provision of care for the poor, and so prevent their turning to crime at all. The many charitable foundations established in the Middle Ages were still active in 1500, and similar organisations were founded throughout the sixteenth century. But in an age of inflation and increasing poverty such voluntary organisations were insufficient, for in years of real difficulty up to two-thirds of the urban population might be in need of regular charitable assistance. In famine years, for example, the Misericordia in Bergamo cared for four times as many people as in normal years. Despite the wide range of assistance available, Rome simply could not cope with the vast scale of need in the early 1590s, and contemporaries describe how the poor died on the streets in horrendous scenes of despair and distress.

Charitable provision in the 1590s therefore seemed to require more finance – and more organisation. When disaster occurred, the governments inevitably became involved, in attempts to repair damage, prevent disease and maintain order. In famine years, all governments tried to increase their control of the grain supply. By encouraging imports, prohibiting exports, by subsidies, warehousing and regular systems of distribution, governments hoped to control price movements. Usually they failed, and the hungry still flocked to the cities demanding charity. In Rome, Pius V and Gregory XIII had both attempted to increase the efficiency of aid by prohibiting street begging and enclosing the poor in special hospitals where they could receive care and be given work. Sixtus V continued this programme by building a hospital near the Ponte Sisto in 1587 as a central repository for all charitable bequests at a cost of some 30,000 *scudi*, nearly as much as the Lateran Palace. His reserve fund in

Castel Sant'Angelo was also used in the 1590s to provide relief during the famines. Similarly, in Florence between 1590 and 1591, the sick were cared for in hospitals, and the able-bodied put to work building the Forte di Belvedere. In Modena the poor were grouped in a special hospital founded in 1592, and by 1600 in Venice orphans, foundlings, prostitutes (and girls at risk), and the sick all had their own hospitals where they could be cared for and trained (where appropriate) for employment outside. The poor were to be institutionalised, begging was to be eliminated. Only in this more organised way, it was argued, could disease and disorder be avoided, and charity be distributed in a more selective manner. With the huge numbers demanding attention, it was becoming increasingly difficult to distinguish the genuinely needy from the fraudulent; so the authorities began to discriminate against those whose credentials were difficult to check. By 1600, able-bodied non-residents in Venice were refused assistance and expelled; in Florence, too, beggars from outside Tuscany were expelled in 1590–1; vagabonds were expelled from Bologna in 1590, and from Rome in 1591 and 1598.

But this development was not simply a response to the requirements of an efficient administration: it reflected as well a growing conviction that poverty was caused by idleness, and idleness was a sin, a rebellion against God. In a sermon of July 1602, Cardinal Bellarmine expressed no surprise that

> today many of the poor appear to have been abandoned by God and die of hunger – because it was they who first separated themselves from God out of love for themselves . . . The poor should not remain idle, living off charity; they should work . . . If they would only be content with their lot in life, God would help them much more than he does now.[36]

A more discriminating form of charity was therefore part of a campaign to moralise society, to isolate sin by expelling the lazy and by segregating the poor who could be trained to work in special institutions. This was a moral crusade on which Church and State agreed. As the constitutions of the Brothers Hospitallers recorded in 1587, 'in order to give health to the body we must first seek the health of the soul'.[37] Relief was thus given only to those who displayed social and moral discipline; it should never be given to those who might disrupt society. Charity should induce gratitude and strengthen the social order. This campaign was not entirely successful. Even in the 1590s the problems of organisation and finance proved too much for most governments; and the poor did not really like being organised. They certainly did not like being expelled. Large, efficient institutions were in fact more likely to alienate the destitute than to induce in them any socially reinforcing gratitude. As Joseph Calasanctius recognised when he set up his first school for the poor in Trastevere in 1597, poverty was frequently a result of illiteracy, not sin; his small-scale charity, inspired by a private perception of need, where the Christian lived with the poor in their own area, was probably more effective in maintaining public order than Sixtus V's massive grants to the hospital near the Ponte Sisto. Clement VIII rapidly reduced the scale of state funding to this hospital after 1592, and in 1596 issued all its able-bodied residents with new licences to beg.[38]

IV

The problems of the 1590s in North and Central Italy had both long- and short-term causes. The bad weather – particularly in the early years of the decade – had a disastrous effect on the harvests, at a time when demand for food in the cities was still growing. The results were predictable: high grain prices, famine, and the spread of disease. Nearly all the records demonstrate that population growth was reversed in the 1590s, before beginning to rise again (though only slowly) after 1600.

These were short-term causes; but they increased the long-term severity of developments that can be perceived well before 1590. Italian manufactured goods had gradually lost their place in foreign markets, and were already suffering the effects of north European competition at home. The drop in domestic demand caused by the difficulties of the 1590s came at the worst possible time. Industries like shipbuilding and textiles suffered as they were forced to cut their profit margins while still paying high taxes. Private investors shifted their funds from industry to office, the money market and land – the one commodity in the 1590s still able to retain its value.

Even where the labour force was able to adapt to these new circumstances, the cost of the 1590s was high. Wages fell behind prices. Many were forced into unemployment, debt, migration, crime and even banditry. Faced by an apparent crisis of urban and rural violence, governments felt obliged to overrule the normal restraints of the law; faced by destitution and despair on the streets, they felt that their duty was to use poor relief to reshape society in a more moral image.

In the long run, the significance of the 'Crisis of the 1590s' in northern Italy may well be found most obviously in the impetus it gave to this enhanced view of government responsibilities. Increasingly, for better or worse, government began to play a more active role in society: in the 1590s it had to act to protect industry and to secure the food supply; taxation was increased; control over local administration and justice was extended. No doubt the effectiveness of such intervention was often limited by financial and political instability; no doubt misguided policies often served only to frustrate more fruitful developments;[39] but this growing sense of government responsibilities can be traced in a number of different areas. After 1580, for example, the Venetian government's blasphemy tribunal, run by the *Esecutori contro la bestemmia*, shifted its interests away from religious to social offences: its trials concentrated more on gaming, immigration, prostitution, scandal and false professions of marriage; in 1593 its control of the press was extended; in 1596 it was given authority to pronounce the death sentence.[40]

By the early seventeenth century, therefore, government exercised a more direct influence over the private lives of its subjects. Not everyone welcomed this – provincial authorities and the guilds frequently objected to growing military demands, for example[41] – but perhaps the most determined opposition came from the papacy. On many matters, of course, governments benefited from close local co-operation with the Church: Church and State both gained, for instance, from the campaign to eliminate popular beliefs in magic and witchcraft. And in his role as temporal ruler of central Italy, the Pope was as keen as any to control his own territories. But, as the Vicar of Christ, he was also anxious to secure his authority over ecclesiastical administration throughout the peninsula, and was therefore deeply suspicious of government attempts to supervise matters previously dominated by the Church – matters of belief and behaviour, the Inquisition, charity and morality. Equally, the State suspected that the Church wished to intervene in secular affairs: as one church sympathiser in Lucca wrote in 1588 to an associate of Cardinal Caraffa, 'anyone here who is conscientious in his devotions is immediately suspect to the government.'[42]

The economic and social difficulties of the last years of the sixteenth century obliged and enabled governments in northern Italy to extend the range of their activities – and so brought them closer into conflict with the Church. Perhaps one of the best known consequences of the 'Crisis of the 1590s' was the Venetian Interdict of 1606.[43]

Notes: Chapter 8

1 Vicenzo Citaredo da Urbino, *Speranza de' poveri* (Urbino, 1588), cited by P. Simoncelli, 'Note sul sistema assistenziale a Roma nel XVI secolo', in G. Politi *et al.* (eds), *Timore e carità: I poveri nell'Italia moderna (Annali della Biblioteca Statale e Libreria Civica di Cremona)*, Vol. 27–30, 1976–9 (Cremona, 1982), pp. 137–56, at p. 151, n. 72. It will be obvious from the notes just how much I have been indebted to the published research of historians like Jean Delumeau, Brian Pullan and Domenico Sella. In addition I am grateful to Dr Richard Mackenney for discussing with me a number of the problems of later sixteenth century Italian history.

2 Paruta's *relazione* is printed in E. Alberi (ed.), *Le relazioni degli ambasciatori veneti al Senato durante il secolo decimosesto*, Vol. 10 (Serie II, Tomo IV) (Florence, 1857); the quotations are from pp. 388, 394.

3 See J. Delumeau, *Vie économique et sociale de Rome dans la seconde moitié du XVIe siècle* (Paris, 1957–9), Vol. 1, pp. 339–46; Vol. 2, pp. 529–33; G. L. Basini, *L'uomo e il pane: Risorse, consumi e carenze alimentari della popolazione modenese nel cinque e seicento* (Milan, 1970), p. 152; B. Pullan, *Rich and Poor in Renaissance Venice: The Social Institutions of a Catholic State, to 1620* (Oxford, 1971), p. 356; E. Cochrane, *Florence in the Forgotten Centuries* (Chicago, Ill., 1973), pp. 98–9; cf. also B. H. Slicher van Bath, 'Agriculture in the vital revolution', in E. E. Rich and C. H. Wilson (eds), *The Cambridge Economic History of Europe*, Vol. 5 (Cambridge, 1977), p. 67.

4 For urban grain requirements, see Delumeau, *Rome*, Vol. 1, pp. 122–4; Pullan, *Rich and Poor*, pp. 356–7; G. Vigo, 'Real wages of the working class in Italy: building workers' wages (14th to 18th century)', *Journal of European Economic History*, vol. 3 (1974), pp. 381–4; D. Sella, *Crisis and Continuity: The Economy of Spanish Lombardy in the Seventeenth Century* (Cambridge, Mass., 1979), pp. 11–13. For other types of food, see Basini, *L'uomo e il pane*, p. 152; R. Montel, 'Un "casale" de la campagne romaine de la fin du XIVe siècle au début du XVIIe: le domaine de Porto d'après les archives du chapitre de Saint Pierre', *Mélanges de l'École Française de Rome*, vol. 83 (1971), pp. 66–72; K. Glamann, 'The changing patterns of trade', in *Cambridge Economic History*, Vol. 5, p. 234; Sella, *Crisis*, p. 19. For population before 1590, see M. Berengo, *Nobili e mercanti nella Lucca del Cinquecento* (Turin, 1965), p. 282; B. Pullan, 'Wage earners and the Venetian economy, 1550–1630', printed in the same author's collection entitled *Crisis and Change in the Venetian Economy in the Sixteenth and Seventeenth Centuries* (London, 1968), pp. 148–55, 170–1; Cochrane, *Florence*, p. 112. It is possible that the rural population was rising rather faster than the urban population; cf. G. Felloni, 'Italy', in C. Wilson and G. Parker (eds), *An Introduction to the Sources of European Economic History, 1500–1800* (London, 1977), pp. 2, 3, 34.

5 See F. Braudel and R. Romano, *Navires et marchandises à l'entrée du port de Livourne (1547–1611)* (Paris, 1951), pp. 94, 107; J. de Vries, *The Economy of Europe in an Age of Crisis, 1600–1750* (Cambridge, 1976), pp. 52–4; Glamann, 'Changing patterns of trade', pp. 196–8; Felloni, 'Italy', p. 10.

6 Delumeau, *Rome*, Vol. 2, pp. 542–3, 554, 614, 616–23; cf. Pullan, *Rich and Poor*, p. 356; Sella, *Crisis*, pp. 35–6; Basini, *L'uomo e il pane*, p. 152.

7 Archivio Segreto del Vaticano, Fondo Borghese, serie IV, 224, fo. 207*v*.

8 Information on grain prices in Delumeau, *Rome*, Vol. 2, pp. 624–5, 695, 743; Pullan, *Crisis*, pp. 14–16, 155–6; Basini, *L'uomo e il pane*, pp. 156–8; Pullan, *Rich and Poor*, pp. 178, 358, 360; B. Pullan, 'The occupations and investments of the Venetian nobility in the middle and late sixteenth century', in J. R. Hale (ed.), *Renaissance Venice* (London, 1973), p. 381; F. C. Lane, *Venice: A Maritime Republic* (Baltimore, Md, 1973), p. 306; Cochrane, *Florence*, p. 113; P. Vilar, *A History of Gold and Money, 1420–1920* (London, 1976), p. 186; Felloni, 'Italy', p. 23; G. Corazzol, *Fitti e livelli a grano: un aspetto del credito rurale nel Veneto del '500* (Milan, 1979), p. 111; R. F. E. Weissman, *Ritual Brotherhood in Renaissance Florence* (New York, 1982), p. 203; cf. also the Siena figures cited in F. McArdle, *Altopascio: A Study in Tuscan Rural Society, 1587–1784* (Cambridge, 1978), pp. 83–5; and Sella, *Crisis*, pp. 25–7, 35. Other food prices also rose in the 1590s, but not so dramatically.

9 Delumeau, *Rome*, Vol. 1, pp. 122–3; Vol. 2, pp. 422–3; Berengo, *Lucca*, p. 282; Pullan, *Crisis*, pp. 150–4; J. R. Hale, 'Terra Ferma fortifications in the Cinquecento', in C. Smith and S. I. Camporeale (eds), *Florence and Venice: Comparisons and Relations*, Vol. 2 (Florence, 1980), p. 178; A. Tagliaferri (ed.), *Venezia e il Friuli: Problemi storiografici* (Milan, 1982), pp. 87–8, 92–2; M. Brozzi, *Peste fede e sanità in una cronaca cividalese del 1598* (Milan, 1982), pp. 14–15.

10 Delumeau, *Rome*, Vol. 1, pp. 341–4; Vol. 2, p. 624, Berengo, *Lucca*, p. 282; Pullan, *Crisis*, pp. 159, 161; Pullan, *Rich and Poor*, p. 358; R. Mols, 'Population in Europe, 1500–1700', in C. M. Cipolla (ed.), *The Sixteenth and Seventeenth Centuries*, Fontana Economic History of Europe (London, 1974), p. 49; Felloni, 'Italy', pp. 3–9; Brozzi,

Peste, pp. 12, 21. For plague, see also R. J. Palmer, 'The control of plague in Venice and northern Italy, 1348–1600', unpublished PhD thesis, University of Kent, 1978.

11 Braudel and Romano, *Navires*, pp. 22, 41, 51, 107, 117; Pullan, *Rich and Poor*, p. 359.

12 AS, Venice, *Sant'Uffizio*, b.24, proc. 'Rosso Pietro'. The problem was not unique to Venice: the Lyons silk industry was developed by Milanese craftsmen at the turn of the century (Sella, *Crisis*, pp. 41–2). For information on Italian foreign trade, see Delumeau, *Rome*, Vol. 1, p. 102; Pullan, *Crisis*, pp. 8–11, 21; Pullan, *Rich and Poor*, pp. 358–9; F. Braudel, *The Mediterranean and the Mediterranean World in the Age of Philip II* (London, 1972), Vol. 1, pp. 222–30, 303–6, 628–36; R. T. Rapp, 'The unmaking of the Mediterranean trade hegemony: international trade rivalry and the commercial revolution', *Journal of Economic History*, vol. 35 (1975), pp. 505–6, 514–17, 519–21; C. H. Wilson, 'The historical study of economic growth and decline in early modern history', in *Cambridge Economic History*, Vol. 5, pp. 33–4; Glamann, 'Changing patterns of trade', pp. 217–18; G. Parker and L. M. Smith (eds), *The General Crisis of the Seventeenth Century* (London, 1978), p. 176; Corazzol, *Fitti e livelli*, pp. 50–1; J.-C. Hocquet, *Le Sel et la fortune de Venise* (Lille, 1979), Vol. 1, pp. 102, 247, 342–3; Vol. 2, pp. 685, 698 and the tables on pp. 317, 323–4, 579; Sella, *Crisis*, pp. 38–42, 79–82.

13 A major exception to this interpretation of demand-led decline was the cotton industry, which lost access to its supplies in territory captured by the Turks. Sugar refining and salt production had to adjust for the same reason.

14 For prices, see Delumeau, *Rome*, Vol. 2, pp. 728, 736–47; C. M. Cipolla, 'The so-called "price revolution": reflections on "the Italian situation"', in P. Burke (ed.), *Economy and Society in Early Modern Europe: Essays from Annales* (London, 1972), pp. 44–5: Vigo, 'Real wages', p. 382; Vilar, *History of Gold*, p. 186; Felloni, 'Italy', p. 23; B. Pullan, 'Poveri, mendicanti e vagabondi (secoli XIV-XVII)', in R. Romano and C. Vivanti (eds), *Storia d'Italia: Annali I: Dal feudalismo al capitalismo* (Turin, 1978), p. 1033.

15 Delumeau, *Rome*, Vol. 2, pp. 834–9; P. Partner, 'Papal financial policy in the Renaissance and Counter-Reformation', *Past and Present*, no. 88 (1980), p. 45.

16 Although there was certainly a timber shortage in the Mediterranean in the later sixteenth century, it is unlikely that many more ships would have been built: difficulties with supplies merely shifted attention to the north European builders.

17 On defence expenditure, see R. Romano, 'Economic aspects of the construction of warships in Venice in the sixteenth century', in Pullan, *Crisis*, p. 80, and the editor's introduction, pp. 7–8; Sella, *Crisis*, pp. 43–5; Hale, 'Fortifications', pp. 169, 176–7; G. Spini, 'Firenze medicea e Venezia di fronte al problema della "organizzazione del territorio"', in Smith and Camporeale, *Florence and Venice*, pp. 195–6. The papal government was an exception, spending less at the end of the century on local defence than in the early 1570s; but, at the same time, Rome was also paying huge sums to subsidise armies abroad: Partner, 'Papal financial policy', pp. 51–5.

18 AS, Venice, *Arti*, b. 726, 'Verieri', p. 109, cap. 137 (I am grateful to Dr Mackenney for bringing this law to my attention); Rapp, 'Unmaking', pp. 505–6, 517–18.

19 For industrial developments, see Braudel and Romano, *Navires*, pp. 20–1; Delumeau, *Rome*, Vol. 1, pp. 129, 256–61, 504–11; Vol. 2, pp. 765–6; M. Carmona, 'Aspects du capitalisme toscan aux XVIe et XVIIe siècles: les sociétés en commandite à Florence et à Lucques', *Revue d'histoire moderne et contemporaine*, vol. 11 (1964), pp. 103–6; Romano, in Pullan, *Crisis*, p. 69; Pullan, 'Wage earners', pp. 154–5, 166–7, and see his introduction in the same volume, pp. 3–4, 7, 11, 16; Pullan, *Rich and Poor*, pp. 16, 358–9, 373; Lane, *Venice*, pp. 306–7, 384–6; Cochrane, *Florence*, pp. 110–11; Rapp, 'Unmaking', pp. 502, 505–9, 522–3; P. F. Grendler, 'The Roman Inquisition and the Venetian press, 1540–1605', *Journal of Modern History*, Vol. 47 (1975), pp. 54–5, 60–4; Vilar, *History of Gold*, pp. 187–8; Wilson, in *Cambridge Economic History*, Vol. 5, pp. 12, 33; Felloni, 'Italy', pp. 12–14; P. F. Grendler, *The Roman Inquisition and the Venetian Press, 1540–1605* (Princeton, NJ, 1977), pp. 3, 6–9, 225, 226, 229; Parker and Smith, *General Crisis*, pp. 184–6; Hocquet, *Le Sel*, Vol. 1, p. 579; D. Lombardi, '1629–31: crisi e peste a Firenze', *Archivio storico italiano*, Vol. 137 (1979), pp. 9–10; Sella, *Crisis*, pp. 16–22, 24–5, 36–9, 41–2; Partner, 'Papal financial policy', pp. 38, 55; J. Goodman, 'Financing

pre-modern European industry: an example from Florence, 1580–1660', *Journal of European Economic History*, Vol. 10 (1981), pp. 418, 423–4.

20 D. Tamilia, *Il Sacro Monte di Pietà di Roma: Ricerche storiche e documenti inediti* (Rome, 1900), pp. 75–6; Delumeau, *Rome*, Vol. 2, pp. 872–4; L. Poliakov, *Jewish Bankers and the Holy See: From the Thirteenth to the Seventeenth Century* (London, 1977), pp. 80–2, 120–2, 145, 168–9, 193–5; J. Viner, *Religious Thought and Economic Society* (Durham, NC, 1978), pp. 81, 86–97; J. Le Goff, 'The usurer and Purgatory', in *The Dawn of Modern Banking (Centre for Medieval and Renaissance Studies, University of California, Los Angeles)* (New Haven, Conn., 1979), pp. 28–43; G. Celata, 'Gli ebrei in una società rurale e feudale: Pitigliano nella seconda metà del Cinquecento', *Archivio storico italiano*, vol. 138 (1980), p. 221; Partner, 'Papal financial policy', p. 58. In 1572 the Apostolic Visitor in Perugia accused the local Monte di Pietà of charging a sinful interest rate of 6 per cent: C. F. Black, 'Perugia and Papal absolutism in the sixteenth century', *English Historical Review*, Vol. 96 (1981), p. 515.

21 Carmona, 'Aspects', pp. 90–2, 95–6, 98–104, 107–8; Pullan, 'Occupations', p. 380; Cochrane, *Florence*, p. 110; De Vries, *Economy of Europe*, pp. 76–7. The only major exceptions seem to have been the Florentine and Lucchese silk industries, which benefited in the 1590s from a form of partnership called an 'accomandita', in which the investor's liability was limited to the amount loaned, and which allowed him to remove that loan at short notice: Carmona, 'Aspects', pp. 85, 90–6, 106–8; Goodman, 'Financing', pp. 424–6, 428–9, 433–5.

22 AS, Venice, *Sant'Uffizio*, b. 31, proc. 'Stichiano fra Aurelio', unpaginated interrogation of 17 October 1549.

23 Tamilia, *Monte di Pietà*, p. 81; Delumeau, *Rome*, vol. 1, p. 515, vol. 2, pp. 765–7, 858–9; Carmona, 'Aspects', p. 103; Pullan, *Crisis*, pp. 19, 167; Pullan, *Rich and Poor*, pp. 111, 138–40; F. Braudel, *Capitalism and Material Life, 1400–1800* (London, 1973), pp. 364–5; Pullan, 'Occupations', p. 388; J. C. Davis, *A Venetian Family and Its Fortune, 1500–1900: The Donà and the Conservation of Their Wealth* (Philadelphia, Pa, 1975), pp. 40–1, 56; Poliakov, *Jewish Bankers*, pp. 163–5, 169–70; Felloni, 'Italy', p. 21; Sella, *Crisis*, pp. 45–6; Celata, 'Pitigliano', pp. 215, 222, 225–6; Partner, 'Papal financial policy', pp. 23–31, 35, 37, 43, 51–3, 55–6.

24 Tamilia, *Monte di Pietà*, p. 77; Delumeau, *Rome*, Vol. 2, pp. 891, 897–904, 925–7, 933–5; Pullan, *Crisis*, pp. 8, 16–19, Pullan, *Rich and Poor*, pp. 564–5, 579–80, 588; Braudel, *Mediterranean*, pp. 476–510; Pullan, 'Occupations', pp. 384–5; Cochrane, *Florence*, pp. 111, 115; Braudel, *Capitalism*, pp. 364–5; Vilar, *History of Gold*, pp. 145, 187–9; Poliakov, *Jewish Bankers*, pp. 94–5, 165, 168, 176–7, 181, 185, 203–4; Felloni, 'Italy', p. 18; Partner, 'Papal financial policy', pp. 25–31, 55, 57, 60–1.

25 Tamilia, *Monte di Pietà*, pp. 76–7; Pullan, *Rich and Poor*, pp. 539–40; Poliakov, *Jewish Bankers*, pp. 203–4.

26 Pullan, *Crisis*, pp. 19–20; Pullan 'Occupations', pp. 380, 388–9; Corazzol, *Fitti e livelli*, pp. 70, 101–5. The rate of interest in Feltre was fixed at 7·2 per cent.

27 G. Fasoli, 'Lineamenti di politica e di legislazione feudale veneziana in Terraferma', *Rivista di storia del diritto italiano*, vol. 25 (1952), pp. 62–4, 70–80; Pullan, *Crisis*, pp. 16, 19, 167; Pullan, *Rich and Poor*, pp. 28, 359; Braudel, *Mediterranean*, pp. 427, 1240; Pullan, 'Occupations', pp. 380–2; Lane, *Venice*, pp. 306–7; Davis, *Venetian Family*, pp. 37–42, 74–80, 93–104; De Vries, *Economy of Europe*, pp. 53–5; Wilson, in *Cambridge Economic History*, vol. 5, pp. 33–4; McArdle, *Altopascio*, pp. 87, 95–6; Hocquet, *Le Sel*, Vol. 1, p. 343; vol. 2, pp. 699, 702; R. T. Rapp, 'Real estate and rational investment in early modern Venice', *Journal of European Economic History*, vol. 8, (1979), pp. 269–73, 280, 284–90; Sella, *Crisis*, pp. 7, 11, 42–5, 93–4, 99, 216; Partner, 'Papal financial policy', p. 61; C. M. Eremo, 'La comunità di Groppazzolo di val Nune nei secoli XVI e XVII', *Archivio storico per le provincie parmensi*, vol. 33 (1981), pp. 156, 171. Other important areas of financial commitment in the later sixteenth century were the purchase of office and dowries, for which see Delumeau, *Rome*, vol. 2, pp. 515–16; B. Pullan, 'Service to the Venetian State: aspects of myth and reality in the early seventeenth century', *Studi secenteschi*, vol. 5 (1964), pp. 119–20; O. M. T. Logan, 'Studies in the religious life of Venice in the sixteenth and early seventeenth centuries', unpublished PhD thesis,

University of Cambridge, 1967, pp. 170–5, 340–59; Pullan, *Crisis*, p. 20; Pullan, 'Occupations', pp. 390, 393–400; Davis, *Venetian Family*, pp. 40–1, 106–11; Partner, 'Papal financial policy', pp. 23–4.

28 Delumeau, *Rome*, vol. 1, p. 126; Romano, 'Construction of warships', p. 76; Pullan, 'Wage earners', pp. 159–60, 162–3, 170; Pullan, *Rich and Poor*, p. 360; Cochrane, *Florence*, p. 113; Vigo, 'Real wages', pp. 382, 386, 388–93; Rapp, 'Unmaking', pp. 513, 523–4; Poliakov, *Jewish Bankers*, pp. 89–91, 178–9, 195–7; Pullan, 'Poveri', pp. 1008–10, 1021–33; Sella, *Crisis*, pp. 27, 29, 44–5; Partner, 'Papal financial policy', p. 45 n. 72. Recent research suggests that Italian guilds may not always have resisted change as fiercely as some earlier interpretations argued: R. S. Mackenney, 'Trade guilds and devotional confraternities in the state and society of Venice to 1620', unpublished PhD thesis, University of Cambridge, 1982.

29 Delumeau, *Rome*, vol. 1, pp. 172, 185–6, 201, 344, 411, 421–8; vol. 2, pp. 542, 554–5, 561, 616, 623, 940; Pullan, *Crisis*, p. 159; Montel, 'Un casale', pp. 80–2, 86–7; Pullan, *Rich and Poor*, pp. 355–6, 358, 361–2, 378; Cochrane, *Florence*, p. 113; Poliakov, *Jewish Bankers*, pp. 132, 149, 181–3; McArdle, *Altopascio*, pp. 83, 96; Pullan, 'Poveri', pp. 991–4, 1008–10; Corazzol, *Fitti e livelli*, pp. 52–3; L. Fiorani, 'Religione e povertà: Il didattico sul pauperismo a Roma tra cinque e seicento', *Ricerche per la storia religiosa di Roma*, vol. 3 (1979), p. 93; Sella, *Crisis*, pp. 8–9, 14–16, 36, 179–81; Eremo, 'Groppazzolo', p. 167; Tagliaferri, *Venezia*, pp. 88, 95–6; Brozzi, *Peste*, p. 14; Simoncelli, 'Note', pp. 146–7; D. Lombardi, 'Poveri a Firenze: Programmi e realizzazioni della politica assistenziale dei Medici tra cinque e seicento', in *Timore e carità*, p. 171; B. Pullan, *The Jews of Europe and the Inquisition of Venice, 1550–1670* (Oxford, 1983), pp. 254–5.

30 *La Piazza Universale li tutte le professioni del mondo* (Venice, 1587), p. 510, cited by Simoncelli, 'Note', pp. 146–7; cf. E. Casali, '"Economica" e "creanza cristiana"', in C. Ginzburg (ed.), *Religioni delle classi popolari*, edizione speciale di *Quaderni storici* n. 41 (Ancona, 1979), pp. 559–75.

31 Sentence cited by C. Povolo, 'Aspetti e problemi dell'amministrazione della giustizia penale nella republica di Venezia: Secoli XVI-XVII', in G. Cozzi (ed.), *Stato, società e giustizia nella republica veneta (sec. XV-XVIII)* (Rome, 1980), p. 236.

32 Archivio segreto del Vaticano, Fondo Borghese, serie IV, 224, fos 196*r*–*v*; cf. AS, Venice, *Sant'Uffizio*, b. 34, proc. 'Mantica Alessandro', for information on the organisation and rivalry of gangs in Pordenone.

33 See, for example, AS, Venice, *Consiglio dei Dieci, Criminal*, reg. 11, fos 159*v*-160*r*, 174*v*-175*r*, 176*r*–*v*, 177*r*, 186*v*, 187*r*, 188*v*, which has information on a series of jail-breaks in Venice between March 1571 and April 1573; the government suspected that the prison warders were responsible.

34 Letter of April 1586 cited by E. F. Guarini, 'Considerazioni su giustizia e società nel Ducato di Toscana del Cinquecento', in Smith and Camporeale, *Florence and Venice*, pp. 153–4.

35 For crime in the 1590s, see Delumeau, *Rome*, vol. 2, pp. 542–64, 622–3; P. Prodi, *Lo sviluppo dell'assolutismo nello Stato Pontificio (secoli XV–XVI)*, vol. 1 (Bologna, 1968), pp. 73–85; Pullan, *Rich and Poor*, p. 358; P. Camporesi (ed.), *Il libro dei vagabondi* (Turin, 1973), pp. 351–61; Cochrane, *Florence*, pp. 98–9; Braudel, *Capitalism*, p. 165; Pullan, 'Poveri', pp. 1011–14; C. Povolo, 'Note per uno studio dell'infanticidio nella republica di Venezia nei secoli XV-XVIII', *Atti dell'Istituto veneto di scienze, lettere ed arti: classe di scienze morali, lettere ed arti*, vol. 137 (1978–9), pp. 122–5; C. Povolo, 'Considerazioni su ricerche relative alla giustizia penale nell'età moderna: i casi di Padova, Treviso e Noale', ibid., pp. 489–97; G. Scarabello, *Carcerati e carceri a Venezia nell'età moderna* (Rome, 1979), pp. 44, 66–9; Fiorani, 'Religione', p. 96; Povolo, 'Aspetti', pp. 164–9, 170–5, 206, 209–10, 213–16, 222, 224–32, 234–7, 240–9, 254; Guarini, 'Toscana', pp. 147–61; A. D. Wright, 'Venetian law and order: a myth?' *Bulletin of the Institute of Historical Research*, vol. 53 (1980), pp. 192–4, 196, 198; Black, 'Perugia', pp. 509, 533–5; Simoncelli, 'Note', pp. 146–9; Pullan, *Jews*, pp. 254–5.

36 Cited by Fiorani, 'Religione', p. 59.

37 Cited by Fiorani, ibid., p. 86 n. 87.

38 *Regesti di bandi editti notificazioni e provvedimenti diversi relativi alla città di Roma e allo Stato*

Pontificio (Rome, 1920–58), vol. 1, nn. 519, 818; vol. 2, nn. 1151, 1402; Delumeau, *Rome*, vol. 1, pp. 344–6, 411–16; vol. 2, pp. 532, 561, 608–16, 622–4; Pullan, *Rich and Poor*, pp. 129, 137, 178–9, 182–4, 186–7, 358–9, 361–2, 369, 639–42; Felloni, 'Italy', p. 29, Pullan, 'Poveri', pp. 990–6, 1008, 1015–20, 1033–7, 1039; M. Rosa *et al.*, 'Poveri ed emarginati: un problema religioso', *Ricerche per la storia religiosa di Roma*, vol. 3 (1979), p. 21; Fiorani, 'Religione', pp. 43–4, 50, 56–9, 85–91, 97, 110–12, 129–31; Partner, 'Papal financial policy', pp. 29–31; B. Pullan, 'The old Catholicism, the new Catholicism and the poor', in Politi *et al.*, *Timore e carità*, pp. 13–19, 22–3; Simoncelli, 'Note', pp. 142–5, 147–9, 151, 153–6; Lombardi, 'Poveri', pp. 168, 170–2; cf. also Poliakov, *Jewish Bankers*, pp. 182–3.

39 Delumeau, *Rome*, vol. 1, pp. 510–14; vol. 2, pp. 767, 939–45; Rapp, 'Unmaking', pp. 506–9.

40 G. Cozzi, 'Religione, moralità e giustizia a Venezia: Vicende della magistratura degli Esecutori, contro la bestemmia' (Padua, typescript, 1967–8), pp. 9, 23–34, 36–8; cf. R. Derosas, 'Moralità e giustizia a Venezia nel '500–'600: Gli Esecutori contro la bestemmia', in Cozzi, *Stato*, pp. 431–528.

41 Hale, 'Fortifications', pp. 182–3; Mackenney, 'Trade guilds', ch. 6.

42 AS, Lucca, *Cause delegate*, vol. 25, fo. 1399; cf. also fo. 1311.

43 For a similar argument, cf. M. J. C. Lowry, 'The Church and Venetian political change in the later Cinquecento', unpublished PhD thesis, University of Warwick, 1971, esp. ch. 6 and pp. 297–300.

9 *Southern Italy in the 1590s: Hard Times or Crisis?*

PETER BURKE

There would be nothing new in discussing the history of Italy, more especially southern Italy in the sixteenth and seventeenth centuries, in terms of 'crisis'; a good many historians have done this in the last twenty-five years or so.[1] Whether it is really illuminating to do so, particularly if one concentrates on a single decade, is less certain. To avoid debasement of the conceptual currency, it is essential to opt for a definition of 'crisis' precise enough to enable some periods to be identified as times of non-crisis. In this chapter, therefore, the term will be used in a sense not too far removed from its original – medical – meaning; that of a short period of acute difficulties, leading to long-term structural changes.[2] In this sense there was no 'crisis of the 1590s' in southern Italy. Acute difficulties, certainly; but the long-term structural changes are harder to discern. If there was, as some Italian historians currently claim, a transition from feudalism to capitalism at this point, it was so gradual that it might be more useful to talk about the persistence of a hybrid form of economic and social organisation throughout the early modern period.

'Southern Italy' is also a rather vague term. I use it here to refer to the peninsula from the Papal States downwards, together with the islands of Sardinia and Sicily. This begs the question of the contrast between the north and the south. The contrast should not be exaggerated; the division between the two Italies was much less sharp than it has become in the last century or so. However, there already was a division. The south had not participated in the rise of the communes in the eleventh, twelfth and thirteenth centuries, a development which made north and central Italy one of the most urbanised parts of late medieval Europe. By the sixteenth century, the trading patterns of the two Italies were very different. The north exported cloth, arms and other craft-industrial products, while the south exported food and other raw materials, notably wool and raw silk; and this trade was largely in the hands of north Italian entrepreneurs. The contrast between the two regions was almost equally marked in agriculture. The south was a land of latifundia, while smallholding, especially share-cropping, was important in much of the north. From the social point of view, another crude but useful contrast may be made between two types of elite, northern patricians (oriented towards towns and trade), and southern barons.[3]

The south was of course far from monolithic, and it is time to distinguish regions within it. There is little to say about Sardinia, for lack of research, despite the existence there – unusual for Italy – of a long series of tithe documents; so it will make no further appearance in this chapter.[4] Nor will Sicily, for which see Chapter 10. There remains the peninsula itself, the southern half of which was divided into two political units, the Papal States and the Kingdom of Naples.

From the economic and social point of view, part of the Papal States, notably Umbria and the Marches, belonged to the north rather than the south; the Romagna was marginal; while Lazio and the Roman Campagna, in particular, should be regarded as southern. Changes in this area in the later sixteenth century were analysed in the 1950s by Jean Delumeau in his important thesis. Delumeau's relative lack of interest in demography and in the productivity of agriculture make the rural sections of this pioneering study seem a little dated now, but the 'Delumeau model' of economic development (or, rather, of failure to develop), is one worth testing for other regions.[5]

As for the *Regno*, the Kingdom of Naples, at this point the *Viceregno* (ruled by the King of Spain's viceroy), this large area, with a population, in the 1590s, of something like 2½ million people, was far from uniform. It was traditionally divided into nine regions; Terra di Lavoro, Principato, Molise, the Abruzzi, Capitanata, Terra di Bari, Terra di Otranto, Basilicata, and Calabria. However, from the economic point of view it may be divided more crudely into three zones, of which the richest and most agricultural was Campania, around the city of Naples, and the poorest, most rocky and most pastoral was Calabria, the toe of Italy, with Apulia (the heel) coming in between.[6] The present state of knowledge of economic and social trends in the *Viceregno* in the early modern period is, to put it mildly, extremely patchy. Sixteenth-century Calabria is known best, thanks to a study based on an important series of documents, the records of the annual receipts of the owners of 'fiefs' (*feudi*), which in the south accounted for a good deal of territory.[7] This example has been followed in studies of the Terra d'Otranto in the generation 1590–1620; of long-term trends in Principato Ultra, 1550–1806; and of a great estate at Leonessa, in Basilicata, which concentrates on the period 1585–1615. In these studies the influence of Marxism (more especially of Witold Kula's analysis of Polish 'feudalism') has been combined with that of *Annales* (notably the attempt, by E. Le Roy Ladurie, J. Goy and others to measure changes in agricultural productivity).[8] However, agrarian trends in much of the south remain to be studied. There are also a few important monographs on south Italian demography in the early modern period, notably on the city of Naples, on Aquila, on the Abruzzi, and on the village of Montesarchio in the Caudine valley.[9] Finally, no survey of the south in the sixteenth and seventeenth centuries can afford to omit the most serious attempt at synthesis, Rosario Villari's book on the preconditions of the Naples revolt of 1647, a study which goes back as far as 1585 and is concerned with the countryside as well as the capital.[10] All the same, the patchiness of the research undertaken so far needs to be borne in mind when reading the discussion which follows. It will be concerned in turn with short-term problems; demography; agrarian trends; and, finally, with political and cultural factors.

I

There can be little doubt about the gravity of the short-term problems faced by the people and the government in the Rome and Naples areas in the 1590s.

In the Papal States, 1578 marks what Delumeau has called the 'coupure fondamentale', the beginning of a sequence of poor harvests which lasted till 1596 and made it impossible to feed the population of Rome – about 80,000 at the time – from the resources of the papal territories. In the Romagna, or at least around Imola, agricultural yield ratios began to decline around 1588–92.[11] The years 1590–3 were years of famine in the whole Papal States. Plague followed, as it so often did, striking Rome in 1591.[12] Mortality was high in the diocese of Sutri, in Lazio, and probably in the whole region.[13] Banditry was a serious problem. Contemporaries suggest that it was at its worst in the decades 1560–90, which makes it likely that the essential explanation was the lack of employment for mercenaries between the peace of Cateau-Cambrésis and the outbreak of war, in 1593, between Hungary and the Ottoman Empire. Clement VIII recruited bandits into the army he raised against the Turk.[14] The problems – not to say 'the crisis' – of the Roman aristocracy were particularly acute at this time. The Orsini, for example, had nearly 500,000 *scudi*'s worth of debts about 1590, compared with an annual income of about 70,000, thanks, it seems, to conspicuous consumption on building and on festivals.[15]

What was to be done? The energetic Sixtus V did his best to deal with the situation. He tried to stamp out banditry, had vagabonds expelled from Rome, organised special loans for the barons, founded a workhouse, set up a 'Congregation' to administer the corn supply, and encouraged silk-weaving and the making of woollen cloth – he planned to turn the Colosseum into a cloth factory.[16] However, Sixtus died in August 1590, and three short papal reigns followed before political affairs settled down again under Clement VIII (1592–1605). There remained too little grain and too many beggars in Rome in the middle 1590s. It was only following the good harvests in the Marches and the Romagna in 1597 and 1598 that the short-term problems became less acute.[17]

Further south, the problems of the decade were if anything even worse. There had been a famine in Naples in 1585, and there was a more or less continuous state of dearth from 1589 to 1595, with 1591, 1592 and 1595 standing out as particularly bad years. The standard loaf, which was 44 *once* in weight in 1560 and 48 in 1599, plunged to 28 in 1592 and to 26 in 1598.[18] As in the Papal States, so in the Kingdom of Naples banditry seems to have reached a peak in the early 1590s. In Bari, plague struck in 1590, 1591 and 1592.[19] In Calabria, the communes could not raise the taxes demanded from them, and the Turks raided them in 1595.[20]

The religious orders and the state both tried to alleviate these problems. In Bari, Lecce and Taranto, poor relief was organised by the Jesuits.[21] In Naples, the Spanish administration issued decrees against both the hoarding and the export of cereals in 1583, 1589, 1590, 1591, 1592, 1593 and 1596.[22] Some two thousand foreign students were expelled from the city in 1591. In the same year, and again in 1595, the native Neapolitans were given ration cards (*cartelle*). Hence the need for censuses, which were carried out in both years and recorded an urban population of 210,834 and 226,399 respectively.[23]

The authorities had good political reasons for taking prompt action. Naples was notoriously prone to disturbance, and the 1585 famine was followed by a riot in which one leading member of the municipal administration, Gio. Vicenzo Starace, was lynched by a crowd.[24] In 1592, placards appeared on the walls of the city inciting the inhabitants to revolt. There was no rising on this occasion, but in 1599 an anti-Spanish conspiracy was organised in Naples and Calabria, with the promise of Turkish support. Campanella, who was involved in the plot, believed that 'everyone was ready for revolt' ('tutti erano disposti a mutatione').[25] His eyes seem to have been fixed on 1600 as the date of the millennium, rather than on the price of bread, which was coming down. In any case, the Turks did not intervene as promised and the plot failed.

II

What of the long-term trends in the economy and society of the south? Demography makes an obvious starting point.

So far as the Papal States are concerned, little can be said about demographic trends in the current state of research. The population amounted to 1,700,000 in 1656, but there are no earlier aggregate figures to compare with this total. In the diocese of Sutri there were sharp peaks in mortality figures about 1590 and about 1620, but it is too early to say whether or not this pattern was typical.[26] The city of Rome increased, presumably as a result of heavy immigration, from about 80,000 people in the 1590s to 100,000 just after 1600, and 120,000 in 1656.[27]

Thanks to the Spanish administration, we are rather better informed about demographic trends in the Kingdom of Naples. Its concern with both taxpaying households and mouths to be fed generated a number of surveys of the population in the sixteenth and seventeenth centuries. Table 9.1 shows the overall trend.

Table 9.1 *Population of the Kingdom of Naples (households)*

1505	255,000
1545	422,000
1595	540,000
1648	500,000
1669	395,000

In other words, the population rose rapidly in the first half of the sixteenth century, more slowly in the second half of the century, but fell in the first half of the seventeenth century, and experienced a sharp decline after the plague of 1656, which was to the south (Rome included) a disaster on the scale of that of 1630–1 in northern Italy.[28]

The general impression left by these figures is one of Malthusian 'crisis', in the sense of a population which had grown too fast, by the mid-sixteenth century, for local resources, leading to undernourishment and vulnerability to plague, which struck Bari in 1590–2 and the whole region in 1656. Delille's study of Montesarchio fills in some of the details for one community, noting the peak in mortality in 1569–70; the peak in the birth-rate about 1585; another peak in mortality in 1590–5; a rise in marriages in 1595–1610; and a higher peak in mortality in 1619–29.[29]

There were of course regional variations, as Table 9.2 should make clear. In other words, the poor regions, notably Calabria, lost population, while the richer regions, the Terre di Lavoro, di Bari and d'Otranto, all gained, presumably by migration. The population of the city of Naples, in particular, rose from about 210,000 in 1547 to 300,000 or even 400,000 by the middle of the seventeenth century.[30] Contemporaries believed that it grew by migration, and a study of marriage registers confirms that this was the case, the migrants coming in the main from the province itself and from Principato (Calabrians preferred to migrate to Messina and Palermo). Here as elsewhere the 'pull' of the great city, with its promise of

Table 9.2 *Population of the Kingdom of Naples (by provinces)*

	1545		*1669*	
	households (thousands)	*percentage of total*	*households (thousands)*	*percentage of total*
Terra di Lavoro	48	11·4	57	14·4
Principato	72	17·0	57	14·4
Molise	14	3·3	13	3·3
Abruzzi	65	15·4	62	15·7
Capitanata	17	4·0	17	4·3
Terra di Bari	36	8·5	40	10·1
Terra d'Otranto	41	9·7	47	11·9
Basilicata	32	7·6	28	7·0
Calabria	96	22·7	82	20·7

cheap food and (however illusory) of employment, was especially great in hard times.[31]

III

What were the long-term trends in the agrarian history of the region? The population figures suggest the hypothesis that the land was more and more intensively cultivated in the course of the sixteenth century, so that the soil was probably exhausted in some places. There are some fragments of evidence which suggest that this exhaustion was the case in some areas. At Leonessa in Basilicata in 1586, it was reported that 'the said fief has been cropped continuously, and so it will not be possible to increase production for some time'.[32] Again, at Marcellinara in Calabria, in 1593, a witness explained the decline of the lump sum for which the feudal dues had been sold by suggesting that 'the land was exhausted by continuous cropping' ('*le terre per le continuo lavoro erano diminuiti et debole*').[33] In Apulia, the productivity of agriculture seems to have fallen in the 1580s.[34] Further north, in the area around Imola in the Romagna, the lowest yield ratios were recorded for the 1590s (which suggests that bad weather was a contributing factor), but the long-term decline in minimum yield fits in with the general picture of overcropping.[35]

In short, the fragmentary evidence seems to support an all too familiar impression of the pressure of population on resources and of an environment deteriorating as a result of the excessive demands made on it by man. However, it would be unwise to end the analysis there, without considering the question of landownership and of the different social groups trying to squeeze a living, or an income, from the soil. Much of the land was in

Table 9.3 *Yield Ratios in the Romagna*

decade	*minimum*	*maximum*
1570–9	4·8	6·8
1580–9	4·5	7·4
1590–9	3·3	5·8
1600–9	3·7	7·7
1610–19	3·5	8·2

noble hands, so we return to the problems of the aristocracy both in the Papal States and in the Kingdom of Naples.

Delumeau's picture of trends in the Papal States is a clear one. The barons, according to him, were in increasing financial difficulties between 1550 and 1600 as a result of increased expenditure on conspicuous consumption. As a result they, or the entrepreneurs who leased their estates, tried to increase profits by shifting from arable to pasture and selling meat, rather than grain, to those Romans who could afford to buy it. One side-effect of this shift was to depopulate the Campagna and to increase the population of Rome still further. As in England, sheep – and cattle – ate up men.[36] Other historians have added a few more touches to this picture, pointing out, for example, that the economic problems of the aristocracy cannot be explained simply in terms of increasing expenditure. At this point wealth and power were flowing away from the Roman baronial families, such as the Orsini and the Colonna, to the families of the popes (Buoncompagni, Peretti, Aldobrandini, etc).[37]

In the south, the barons seem to have been faced with broadly similar problems. They began to abandon their country estates for town houses from about 1530 onwards, in order to live near the court of the viceroy. In Naples they competed with one another in conspicuously expensive consumption. One observer commented in 1594 that, rich as they were, the aristocrats of Naples were living beyond their means.[38]

As a result, some of the barons were forced to sell land in the period 1560–1620.[39] There is also evidence that some of them tried to increase their revenue from feudal dues. In Principato Ultra, for example, revenue from this source increased steadily throughout the period 1550–1630 (as it did in Montesarchio 1570–1620).[40] In Apulia, the barons are said to have preferred squeezing more out of the feudal dues to reorganising their estates on a more commercial basis.[41] As for Calabria, a recent study speaks of the 'intensified feudalism' ('la rafforzata feudalità') of the last decades of the sixteenth century.[42]

Tommaso Campanella seems to have been essentially right in his analysis of the ills of the south in his day:

> The barons . . . come to Naples, and to the court, and there spending their money profusely and lavishly, they make a great show for a while . . . and at length having spent all, they return poor home, and make prey of whatsoever they can, so that they make themselves whole again, and then they return to Court again; running round still, as it were in the same Circle; in so much that we see these men's territories much more desert and naked, than the King's in Italy are; all through the default of the barons themselves.[43]

What about the other social groups? Campanella wrote elsewhere that the people of Italy were oppressed and exploited by the King of Spain.[44] Even less is known about the changing social impact of taxation than about agricultural and demographic trends in southern Italy in the sixteenth and seventeenth centuries, but the evidence suggests that the tax burden became heavier. The taxpaying inhabitants of the Papal States suffered from the shift in the economic base of the papacy from spiritual revenues to temporal ones. Tax grievances underlay the revolt of Fermo in 1648.[45]

As for the Italian subjects of the King of Spain, they suffered from his need to raise money to pay for involvement in the Eighty Years War, as the Dutch call the period 1568–1648. In Naples, a tax on fruit, the staple diet of the poor, had been proposed during the difficult times of the 1590s; it was actually levied during the equally difficult times of the late 1640s, thus triggering one of the major upheavals of that disturbed decade, the revolt of Masaniello.[46] The provinces suffered as well as the capital. A study of the city of Aquila in the Abruzzi suggests that the weight of taxation there grew heavier in the course of the sixteenth century.[47] In Calabria, the tax burden encouraged emigration. In 1590, for example, the commune of Terranova complained that it was dwindling 'owing to the emigration of many citizens, who could not afford such high taxes'. The burden on those remaining was all the greater, since communes were assessed for particular quotas and assessments were hard to modify. It has also been suggested that taxation was a factor in the decline of the Calabrian silk industry at the end of the sixteenth century.[48] It is unfortunate that in the present state of knowledge a general discussion of trends in trade and industry is impossible.

No discussion of the problems of southern Italy in the early modern period can afford to omit the Church. From Campanella to Trevor-Roper, diagnoses of the ills of the south – as of Spain – have referred to the inflated numbers of unproductive clergy. Exaggerated figures are in circulation, but moderate estimates are striking enough. It is likely that the clerical population of the cities (including nuns) varied between 6 and 8 per cent, and also that it increased between 1550 and 1650. This increase may well be a response to the economic recession; the Church offered the safest jobs going and exemption from taxation into the bargain. It was said at the time that some men had turned clerical for fiscal reasons.[49] Whether the Church also contributed to the recession by encouraging people to leave trade and industry is a more awkward question, depending as it does on an unverifiable estimate of the opportunities for productive employment at the time.

A more subtle diagnosis of the economic harm done by the Church was offered by an acute if prejudiced Protestant visitor to the south in the 1680s. Gilbert Burnet explained the 'decay of trade' and the 'dispeopling' of Italy partly, as so many foreign tourists did, by 'the sloth and laziness of this people'; partly by 'the severity of the taxes'; but also by the 'vast and dead wealth that is in the hands of the Churchmen', wasted on building churches and filling them with 'prodigious masses of plate', a misuse of resources, according to him, which does 'sink their trade extremely'.[50] There is no doubt something in this striking seventeenth-century variant on the Delumeau model, and indeed on the Weber thesis, but it might equally well be argued that 'hard times' were the cause, rather than the result, of investment in the hereafter.

IV

Two points emerge clearly from this survey: that the 1590s were an unhappy decade for the south Italians, and that long-term changes were also, in the sixteenth and seventeenth centuries, generally for the worse. However, two problems remain. Do the 1590s usher in a long-term recession (making them a 'crisis' in the strict sense)? And are the long-term problems of southern Italy in the sixteenth and seventeenth centuries problems of the transition from feudalism to capitalism? It would be convenient – in the sense of giving us a clear and simple explanation of the phenomena – if the answer were 'yes' in both cases; but there are difficulties in the way of such an affirmation.

To begin with the question of dating. When were the long-term economic problems at their worst? After the mid-1590s, there seems to have been a generation of reprieve. 1622, however, was a year of famine and disturbances in Naples, and the years around 1620 can be described with more reason than the years around 1590 as a crisis for the Italian economy, in the sense of years of difficulty followed by a change in long-term trends, of which the most important were declining productivity and increasing involution.[51] In Principato Ultra, for example, 1630 marked the beginning of a ninety-year period of decline in the revenue from feudal dues. The late 1640s were not only a time of bad harvests (one of the 'preconditions' for the revolts of Fermo, Naples and Palermo), but also a time of a downturn in the agricultural production of the relatively rich region around Naples, which until that time had remained prosperous. In 1656, plague ravaged Rome and Naples. This disaster was to the south what the plague of 1630–1 had been to the north, a catastrophe from which it would take the best part of a century to recover.[52]

The second problem is whether the long-term economic and social problems of the region can be explained, as some historians have explained so many of the problems of early modern Europe, in terms of the transition from feudalism to capitalism. I must admit to an initial suspicion that this phrase is too glib – partly because it is invoked to explain so many changes between the fourteenth century and the eighteenth, if not beyond, and partly because each of the key terms has a whole range of different meanings. In any case, the population figures quoted above do suggest that the basic explanation for the problems of the south in this period was a Malthusian one; the pressure of population on resources.

However, this explanation is unlikely to be the whole story. In the increasingly severe competition for resources, some individuals, families and social groups had better chances than others. Besides, the resources were not fixed by God or nature; if agricultural productivity was not raised in southern Italy, or if industry (silk-weaving, for example), was not developed as a substitute, this lack of development has itself to be explained.

In the case of the south, it is difficult to discuss the possible transition from feudalism to capitalism not only because the concepts are elusive but because of the lack of information about land tenure, landownership, and crops, especially the lack of statistics for the whole area. I hope that even specifying our ignorance more precisely than before may make a small contribution to our understanding of these problems.

It has often been argued that the fundamental economic and social process in the south at this point was not the transition to capitalism but its opposite: 'refeudalisation', a term of undoubted convenience, but one which is unfortunately used in two or more senses. In the first, more precise sense, refeudalisation refers to the increasing importance of the *feudo*, the fief or great estate (not necessarily the same thing). Much of southern Italy – how much, we do not know – was composed of great estates, and most great estates were fiefs. But, as one historian has pertinently asked, had there ever been any 'defeudalisation' in the south? There may have been a trend towards latifundia; if there was such a trend, it would not be difficult to explain it, as has been done in the case of England, as a result of hard times, which the rich can survive better than the poor.[53] However, it remains to be shown that there was such a trend, rather than a steady state.

The objection might be countered by using the term 'refeudalisation' to refer simply to the increased importance of feudal dues as opposed to other forms of income from the estate. In this case there seems little doubt about the trend, but the explanation is less sure. Historians of what used to be called the 'feudal reaction' in late eighteenth-century France have noted that feudal dues were sometimes increased because a noble estate had passed into the hands of a bourgeois who was concerned to get a good return on his investment.[54] In southern Italy in our period, when financiers were buying fiefs, it is at least worth asking whether the increase in feudal dues could be explained in these terms.

The word 'refeudalisation' is also used in a wider sense to refer to the 'revival' of the landed aristocracy at the expense of the bourgeoisie. This formula may be a useful one for characterising changes in northern Italy, but it is awkward to adapt it to southern conditions. In the first place, the local bourgeoisie had never risen. In the second place, we do not know what proportion of the land was in aristocratic hands at different times, so it is difficult to know whether 'revival' or 'stability' is the better term. In the third place, it is difficult to know who should be counted as an aristocrat. In the Kingdom of Naples, as in Lawrence Stone's England, this was not only a time when the old families often found themselves in difficulties, but also one in which many new men entered the aristocracy, notably financiers of foreign origin (often Genoese, sometimes Portuguese). It seems odd to describe the process by which such men bought themselves large estates as 'refeudalisation'.[55]

If this term is not an altogether happy one to characterise change in the south, what about the rise of capitalism? Unfortunately, 'capitalist' is of course a term with almost as many meanings as 'feudal'. Again, it may be useful to distinguish two interpretations or models of social change in which the term might reasonably be used. The first might be called the 'Wallerstein model'; it suggests that in this period the south was sucked into the capitalist world-economy as part of a periphery which was increasingly 'underdeveloped', that is to say reduced to exporting raw materials such as grain and silk and importing industrial products in return.[56] This explanation is attractive in the sense that it accounts, simply and economically, for the particular blend of change and continuity that we find in the south at this time. However, it has a major difficulty to surmount: given the rise of population, southern Italy, unlike Poland, say, will not have had a grain surplus to export.

Alternatively, we might talk about the rise of capitalism in the more limited sense of increasing orientation to the market by landowners in this period, in the Roman Campagna and also further south. It is likely that there was a shift in this direction, but we are not in a position to say who was responsible. Were the barons changing their attitudes and becoming interested in profit, or were they, like Kula's Polish magnates, interested only in a fixed income? If the latter, were the changes the work of stewards and bailiffs rather than landlords? Or should we be thinking in terms of the model which Lucien Febvre set up to explain change in sixteenth-century Franche-Comté? In this case the traditional nobility failed to cope with change, went under and sold land to a bourgeoisie which, whether ennobled or not, exploited the land – and the peasants – more efficiently than their predecessors.[57] It would be interesting to know whether the new men, like the Grimaldi and the Spinola, who bought land in this period, were more interested in productivity and profitability than older families; whether they were interested in new crops; or whether they believed that the way to maximise profit was to concentrate on raising feudal dues. The problem of the lack of investment in the land remains. Was there not a productive outlet for capital, say, irrigation schemes? No one at the time seems to have thought so. In this society, population growth was not a stimulus to technological change; hence it remained caught in the Malthusian trap.

The problems of the south in this period do not seem too difficult to diagnose. A rising population, an indebted aristocracy, new landowners on the make, and an insolvent government all made increasing demands on the land and the peasantry, demands which it was impossible to satisfy and only possible to escape by leaving the land for the cities. However, it is difficult to classify this society as either 'feudal' or 'capitalist'. The large estates, with their economies of scale, were in a sense capitalist because they were feudal, and the landowners who increased feudal dues were perhaps feudal because they were capitalist. There was urbanisation, but it reflected economic decline rather than economic growth; Rome, Naples and Palermo were, as Sombart pointed out long ago, 'consumer' not 'producer' cities.[58] The terms 'feudalism' and 'capitalism' – like 'crisis' – were not coined to deal with situations like these, and perhaps the south is better off without them.

Notes: Chapter 9

1 F. Caracciolo, *Il Regno di Napoli nei secoli XVI e XVII* (Rome, 1966), p. 353 ('una lunga crisi di quasi cento anni'); G. Galasso, *Economia e società nella Calabria del '500* (Naples, 1967), p. 8; R. Villari, *La Rivolta anti-spagnola a Napoli* (Bari, 1967); R. Romano, *Tra due crisi* (Turin, 1971), a study of Italy from the fourteenth century to the seventeenth; A. De Matteis, *L'Aquila e il contado* (Naples, 1973), p. 141 (on the seventeenth century as 'secolo di crisi' in the south); most recently, A. Lepre, 'La crisi del XVII secolo nel Mezzogiorno', *Studi storici*, vol. 22 (1981), pp. 51–77.

2 cf. R. Starn, 'Historians and crisis', *Past and Present*, no. 52 (1971), pp. 2–22; T. K. Rabb, *The Struggle for Stability in Early Modern Europe* (New York, 1975), ch. 4.

3 On the underdevelopment of the south, Caracciolo, *Napoli*, pp. 149 ff.; on land tenure, G. Giorgetti, *Contadini e proprietari nell'Italia moderna* (Turin, 1974), pp. 72 ff.

4 The tithe documents have been studied by B. Anatr *Quaderni Sardi*, 3 (1981–3) 4. M. Le Lannou, *Pâtres et paysans de la Sardaigne* (Tours, 1941).
5 J. Delumeau, *Vie économique et sociale de Rome dans la seconde motié du XVIe siècle* (Paris, 1957–9). For a sample of the historical demography of the region, see R. Ago, 'La diocesi di Sutri', *Mélanges de l'École Française de Rome*, vol. 86 (1974). Jacques Revel's study of the great estates of the region in the seventeenth century is eagerly awaited.
6 For a historical geography of the region in the eighteenth century, see P. Macry, *Mercato e società nel Regno di Napoli* (Naples, 1974), pt 2.
7 Galasso, *Calabria*.
8 M. A. Visceglia, 'Rendita feudale e agricoltura in Puglia', *Società e Storia*, no. 9 (1980), pp. 527–60; M. Benaiteau, 'La rendita feudale nel Regno di Napoli', ibid., pp. 561–611; S. Zotta, 'Momenti e problemi di una crisi agraria', *Mélanges de l'École Française de Rome*, vol. 90 (1978), pp. 715–96.
9 C. Petraccone, *Napoli dal '500 al '800* (Naples, 1974); De Matteis, *L'Aquila*; G. Delille, *Croissance d'une société rurale* (Naples, 1973).
10 Villari, *La Rivolta*.
11 C. Rotelli, 'Rendimenti nell'Imolese', *Rivista storica italiana*, vol. 80 (1968), pp. 107–20. For Rotelli this decline marks the first phase of 'the great agricultural crisis of 1588–1606'.
12 Delumeau, *Rome*, Vol. 2, pp. 608 ff.
13 Ago, 'La diocesi di Sutri', graph 1A.
14 L. Pastor, *History of the Popes*, 6th edn (London, 1938–53), Vol. 21, pp. 76 ff.; Vol. 23, pp. 265 ff.; Vol. 24, pp. 374 ff.; Delumeau, *Rome*, Vol. 2, pp. 543–65.
15 Delumeau *Rome*, Vol. 1, pp. 471 ff.
16 Pastor, *Popes*, Vol. 21, pp. 99, 106–7; Delumeau, *Rome*, Vol. 1, pp. 501 ff., 403 ff.
17 Pastor, *Popes*, Vol. 24, p. 371; Delumeau, *Rome*, Vol. 1, pp. 405 ff. Many more details on the problems of the 1590s are to be found in a source Delumeau does not seem to have used: AS, Rome, Tribunale del Governatore, Processi. I am currently working on these records.
18 *Storia di Napoli*, Vol. 5 (Naples, 1970), pp. 699 ff.
19 J.-N. Biraben, *Les Hommes et la Peste en France et dans les pays européens* (Paris, 1975), Vol. 1, p. 398.
20 Galasso, *Calabria*, pp. 353 ff., 105.
21 M. Rosa, *Religione e società nel Mezzogiorno* (Bari, 1976), pp. 245 ff. Rosa notes that the Annual Letters of the Jesuits provide a valuable source for the study of the problems of the 1590s.
22 *Storia di Napoli*, Vol. 5, p. 710.
23 N. Faraglia (ed.), 'Descrizione delle parrocchie di Napoli fatto nel 1598', *Archivio storico per le provincie napolitane*, vol. 18 (1898).
24 Villari, *La Rivolta*, pp. 42 ff.
25 L. Amabile, *Fra Tommaso Campanella* (Naples, 1882), Vol. 1, p. 153.
26 Ago, 'La diocesi di Sutri', graphs 1A, 1B.
27 K. J. Beloch, *Bevölkerungsgeschichte Italiens*, Vol. 2 (Berlin, 1940), p. 122.
28 ibid., Vol. 1 (Berlin, 1937), p. 212.
29 Delille, *Croissance*, pp. 68–79.
30 Petraccone, *Napoli*; cf. R. Romano, *Napoli dal Viceregno al Regno* (Turin, 1976), pp. 3 ff.
31 Petraccone, *Napoli*, pp. 111 ff.; Galasso, *Calabria*, p. 101.
32 Zotta, 'Momenti e problemi', p. 716.
33 Galasso, *Calabria*, p. 124.
34 Visceglia, 'Rendita feudale', p. 542.
35 Rotelli, 'Rendimenti'.
36 Delumeau, *Rome*, Vol. 2, pp. 566 ff.; cf. J. Revel, 'Les privilèges d'une capitale: l'approvisionnement de Rome à l'époque moderne', *Annales ESC*, Vol. 30 (1975), pp. 563–73.
37 G. P. Carocci makes this point in his review of Delumeau in *Rivista storica italiana*, Vol. 69 (1957), pp. 604–13; cf. his *Lo stato della chiesa nella seconda metà del '500* (Milan, 1961).

38 G. Labrot, 'Le comportement collectif de l'aristocratie napolitaine du 16e au 18e siècle', *Revue historique*, vol. 258 (1977), pp. 45–71; and the same author's *Baroni in città* (Naples, 1979), pp. 19 ff., 61 n.
39 Caracciolo, *Napoli*, pp. 306 ff.
40 Benaiteau, 'La rendita feudale'.
41 Visceglia, 'Rendita feudale', p. 554.
42 Galasso, *Calabria*, p. 294.
43 T. Campanella, *Monarchia Hispanica* (Amsterdam, 1640), p. 121; quoted in the contemporary English translation (London, 1660), p. 61.
44 G. Bock, *Tommaso Campanella* (Tübingen, 1974), pp. 91 ff.
45 Y. M. Bercé, 'L'émeute de ferme', *Mélanges archéologie histoire*, vols 73–4 (1961–2), pp. 471–505, 759–89.
46 Villari, *La Rivolta*; cf. A. Musi, *Finanze e politica nella Napoli del '600* (Naples, 1976).
47 De Matteis, *L'Aquila*.
48 Galasso, *Calabria*, pp. 354, 105–6, 146.
49 H. R. Trevor-Roper, *Religion, the Reformation and Social Change* (London, 1967), pp. 36 ff.; cf. P. Sposato, 'Dati statistici sulla popolazione nel Viceregno di Napoli', *Annali della Scuola per Archivisti*, vol. 5 (1965), on the numbers of clergy.
50 G. Burnet, *Some Letters* (Rotterdam, 1686), pp. 176 ff.
51 A. De Rubertis, 'Carestia e fame a Napoli nel 1622', *Annali Scuola Normale Pisa*, vol. 17 (1948); R. Romano, 'L'Italia nella crisi del secolo XVII', *Studi Storici*, vol. 9 (1968).
52 On the plague, see P. Savio, 'Ricerche sulla peste di Roma degli anni 1656–7', *Archivio Società Romana Storia Patria*, vol. 95 (1972). On the demographic consequences, see Beloch, *Bevölkerungsgeschichte*.
53 On the lack of defeudalisation, see Galasso, *Calabria*, pp. 53 ff., 376 ff. On England, see H. J. Habakkuk, 'English landownership, 1680–1740', *Economic History Review*, 1st ser., vol. 10 (1939–40), pp. 2–17.
54 See, for example, A. Cobban, *The Social Interpretation of the French Revolution* (Cambridge, 1964), ch. 5.
55 On the financiers, see Villari, *La rivolta*, and Musi, *Finanze*.
56 I. Wallerstein, *The Modern World-System*, vol. 2 (New York, 1980), pp. 146 ff.
57 W. Kula, *Economic Theory of the Feudal System* (1962); English trans., London, 1976). Kula's approach has been applied to Sicily by Maurice Aymard, and to southern Italy by A. Lepre, *Feude e masserie* (Naples, 1973). L. Febvre's model is put forward in *Philippe II et la Franche-Comté* (Paris, 1912), pt 2.
58 W. Sombart, *Luxury and Capitalism*, trans. W. R. Dittmar (Ann Arbor, Mich., 1967).

10 *Village-Building in Sicily: an Aristocratic Remedy for the Crisis of the 1590s*

TIMOTHY B. DAVIES

Between the sixteenth and eighteenth centuries Sicily's transition from feudalism to capitalism was irreparably blighted. In the late sixteenth century large quantities of Sicilian wheat, sugar and silk were sent abroad but a hundred years later exports were comparatively insignificant and most of the island's wheat was consumed by the Sicilians themselves. During this long-term recession or 'general crisis' (to use E. J. Hobsbawm's term) the feudal aristocracy became stronger,[1] and its position was not seriously threatened by the revolutions at Palermo and Messina, the only major upheavals of the seventeenth century. The aristocracy could count on the support of the untitled holders of capital, such as grain merchants and lawyers, most of whom aspired to join its ranks.[2] This alliance of interests was not fortuitous but was brought about by the changes which occurred in the late sixteenth century. Sicilian aristocrats hoped to secure enough income to cover social needs since their capital resources were largely eaten up by younger sons and daughters in the form of portions and dowries, so they wanted above all to ensure that the *gabelloti*, the middlemen to whom they leased out their estates, would continue to shoulder the risks of agrarian production. Difficulties became increasingly apparent both to aristocrats and *gabelloti* in the closing decades of the sixteenth century because of the growing indebtedness of the peasant cultivators, to whom credit always had to be given.

My intention is to show how the famine years between 1590 and 1610, the 'crisis of the 1590s', were a critical period for the Sicilian aristocracy, in so far as many families tried to make the best of a bad situation by building new villages on their estates. I shall argue that the production and distribution failures of these years favoured this type of activity.

I

By the early 1580s the population of Sicily, about 1 million, was concentrated in 187 townships. There were few villages as small as those to be

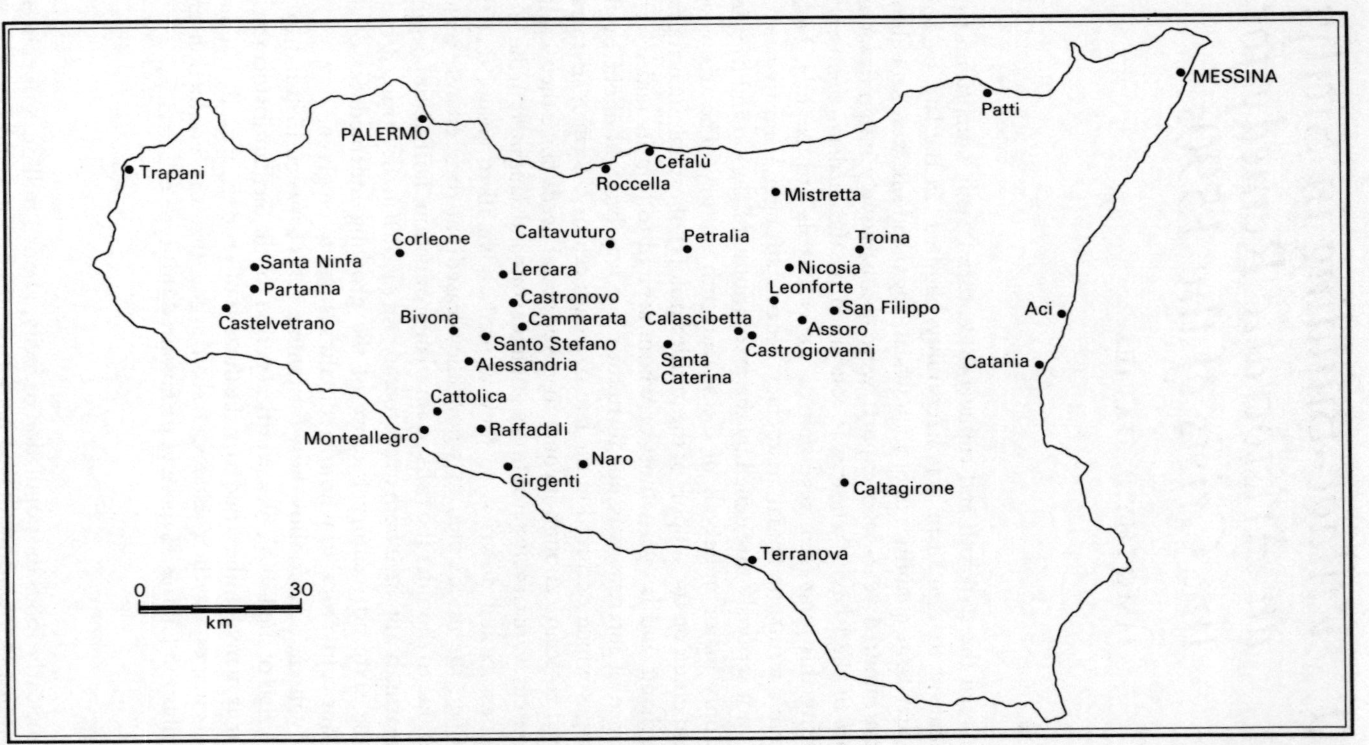

Sicily in the 1590s

found all over England at this time. According to the census of 1584, only about one-third of the island's towns had less than 2,000 inhabitants whereas 53 towns had more than 5,000 inhabitants and 18 more than 10,000. Most of the smaller towns with under 5,000 inhabitants were situated in the north-eastern third. It was in this predominantly mountainous and silk-producing area that the medieval peasant communities had fared best after the catastrophic loss of population in the fourteenth century. Elsewhere, particularly in the flatter west and centre of the island, small hamlets or *casali* had been deserted on a vast scale during the late Middle Ages.[3] In the sixteenth century their sites were indicated by mills, isolated chapels, or wayside inns, which were the only landmarks in a countryside without trees and houses.

From researches in the Sicilian census books (*riveli*) of the early modern period, M. Aymard has built up a fairly accurate picture of the island's population trends.[4] During the sixteenth century the total number of Sicilians increased by between 65 and 75 per cent. This tremendous growth, which was levelling off by the 1570s, was absorbed by the ancient towns. Although every locality gained in numbers the western towns expanded most. Between 1550 and 1580 the population of most localities in Western Sicily increased by over 50 per cent compared with a rate of only 20–30 per cent in the east. At least up to the middle of the sixteenth century, more than enough wheat to meet local demand was harvested from the upland plains of western Sicily in good years, even though a great deal of land was not cultivated or left as pasture. The lower growth rates of the mountainous north-east reflected, by contrast, the inadequacy of local wheat supplies. The people of the north-east could not afford to be fussy about eating bread made of rye or chestnuts for wheat prices were higher here than in the west of the island.[5] The numerous hamlets or *casali* which emerged in this region from the middle of the sixteenth century represented attempts to relieve the pressure of too many people on limited food supplies. The process seems to have gathered momentum in later decades of the century. This happened near the towns which, by the early 1580s, had more than 5,000 inhabitants, from Mistretta and Patti on the northern coast down to Aci and Catania in the east. The new hamlets apparently developed without any direction from above but it is likely that the ruling elites of all the ancient towns tried to encourage some of their fellow townsmen to settle there. According to a contemporary observer, the inhabitants of these *casali* of Messina were forbidden to resettle in the mother town.[6]

In this period the food supplies of the towns of the interior also became more precarious. It is not obvious why this was so. Population was increasing rapidly at this time but so was the area of land under wheat cultivation, although no figures exist to compare the two movements. Wheat exports abroad, moreover, continued to remain high in the 1570s and 1580s since the north Italian cities were largely forced to rely on Sicily for their supplies. Between 1576 and 1590 yearly wheat exports were at least 120,000 *salme* and sometimes as much as 150,000 (one *salma* was equal to 2 quintals or 7·5 bushels).[7] Increases in cultivated land in the late sixteenth century are shown by rising nominal income which many feudal lords were able to realise from their estates. This was threefold in many cases between 1550 and 1590.[8] Everywhere in western Sicily men were tilling land which had formerly been pasture. This could be seen especially clearly in the case of the land on which all the townspeople, in theory, had rights of pasturage.[9] Large tracts of such land passed out of municipal control through 'enfeoffment' to a small group of prominent local families.

Food supply became more complicated, however, because of the shortcomings of the town provisioning system, the growing monopolisation of the means of production in the hands of the *gabelloti* and the pauperisation of the independent cultivators. In the first place, the crucial relationship between town and countryside became increasingly strained during the sixteenth century. In Sicily, as in the rest of Italy, each town held economic sway over the surrounding countryside within its territory.[10] The importance of the municipal territory was very clear to Sicilians in the late sixteenth century even though the boundaries were frequently a matter for local dispute. Town officials, known as the *giurati*, expected to obtain adequate food supplies from the territory they controlled and to receive the assent of the Royal Patrimony, the institution responsible for Sicily's financial administration, if they were obliged to buy wheat from outside. They were entitled to buy up the wheat necessary for the town provision from the municipal territory at the price of the *meta*. This was not the market price but a rate which was fixed every year in each town to reflect the state of the harvest within its territory.

The large wheat surpluses accumulated by the *gabelloti* and other large producers made them unwilling to sell at the fixed prices established in the locality. This was increasingly so after 1550 as feudal lords stopped managing their estates directly and rented them out to *gabelloti* in return for an annual rent or *gabella* in money. Both feudal lords and *gabelloti* were confident that income from land would continue to rise. The *gabelle* were driven up by the *gabelloti* themselves, who outbid each other to gain control over the land.[11] Not only were they willing to make advance payments to the feudal lords but also to carry out small improvements within the fiefs, by building warehouses or drinking troughs for example. These *gabelloti* were not a separate bourgeois class but came from different backgrounds. They were often themselves feudal lords or relatives of such. Many of them belonged to the office-holding patriciate of Palermo. It was to Palermitans that the Barresi family, from 1560 onwards, continuously rented out their barony of Pietra d'Amico. It was to relatives who were also members of the local town oligarchy of Castrogiovanni (Enna), on the other hand, that the Grimaldi rented out their fiefs in central Sicily. *Gabelloti* could also be rich peasants, a phenomenon which was to be increasingly in evidence during the seventeenth century.

The higher profits of the *gabelloti* were gained at the expense of the peasant cultivators, the *borgesi*. The demographic growth of the early sixteenth century resulted in greater subdivision of smallholdings and made it necessary for many cultivators to earn a subsistence wheat ration by working as day-labourers (*giornatari*). In the opening years of the century the *borgese* had been a relatively well-to-do smallholder, managing to provide his own 'cultivation capital' and sell his own wheat.[12] By its closing years, however, he had become entirely dependent on the *gabelloto* for advances (*soccorsi*), which he had to pay back at interest, or upon one of the handful of families in his town who made a good living out of usury. Between 1550 and 1580 the rents in kind (*terraggi*) paid to the *gabelloto* by the *borgesi* of Terranova increased from 1 to 4 *salme* of wheat per *salma* of land (or from 0·5 to 2·4 quintals per hectare).[13] By the 1570s the mounting indebtedness of the *borgesi* had reached levels so high that they could neither pay the *terraggi* nor the excessive interest on the 'cultivation capital'. By the early 1580s the whole system of agrarian credit threatened to collapse. In 1583 the *borgesi* of the Duke of Terranova, embittered by the seizure of their small stocks of grain and animals by creditors, refused to accept the terms of the *gabelloti*. Not only did their resistance make it impossible, at least temporarily, to cultivate more land, but it also threatened to block the income of the feudal lord at a time when his own debts were reaching unprecedented heights.[14] Even before the years of famine, then, a 'cultivation crisis' was already in operation, and this may have considerably worsened the prospects which each municipality had of finding enough wheat in its territory to make up its provision. One indication of this, in central Sicily, was the decision by the *giurati* of Castrogiovanni in 1580 to abolish the duty which they had traditionally levied on grain brought into the town's territory from outside.[15] The problem of municipal shortfall now gave greater cause for concern, however, because of the greater unwillingness of local *gabelloti*, especially the ones excluded from the urban oligarchies, to sell wheat to the local town at the obligatory fixed price.

II

By the difficult closing years of the sixteenth century, the economic problems of the Sicilian nobility were greater than before. At the same time those with capital to invest were associating themselves more closely with the interests of the aristocracy. A long period of uncertainty in the late sixteenth century was reflected, on the one hand, by the trend of rising feudal indebtedness which made many families sell off hereditary lands, and, on the other, by the greater extent to which capital was invested in land rather than in other economic activities. Since the fourteenth century, Sicilian lords had been free to sell or alienate their feudal lands provided they had not been entailed. Although no systematic study has yet been made of the land market in Sicily, it seems likely that the tremendous increase in land transactions during the sixteenth century reached a peak by the 1580s, and fell off thereafter. The turnover of sales of feudal land revealed the ineffectiveness of *fidecommessi* or entails which were intended to keep feudal estates in the same hands. Legal safeguards of this kind were embodied in the wills and marriage contracts drawn up by successive generations of feudal lords. On the other hand, many land transactions did not give secure possession to the buyer. Fiefs were often sold only on the understanding that they could be bought back at the same price later on and the right to repurchase might be given away separately, as a dowry for example.

All feudal families, from whatever sources they derived their income, became saddled with heavier debts in the sixteenth century. To pay for dowries and portions and purchases of feudal land they were always trying to raise long-term mortgages or *soggiogazioni*. The value of the *soggiogazioni* contracted by the Aragona of Terranova, one of the premier families of Sicily, increased nearly five times between 1569 and 1590. They were worth a total nominal capital of 33,000 *onze*, and nearly 70 per cent of it was used to create annuities for the payment of dowries and dower settlements.[16] The *soggiogazioni* on the estates of the more recently established family, the Barresi of Alessandria, trebled between 1562 and 1598, rising from 4,160 to 12,720 *onze*.[17] The problem of indebtedness was such that, in order to check the rate at which indebted families would have to sell parts of their landed patrimony, an institution known as the Deputazione degli Stati was set up by the government in 1598. Deputies were appointed to administer the estates of indebted feudal lords who were then only able to draw upon a subsistence pension for their families.[18]

The extent to which feudal lords contracted debts and sold off their estates was paralleled by the willingness with which those with capital invested it in buying land and annuities on noble family patrimonies. This was mainly caused by the long-term decline in the profits which could be realised from investment in commerce and non-agrarian activities. From capital invested in *soggiogazioni* a return of 8 or 9 per cent could be expected in the 1570s and 1580s, compared with only 5 per cent from sugar production.[19] The long-term trend is illustrated by the changing investment patterns of the Mastiani, a non-noble family whose members regularly held civic office at Palermo between 1560 and 1640. From 1577, or even earlier, until 1597 they held the lease of a sugar-mill at Roccella near Cefalù on the northern coast. Their marketing problems may have been eased by the fact that, between 1585 and 1591, one of the family seems to have farmed the export duties on sugar.[20] But they had to be content with declining profits, partly because they were undercut by Brazilian competition and partly because they were handicapped by diminishing supplies of wood. In the middle of the century demand for sugar had been high enough for a new mill to be built at Roccella and between 1577 and 1582 the mill was leased at 5,200 *onze* yearly. By 1609 the same mill, together with the barony in which it was situated, was leased out to a Ragusan merchant at only 2,000 *onze* yearly.[21] From the 1570s the Mastiani assiduously invested in *soggiogazioni*.

III

The distress of the years between 1590 and 1610 was primarily caused by very poor wheat harvests. No production figures are available, but the trend in these years is reflected very clearly by the acute upturn in the price rates (*mete*) for wheat. At Palermo the price rates of wheat, compiled by Aymard, averaged between 55 and 65 *tarì* per *salma* during the crisis decades, contrasting strongly with the years before and the decade after (1611–20) when the rates never rose, on average, to more than 43 *tarì*.[22] We can also follow the production difficulties after 1590 from the price rates of wheat at Trapani and from a list of wheat prices at Catania.[23] From these sets of data the period between 1590 and 1610 falls into three phases: catastrophe in 1590–91; slow recovery in the rest of the 1590s; further catastrophe in the first decades of the seventeenth century, possibly even more severe than in the 1590s (see Figure 10.1). In 1591 wheat was brought by the senates of Palermo and Messina at 240 and 480 *tarì* respectively.[24] At Messina dearth of wheat seems to have caused rioting in 1594. In contrast, the more favourable harvests of the later 1590s are clearly shown by the price data for Palermo and Catania. At Trapani it is probable that all the harvests of these years, except that of 1596, were fair, given the diminished quantities of seed available for sowing. The harvests reflected yields on the seed of 7 or 8 to 1 but the price rates remained fairly high in these years and only in 1600 was the rate again less than 40 *tarì*. Between 1602 and 1608 harvests were once more very bad, since the price rates at Trapani were never less than 50 *tarì*. None of the harvests in these years was good enough to allow much more than 40,000 *salme* to be exported in any year. At Trapani the harvest of 1606 was apparently so bad that no attempt was

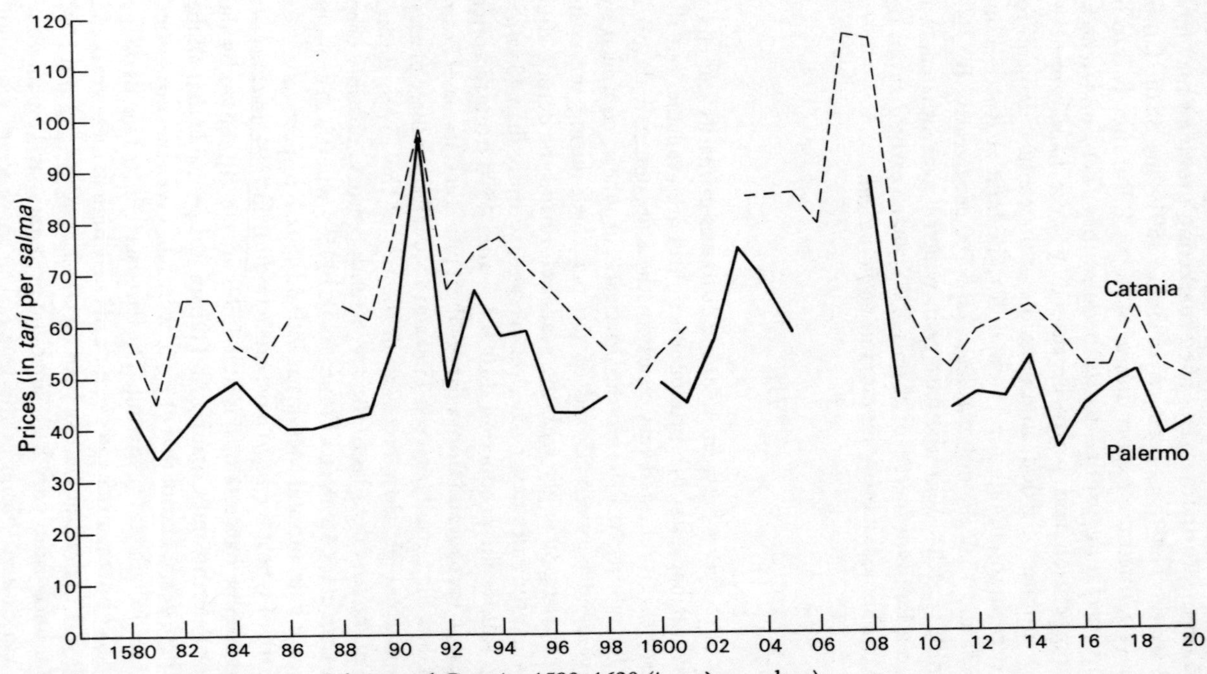

(Figure 10.1 *Wheat prices at Palermo and Catania, 1580–1620 (in* tarì *per* salma).

Sources: Palermo – unpublished data from the Archivio del Comune di Palermo. I am grateful to Professor M. Aymard for allowing me to use them. Catania – A. Petino, 'Primi assaggi sulla rivoluzione dei prezzi in Sicilia nei secoli XVI e XVII', in *Studi in onore di Gino Luzzatto, II* (Milan, 1950), pp. 208–9.

made to fix a rate in that year, and at Catania wheat was sold for no less than 448 *tarì* per *salma*.[25]

The frequency of dearth resulted from an unfortunate combination of drought and heavy rain. The years 1585, 1589 and 1590 are all recorded as having been dry years.[26] The meagre harvest of 1590 was followed by a long spell of drought until March 1591 when torrential rain fell throughout the spring months and caused the seeds to rot.[27] Bread made from the rotten wheat caused typhus to break out and sweep the island.[28] 1606 and 1607 were excessively dry. In March 1607 large numbers of people went in daily procession through the streets of Palermo to pray for rain.[29]

The dearth of 1590–1 affected some localities much more severely than others. Although little research has been carried out to show the extent of mortality in the early 1590s, this is indicated by the disappearance of about 70,000 people between 1583 and 1593, a loss of 9 per cent of the total population. From a comparison of the censuses of these years it is clear that mortality was much higher in the more densely populated north-east of Sicily where little wheat was grown. Here, population in most localities fell by up to 20 per cent, and in the vicinity of Patti, by nearly 30 per cent.[30] Parts of central Sicily, especially the eastern localities, were also very seriously affected. There were losses of at least 20 per cent at Castrogiovanni, Calascibetta, Troina and Assoro, and nearly 40 per cent at Nicosia. In the west of the island, by contrast, mortality was much less serious, to judge from the minimal losses or even gains recorded between 1583 and 1593. In every locality, however, some towns suffered more heavily than their neighbours, often because they were more remotely situated. For example, the mountain towns of Naro, Cammarata and Caltavuturo, in western Sicily, lost between 20 and 30 per cent of their inhabitants. The harvest failures of 1606 and 1607, on the other hand, seem to have ravaged the population of Sicily less seriously than the famine of 1590–1. This is shown, above all, by the absence of any substantial check to the island's long-term population growth. By 1607 the overall population was nearly 4 per cent higher than in 1583, and by 1623 it was 7 per cent higher. By 1607 the population of the north-east, where losses had been heaviest in 1590–1, had almost regained its 1583 level; and by 1616 it was slightly higher than in 1583. In the west of the island, however, population was about 20 per cent higher by 1623 than it had been in 1583.[31] In the south-east, however, the population was no higher in 1623 than it had been in 1583, and the same was probably true – although here the census information does not exist – of the populations of Palermo and Messina between these dates. Such trends suggest that, at least from the late 1590s, wheat cultivation in western Sicily was expanding and that considerable quantities of wheat were made available in the wheat-deficient north-east of Sicily, so allowing, at least in the short term, population in this region to grow.

The widespread misery caused by frequent harvest failure was made much worse, especially in 1590–1, by export of wheat from Sicily and by large-scale hoarding. In the first place, more wheat seems to have left Sicily in the late 1580s, despite the mediocre harvests of these years, in response to greater provisioning demands made by the Spanish government. The consequences of this proved to be particularly serious after the very poor harvest of 1590.[32] The experience of 1590 made the Sicilian authorities much more cautious in their approach to the question of how much wheat was to be exported, and only once in the following decade, after the harvest of 1598, were more than 120,000 *salme* exported. Virtually no wheat was exported after the harvests of 1606, 1607 and 1608, with the exception of the duty-free quotas already pledged for the provisioning of Malta (see Table 10.1).

Table 10.1 *Wheat Exports from Sicily between 1598 and 1612* (*in* salme)

Year	*Total Exports*	*Year*	*Total Exports*
1598–9	126,187	1605–6	78,988
1599–1600	97,736	1606–7	nil
1600–1	38,515	1607–8	7,250
1601–2	36,020	1608–9	5,950
1602–3	41,927	1609–10	52,948
1603–4	6,808	1610–11	23,559
1604–5	53,351	1611–12	30,094

Source: *Spadofora*, ser. II, 61, fos 384–421, 'Relatione dell'estrattioni'.

Little could be done by either government or municipalities to check hoarding. The government commission appointed to look into this in 1603–4 seems to have been relatively ineffective. This reflected the greater importance in these years of the few who had grain stocks to sell, namely the local merchants or *gabelloti*. They preferred to keep their wheat buried or stored in warehouses in the countryside rather than sell at the fixed rates. Disproportionate quantities of wheat were probably attracted to Palermo during these years because of the higher prices that were offered.

The effects of the famine years were felt more severely by those who could not possibly save any food reserves, the day-labourers and share-croppers. Throughout the famine decades their misery expressed itself in widespread subsistence migration. Palermo was always a magnet which in the late 1580s attracted thousands of vagrants hoping to benefit from its superior provisioning system. In 1590 the city authorities appointed and paid new officials known as *censori* to round up suspected vagrants.[33] After the famine of 1591 they ordered all 'strangers' to leave the city.[34] In any case, long-distance migration seems to have been limited in comparison with the short-distance journeys – usually over less than 15 km – made by dwellers of the old towns of western and central Sicily to one of the many feudal settlements which were being launched at the time throughout this region. By 1593 Monteallegro and Alessandria, villages founded in 1574 and 1583, had each gained just over 300 inhabitants. Most of the inhabitants of Alessandria were from the neighbouring towns of Bivona and Santo Stefano.[35] From the *riveli* of 1616 and 1623, which were usually the earliest censuses to be taken in the 'new foundations' of the famine years, it is clear that these short-distance journeyings had reached a peak by the first decade of the seventeenth century. The place of origin was frequently declared, but when it was not one can usually assume it was the same as the place where debts were owed or where property was held. Migrants came from both feudal and domanial towns. At least 50 per cent of those who settled at Santa Ninfa in western Sicily were natives of the feudal towns of Partanna and Castelvetrano, and, similarly, many of the earliest inhabitants of Cattolica (near Agrigento) were from the feudal town of Raffadali. Over 80 per cent of those who migrated to Santa Caterina in central Sicily originated from Castrogiovanni or from the domanial towns of the Madonie mountians. A similar proportion of the first settlers at Leonforte, a little farther to the east, were from the feudal town of Assoro and the domanial towns of San Filippo and Nicosia.[36]

The majority of those who quit or rather 'fled' their home towns had little choice before them but to start a barely improved life in the new settlements, even though they were under few illusions as to the 'concessions' offered by their founders. As the Marquis della Motta pointed out in 1610, those who remained had little prospect of being able to support a family and were thus unlikely to increase the populations of these towns.[37] Poverty-stricken widows were probably most representative of the *miserabili* who could not emigrate, because they had no contribution to make in the new villages. There were 1,279 of them at Castrogiovanni in 1607, accounting for about one-third of the total number of households in the town.[38] A small number of the migrants to the new villages were better off than the rest, however. They often took with them small stocks of agrarian capital. For example, the d'Amico family, who settled at Santa Caterina in 1607 or 1608, brought several oxen and cattle with them from their native town of Petralia in the Madonie.[39]

IV

The gruelling experience of prolonged dearth not only emphasised the vulnerability of the ancient towns, but also impressed upon all Sicilians the need for more systematically organised sources of food supply and agrarian credit. By building villages which at least partially met this need the feudal lords of western and central Sicily hoped that they, or rather the *gabelloti*, would be able to exploit their resources more quickly. At a time when noble family economies were reeling under the weight of debt, feudal lords welcomed even the marginal benefits which colonisation projects might bring them. Between 1595 and 1610, during the decades of dearth, about 24 villages were founded. In the following decades, especially after 1620 with the 'price reversal', the number of new settlements tripled. During the half-century between the catastrophe of 1590–1 and the lean years of the late 1640s, about 70 villages were built compared with perhaps 20 between 1500 and 1590 and perhaps 30 between 1650 and 1800. They were most numerous in western and central Sicily.[40]

All these villages were built on a gridiron plan reminiscent of the colonial towns of Spanish America. Rows of one- or sometimes two-storey houses were erected around one or possibly two central *piazze*, and these mean dwellings were dominated by the baronial palace or castle and by the church. With one or two notable exceptions, none of these villages seems to have been planned by an architect. In many new villages it is likely that a master builder, working from a pattern book, would have had the task of making sure that the building followed the regular plan. As in architectural design, so in other aspects of its earliest years, each 'new foundation' conformed to a similar overall pattern. Before founding the village, the founder was careful to obtain a special licence from the Royal Patrimony at Palermo (after 1611 it could be obtained only from Madrid). This *licentia populandi* gave him permission to colonise one or more of his officially uninhabited fiefs. The importance of the licence was that it conferred on the founder jurisdictional rights over the future inhabitants and recognised the territorial autonomy of the new village. To attract settlers each founder proclaimed that moratoria would be granted to debtors who became his vassals, but it is unlikely that this greatly swelled the numbers of immigrants. After the foundation, the feudal lord divided up part of the estate being colonised (often a fief or two out of an entire barony) into small plots of land and granted them in emphyteusis to each of the immigrant households, who were obliged to plant vines. The rest of the territory of the new village continued, as before the foundation, to be rented out to *gabelloti*, who would sub-rent the land to the immigrants in return for rents in wheat. At the time of the foundation, many founders were careful to lay down the monopoly rights which they claimed. This was often done by making formal agreements (*capitoli*) to this effect with the first settlers in the village.

Detailed information exists for only a handful of the seventeenth-century 'new foundations'. Probably much more existed in the many family archives which have been lost or destroyed. It can be suggested, however, that the benefits of village-building became more apparent to potential founders after the dearth of 1590–1. The frightening levels of aristocratic indebtedness meant that their investment in colonisation would have to be made at the expense of others, because their own capital resources were already committed.[41] Potential founders had good reason to believe that building costs could be kept low if they could provide the necessary building materials – especially wood – and exercise the right degree of social control over the poverty-stricken immigrants. Each founder counted on getting most or all of the houses and smaller buildings erected by the immigrants. He did this by granting to each peasant household a plot of land on which, by the terms of a contract, one or more houses were to be built. The lord assumed that within a year or two of the foundation the influx of labour would make it possible to harvest a substantial wheat surplus which could then be used to pay for the other buildings: palace, church, mill, oil-press, fountains, prison.[42]

The difficulties of the 1590s prompted Giulio Grimaldi to build the village of Santa Caterina in his barony of Risichillia near Castrogiovanni. Because of his political influence at Castrogiovanni his application for a licence, in 1602, was unopposed. We do not know how much Giulio spent in building the village since the only evidence for this comes from affidavits in a lawsuit during the 1620s. According to some of these statements, the total cost was 3,784 *onze*, while according to others it was 5,474 *onze*. Although these estimates cannot be taken literally, they give us some idea of the relative values of the buildings. Nearly 40 per cent of the alleged expenses were for building houses and 30 per cent for building the baronial palace. Next on the expenditure scale come the drinking fountain (11 per cent), inn (9 per cent), church (7 per cent) and prison (1·5 per cent). At least 100 houses, and no doubt some of the other small buildings in the village as well, were built by the newcomers themselves. According to a notarial document probably dating to the time of the foundation, each of the settlers at Santa Caterina received a beam of wood and some bricks as *soccorsi* with which to build a house. He was then required to pay these back, in wheat, at the end of periods which varied from one to four years.[43]

Some feudal lords were unsuccessful in their attempts at colonisation. About ninety *licentiae populandi* were issued between 1595 and 1650. Of these, twenty did not give rise to a village. In the sixteenth century, by contrast, the number of licensed building projects which proved abortive equalled the number of successful ones: between 1571 and 1590 there were five successes and four failures, and earlier, between 1501 and 1540, sixteen successes and fifteen failures. Admittedly, the existing documentation is by no means complete. Many applications for licences by prospective founders were rejected by the Royal Patrimony out of deference to local opposition, whether from domanial town or feudal lord, where this was especially vehement. Some building projects failed or were delayed as a result of the founder's sudden death. Such was the case at Lercara, begun in 1605 by Baldasar Gomez de Amescua but virtually refounded in the 1660s by one of his successors.[44]

Village-building was more likely to be successful after the 1590s both because of the particular economic conditions arising from the famine and because of the more favourable political circumstances. In the first place, feudal lords did not need to attract their new vassals since hunger was driving them from the old towns. Neither did they have to attract potential lenders of 'cultivation capital'. In most cases the indebtedness of feudal lords was now such that they could not afford to be indifferent to the possibilities offered by colonisation or carry out building projects half-heartedly. Secondly, most of the chief citizens of the old towns were more willing to swallow their pride and accept the emergence of the 'new foundations' in their midst, even though this meant loss of jurisdiction and territory. The problems of the hopelessly indebted cultivators must have been such that the municipalities, who could not give them any hope of being able to feed themselves, were glad to see many of them depart to the new villages. Generally speaking, it was not until after 1615 that the old towns attempted to re-attract their lost populations, and this may be indicative of a more flexible attitude towards colonisation in the decades of dearth. Caltagirone and Corleone, for example, announced that moratoria would be available for indebted 'returnees' in 1615; Castronovo did the same in 1619, Girgenti (Agrigento) in 1623 and Castrogiovanni in 1624.[45] Throughout the 'peak' period of colonisation, however, feudal lords with the right political connections with the local town oligarchy found it easiest to build villages. Those without such connections were often able to carry out their projects only in the face of protracted local opposition.

After the famine of 1590–1 village-building was also assisted by the Spanish government's greater willingness to grant the necessary *licentiae populandi*. The government was worried about the drastic fall in wheat exports. It was also more concerned about social unrest, and possibly more anxious to stop the population of Palermo expanding any further. This does not mean that there was ever an official policy on internal colonisation in Sicily, however. Officials probably thought much less about the question than about how to defend the island against Turkish and north African privateers. They had good reason, for at least eighty enemy landings were made between 1581 and 1611.[46] But Sicilian and Spanish resources employed in the 1590s in defence were extremely modest compared with what they were to be in the 1620s and 1630s.[47]

In the short term the most remunerative of the markets for wheat from the new villages was probably north-eastern Sicily. However, this was the case only so long as there continued to be steady demand in northern Italy for Sicilian silk. It was the arrival of wheat from western Sicily which allowed population levels in the north-east to recover in the generation after the famine of 1590–1 and, in many localities, to continue growing until the 1650s or 1660s, when foreign demand for Sicilian silk definitely declined. Much of the wheat came by sea on tiny vessels, and the growing, though short-lived, importance of the coasting trade in wheat is shown by the fact that a tax was levied on it by the government, for the first time, in 1636. Considerable quantities of wheat were also transported to the north-east overland, in spite of the difficult terrain. From the account books of the Branciforti family it is clear that surpluses produced by the new village of Leonforte were regularly loaded on to mule-trains and sent to the north-eastern town of Raccuia.[48] For some founders, or rather for their *gabelloti* and agents, more localised markets also offered scope for profit. Wheat surpluses produced in the territory of the new village did not have to be sold to the local town at the fixed rate given to local producers but could be sold at prices asked by the *gabelloti*. By levying feudal taxes on goods extracted from the territory of the village, founders could discourage peasant cultivators with small surpluses from marketing their produce independently of the *gabelloti* as they might have done before the building of the village.

V

Diminishing opportunities for profit in the late sixteenth century raised the question of how this would affect the fortunes of the aristocracy. Since the 1570s and 1580s it was clear to many feudal lords that income from land was not going to rise fast enough for them to meet financial commitments which were unavoidable if social prestige and family honour were to be maintained. Their standard of living was put in jeopardy when the *gabelloto* was unable to count on makng an attractive profit from the cultivation enterprise. This probably became an increasing worry during the years of dearth from the late 1580s when some *gabelloti* failed to respect the terms of the *gabella* because the return given by the harvest was so meagre. From the late 1590s onwards feudal lords took advantage of the greater difficulties of the landless cultivators to found villages which gave the middlemen greater scope for making modest profits. The feudal lord guaranteed that a supply of labour would be available and that it would be largely excluded from the possibility of profit-sharing because of the baronial monopolies which discouraged the independent marketing of produce. Village-building was thus a rational response to a situation of uncertainty. The logic behind it was vindicated with the reversal of the long-term trend from 1615–20 onwards. After the 1620s annual wheat exports were never more than one-third of what they had been in the 1570s and 1580s. This was not because Sicily could not produce the wheat but because of the increasingly difficult terms of trade which the island had to accept *vis-à-vis* more successful countries. Consequently, more wheat was directed to the home markets, particularly to the north-east. After the 1620s feudal lords also had to come to terms with the prospect of a long-term stagnation in real income and, because of this, the increasing reluctance on the part of former *gabelloti* to take on the *gabelle* any longer. Feudal lords had no option but to rely more and more on peasant 'brokers', who, operating with marginal assets, were content with the reduced profits that were to be made from agriculture. The peasant elite from which these men were drawn enjoyed opportunities for self-advancement within every new village, right from the time of the foundation. Because they were able to lend 'cultivation capital' to other settlers in the village, they were 'rewarded' by the feudal lord with opportunities to become richer at the expense of others. The descendants of this peasant elite, moulded by the 'crisis of the 1590s', were to play an increasingly larger part in shoring up the power of the Sicilian aristocracy.

Notes: Chapter 10

1 M. Aymard, 'Amministrazione feudale e trasformazioni strutturali tra '500 e '700', *Archivio storico per la Sicilia orientale*, vol. 71 (1975), pp. 14–41; M. Aymard, 'La transizione dal feudalesimo al capitalismo', *Storia d'Italia, Annali*, Vol. 1 (1978) pp. 1133–92.

2 cf. F. Braudel, *The Mediterranean and the Mediterranean World in the Age of Philip II* (London, 1972), vol. 2, pp. 724–30; I. Wallerstein, *The Modern World-System: Capitalist Agriculture and the Origins of the European World-Economy in the Sixteenth Century* (New York, 1974), pp. 83, 160–1, 256.

3 M. Aymard and H. Bresc, 'Problemi di storia dell'insediamento nella Sicilia medievale e moderna, 1100–1800', *Quaderni storici*, vol. 24 (1973), pp. 945–76.

4 M. Aymard, 'Une croissance sélective: la population siciliene aux XVIe–XVIIe siècles', *Mélanges de la Casa de Velazquez*, vol. 4 (1968), pp. 303–27; M. Aymard, 'In Sicilia: sviluppo demografico e sue differenziazioni geografiche, 1500–1800', *Quaderni storici*, Vol. 17 (1971), pp. 417–46.

5 M. Aymard and H. Bresc, 'Nourritures et consommation en Sicile entre XIVe et XVIIe siècles', *Annales ESC*, vol. 30 (1975), p. 592.

6 A. Crivella, *Trattato di Sicilia (1590)* (Caltanissetta/Rome, 1970), p. 76.

7 M. Aymard, *Venise, Raguse et le commerce du blé pendant la seconde moitié du XVI siécle* (Paris, 1966), pp. 134 ff.; O. Cancila, 'I dazi sull'esportazione dei cereali e il commercio dei grani nel Regno di Sicilia', *Nuovi quaderni del Meridione*, vol. 28 (1969), pp. 23–4.

8 O. Cancila, 'Della rendita fondiaria in Sicilia nell'et moderna', *Archivio storico per la Sicilia orientale*, vol. 24 (1978), pp. 385–463.
9 L. Genuardi, *Terre comuni ed usi civici* (Palermo, 1907), Documenti per servire alla storia di Sicilia.
10 cf. D. Sella, *Crisis and Continuity: The Economy of Spanish Lombardy in the Seventeenth Century* (Cambridge, Mass., 1979), pp. 29–30.
11 Cancila, 'Della rendita', pp. 402–4.
12 M. Aymard, 'Il commercio dei grani nella Sicilia del '500', *Archivio storico per la Sicilia orientale*, vol. 72 (1976), p. 25.
13 M. Aymard, 'Une famille de l'aristocratie sicilienne aux XVIe et XVIIe siècles: les ducs de Terranova', *Revue historique*, vol. 247 (1972), pp. 29–66.
14 ibid., pp. 64–5; cf. Aymard, 'La transizione dal feudalesimo', p. 1185.
15 AS, Palermo, *Protonotaro del Regno*, 371, fo. 271, 15 May 1580.
16 Aymard, 'Une famille', p. 58
17 *Spadafora*, ser. II, 82, fo. 16; ser. II, 288, fos 243 ff., 4th February 1625.
18 G. Tricoli, *La Deputazione degli Stati e la crisi del baronaggio siciliano dal XVI al XIX secolo* (Palermo, 1966), pp. 41–52.
19 AS, Palermo, *Trabia*, ser. I, 52, fos. 14 ff., 7 November 1589.
20 Biblioteca Comunale, Palermo, 2Qq.G.96, fos 934 ff.; BL, Add. MS 28,396, fo. 483.
21 Biblioteca Comunale, Palermo, 2Qq.G.90, fos 109ff.; 2Qq H.111, fo. 443, eighteenth-century MSS.
22 M. Aymard, 'Une famille', p. 66.
23 O. Cancila, *Aspetti di un mercato siciliano: Trapani nei secoli XVII–XIX* (Caltanissetta/Rome, 1972), pp. 19, 174–5, 247–8.
24 H. G. Koenigsberger, *The Government of Sicily under Philip II of Spain* (London, 1951), p. 113; Braudel, *Mediterranean*, vol. 1, p. 603.
25 Cancila, *Aspetti*, p. 175; F. Ferrara, *Storia di Catania sino alla fine del secolo XVIII* (Catania, 1829), p. 151.
26 G. E. di Blasi, *Storia cronologica de'Vicerè* (Palermo, 1790), vol. 2, pt I, pp. 331, 341.
27 G. E. di Blasi, *Storia del Regno di Sicilia* (Palermo, 1833), vol. 20, p. 65; Biblioteca Nazionale, Palermo, MS. VII. E. 7, fos 92 ff., 'Discorso di dove nascè il mancamento del seminerio et il remedio che c'è bisogno', about 1605.
28 M. Aymard, 'Epidémies et médecins en Sicile à l'époque moderne', *Annales cisalpines d'histoire sociale*, vol. 4 (1973), pp. 9–37.
29 F. Paruta, 'Diario della Città di Palermo', in G. di Marzo, *Biblioteca Storica e Letteraria di Sicilia* (Palermo, 1869), 1st ser., Vol. 2, pp. 3–8.
30 Aymard, 'Une croissance sélective', pp. 220–1.
31 ibid.
32 Koenigsberger, *Government of Sicily*, p. 113.
33 F. Paruta and N. Palmerino, 'Diario della Città di Palermo', in G. di Marzo, *Biblioteca*, 1st ser., vol. 1, p. 122.
34 Di Blasi, *Storia cronologica*, vol. 2, pt I, p. 341; F. Perino, 'Varie Notizie di . . . Palermo . . . all' anno 1606', BL, Add. MS. 19,326.
35 AS, Palermo, Tribunale del Real Patrimonio, *Riveli*, Alessandria, 11 May 1593.
36 Aymard, 'In Sicilia: sviluppo demografico', pp. 442–3; see also AS, Palermo, Tribunale del Real Patrimonio, *Riveli*, Santa Caterina, 1616; Santa Ninfa, 1616.
37 *Relazione* in V. Titone, *La Sicilia spagnuola, saggi storici* (Palermo, 1948), p. 196.
38 AS, Palermo, Tribunale del Real Patrimonio, *Riveli*, Castrogiovanni, vols, 2008–10, 1607.
39 AS, Palermo, Tribunale del Real Patrimonio, *Riveli* Santa Caterain, vol. 259, 1616, fos 19, 51, 111, 151, 197.
40 See Aymard and Bresc, 'Problemi di storia dell'insediamento', and also my forthcoming general survey of the problem in *Storia d'Italia, Annali.*
41 cf. W. Kula, *An Economic Theory of the Feudal System: Towards a Model of the Polish Economy, 1500–1800* (London, 1976).
42 AS, Palermo, Villarosa, 315, passim, 11 October 1624, *Testes recepti.*
43 AS, Enna, Notari Diversi, 84, undated.

44 AS, Palermo, *Palagonia*, 518, fos 93–5, 12 December, 1603.
45 See AS, Enna, *Notari diversi*, 20 *passim*, 30 Sept 1615; AS, Palermo, *Protonotaro del Regno*, 511, fo. 216, 1615; 523, fo. 234, 19 October 1619; 537, 27 May 1624; AS Palermo, *Conservatoria del Registro (Mercedes)*, 304, fo. 65, 21 July 1623.
46 R. Gregorio, *Opere scelte*, 3rd edn (Palermo, 1845), p. 561.
47. M. Aymard, 'Bilancio d'una lunga crisi finanziaria', *Rivista storica italiana*, vol. 84 (1972), pp. 998–1021.
48 The importance of the internal market in the short term is discussed in my article, 'Changes in the structure of the wheat trade in seventeenth-century Sicily and the building of new villages', *Journal of European Economic History* vol. 12 (1983), pp. 371–405.

11 *Spain: a Failed Transition*

JAMES CASEY

The end of Spanish hegemony is an outstanding feature of European history in the seventeenth century. Though political and military defeat could be staved off for several more generations, it was from 1600 that a group of Spanish writers – the famous *arbitristas* – began to highlight the underlying economic weakness of their country: depopulation, decline of agriculture, collapse of manufactures. Some of these developments – notably the deindustrialisation of the peninsula – can be attributed in part (paradoxically enough) to increasing prosperity, as a structurally weak economy was drawn into closer commercial contact with her more advanced northern neighbours after the Discoveries in the New World.[1] But the pattern is confused because, at the same time as this long-term transition was taking place, imperial Spain was subjected to a concatenation of natural and man-made disasters. The defeat of the Armada in 1588 and the major struggle against the Dutch, the English and the French which reached a new peak in the 1590s ushered in a frantic search for more taxes that fell awkwardly on a population decimated by bad harvests and between 1596 and 1602 one of the worst outbreaks of plague in its history.[2] The task facing a historian of the 1590s in Spain, therefore, is that of determining whether the exacerbation of difficulties in that decade constituted the heart of the 'crisis', in the sense of a turning point in the economic and social development of the country, or whether the Spanish malaise had deeper roots.

A basic test is population, perhaps the chief victim of the ravages of the 1590s. The population of Spain as a whole probably rose from 7½ to 8½ million people between 1541 and 1591, then fell to 6½ million by 1650.[3] Greater precision can only be found within the local context. Here, within the last few years, it has become evident just how complex and variable the pattern can be, with the 1590s falling into place as not the only and not even the most important phase of Spain's depopulation. As regards Old Castile it is likely that the growth of population as measured by the baptismal curves was finished as early as the 1550s.[4] By 1575 the same slowing down is visible in much of the rest of the peninsula, though there were areas around Toledo and Murcia where growth continued until about 1600, and parts of Valencia and Catalonia until about 1620. A falling trend in the numbers of baptisms comes a generation or so after the onset

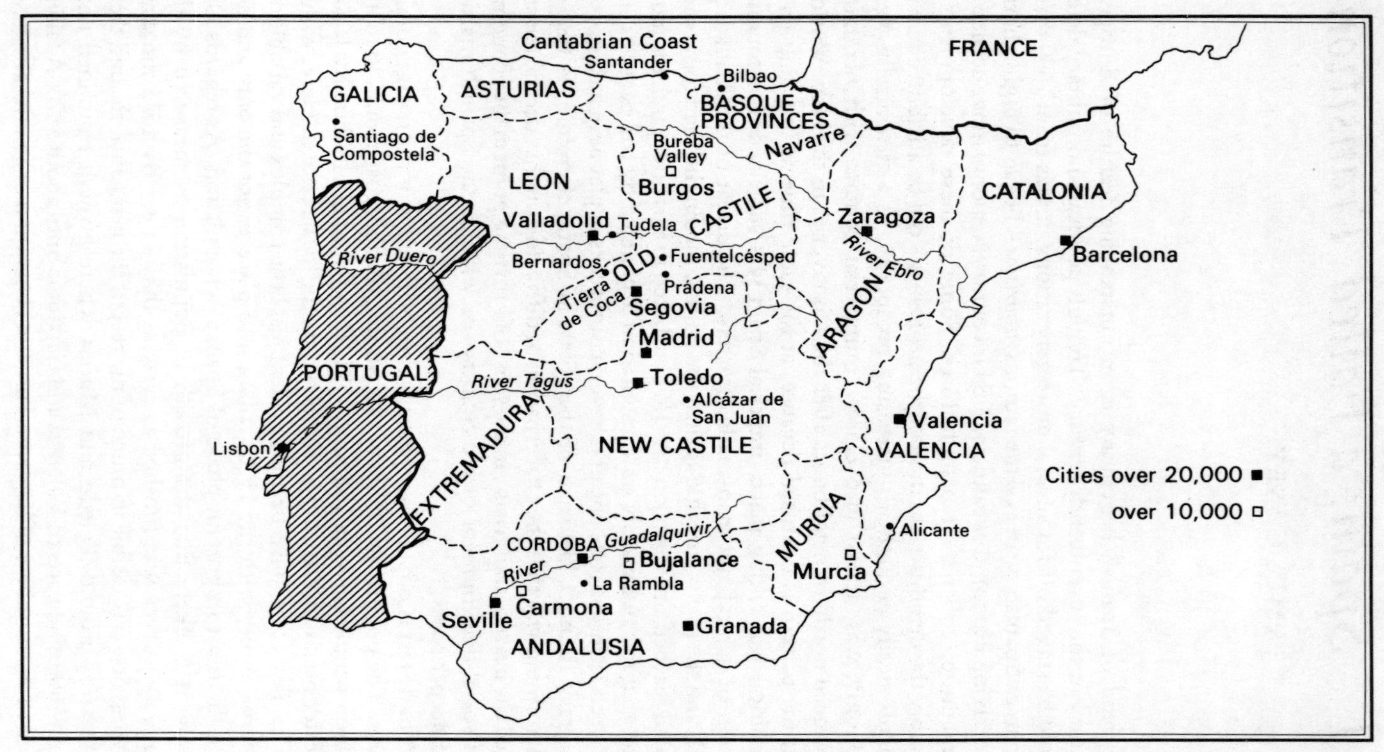

Spain in the 1590s (places mentioned in the text)

of stagnation – in Old Castile from the 1590s, in New Castile from 1600–10, on the Mediterranean seaboard (Valencia, Murcia) not until 1620–30. Indeed, in many parts of Castile as well a clear falling off in baptisms and marriages is visible only from 1620–40.[5] This last piece of evidence is particularly surprising, because it was Castile which suffered most from the ravages of hunger and disease in the 1590s.

The bad harvests of the early 1590s, especially those of 1593–4, led to a doubling or trebling of deaths throughout the Castiles. Mortality reached a paroxysm in 1599, when plague and famine carried off about one person in ten in the region, or 8 per cent of the Spanish population as a whole. True, there was a boom in marriages after the catastrophe (in a fashion familiar to demographic historians) to help repair the breach. But these alliances of widows and widowers were very infertile: the coefficient of baptisms and marriages in three Cordoban parishes sank from 4·21 in 1581–5 to only 2·8 in 1600–4.[6] The damage done by the plague could be contained, but only at great cost. Whether that cost ultimately proved supportable or not seems to be linked to the general economic context. After all, though 1599 was the single worst year in modern Spanish history, it was not unusual in kind. Subsistence crises were a recurrent feature of Castilian life, and actually more generalised in the eighteenth century than in earlier periods: yet they failed to stop the growth of population.[7]

Many Spanish communities were stagnating demographically for a generation before the great mortality of the 1590s. On the other hand, some continued to thrive, not just for a short period afterwards, but throughout succeeding generations. The sense of crisis, even in the heart of the storm (Old Castile), disappears or is very muted in towns which managed to provide a new means of livelihood for their populations, like Fuentelcésped with its vines, or Prádena with its herds, or Bernardos with its textiles.[8] Round Valladolid the thriving vineyards of Tudela de Duero enabled this village to weather the crisis well: between 1592 and 1600 baptisms exceeded burials by around a third.[9] Migration towards economic opportunity is a key feature of the story, and very evident in the case of Catalonia, whose population was kept buoyant until the 1620s by a massive influx of French workers.[10] The Cordoban towns of La Rambla and Bujalance seem to have been less affected by the crisis than their neighbours because of their healthier agricultural and industrial base.[11] The question therefore is this: What were the weaknesses in the Spanish economy generally which made the losses of the 1590s more of a running sore than they need otherwise have been?

Historians have for some time seen the late sixteenth century as a period of difficulty for Castilian agriculture. Contemporary concern was reflected in the petitions of the Cortes, with their complaints of falling production, of the lack of equipment of the peasantry, and of the latter's bankruptcy and forced sale of land.[12] Within the last few years our understanding of the problem has been transformed by the quantitative studies of younger historians working with tithe records. Round Segovia the 1590s witnessed the dramatic beginnings of a fall in grain output, culminating in the very low yields of the 1630s. In another part of Old Castile, the Bureba valley, wheat production fell by one-fifth, barley and wine by even more, over the last quarter of the century.[13] On the Mediterranean seaboard, in Valencia and Murcia, the keynote of the later sixteenth century was stagnation, before the tithes began to fall during the 1600s.[14]

Already in 1578 Juan de Arrieta had given voice to the fears of the Castilian peasantry that 'the land is becoming exhausted and the fields are not as productive as they once were'.[15] Had the expansion of population gone too far, and was Castile beginning to pay the price of a growing imbalance between pasture and arable? It is difficult to accept this interpretation in any absolute sense. Complaints about the decline of pasture and woodland are recurrent in Castilian history; one finds them as early as the 1480s and 1530s.[16] On the other hand, with no great change in her agrarian system, Spain managed to push her population up by nearly 40 per cent above its maximum in Habsburg times, to 11½ million souls by the end of the eighteenth century, most of whom were being kept alive (albeit badly) from domestic grain production.[17] In the 1590s the extent of vacant land in the peninsula was still enormous. One has only to think of the marshlands of Valencia, not properly exploited until the great expansion in rice cultivation during the eighteenth century, or the huge tracts of waste denounced by Enlightened reformers under the Bourbons – one-third of Extremadura, two-fifths of Segovia, two-thirds of Andalusia.[18] Despite the beginnings of a break-up and sale of the common lands under Philip II (1556–98) – nearly one-fifth of the Tierra de Coca in Old Castile came under the hammer in this way – it was not until the liberal legislation of the mid nineteenth century that enclosure became at all general in the peninsula.[19]

One cannot deny, however, that there *was* an increasing imbalance between arable and pasture towards the later sixteenth century. The transhumant herds of the Mesta fell from under 3 million to under 2 million head between 1550 and 1620.[20] Though we know less about the non-migratory flocks, which were possibly four times the size of those of the Mesta, inquiries of 1575 leave no doubt about a substantial decline here too. And it is from 1570 that the cattle tithes of Valencia show a clear tendency to fall.[21] To understand why, one has to remember that both farmer and shepherd were wastefully extravagant in their use of the available resources. Extensive farming, of course, is almost a law of nature in Castile, with the peasant even today only working about half the land he occupies every year under the system of biennial fallow. Cold dry winters, characteristic of the central tableland, following hard on the heels of hot dry summers, lead to intense evaporation from a soil low in humus. The land needs to wait over the winter until the rains soften it for ploughing.[22] The fallow could be and occasionally was 'robbed' by planting root crops, but these are difficult to market in an under urbanised region. Low productivity can and did lead in the sixteenth century to patterns of shifting cultivation, with the peasantry felling trees or burning pasture, scattering the ashes as a fertiliser, and then moving on after a few years of tillage.[23] The burning of the scrub sometimes led to fires, in fact, which destroyed more pasture than was intended.[24] I think it is probably in this context of social conflict between sheep-herder and dirt-farmer that one has got to understand the great series of legislative enactments of the Spanish kings, designed to protect the waste: the law of 1501 which allowed the Mesta to occupy permanently any pasture once held, at the rent originally agreed for it; the ordinance of 1633 that all pasture converted to arable since 1590 was to be restored. As Julius Klein remarked years ago, such measures were bad for the pastoralists themselves, because 'the best pasturage which the Mesta flocks could find anywhere was not the open unkempt waste lands, nor the perennially denuded leased pastures, but the stubble straw, the vine leaves left after the grape harvest, and the fertile balks and fallow strips between cultivated patches'.[25] The Spanish Cain and Abel should have been able to profit by each other's services; instead they were at each other's throats.

It was a sign of trouble when, in the name of safeguarding productivity and with the argument that the soil was 'tired' (an evocative but misleading image), the town council of Cordoba decreed a fallow of two years in three instead of one in two after 1598.[26] Yet we know that the productivity of the arable could be just as high in this territory under Philip II as under Charles III two centuries later. Focusing on yields from forty-five big farms round Cordoba, Ponsot has demonstrated the elasticity of yields rather than their unilinear improvement over time. By simply observing the traditional precepts of the writers of the period, the sixteenth-century Castilian farmer could nearly double his yield of barley and significantly increase that of wheat.[27] The difference between high and low depended on an adequate preparation of the fallow. The constant theme in the Castilian farming manuals – Herrera (1513), Arrieta (1578), Lope de Deza (1618) – is that good farming consists of counteracting the effects of a drought-prone climate on a humus-poor soil. The constant battle involves frequent ploughings on the fallow (one in the autumn, one or two in the spring, one at sowing) and regular manuring every two years, to improve the texture and moisture-retaining capacities of the soil. Otherwise, as

Arrieta pointed out, 'since they have not grasped this idea and do not follow it in Andalusia and elsewhere, they lose the grain harvest, one year because it rains too little, the next because it rains too much'.[28] In other words, the badly worked fields were prone to both waterlogging and evaporation – a remark which warns us against too much historical determinism when we come to assess the influence of climatic change on agriculture.

Certainly the 1590s were a decade of extremely bad weather in Spain. Working with chronicles and tithe records for Valencia and Murcia in the period 1580–1630, Wendy Bell has found that these regions experienced an exceptional run of wet years between 1589 and 1598, followed by unusually prolonged drought between 1603 and 1614.[29] But bad weather has to be seen in the context of the peasants' failure to respond to the crisis. As in Cordoba, the answer seems to have been the reverse of what was required: to farm more extensively and inefficiently instead of tilling and cleaning the fallow year in year out. Obviously the farmer was in a cleft stick: the herds were in decline anyway and manure was in too short supply, and the fall in population after the plague of 1599 pushed up real wages pretty dramatically.[30] Hence the temptation to go towards ever more wasteful shifting cultivation must have been irresistible.

The fullest contemporary analysis of the peasant plight is that of Lope de Deza in 1618 – a strange man, who, among some acute observations, advocated a cabinet of astrologers in Madrid to warn the countryman of bad weather ahead. Broadly his argument was that farming had become unprofitable because of high overheads (wages, debts, taxes) and low returns (the *tasa* or government price for grain which fixed a maximum, combined with the flooding of the market by cheap grain stored by municipal governments against hard times).[31] One could add the heavy burden of rents, especially to landlords (feudal dues were rather insignificant outside Catalonia and Valencia): where the peasant had to lease his land, he could find himself paying effectively between a third and a half of his harvest to his master, depending on whether he used biennial or triennial fallow.[32] This problem seems to have been growing over the later sixteenth century, as more and more land passed into the hands of non-peasant cultivators. The mechanism has been well enough described, with the peasant mortgaging his holding in order to make ends meet, only to see the creditor step in and take over when he fell behind with interest payments in years of bad harvest.[33]

Already in 1552 the Cortes had asked for a reduction of interest on these *censo* loans. But it was really from the 1570s round Valladolid that the peasantry or their villages began to borrow on a large scale to buy bread.[34] The government intervened in 1575, 1608 and 1621 (possibly with the nobility rather than the peasantry in mind) to reduce interest first to just over 7 and then to 5 per cent. But it was after the disastrous harvest of 1593 that it made its biggest move to help the peasant, refurbishing old medieval laws that prohibited the seizure of the farmer's plough or crops, except for arrears of rent or taxes, and innovating to the extent of safeguarding the person of the cultivator from gaol for debt during the 'harvest months' of July through to December. At the same time distraint on the peasantry for the debts of their feudal lords was disallowed (a measure grudgingly extended to Valencia – but only to the new settlements – after the expulsion of the *moriscos*, in 1614).[35]

Rural debt is a key feature of the crisis of the 1590s – a significant way in which short-term reverses could mortgage the future. But it was not only a reflection of hard times. Lope de Deza also blamed the urbanisation of the countryside, the new demand for the services of tailors and lawyers. The lawsuit proved only too adaptable to the timeless feuds of rural Spain: peasants 'are fearful and envious of their neighbours, and for most of their grievances see no better vengeance, no better triumph and satisfaction than going to court'.[36] Nor was the penalty of indebtedness – loss of land – necessarily as threatening and decisive as we might assume. Not all – perhaps not even most, if we are to judge by testaments – peasant obligations were secured by mortgage in the first place. A good half of peasant land belonged anyway not to the head of the household but to his wife, thanks to the operation of dowry, inheritance and jointure. The Cortes of 1579–82, 1583–5 and 1607–11 actually had to address themselves (without result) to the thorny problem of protecting the creditor against the malicious appeal by a wife that the family property was hers and had been wrongfully mortgaged by her husband![37] The debt problem led to no clean surgical operation, but to a messy conflict round 1600, in which uncertainty about rights and obligations inflicted the maximum damage with the minimum gain on Castilian agriculture. The Cortes of 1586–8 pointed out that the peasants were selling off their holdings cheap only to receive them back from the new owner on lease – which seems to bear more resemblance to a revival of serfdom than to an extension of capitalism in the countryside. Round Segovia, where two-thirds of the land was owned by the Church, the nobility and the bourgeoisie in the mid-eighteenth century, the peasantry continued to outnumber wage labourers, though now as tenant farmers mostly on the big holdings.[38]

It is still rather difficult to gauge what structural change did occur in landholding as a result of the crisis of the 1590s. In particular, leasehold, an unfamiliar new development, could be assimilated in the peasant mind (and in that of the courts) to emphyteusis. Though the written contracts specify a term of years – generally from four to six – it was costly to get rid of a tenant in Habsburg Spain since all improvements the latter had made (plantations, buildings, manure) had to be reimbursed. In Galicia and Asturias the *foro* (rather like the *domaine congéable* in Brittany) was a particularly ambiguous combination of emphyteusis and lease, being a concession of land nominally for three lives. As in Brittany in the same period, the arrangement began to break down in the later seventeenth century as the landlords began to insist on their strict proprietary rights of taking back the property at the expiry of the lease.[39] To the end of the old regime, the Spanish monarchy proved incapable of clearly distinguishing between tenant and serf in practice: in 1770 it affirmed the right of the owner to recover the land on reimbursement of improvements, but then in 1785 it specified that no incumbent was to lose his tenancy, even when the agreed time was up, unless the owner was going to cultivate the property himself.[40]

Yet clearly the spread of urban property-holding in the countryside was part of that general urbanisation of the peasantry about which Lope de Deza was complaining in 1618. Cloth-working in the later sixteenth century round Valencia, Toledo and Cordoba and the spread of viticulture in piecemeal fashion throughout Castile were tributes to this growing interpenetration of town and country.[41] One more reflection of the same trend was the spread of the mule as the typical beast of burden in Spain as in other parts of the western Mediterranean at this time. In spite of the fears of some contemporaries that the mule ploughed less deeply than the ox (the mule could only drag a ploughshare through the soil to the depth of a hand span 'between forefinger and thumb', while the ox could go in half a yard, and consequently yields were up to a half lower in the case of grain than with the ox), the evidence suggests that this lighter, more mobile animal was used only on shallower soils anyway. Above all, it came in to cultivate vineyards and olive groves, where it has a decided advantage over the lumbering ox with its dangerous addiction to green foliage, and to transport the increasing flow of goods of all kinds between town and country.[42] Arrieta surely confused cause and effect when he accused the mule in 1578 of contributing to the spread of vineyards – and of drunkenness and moral decay in the Spanish village!

In agriculture, then, the picture was not all gloom. The crisis of the 1590s reflected, perhaps, the transition towards private property in the countryside with its attendant uncertainty about pastoral rights and about the obligations of tenants, aggravated by exceptional losses of manpower and crops. Yet the breakdown of rural autarky proved woefully incomplete, as the urban market itself went into decline. Though agriculture was the basis of the traditional economy – 64 per cent of the gross national product of Castile according to one bold estimate[43] – Spain had an important industrial and commercial sector based on the manufacture of wool and silk, and on the Indies trade through Seville. Though much of this industry was geared for domestic consumption, parts of it seem to have achieved very high standards of quality: the woollen textiles of Cordoba, for example, were exported to Seville and Lisbon, presumably for shipment overseas, and Valencia was renowned for its velvets.[44]

But by the 1580s the vital woollen manufactures – in Cordoba, in Segovia – were beginning a slow decline, though the recession only became marked from around 1620.[45] In Toledo woollen and linen output dropped after 1606–7 and then again after 1619–20; in Murcia the textile industry seems to have reached the limits of growth by the 1580s; in Valencia silk manufacture reached a peak around 1580, then slipped seriously after 1620.[46] It is perhaps no accident that these years also marked turning points in the activity of the Spanish ports – the turnover in the customs of Valencia stagnating from 1570, and the great expansion in the tonnage through Seville levelling off after 1590, before both ports experienced recession after 1620.[47]

Spain may have felt the effects of the European recession of the 1590s and 1620s. But clearly she was also a victim of a growing internal pauperisation. The English merchants, when they resumed trade with the peninsula after the Peace of 1604, found it poor and denuded of silver, a good market only for foodstuffs like grain and fish.[48] In Cordoba the artisans, finding times hard, were resorting to inferior materials – using cheaper dyes for their cloths, for example.[49] Real wages were inevitably very high in the wake of the great plague of 1599. In all of these ways the demographic and agrarian crisis directly affected industry. The trouble was probably aggravated by the decline of the independent craftsman over the sixteenth century. In Cordoba the merchants controlled the supply of raw silk from faraway Murcia, and though the woollen weavers could buy their own wool locally the marketing of the finished product in distant markets was inevitably in the hands of entrepreneurs, who also increasingly had to advance the money which the weaver needed to set up his loom.[50] In a familiar enough fashion, then, growing commercialisation led to the breakdown of the old guild economy. But the transition remained incomplete, because the city fathers in Cordoba, of aristocratic rather than merchant origin themselves, insisted on maintaining the guilds in the interests of social harmony and discouraged entrepreneurs from using unqualified or domestic labour or selling unstamped wares.[51] In fact, the master craftsman at his loom, though backed up now by entrepreneurial capital, was to remain typical throughout Spain until the end of the eighteenth century, retaining a rough equality in numbers with journeymen.[52] Indeed, the merchants themselves seem to have preferred this arrangement, since it gave them greater flexibility. Thus the merchants of Segovia shifted their investments from local manufacture to export of raw wool, depending on the state of the market. The old picture of a conflict between them and the wool exporters of Burgos is therefore perhaps overdrawn. Certainly it was out of the profits they made in the raw wool trade that the Segovian industrialists financed a revival of manufactures in the eighteenth century.[53]

But the problem facing Spanish industry round 1590 was indeed that too much raw material was leaving the country unworked, a development facilitated by the control over supply which the merchants had built up in previous years – the nemesis of 'power without responsibility', of the incomplete capitalisation of the textile manufactures. The Cordoban artisans had to fight the Burgos and Seville merchants for access to raw wool, and the battle was lost as they themselves became pauperised and as the herds declined round 1580. Silk was, if anything, more directly dependent on the fortunes of agriculture. Floods in 1590 and 1626 did enormous damage to Valencian mulberry. The attitude of the government to these problems was ambiguous. Its revenues depended heavily on the strength of the Mesta and the prosperity of wool export. Likewise it had a commitment to defend the interests of landlords by prohibiting the import of raw silk when prices rose too high. There was a furious debate in the Cortes of 1619–20 on this issue, with the great silk-weaving city of Toledo demanding cheaper imports and denouncing Valencian attempts to seal off the market. By what right, it wanted to know, could the Valencian mulberry growers – who lived in a separate kingdom – claim any better access to Castile than the realms of 'China, Naples, Sicily or Italy'?[54]

On the other hand, the government did take steps to limit the export of the raw material. Already in 1462 Castilian weavers had been granted the right of first refusal on one-third of the wool clip; and the Cortes of 1551 got the Crown to increase this to one half, a measure extended to Valencia in 1572.[55] In 1552 silk-weavers were allowed to buy back, at cost price, any raw silk which a merchant had acquired for export, a provision extended to Valencia in 1587 and reaffirmed as late as 1760.[56] Other measures forbade the resale of wool or silk without some reworking, another attempt to safeguard the employment of the artisan. Despite all this, shortage of raw material remained to plague the Spanish weaver – especially as he grew poorer in the 1590s, as bread prices rocketed and herds and mulberry declined.

The other side of the coin, the growing import of foreign manufactures, was an inevitable consequence of the decay of native textiles (because I think we have to talk of decay and not just inadequate quality of the Spanish product). From 1540 the government was being apprised of the problem; by 1582 the Cortes were asking for a total ban on the import of woven silk stuffs; in the Cortes of 1588–92 protectionism was a major issue.[57] The Spanish customs was overwhelmingly a revenue-collecting machine, a simple toll with no clear discrimination between exports and imports. The famous blunder of 1548–58 when, to counter high prices, the government allowed the import of foreign textiles while forbidding the export of native, was short-lived. More serious was the cutting of Castile, Andalusia, Aragon and Cantabria into self-contained tariff zones. Though exact comparisons are difficult, it may have been more expensive to send Valencian raw silk to the weavers of Toledo than to her great competitor, Lyons. The major overhaul of the Castilian tariffs in 1564–7, bringing them close to a general rate of 7·5 per cent *ad valorem* on trade through the Cantabrian ports and 10 per cent through Andalusia or Aragon, streamlined the system but did not reform its basic deficiency.[58] It is, of course, true that Spain did have protectionist laws. From the Middle Ages bullion was a prohibited export, raw silk a forbidden import, and Castilian ships were supposed to be loaded before foreign vessels in Castilian ports. A comprehensive edict of 1623 stopped the import of almost all silk or woollen cloth. But the Spanish monarchy seems to have been rather irregular about the enforcement of its own laws; certainly it cracked down on the shipping and goods of countries with which it was at war increasingly in the seventeenth century, but it failed to stop the flood of foreign textiles.[59]

It is indeed, no longer possible to talk about the 'treason of the bourgeoisie' in sixteenth-century Spain in view of all the evidence emerging about the relative compatibility between large-scale trade and status.[60] But perhaps we can still remark the absence from the Spanish scene of a 'progressive managerial class' and agree with Immanuel Wallerstein that what was really lacking was a state system geared to the interest of the trader.[61] Round 1590 the Spanish urban sector was in crucial need of active, aggressive protection on foreign markets, as its own demographic and agrarian foundations began to fail it. Instead of that it received a double dose of punishment from a monarchy committed fundamentally to agrarian exporters, and to costly wars fought in large part for reasons of dynastic prestige. For between 1586 and 1607 Spanish military expenditure in northern Europe, against Dutch rebels and their French and English allies, reached a new peak.[62]

The 1570s are probably a turning point in the history of Castilian finance. Philip II had already inherited a critical situation on his accession to the throne in 1556. In the Cortes of 1573–5 the reality came home to the public as big new tax quotas were assigned to the Castilian towns – Seville liable for three times her previous amount, Segovia for two and a half times, Cordoba for a similar rise. But the full significance of the changes has to be grasped at the local level: in Segovia, thanks to depopulation, each family found itself paying six times by 1584 the quota in direct taxes required in 1561.[63] Though these new taxes were scaled down in 1577, the twenty-three communities of the territory of Cordoba still found themselves paying in 1590–5 some 13·6 million *maravedís* as against 4·5 million in 1557–61.[64] On top of this, the notorious excise, the *millones*, was introduced in 1590 as a response to the disaster of the Armada two years before. And worse was to come as the rates were progressively raised in the early seventeenth century – Segovia's quota 2½-fold between 1590 and 1633. After 1580 the government also began to extort benevolences from seigneurs and towns on an increasing scale.

None of this effort seems to have done much to halt the downward spiral of the crown's finances. Long-term government debts amounted to 30 million ducats at the accession of Philip II; by 1607 they may have reached 160 million.[65] The result was that the basic royal tax, the *alcabala*, was virtually mortgaged in interest payments to prominent local citizens wherever it was collected in Castile.[66] Since many Castilian towns made themselves responsible as a community for the payment of this tax, collecting it thereafter from their own citizens themselves, they resorted to borrowing as times became difficult. In fact, the growing bankruptcy of the towns was more directly worrying than that of the Crown, because more immediate in its social consequences. The interest on the Cordoban debt was 5 million *maravedís* a year around 1580, or double the annual *alcabala* tax bill, and most of this was due to the need to supply cheap bread to the poor. In Valencia it was a similar problem: heavy borrowing to feed the poor was the prime cause of the collapse of the city bank or *Taula* by 1614. In Murcia, with expenditure rising by 50 per cent between 1577 and 1596 and no growth at all in income, the council had to borrow to bridge the gap.[67] The danger was that this process became self-fuelling; inadequate accounting meant that the servicing of debts became the occasion for borrowing yet vaster sums, especially since bad harvests threw tax-collecting in most of these towns out of gear. Need one add that even the landed aristocracy were facing similar problems just about this time? With the stagnation of rural rents, familiar hand-to-mouth borrowing was converted increasingly from the 1580s into long-term mortgages, the servicing of which fell heavily in arrears by the 1600s. In Castile in 1594 and in Valencia in 1614 the Crown had to intervene to stop bailiffs seizing the goods of the peasant for the debts of his master.[68] For municipal bankruptcies there was less relief; if a town did not have commons, its citizens might well find their individual properties seized for the debts of the town hall.

As we have indicated, much of this burden had been contracted not for royal taxation alone but for the feeding of the poor. One might have expected echoes of Spain's difficulties around this time in social tension and revolt. It is from the 1580s, significantly enough, that one gets an increasing preoccupation on the part of the authorities with banditry in Valencia and Catalonia.[69] Even the more overtly political disturbances in Aragon in 1591 have to be set against a background of rural feuding on the Villahermosa estates. Bread riots in Valencia in 1605 were followed by half a century of political strife surrounding control of the municipal granary. Crime in the mountains of Toledo appears to increase with the hard times round 1610–20. Certainly in 1610 the Cortes were complaining of the hordes of well armed gypsies stalking the kingdom, and in 1611 of the problem of the sturdy beggars.[70] Yet the terrible economic reverses of these years led to very little generalised unrest. How did the government manage to weather the storm?

Fixing the price of food had played an increasing role in public policy during the sixteenth century. But there seems to be general agreement that the *tasa* was simply not respected, not even by government officials themselves, especially since transport costs could always be added on to the base price anyway.[71] Of equally doubtful efficacy were prohibitions on the export of wheat from a disaster area. Cordoba tried to use such embargoes from time to time in the sixteenth century, only to protest to the Royal Council when other towns tried to use similar prohibitions against herself. In fact, the government seems to have discouraged municipalities from arrogating authority to themselves in this way.[72] In any case privileged individuals were too numerous for any ban to work effectively. The Church refused secular jurisdiction over movement of the tithe; while in a town like Carmona, where most of the best grain lands were in the hands of absentee nobles living in Seville, most wheat was exported not by sale but in rent, which was inviolable.[73]

Actually Castile, like Valencia where there was no *tasa*, seems to have relied more on municipal granaries to hold prices down. Burgos, for example, fed a third of its citizenry with bread from its own store in 1584, while Cordoba was selling bread at 10 *maravedís* a pound in 1571 when the market price was nearer 30.[74] Already in 1491 the Crown had ordered the construction of *alhóndigas* for the better regulation of grain sales, and in 1528 allowed these granaries preference over private individuals in buying up wheat for the municipality.[75] Madrid was among the first towns in Castile to found what was properly known as a *pósito* – a deposit of wheat held by the municipal council against hard times – this as early as 1504. Combined with a system of forced provisioning from villages up to twenty or fifty miles away, it ensured a regular supply of food for the capital in Habsburg times and avoided bread riots until the one of 1699.[76] In 1555 the Cortes were asking that there should be a granary in every Castilian town. But whether this was actually achieved may be questioned. The smaller communities, at least, seem to have been without such resources if we are to judge by the demand of the Cortes of 1592–8 for municipal councils to be required to lend out grain to their peasantries for sowing, in order to halt the decline in agricultural production.[77] *Pósitos* were expensive and certainly no universal solution to bad harvests. Indeed, some commentators in the seventeenth century were criticising them as a prime cause of municipal indebtedness and a source of unfair competition to the ordinary farmer with grain to sell.[78]

Above all, they were too little help to the indigent, since the grain had to be bought (only in time of plague might it be given away). The Castilian laws on begging dated mostly from the Black Death and from the first half of the sixteenth century. The major series of measures approved by the Cortes of 1523 was periodically reissued in 1525, 1528, 1534 and 1540, and summarised in the great edict of 1565. Begging was prohibited in Castile without a licence, issued by the justices on the recommendation of the parish priest and to be reserved for the old and infirm. Pauper children were to be apprenticed. Sturdy beggars were to be dealt with by the criminal law, which specified conscription for work, whipping, or expulsion from the community. These older penalties were replaced in 1552 and 1565 with four years in the galleys for the first offence, eight years and a hundred lashes for the second, and life in the galleys for the third. Meanwhile edicts of 1544 and 1558 ordered local authorities to get beggars of all kinds off the streets and into hospitals – if there was the money to do so. In fact, the Cortes of 1592–8 rejected a proposed amalgamation of charitable endowments which had this aim in mind, on the grounds that it would override the pious will of the founders and lead to remote, inefficient administration.[79]

The crisis of the later sixteenth century gave a greater urgency to the search for some satisfactory form of 'hospitalisation' of the poor. A model *casa de misericordia* was established at Toledo in 1584, with 600 inmates funding themselves in theory through their work, and another was set up in Saragossa in 1606.[80] More common, because less costly, may have been the *albergues*, proposed by the famous doctor Cristóbal Pérez de Herrera. These were night shelters to which the licensed indigent could retreat to sleep, maintaining themselves by begging during the day. Herrera's ideas were expounded in a treatise published in 1598, and sponsored by the Cortes, which recognised at this difficult time that 'the indigent pay little heed to living regular and decent lives, causing charity to freeze'.[81] His shelters were set up in Madrid and elsewhere, but met accusations of being too expensive and apparently proved even less enduring than the *casas de misericordia*. In fact, the burden of poor relief under the Habsburgs remained firmly with the Church and private institutions. In harmony with developments in other parts of Catholic Europe, the age of the Counter-Reformation saw the proliferation of brotherhoods in Spain to care for the indigent. The Hermandad del Refugio, set up by six Robe nobles and clergymen in Madrid in 1618, collecting alms and distributing outdoor relief to carefully screened 'deserving' poor, was a model of its kind.[82] It was not really until 1766 that the Crown, faced with urban riots and a growingly dangerous proletariat, began to interest itself again in the problem of poor relief, as an urgent matter of public order. It then began to use government agents to co-ordinate funds for the establishment of official workhouses, and set up public organisations, the Diputaciones del Barrio, to handle the administration of charity to people living at home.[83]

The problem with all institutionalised systems of poor relief at an earlier period had been that the dividing line between casual labour, migrants and vagabonds was a rather fine one. Perhaps 25,000–30,000 men and women – 3 per cent of the local population – left Galicia every year for seasonal work in the harvests of Castile and Portugal.[84] On the other hand, the actual size of the dependant populations in the towns is not entirely clear. In 1665 the 240 inns and hostels of Madrid contained some 1,824 transients, in an urban population of perhaps 150,000 – but this figure would not include those sleeping rough. Paupers, defined as those who could not pay for their own burial, possibly constituted about 20 per cent of the inhabitants of Madrid in the later seventeenth century; but only about a quarter of this number ultimately found no one, no kinsman, patron or guild, to bail them out in this extremity, being thrown on to the charity of the parish.[85] A very extensive network of guilds, in fact, protected at least the artisan against the worst hardships of illness, and even (but only in a handful of cases) against widowhood and unemployment.[86] Going beyond this institutionalised protection was a certain solidarity of family and neighbourhood. Even the migrant labourers – Frenchmen and Galicians in Granada, Portuguese in Cordoba – developed personal ties with their employers, if they stayed long enough, and in any case usually had cousins already established in town. One French tavern-keeper, selling the wine produced by a local priest, left the latter three pigs at his death in satisfaction of any accounts betweeen them, 'in view of his great Christianity and the confidence I have in his plain dealing'; a Portuguese labourer, serving as foreman to a Cordoban priest, specified that 'the priest's word is to be taken for any wages owing to me'.[87] Informal loans among artisans and peasants were frequent and often against the security of a friend's word. There were attempts under Philip II and Philip IV to set up public banks – the so-called *erarios publicos* – to provide cheap loans for both individuals and government, but they came to little. It was only in 1702 that the first *Monte de Piedad* – prototype of the municipal pawnshop and an imitation of institutions employed for centuries in the communes of northern Italy – was set up in Madrid, and only in 1743 that the next one was founded in the provinces.[88] Indeed, even the charitable brotherhoods numbered only about a dozen foundations throughout Spain, as far as one can tell, during the seventeenth century. No doubt a very powerful Church and the emphasis in government policy on the *pósitos* or municipal granaries help account for the apparent sluggishness of the Spanish response to the problem of poverty.

In social policy, then, the great crisis of the late sixteenth century does not seem to have marked a turning point. Rather it reinforced the structures of a traditional Spain. The misery created by the fatal decade of the 1590s, though, hastened on structural transformations in other areas: the peasants lost more and more of their land, the artisans sank further and further into dependence. Possibly this was anyway an inevitable outcome of the growth of the population and commerce earlier in the century. The problem was that this transition was frozen: peasants and artisans were both pauperised, but they stayed by and large in control of agriculture and manufactures, a handicap for future growth. The classes which had the wealth remained prisoners of the past, trapped in the service of a horribly costly and inefficient agrarian monarchy. The crisis of the 1590s in Spain was not just a series of short-term reverses; the damage done by plague and bad harvest was slowly repaired in the seventeenth century, but the economy continued to stumble on through a succession of similar crises later, a constant prey to population problems and harvest failures throughout the eighteenth and nineteenth centuries. In that sense the problems of the 1590s were never solved, only shelved. Those difficulties were in part the outcome of a decline of older economic structures: rural and guild autarky had reached the end of the road in Spain as elsewhere in Europe by the later sixteenth century, bursting under the pressure of economic growth. But Spain's peculiar failure was an inability to complete the transition to a more urbanised economy. One can identify structural handicaps, of course: the country was one of the more barren in Europe, scantily populated, with an inferior transport system and a social structure geared to the interests of sheep-herders and warriors, which had greatness thrust upon it by the discovery of America. But to stop at this would be a caricature of reality and would ignore a healthy urban tradition with a fine standard of workmanship in textiles and steel. An opportunity was missed in the late sixteenth century, and Spaniards themselves after 1600 were prolific in their writing on the economic malaise. 'Decline' may be the wrong word to use; but a relative retardation as compared with northern Europe, a failed transition to urbanisation, there does seem to have been. The wreckage of the old without anything better to replace it – that was the real significance of the crisis in Spain.

Notes: Chapter 11

1 H. Kamen, 'The decline of Spain: a historical myth?', *Past and Present*, no. 81 (1978), pp. 24–50; cf. critique by Jonathan Israel, and Kamen's reply, in ibid., no. 91 (1981), pp. 170–85.

2 J. H. Elliott, *Imperial Spain, 1469–1716* (London, 1963), pp. 279–95.

3 A. Domínguez Ortiz, *La sociedad española en el siglo XVII*, vol. 1 (Madrid, 1963), p. 112; J. Nadal, *La población española: siglos XVI a XX* (Barcelona, 1966), p. 20.
4 B. Bennassar, *Valladolid au siècle d'or* (Paris, 1967), pp. 176–7; A. García Sanz, *Desarrollo y crisis del antiguo régimen en Castilla la Vieja: economía y sociedad en tierras de Segovia, 1500–1814* (Madrid, 1977), p. 54; A. Marcos Martín, *Auge y declive de un núcleo mercantil y financiero de Castilla la Vieja: evolución demográfica de Medina del Campo durante los siglos XVI y XVII* (Valladolid, 1978), p. 64.
5 M. Weisser, 'The decline of Castile revisited: the case of Toledo', *Journal of European Economic History*, vol. 2 (1973), pp. 614–40; F. Chacón Jiménez, *Murcia en la centuria del quinientos* (Murcia, 1979), pp. 118–25; C. R. Phillips, *Ciudad Real, 1500–1750* (Cambridge, Mass., 1979), pp. 24–5; J. Casey, *The Kingdom of Valencia in the Seventeenth Century* (Cambridge, 1979), pp. 11–13; A. Rodríguez Sánchez. *Cáceres: población y comportamientos demográficos en el siglo XVI* (Cáceres, 1977), p. 94.
6 J. I. Fortea Pérez, *Córdoba en el siglo XVI: las bases demográficas de una expansión urbana* (Córdoba, 1981), pp. 162–3; cf. Bennassar, *Valladolid*, p. 197.
7 The major new study of the performance of the Castilian population in the early modern period, based on an analysis of some seventy-nine separate parish registers, is V. Pérez Moreda, *Las crisis de mortalidad en la España interior: siglos XVI-XIX* (Madrid, 1980), pp. 245–65, 266–81 and 294–326.
8 García Sanz, *Desarrollo y crisis*, pp. 63–71.
9 Bennassar, *Valladolid*, pp. 180–3.
10 J. Nadal and E. Giralt, *La Population catalane* (Paris, 1960), pp. 79–82.
11 Fortea Pérez, *Córdoba*, p. 130.
12 *Actas de las Cortes de Castilla*, vol. 6 (Madrid, 1867), petitions 72 and 74; vol. 7 (1866), petition 20; vol. 9 (1885), petition 54; vol. 16 (1890), petition 72; vol. 26 (1906), petition 38.
13 García Sanz, *Desarrollo y crisis*, pp. 91–110; F. Brumont, *La Bureba à l'époque de Philippe II* (New York, 1977), pp. 70–4.
14 Chacón Jiménez, *Murcia*, pp. 167–8 and 256; Casey, *Valencia*, p. 66; cf. Modesto Ulloa, 'La producción y el consumo en la Castilla del siglo XVI', *Hispania*, vol. 31 (1971), pp. 5–30, for an overview of the royal share of the tithe under Philip II. Though mostly for later periods, there is a vast section on Spain in J. Goy and E. Le Roy Ladurie (eds), *Prestations paysannes, dîmes, rente foncière et mouvement de la production agricole à l'époque préindustrielle*, vol. 1 (Paris, 1982), pp. 295–461.
15 *Despertador*, reprinted in G. Herrera, *Agricultura General*, vol. 2 (Madrid, 1818), p. 217.
16 S. Haliczer, *The Comuneros of Castile: The Forging of a Revolution, 1475–1521* (Madison, Wis., 1981), pp. 12–13, 56–9 and 127–8, gives evidence of land hunger at this early period. See also Fortea Pérez, *Córdoba*, p. 135.
17 M. Colmeiro, *Historia de la economia política en España* (1863), re-ed. G. Anes, vol. 2 (Madrid, 1965), pp. 670–1.
18 M. Defourneaux, 'Le problème de la terre en Andalousie au XVIIIe siècle', *Revue Historique*, vol. 217 (1957), pp. 42–57; Colmeiro, *Economía política*, vol. 2, p. 703.
19 García Sanz, *Desarrollo y crisis*, pp. 142–6; D. E. Vassberg, 'The sale of *tierras baldías* in sixteenth-century Castile', *Journal of Modern History*, vol. 47 (1975), pp. 629–54; J. García Fernández, 'Champs ouverts et champs clôturés en Vieille-Castille', *Annales ESC* (1965), p. 715.
20 J. Klein, *The Mesta: A Study in Spanish Economic History, 1273–1836* (Cambridge, Mass., 1920), pp. 26–7; J.-P. Le Flem, 'Las cuentas de la Mesta, 1510–1709', *Moneda y Crédito*, vol. 121 (1972), pp. 23–104.
21 N. Salomon, *La vida rural castellana en tiempos de Felipe II* (Barcelona, 1973), pp. 68–71; Casey, *Valencia*, p. 71.
22 J. García Fernández, *Aspectos del paisaje agrario de Castilla la Vieja* (Valladolid, 1963), pp. 30–1.
23 M. Caxa de Leruela, *Restauración de la abundancia de España* (1632), re-ed. J.-P. Le Flem (Madrid, 1975), pp. 78–9.
24 Colmeiro, *Economia política*, vol. 2, p. 703.
25 Klein, *Mesta*, p. 328.

26 Fortea Pérez, *Córdoba*, pp. 454–6.
27 P. Ponsot, 'Rendement de céréales et rente foncière dans la Campiña de Cordoue au début du XVIIe siècle et au début du XIXe siècle', in M. A. Ladero Quesada (ed.), *Andulucía de la Edad Media a la Moderna* (Madrid, 1977), pp. 475–89.
28 *Despertador*, vol. 2, p. 275.
29 W. T. Bell, 'The climate of south-east Spain, 1580–1630'. Final Report for the Rockefeller Foundation Fellowship in Environmental Affairs (unpublished), 1980.
30 E. J. Hamilton, *American Treasure and the Price Revolution in Spain, 1501–1650* (Cambridge, Mass., 1934), pp. 272–82.
31 Lope de Deza, *Govierno polytico de agricultura* (Madrid, 1618).
32 Salomon, *Vida rural*, pp. 248–9.
33 C. Viñas y Mey, *El problema de la tierra en la España de los siglos XVI-XVII* (Madrid, 1941), pp. 33–53.
34 Bennassar, *Valladolid*, p. 261.
35 *Novísima Recopilación* 10/11/6; Colmeiro, *Economía política*, vol. 2, p. 659; F. de Cárdenas, *Ensayo sobre la historia de la propiedad territorial en España*, vol. 2 (Madrid, 1873), pp. 346–62.
36 *Govierno polytico*, pp. 37–8*v*. On the extent of the problem, see R. L. Kagan, *Lawsuits and Litigants in Castile, 1500–1700* (Chapel Hill, NC, 1981), pp. 12–15.
37 *Actas*, petitions 36, 25 and 19 of the respective dates.
38 García Sanz, *Desarrollo y crisis*, pp. 264 and 376.
39 J. F. de Castro, *Discursos críticos sobre las leyes y sus intérpretes*, vol. 1 (Madrid, 1765), pp. 191–202.
40 A. Domínguez Ortiz, *Sociedad y estado en el siglo XVIII español* (Barcelona, 1976), p. 422.
41 Weisser, 'The decline of Castile', pp. 630–1; Casey, *Valencia*, p. 89; Fortea Pérez, *Córdoba*, pp. 281–8.
42 The literature on this intriguing subject is fragmented. See A. López Ontiveros, *Emigración, propiedad y paisaje agrario en la campiña de Córdoba* (Barcelona, 1974), pp. 293–4, or J. M. Casas Torres, *La vivienda y los núcleos de población rurales de la huerta de Valencia* (Madrid, 1944), pp. 107–8, among other useful contributions from historical geographers. The best overall view is still that of Arrieta, but more especially Deza, *Govierno polytico*, fos 34*v*-6: '[the mule] earns as much on a day off as when he is ploughing' – that is, thanks to carting services.
43 J. Gentil da Silva, *En Espagne: développement économique, subsistance, déclin* (Paris, 1965), pp. 92–3.
44 Fortea Pérez, *Córdoba*, 358–77.
45 F. Ruiz Martín, 'La empresa capitalista en la industria textil castellana durante los siglos XVI y XVII', *Third International Conference of Economic History* (Munich, 1965), pp. 267–76; J.-P. Le Flem, 'Vraies et fausses splendeurs de l'industrie textile ségovienne', *Produżione, commercio e consumo dei panni di lana: atti della seconda settimana di studio di Prato* (Florence, 1976), pp. 525–36.
46 R. Ling, 'Long term movements in the trade of Valencia, Alicante and the western Mediterranean, 1450–1700', unpublished PhD thesis, University of California, 1974, pp. 62, 73; Chacón Jiménez, *Murcia*, pp. 360–1; Weisser, 'The decline of Castile', p. 631.
47 P. Chaunu, *Séville et l'Amérique* (Paris, 1977), pp. 270–1; A. Castillo, 'La coyuntura de la economía valenciana en los siglos XVI y XVII', *Anuario de Historia Económica y Social*, vol. 2 (1969), pp. 4–13.
48 H. Taylor, 'Price revolution or price revision: the English and Spanish trade after 1604', *Renaissance and Modern Studies*, vol. 12 (1968), pp. 5–32.
49 Fortea Pérez, *Córdoba*, pp. 289–306.
50 ibid., pp. 358–77.
51 ibid., pp. 378–88. Of course the Spanish experience in this respect was not at all unique. The commitment of municipal magistrates to the maintenance of the guilds in the interests of public order emerges from C. R. Friedrichs, 'Capitalism, mobility and class formation in the early modern German city', *Past and Present*, no. 69 (1975).
52 V. M. Santos Isern, 'Sederia i industrialitzacío: el cas de València 1750–1870', *Recerques*,

vol. 5 (1975), pp. 111–35; M. Garzón Pareja *La industria sedera en España* (Granada, 1972), p. 112; García Sanz, *Desarrollo y crisis*, pp. 216–20.

53 García Sanz, *Desarrollo y crisis*, pp. 234–5. The proto-capitalist phase of both Segovian and Cordoban weaving seems to bear out recent interpretations of the remarkable resilience of the artisan economy in continental Europe generally. See R. Du Plessis and M. C. Howell, 'Leiden, Lille and the early modern urban economy', *Past & Present*, no. 94 (1982), pp. 49–84.

54 *Actas*, vol. 35, pp. 384–5.

55 R. Carande, *Carlos V y sus banqueros*, vol. 1 (Madrid, 1949), p. 109.

56 A. Martínez Sarrión and A. García Sanz, 'La decadencia del cultivo de la seda', *Saitabi*, vol. 6 (1948), pp. 154–5; Garzón Pareja, *La industria sedera*, pp. 160–1.

57 Le Flem, 'Vraies et fausses splendeurs', p. 533; V. Vázquez de Prada, *Historia económica y social de España*, vol. 3 (Madrid, 1978), p. 580.

58 M. Ulloa, *La hacienda real de Castilla en el reinado de Felipe II* (Madrid, 1977), chs 6–9.

59 J. Israel, 'A conflict of empires: Spain and the Netherlands, 1618–48', *Past & Present*, no. 76 (1977), pp. 34–74; Casey, *Valencia*, pp. 96–8.

60 R. Pike, *Aristocrats and Traders: Sevillian Society in the Sixteenth Century* (Ithaca, NY, 1972), pp. 99–129; H. Kamen, *Spain in the Later Seventeenth Century, 1665–1700* (London, 1980), pp. 261–6.

61 I. Wallerstein, *The Modern World-System*, vol. 1 (New York, 1974), pp. 191–7.

62 G. Parker, 'The economic costs of the Dutch revolt', in J. M. Winter (ed.), *War and Economic Development: Essays in Memory of David Joslin* (Cambridge, 1975), p. 55.

63 Ulloa, *La hacienda de Felipe II*, pp. 211–13; García Sanz, *Desarrollo y crisis*, pp. 330–2.

64 Fortea Pérez, *Córdoba*, p. 139.

65 I. A. A. Thompson, *War and Government in Habsburg Spain, 1560–1620* (London, 1976), p. 72.

66 Bennassar, *Valladolid*, p. 254; Chacón Jiménez, *Murcia*, pp. 229–31.

67 Fortea Pérez, *Córdoba*, pp. 207–8, Chacón Jiménez, *Murcia*, p. 242; Casey, *Valencia*, pp. 163–5.

68 C. Jago, 'The crisis of the aristocracy in seventeenth century Castile', *Past & Present*, no. 84 (1979), pp. 60–90.

69 J. Reglà, *El bandolerisme català del barroc* (Barcelona, 1966), pp. 91 ff.; S. García Martínez, *Bandolerismo, piratería y control de moriscos en Valencia durante el reinado de Felipe II* (Valencia, 1977), pp. 61 ff.

70 *Actas*, vol. 26, pp. 163–5; M. Weisser, *The Peasants of the Montes* (Chicago, Ill., 1976), p. 106. There were also riots in Madrid in 1591, and unrest in Toledo and Seville – quite apart from the tenacious opposition of the Cortes to the Crown's fiscal demands in this decade. See G. Parker, *Philip II* (Boston, Mass., 1978), pp. 183–5.

71 Vázquez de Prada, *Historia económica*, pp. 544–5; Chacón Jiménez, *Murcia*, p. 287.

72 Cárdenas, *Propiedad territorial*, vol. 2, p. 326; Fortea Pérez, *Córdoba*, pp. 211–13.

73 M. González Jiménez, *El concejo de Carmona a fines de la edad media* (Seville, 1973), pp. 259–60.

74 Ulloa, 'Producción y consumo', pp. 16–17; Fortea Pérez, *Cordoba*, p. 205.

75 Haliczer, *Comuneros*, p. 51; Cárdenas, *Propiedad territorial*, vol. 2, p. 326.

76 C. L. Carlson, 'The vulgar sort: common people in siglo de oro Madrid', unpublished PhD thesis, University of California, 1977, pp. 79–83.

77 Actas, vol. 16, petition 88.

78 Deza, *Govierno polytico*, fos 58*v*–9*v*, though balanced in his own opinion, summarises the main arguments against.

79 *Novísima Recopilación* 7/39/1–26, 7/38/3 and 12/21/4; J. Soubeyroux, *Paupérisme et rapports sociaux à Madrid au XVIIIe siècle*, vol. 1 (Paris, 1978), pp. 324–5. Some development towards consolidation was under way, though: cf. W. A. Christian, Jr, *Local Religion in Sixteenth Century Spain* (Princeton, NJ, 1981), pp. 168–9.

80 M. Jiménez Salas, *Historia de la asistencia social en España en la edad moderna* (Madrid, 1958), pp. 99–102 and 196. On Toledo see now L. Martz, *Poverty and Welfare in Habsburg Spain*' (Cambridge, 1983).

81 ibid., pp. 103–11; cf. M. Cavillac, 'Noblesse et ambiguïtés au temps de Cervantes: le cas du docteur Cristóbal Pérez de Herrera', *Mélanges de la Casa de Velázquez* vol. 11 (1975), pp. 177–212.

82 W. J. Callahan, *La Santa y Real Hermandad del Refugio y Piedad de Madrid, 1618–1832* (Madrid, 1980), cf. Brian Pullan, 'Catholics and the poor in early modern Europe', *Transactions of the Royal Historical Society*, 5th ser., vol. 26 (1976), pp. 15–34.

83 Soubeyroux, *Paupérisme*, vol. 2, ch. 11; W. J. Callahan, 'The problem of confinement: an aspect of poor relief in eighteenth century Spain' *Hispanic American Historical Review*, vol. 51 (1971), pp. 11–12.

84 A. Mejide Pardo, 'La emigración gallega intrapeninsular en el siglo XVIII', *Estudios de Historia Social de España*, vol. 4 (1960), pp. 461–606.

85 C. Larquié, 'Une approche quantitative de la pauvreté: les madrilènes et la mort au XVIIe siècle', *Annales de démographie historique* (1978), pp. 175–96; J. Fayard and C. Larquié, 'Hôtels madrilènes et démographie urbaine au XVIIe siècle', *Mélanges de la Casa de Velázquez*, vol. 4 (1968), pp. 229–58.

86 A. Rumeu de Armas, *Historia de la provisión social en España* (Madrid, 1942), p. 363.

87 Archivo de Protocolos de Granada, *escribanía* Nicolás González 1740, fos 472–5*v*; Archivo de Protocolos de Córdoba, *escribanía* Baltasar del Castillo 1638, fos 126*v*–8*v*.

88 Rumeu de Armas, *Previsión social*, pp. 418–19; Colmeiro, *Economia política*, vol. 2, pp. 1093–9. There were, of course, political reasons to explain the failure of the *erarios* since they were designed to get the municipal elites to pay more money to the government through this medium.

PART TWO

12 Demographic Crisis and Europe in the 1590s

DAVID SOUDEN

Few European countries escaped the ravages of sharply increased mortality, with dramatic surges in numbers of deaths in particular years, at the tail end of the sixteenth century. Combined with widespread military activity, climatic change, and general economic difficulties, mortality conditions help mark the 1590s as a 'crisis' decade. Inadequate food supplies through the failure of harvests, the action of epidemic disease and the depredations of war, provide the basis for these mortality surges. The purpose of this chapter is to provide a framework for comprehending the nature of 'crisis mortality' and its extent over the Europe of the 1590s. What should also emerge is that the importance of crisis mortality *per se* has often been overplayed, particularly in looking at turning points in the growth of regional populations, and that the characteristics of mortality crises are often misunderstood.

Thus, as many of the contributions to this book amply demonstrate, the mortality conditions which prevailed do not of themselves constitute a 'general crisis' – but in combination with other features they could add to such a crisis. It is unfortunate when attempting a commentary such as this that records of greatest utility to the demographic historian are scarce or non-existent for the period. Some interpretative difficulties are the result of using available sources uncritically. Reference to the experience of other periods and regions and the application of logic may help remedy some of these difficulties.[1]

A primary and obvious handicap to such a venture is the paucity of systematic series of parish or other vital registrations of births, marriages and deaths. Many if not most regions have few such data series which are the essential means of gauging the characteristics, and something of the impact, of the enormous upward leaps in numbers dying in a given period. For many areas we are forced back upon contemporary descriptions and incomplete data which, as we shall see, require of the historian a particular level of critical awareness of the nature and characteristics of 'crisis' mortality. Even where parish registers are available we must be cautious; baptismal registers tended to appear before burial registers, and the registration of burial of infants and children may lag significantly behind that of adults.[2]

The occasional existence of nominal listings, *libri status animarum*, produces quantitative evidence for age- and status-structural change in local populations. Such sources have been little studied, and are often of only limited utility, but they do provide an estimation of 'populations at risk' and can, in the absence of other information, provide some clues to the causation and impact of demographic change.

Since scarce sources prevent us from examining most mortality crises of the 1590s directly, this commentary is aimed elsewhere – at the specification of problems in the identification and nature of crisis, isolating likely causes, interconnections and effects, and at squashing some of the myths and misunderstandings which often surround this subject. There is some danger in using evidence from more recent populations and from other cultures in an attempt to illuminate the character of mortality crisis at the end of the sixteenth century, but demography is a study based partly upon physiological and biological attributes which are likely to be constant, and partly upon the art of the possible. Although this discussion may play down the effects of 'pure' demographic crisis, particularly its longer-term effects, a careful specification of what one should look for, and may expect to find, in this subject will be of benefit.

I

The contributions to this volume show something of the chronology of crisis mortality. Crises of subsistence and 'famine' especially mark southern Europe in the early 1590s, northern Europe in the later. Reports of mortality crises from inadequate harvests are found for example in the Po valley in 1591, Tuscany 1590–2, Naples 1591–5, Sicily 1590–1;[3] for Spain in 1590–2, and again 1593–4;[4] and for southern France in 1590–3, especially in 1592.[5] Then over the years 1596–8 subsistence crises and famines are recorded for Scotland,[6] for northern and western England,[7] for northern France, especially the Beauvaisis, Anjou and the Île de France,[8] in Sweden,[9] in the southern Netherlands[10] – generally across Europe.[11] Commentators are usually agreed that the failure of the food supply was a common cause of widespread deaths, the result of acute pressure of population upon increasingly scarce economic resources. Whilst reports of high grain and other food prices do not necessarily entail dearth-related mortality crises, contemporary commentary and subsequent analysis do suggest some link. Moreover, it is often held that a population weakened by the failure of its food supply was inherently more susceptible to diseases.

Whether or not that was the case, disease, and especially bubonic plague, hit many regions of Europe in the decade. Severe outbreaks of plague in Catalonia, and particularly Barcelona, occurred in 1589–91, whilst plague ravaged Bari and other areas of Italy in 1590–2.[12] In the same years typhus affected Tuscany, accompanying the dearth crisis there.[13] The years 1592–3 saw bubonic plague in England and elsewhere.[14] In 1595–8 Switzerland, eastern France and south-west Germany were hit by plague, especially in the towns, whilst northern France experienced plagues in 1596–8, and southern France in 1597–8.[15] Rural Castile was particularly hard hit, with plague (and possibly other diseases) raging through the period 1597–1602.[16] Plague is noted again in Italy with outbreaks in Savoy in 1599.[17] As the range of diseases widened and the spread of transmission undoubtedly increased – the result above all of more extensive trading and communications within and outside Europe[18] – so the virulence and general impact of many diseases seems to have been heightened. Certain diseases such as smallpox would hit indiscriminately a population which had not yet acquired sufficient immunity to withstand it (and thus would produce a far greater overall impact upon the population), whilst relatively irregular epidemics such as bubonic plague, particularly in northern areas of Europe, were of sufficient intensity to produce widespread mortality and to have a high case-fatality rate.[19]

Climatic variation is a clear link between the two phenomena of dearth and disease. 'Blocking' conditions characterise the decade's weather with long severe winters and wet alternating with drought summers a marked feature. Not only would this have had a deleterious effect upon harvests of most food crops, and upon animal stocks, but it would also promote certain ranges of diseases – respiratory complaints and perhaps typhus in winter months, waterborne infections and bubonic plague in summer.[20]

Added to this catalogue of disasters is the mortality effect of extensive and prolonged warfare, especially in France.[21] Some areas were ravaged by armies: settlements were attacked, destroyed or deserted, resources were confiscated and work routines disrupted, and food supplies were interrupted.[22] The combination of warfare, plague and dearth, as in Burgundy and in Brittany in the late 1590s, could prove a devastating mixture.[23]

Our sources and the work of historians therefore provide us with both a chronology of major increases in numbers dying and an outline of the causal factors behind it. Nevertheless, we need to go much further, to investigate more of the characteristics of mortality and of crises, and to test some of the assumptions that historians tacitly or explicitly use.

II

A priority must be to assess the nature of mortality conditions, and how we might define a 'crisis' within those conditions. Only by attempting to distinguish the normal from the abnormal may we begin to understand the character of this particular demographic regime. We need to know the frequency with which crises occurred, and the patterns of diffusion by which the causes of those crises may have spread. Since spreading presupposes the occurrence of crisis in more than one location, knowing the number and characteristics of places affected and the relative intensity of those crises is of great utility. That provides not only evidence for the causation of crises (on which we are commonly less than sure), but also a means of comparing place with place, time period with time period.

Even in a population with stable levels of mortality, stochastic variation will produce short-run variance in numbers of deaths, and chance is likely to produce a very occasional sharp upward or downward movement in those numbers. The historian who has available running series of deaths needs ways of determining whether or not perturbations in these time series are likely to be the product of random variation, or to be the result of abnormal conditions. Several means of measuring such variability have been devised, deciding whether or not a particular deviation represents a 'crisis' in the sense of a significant deviation from a 'normal' prevailing level. Those methods have been of varying degrees of sophistication.[24] Whilst many are content to take a doubling of numbers of deaths over a year compared with a group of preceding years,[25] others contend that this does a disservice. Although any distinction between 'normal' and 'crisis' is necessarily arbitrary, one can choose from methods involving moving averages (weighted or unweighted)[26] or movement outside bounds marked by standard deviations;[27] methods using two passes at the data so as to eliminate crisis years which hide other crises or sequences of high mortality years;[28] and complicated formulæ taking the size of the total population and some measure of psychological impact to produce a comparative measure of intensity for crises.[29] But in few areas do we possess anything approaching a consistent set of vital registrations, and in even fewer areas a set of population totals.

Thus we are left with problems that are often intractable. Only for England is there a demographic series that may be treated as a national one, based upon a representative sample of local series.[30] In some countries we have a number of such local data series, in others few or none. Although contemporaries provided information and commentary on the incidence of crisis, and expressed their horror at the effects of surges in mortality, we need to know more about the prevailing mortality conditions. Terms such as 'plague' could cover a multitude of diseases, whilst contemporaries' or historians' concentration upon untypical cases or places may produce a false impression of the scale and incidence of crises.[31] Carefully examining underlying assumptions about the nature and impact of crisis mortality, and testing those assumptions against available data, produces a more coherent analysis.

It is easy, but fallacious, for example, to conflate *variance* and *level* in mortality trends. The fact that numbers of deaths peak in certain years does not necessarily mean that levels of mortality are high except in the very short run. A naive example may help. Assuming a population which will have 1,000 deaths distributed over ten years, those deaths may be evenly distributed (100 per annum) or unevenly – say, 40 in each of five years, 100 in each of another three years, 200 in another year, and 300 in another. Whilst the mortality outcome, other things being equal, remains the same, the difference between the two instances in terms of annual variation is extreme. Moreover, over another ten-year period the number of deaths may be doubled but the proportional distribution of deaths could remain the same. In other words, there is not a necessary relationship between moving totals of deaths and medium-to-long-term measures of mortality, between variance and level. This is demonstrated particularly well for England, on which considerable information is now available. The 1590s witnessed an especially concentrated set of mortality crises. Although particular years were by no means the worst in a ranking of mortality crises in England during the sixteenth, seventeenth and eighteenth centuries, the number of years affected by crises and the widespread nature of those crises is striking. National death rates rose significantly, measured on an annual basis: but expectations of life at birth were little altered except in the very short term. Moreover, those expectations of life were remarkably high – the seventeenth century saw a deterioration in overall mortality conditions, and the late-sixteenth-century heights were not to be regained on a national basis until the second quarter of the nineteenth century.[32] The assumption that Europe moved from high mortality marked by high variance to lower and more stable mortality over the early modern period is a dangerous one.[33]

Caution must again be exercised in determining the number and the character of locations affected by crises. In any widespread mortality surge, not all places would be equally affected, whilst in a series of such calamities some places might be hit once, others hit on each occasion, and others emerge unscathed. The clearest statistical evidence for this again comes from England; five of the 404 parishes in Wrigley and Schofield's sample escaped without a single month of crisis mortality in the long period that they cover. In 20 per cent of the parishes there were fewer than three months per century, and in another 20 per cent more than twenty months per century, a mortality crisis.[34] Other countries might not have such extensive data coverage, but there is evidence of the variability of mortality experience within as well as between regions. The evidence from the typhus epidemics of 1590–2 in Tuscany shows that, of eighteen burial series, sixteen saw a mortality crisis (defined as 40 per cent or more excess mortality). Of those, four series saw a quadrupling, four a trebling and three a doubling in numbers dying during the crisis.[35] Moreover, regional differences are highlighted by the fact that for the years 1580–1600 the whole of Italy experienced 30 years of crisis per 1,000 years (defining a crisis as a 50 per cent increase) whilst Tuscany experienced 57 per 1,000 (on a 100 per cent increase definition).[36]

In Spain, a number of places which had been affected by the mortality surges of the early 1590s escaped the great ravages of plague mortality in the last years of the decade comparatively lightly. The geographical extension of that latter epidemic is clearly marked, covering northern and southern coastal areas, a major concentration in the northern interior, and possibly also covering much of Portugal.[37] The variability of timing and impact of mortality crisis within the Pays Nantais is highlighted by Dupâquier's analysis.[38]

That mortality crises did not necessarily strike everywhere, or were of widely varying degrees of severity, may be obvious but is often overlooked. The fact that contemporaries would have been more likely to comment upon or report the most severe occurrence of a crisis may lead to an overstatement of its magnitude, or a misunderstanding of its characteristics. Concentration upon the very heavy plague mortality in the town of Santander in 1599, for example, has often disguised the fact that the most widespread and deadly plague epidemics occurred in rural areas of central Spain at that time.[39] Particular forms of widespread mortality peaks may also disguise the extent of those crises: plague epidemics have often received more attention since they tended to be concentrated in larger urban centres and to have identifiable and lethal characteristics, whereas subsistence crises in marginal regions away from political centres and lines of communication may have been less readily recognised.[40]

The evidence suggests that the lethal character of mortality crises is often overemphasised. Although mortality levels may be very high in the short run, this is by no means necessarily the case in the longer term. As we shall see, we are rarely able to 'predict' a demographic outcome simply on the basis of the existence of a mortality crisis. Moreover, even when a country or region was hit hard by mortality crisis, by no means all places were affected, or affected with equal severity – and in successive crises it was rare for the same areas to be affected on each occasion.[41]

III

We must be cautious in reaching conclusions about the nature of mortality crises – but must exercise even greater care in linking mortality conditions with other demographic phenomena, in positing links between subsistence and disease, between nutrition and fertility.

The belief is widespread that those who are malnourished, either as a result of continued low nutritional levels or in the wake of severe harvest failure, are more susceptible to, and more likely to die from, infectious diseases than are those who are well nourished.[42] This is initially plausible but the assumption is based more upon reiteration than upon evidence, with the expectations of association between the two being so widely held that they have moulded scholars' views. The dramatic nature of epidemic and of subsistence crisis may help exaggerate the coincidence of their occurrence.

For human populations the evidence is sparse and inadequate. Studies of Third World populations in which a substantial proportion are malnourished and in which disease is a major factor in mortality have produced inconclusive results. The differentials between the mortality patterns of particular groups is as much a result of other social and economic attributes as it is of nutritional status. In the case of infants and children, the evidence does seem clearer that their mortality is increased by chronic malnutrition. Even this conclusion is not as clear-cut as it may seem: in modern Bangladesh, for example, recognised areas of chronic malnourishment have only some 10 per cent of their children actually diagnosed as severely malnourished. Given the economic conditions of Europe at the time with which we are here concerned, that would seem an unduly severe comparison to make.[43] European experience during the Second World War similarly questions assumptions that nutrition levels and disease are intimately linked – notably in the case of the resilience of the Dutch population in the face of famine, and the evidence of long-term survival of those incarcerated in the Warsaw ghetto.[44]

The association of some diseases, notably typhus, with subsistence crises is common.[45] Here again we must guard against confusing cause and effect. Conditions which produce one may well produce the other, whilst the upheaval accompanying a subsistence crisis, usually through the process of migration, may aid the spread of disease. The manner in which bubonic plague commonly affected poorer areas more than wealthy areas in a town probably has less to do with the nutritional status of those groups, than with the fact that in poorer areas overcrowded housing and an inability to flee prolonged exposure to the contagion.[46]

The evidence on the interrelationship between poor nutrition and disease is inadequate: intermediate variables usually appear more important in explaining the coincidence of the two varieties of crisis.[47] Until more evidence is forthcoming, the historian should be sceptical of conclusions that epidemics would tend to hit – and hit hardest – a population weakened by the failure of subsistence.

Evidence on the follow-through from diminished nutrition to subsequent fertility similarly needs sceptical attention. For in recent years historians have been interested in the possible links between food supplies and fertility. Popularised by Emmanuel Le Roy Ladurie, the concept of 'famine amenorrhoea' has been widely employed to explain depressed fertility accompanying and following harvest failure and famine conditions.[48] In conditions of chronic malnutrition, ovulation may cease.[49] Taking that further, some have suggested that chronic or endemic malnourishment will result in depressed female fertility, the consequence of longer periods of post-partum amenorrhoea (the infertile period after the birth of a child) and of a greater frequency of anovulatory cycles.[50] Initially attractive as a means of explaining differential levels of fertility, and of explaining demographic behaviour in the wake of a mortality crisis (particularly when populations failed to grow and recoup losses through mortality), this interpretation does not withstand critical examination.[51] At any given duration of breast-feeding amongst women studied in Guatemala and Bangladesh, for example, there is little difference in the length of post-partum amenorrhoea irrespective of nutritional status, and little difference in the period of 'waiting time' to the next conception.[52] Breast-feeding practices (in extending periods of post-partum amenorrhoea and in reducing levels of infant mortality) and sexual abstinence (whether voluntary or resulting from the temporary absence of one partner) are commonly found to be the most important intermediate variables in explaining differential fertility in non-contracepting populations. The use of information from modern developing nations may again appear gratuitous, but the links which have been postulated between nutrition and fertility are essentially physiological ones, and thus basic relationships should not differ in fundamentals from one population to another.[53]

The available evidence therefore suggests that close and direct links between nutrition levels and fertility are not found except in the most savage conditions of famine and malnourishment. This is not to deny the fact that mortality crises were often accompanied by contemporaneous falls in numbers of conceptions, but such falls are almost certainly the result of the postponement of marriages, the temporary absence of a spouse in an attempt to find work or food, and of diminished coital frequency either from deliberate abstention or a loss of sexual appetite. Biological control mechanisms in the form of amenorrhoea and increased foetal wastage seem to be of little importance in such crises except the most catastrophic.

IV

If some of the biological features often assumed to be part of the demographic follow-through of a mortality crisis turn out to be suspect, what may we say of other features? We have already seen that a mortality crisis was not necessarily a major blow to the dynamic of a population and its rate of increase: for reasons that have been outlined, a short-run sharp upward fluctuation in a mortality series may have had few lasting repercussions; a high degree of variance in a low-level mortality environment, in which deaths are packed into certain years, may mean that some lives have been curtailed, but others lengthened, measured against their expected lifespan. The ability of a population to regain lost members through a fertility 'bounce back' is well known, a result of the combination of postponed and current marriages and fertility.[54] The extent of the recovery would depend at least in part upon the mortality characteristics of the crisis: whilst little net effect would result from heightened mortality of the elderly and of infants, the considerably increased mortality of an adolescent and young adult age-group would result in a 'hollow generation' with depressed total fertility.[55] The belief of Italian demographers that the population of their peninsula was kept in check in the long term relies upon their contention that repeated mortality crises had just these total-fertility-depressing characteristics.[56] Until we know more of the characteristics and age-specific patterns of mortality in these crises, such conclusions remain tentative.

It is a commonplace in the literature to regard the mortality crises of the 1590s as 'Malthusian visitations', as the operation of the positive check envisaged by Thomas Malthus upon a population which had grown rapidly through much of the sixteenth century in most European regions. The pressure of numbers upon relatively scarce economic resources, particularly the food supply, would lead to a thinning of the ranks. Irrespective of the fact that population losses in the 1590s were often temporary, this interpretation ignores the accidental nature of most of the mortality crises. Unless we accept the principle of a guiding hand, we cannot necessarily expect or predict natural phenomena – climatic variation, harvest failure, particular forms of contagion – and the calamities they may bring.[57] Perhaps only at the most extreme level of population pressure are 'positive checks' of widespread mortality bound to occur; the likelihood is that 'preventive checks', adjustment within the population itself, would intervene long before that position was reached.

What thus are we to make of the belief that mortality crises often represent not only a check upon the growth of a population but also a turning point? Catastrophic mortality crises of the late sixteenth and early seventeenth centuries have generally been accepted as one of the decisive factors in the decline of Spain.[58] This ignores the fact that some regions which were hit hardest by crises still had buoyant populations until well into the seventeenth century whilst other, less clearly affected, areas were already in decline.[59] Similarly in France, various chronologies of growth and stagnation are found which operate independently of the incidence of crises.[60] The processes of demographic growth are an epiphenomenon of wider economic trends, and are reflected for example in migration trends. In a buoyant population positions vacated by deaths in a mortality crisis might be filled from elsewhere, but in economically less beneficial circumstances would often be left unfilled.[61]

Changes wrought within a population through shifts in fertility and migration patterns, rather than exogenous factors, may thus be a potent element in the growth or stagnation of populations that we see buffeted by the (external) mortality crises of the 1590s. The occurrence of mortality crises may well disguise the true demographic turning points in populations which did decline. The case for falling fertility levels has been argued persuasively for England in the seventeenth century.[62] Studies of Bergamot villages in northern Italy suggest that fertility restriction (above all through an increased unmarried proportion in the adult population) rather than emigration or generational mortality effects are the key to population decline there in and after the 1590s. Similar claims could be made for Spain, and for seventeenth-century Flanders, for example.[63]

So the evidence presented here suggests that mortality crises rarely had an overwhelming effect *in themselves* upon early modern European populations, not least in the critical decade of the 1590s. The ability of those populations to make good their losses was considerable – in some circumstances the population decided not to use those resources for recovery or, in the face of economic adversity, were already undergoing change.

V

The 1590s occupy a prime position in the mortality peaks of the sixteenth century. Although it may be tempting to do so, these crises should not be seen as cataclysmic nor as unduly representing Malthusian solutions. The main consideration in this brief commentary has been with the *demographic* aspects of mortality crises – their political and economic repercussions, which were usually of greater significance, are considered extensively in many of the other contributions. The absence of detailed demographic information for most European countries at this time should make the historian especially cautious: that absence has often resulted in cavalier assumptions being made and inappropriate conclusions being reached. The intention of this commentary has been to examine critically the assumptions and preconceptions which historians have had, by looking at the nature of crises, their components and their likely longer-term effects, at their local and national incidence, and at the interaction between various demographic phenomena. For mortality crises have often had to bear more weight in interpreting the course of economic and political change in this period than they warrant.

> La mortalité finie, les hommes l'oublièrent;
> Ceux qui n'avaient pas de femme, la cherchèrent;
> Les femmes restées veuves se remarièrent,
> Jeunes ou vieilles de même se portèrent.[64]

Notes: Chapter 12

1 This commentary is based upon an oral presentation at the Leicester conference in 1981. I wish to thank Peter Clark, Peter Burke and other participants in the conference, Richard Smith, Roger Schofield and Jessie McLeman for advice before and after the event.

2 M. Livi-Bacci, *La Société italienne devant les crises de mortalité* (Florence, 1978), pp. 38–47: almost half of the Italian dioceses first had parish registers kept within them in the period 1550–99, but burial registers were not widely kept except in northern towns; V. Pérez Moreda, *Las crisis de mortalidad en la España interior, siglos XVI–XIX* (Madrid, 1980), pp. 27–44; M. P. Gutmann, *War and Rural Life in the Early Modern Low Countries* (Princeton, NJ, 1980), p. 155; E. A. Wrigley and R. Schofield, *The Population History of England, 1541–1871: A Reconstruction* (London, 1981), p. 57, show 80 per cent of their 404 parish register sample to be in observation by 1600.

3 A. Belletini, 'La démographie italienne au XVIe siècle: sources et possibilités de recherche', *Annales de démographie historique* (1980), pp. 19–38, esp. pp. 36–7; Livi-Bacci, *La Société italienne*, p. 51; see P. Burke, above, p. 180; T. Davies, above p. 197.

4 Pérez Moreda, *Las crisis de mortalidad*, p. 255.

5 M. Greengrass, above, pp. 116, 127.

6 M. Flinn *et al.*, *Scottish Population History from the Seventeenth Century to the 1930s* (Cambridge, 1980), pp. 116–17.

7 A. B. Appleby, *Famine in Tudor and Stuart England* (Liverpool, 1978), pp. 109–54; Wrigley and Schofield, *Population History*, pp. 670–2.

8 P. Goubert, 'Recent theories and research in French population between 1500 and 1700', in D. V. Glass and D. E. C. Eversley (eds), *Population in History* (London, 1965), pp. 457–73, esp. pp. 463–6. J. Jacquart, *La Crise rurale en Île-de-France, 1550–1670* (Paris, 1974) pp. 179–82, 597–608; P. Benedict, above, p. 95.

9 G. Ütterstrom, 'Climatic fluctuations and population problems in early modern Europe', *Scandinavian Economic History Review*, vol. 3 (1955), pp. 3–47, esp. pp. 27–8.

10 L. Noordegraaf, above, p. 77.

11 Appleby, *Famine*, pp. 133–4.

12 Pérez Moreda, *Las crisis de mortalidad*, pp. 253–5; Burke, above, pp. 179, 181.

13 Livi-Bacci, *La Société italienne*, p. 51.

14 Wrigley and Schofield, *Population History*, p. 675.

15 E. A. Eckert, 'Boundary formation and diffusion of plague: Swiss epidemics from 1562 to 1669', *Annales de démographie historique* (1978), pp. 49–80, esp. pp. 52–5; Benedict, above, p. 95; Greengrass, above, p. 117; H. Schilling, above, p. 137.

16 Pérez Moreda, *Las crisis de mortalidad*, pp. 245–93.

17 Eckert, 'Boundary formation and diffusion of plague', p. 53.

18 E. Le Roy Ladurie, 'Un concept: l'unification microbienne du monde (XIV$_e$–XVII$_e$ siècles)', *Revue suisse d'histoire*, vol. 23 (1973), pp. 627–96.

19 J.-N. Biraben, *Les Hommes et la Peste en France et dans les pays européens et méditerranéens* (Paris, 1975), Vol. 1.

20 See, for example, the disease 'check list' in R. S. Schofield, 'An anatomy of an epidemic: Colyton, November 1645 to November 1646', in *The Plague Reconsidered: A New Look at Its Origins and Effects in Sixteenth and Seventeenth Century England*, Local Population Studies suppl. 3 (Matlock, 1977), pp. 95–126, esp. p. 121.
21 Benedict, above, pp. 91 ff; Greengrass, above, pp. 115 ff.
22 Jacquart, *La Crise rurale*, pp. 179–82.
23 Gutmann, *War and Rural Life*, pp. 152–6, shows (albeit for a later period) that war in itself was not a particularly significant factor behind widespread mortality crisis, but was especially important in combination with other factors, above all harvest failure.
24 The widest-ranging discussion of this is in H. Charbonneau and A. Larose (eds), *The Great Mortalities: Methodological Studies of Demographic Crises in the Past* (Liège, 1979).
25 cf. the pioneering work of J. Meuvret, 'Les crises de subsistance et la démographie de la France de l'Ancien Régime', *Population*, vol. 1 (1946), pp. 643–50, and the recent work of F. Lebrun, 'Les crises demographiques en France aux XVIIe et XVIIIe siècles', *Annales ESC*, vol. 35 (1980), pp. 205–34.
26 Wrigley and Schofield, *Population History*, pp. 332–42.
27 L. del Panta and M. Livi-Bacci, 'Chronologie, intensité et diffusion des crises de mortalité en Italie, 1600–1850', *Population*, vol. 32 (1977), pp. 401–46.
28 J. Dupâquier, 'L'analyse statistique des crises de mortalité', in Charbonneau and Larose, *The Great Mortalities*, pp. 83–112.
29 T. H. Hollingsworth, 'A preliminary suggestion for the measurement of mortality crises', in Charbonneau and Larose, *The Great Mortalities*, pp. 21–8.
30 Wrigley and Schofield, *Population History*.
31 See the concluding comments in L. Noordegraaf, above, pp. 80–1, on contemporaries' and historians' views upon the relative situation in northern and southern Netherlands.
32 Wrigley and Schofield, *Population History*, pp. 230–1, 242–3, 528, 531.
33 M. Flinn, 'The stabilisation of mortality in pre-industrial Western Europe', *Journal of European Economic History*, vol. 3 (1974), pp. 285–318.
34 Wrigley and Schofield, *Population History*, pp. 685–6. Distance from a market town and population size were the most important explanatory variables for this phenomenon: pp. 691–3.
35 Livi-Bacci, *La société italienne*, p. 51.
36 Ibid., pp. 58–9.
37 Pérez Moreda, *Las crisis de mortalidad*, pp. 125–7, 259, 277–8. Also V. Pérez Moreda, 'The intensity of mortality crises in Spain: an outline of their regional differences over time', in Charbonneau and Larose, *The Great Mortalities*, pp. 179–98; B. Bennassar, *Recherches sur les grandes épidémies dans le nord de l'Espagne à la fin du XVIe siècle: problèmes de documentation et de méthode* (Paris, 1969).
38 Dupâquier, 'L'analyse statistique', pp. 99–100, using data from A. Croix, *Nantes et le pays nantais au XVIe siècle: étude démographique* (Paris, 1974).
39 Pérez Moreda, *Las crisis de mortalidad*, p. 120.
40 See particularly Appleby, *Famine*, and J. Ruwet, 'Crises démographiques: problèmes économiques ou crises morales? Le pays de Liège sous l'Ancien Régime', *Population*, vol. 9 (1954), pp. 451–76. The political dimensions of mortality crises and dearth are discussed in R. B. Outhwaite, above pp. 32 ff, and in P. Clark, above, pp. 57 ff.
41 In England the epidemic mortality of 1603–4 predominantly affected the south and east of the country, whilst the subsistence crisis of 1596–7 resulted in excess mortality principally in the north and west: Wrigley and Schofield, *Population History*, pp. 672–4.
42 This view is enshrined in the World Health Organisation's survey of the then available literature: N. W. Scrimshaw, J. E. Gordon and C. E. Taylor, *The Interactions of Nutrition and Infection*, WHO monographs no. 77 (Geneva, 1968).
43 E. van de Walle and S. Watkins, 'On the unlikelihood of Malthusian equilibria in history', paper presented at 'Hunger and History' conference, Bellagio, 1981, pp. 17–25; G. R. Solimano and M. Vine, 'Malnutrition, infection and infant mortality', in S. H. Preston (ed.), *Biological and Social Aspects of Mortality and the Length of Life* (Liège, 1982), pp. 83–112.
44 Z. Stein *et al.*, *Famine and Human Development: The Dutch Hunger Winter of 1944–45* (Oxford, 1975).

45 Livi-Bacci, *La Société italienne*, pp. 48–53; C. Bruneel, *La Mort dans les campagnes: le duché de Brabant aux 17e et 18e siècles* (Louvain, 1977).
46 This is demonstrated, for example, in P. Slack, 'The local incidence of epidemic disease: the case of Bristol, 1540–1650', in *The Plague Reconsidered*, pp. 49–62.
47 Of course, the two do not always or necessarily coincide: Wrigley and Schofield, *Population History*, pp. 349–53.
48 E. Le Roy Ladurie, 'L'aménorrhée de famine (XVIIe–XXe siècles)', *Annales ESC*, vol. 24 (1969), pp. 1589–1601.
49 cf. Stein *et al.*, *Famine and Human Development*, pp. 73–6.
50 Summarised in R. E. Frisch, 'Population, food intake and fertility', *Science*, vol. 199 (1978), pp. 22–30. T. McKeown, *The Modern Rise of Population* (London, 1976), for example, uses this literature to explain depressed fertility in many historical populations.
51 J. Bongaarts, 'Does malnutrition affect fertility? A summary of evidence', *Science*, vol. 207 (1980), pp. 564–9; J. Mencken, J. Trussell and S. Watkins, 'The nutrition fertility link: an evaluation of the evidence', *Journal of Interdisciplinary History*, vol. 11 (1981–2), pp. 425–41.
52 ibid., pp. 435, 438.
53 For a demonstration of this with historical populations, those of England and also of Belgium and Germany, see C. C. Wilson, 'Marital fertility in pre-industrial England', unpublished PhD thesis, University of Cambridge, 1982.
54 This is investigated statistically by Ron Lee in his contribution to Wrigley and Schofield, *Population History*, pp. 356–401, esp. pp. 359–66.
55 These effects are explored in H. Le Bras, 'Retour d'une population à l'état stable après une catastrophe', *Population*, vol. 24 (1969), pp. 861–96.
56 Livi-Bacci, *La Société italienne*, pp. 80–4; L. del Panta, *Le epidemie nella storia demografica italiana (secoli XIV–XIX)* (Turin, 1980).
57 T. R. Malthus, *An Essay on the Principle of Population* (London, 1798; reprinted for the Royal Economic Society, 1926), pp. 63–73, is the basis for the 'positive check' interpretation. Malthus modified his position in later editions. Amongst recent commentators, see D. B. Grigg, *Population Growth and Agrarian Change: An Historical Perspective* (Cambridge, 1980), pp. 11–13, 40–7; van de Walle and Watkins, 'On the unlikelihood of Malthusian equilibria'.
58 See the comments in Pérez Moreda, 'Intensity of mortality crises in Spain', p. 179.
59 Pérez Moreda, *Las crisis de mortalidad*, pp. 246–7; J. Casey, above, p. 211.
60 Benedict, above pp. 96 ff.
61 A. Humm, *Villages et hameaux disparus en Basse-Alsace: contribution à l'histoire de l'habitat rural (XIIe–XVIIIe siècles)* (Strasbourg, 1971), pp. 32, 71, showing how villages which disappeared were already in decline, the process being accelerated rather than caused by war and mortality crises. Also see Gutmann, *War and Rural Life*, pp. 148–50.
62 Wrigley and Schofield, *Population History*.
63 D. Sella, 'A Malthusian crisis in late sixteenth century Italy: the case of two rural communities', paper presented to Asilomar conference, March 1982; Casey, above, p. 211; Bruneel, *La Mortalité dans les campagnes*, p. 615, concludes after his lengthy examination of mortality conditions: 'La crise n'est qu'un frein de portée limitée. Les rênes sont ailleurs, du côté de la fécondité.'
64 Ranallo Buccio on Aquila, quoted in Livi-Bacci, *La Société italienne*, p. 67.

13 Popular Disorder

C. S. L. DAVIES

It would have been astounding if the *fin de siècle* economic crisis had not produced its share of popular disorders. A series of bad harvests or, worse, devastating outbreaks of plague, compounding a long-term deterioration in living standards to produce what may well have been the low point in the living standards of the mass of the European population at any rate since the Black Death, would seem an infallible formula for massive popular unrest which must challenge the social order. And it is not difficult to piece together an impressive-looking series of revolts and disturbances, the more especially if the 'nineties' for this purpose can be stretched to begin in 1585 and to drag on in some circumstances into the first decade of the next century.

The *bilan* has been memorably drawn up by Henry Kamen (who suggested that 'never before in European history had so many popular rebellions coincided in time') and by Winfried Schulze; further details can be added from the contributions to this volume. For France not merely the 1594–5 rising of the Croquants in Limousin and Périgord could be instanced, but also the whole extraordinary phenomenon of a social revolutionary urban Catholicism in Paris and in other Leaguer towns. Upper Austria, the area around Linz, in which peasant revolt seems to have been endemic, was in open revolt between 1595 and 1597. Revolt spread into Lower Austria, the normally much more peaceful area around Vienna, in 1596–7; properly organised peasant armies, stiffened by a number of deserters from the Turkish war, were dispersed by the traditional mixture of military force and largely spurious promises of relief. In Naples in 1585 a crowd lynched and ritually dismembered a magistrate during a riot over the price of bread; 820 were involved in the subsequent trials, and, allegedly, 12,000 (out of a total population of a quarter of a million) fled the city. The rural subjects of the city of Basle refused, for the years from 1591 to 1594, in the so-called 'Rappenkrieg' ('farthing war'), to pay a tax levied for the indemnity owed by the city for its recent quarrel with the bishop. Transylvanians (1595), Moldavians and Wallachians (1593 onwards), and Bulgarians (1598) rose against their Turkish overlords. There were serious rebellions in Istanbul and in Anatolia. There were risings in the Polish Ukraine in 1591–4 and in 1595–6; and the 'Club War' in Finland in 1596. The years 1601–4 saw the Russian Time of Troubles.[1]

Disorder on a lesser level than full-scale revolt was also widespread; see for instance, the meticulous list for England drawn up by Peter Clark, or the note on German towns by Heinz Schilling.[2] Banditry was clearly at a peak both in Naples and in the Papal States in the late 1580s, and also in Catalonia in the 1590s.[3] Anatolia was plagued by the brigandage of the *levendat*, bands of landless men, including uprooted peasants and deserters from the Ottoman army.[4] More generally, criminal statistics, in so far as they can be trusted, tend to show at least an increase of indictments for theft in years of bad harvests, reflecting, no doubt, in part heightened anxiety and readiness to prosecute on the part of the authorities, but also probably, some degree of actual increase in crime as necessity drove men and women to desperate measures.[5] There is evidence too for a rise in prosecutions for witchcraft – most strikingly, the epidemic in Scotland in 1597, but also, for instance, in the Rhineland, in Bavaria, and in Franche-Comté.[6]

The list is an impressive one; the 1590s were clearly a period of severe social dislocation. But it is perhaps more surprising that the effects were not much more dramatic. England, after all, saw, in Peter Clark's phrase, a 'crisis contained'.[7] Scotland suffered severely from famine between 1594 and 1598 and from plague from 1597 to 1599, and this may be linked to the witchcraft craze. But the only large-scale disorder seems to have been the riot in Edinburgh in December 1596; presumably hunger and desperation were a contributory factor, although the riot itself was caused by rumours of a popish plot to massacre king, councillors, and ministers. In the event James VI was able to turn the incident to his advantage against the advanced Presbyterians who had associated themselves with the more 'popular' party in Edinburgh politics.[8]

Norway (where there had been severe peasant revolt in the 1570s) was apparently quiet, as was Sweden; both countries hard hit by the famine of 1596–7 which was background to the Finnish 'Club War'.[9] Poland was called on to provide additional exports to the west, which both provoked a very large rise in grain prices locally and added to the attraction of large-scale cultivation on noble estates which was reducing the Polish peasantry to a condition of serfdom. Nevertheless there seems to have been extraordinary inertia on the part of both townsfolk and peasants, in spite of attempts to stir up revolt by the Ukrainian Cossacks.[10] As for Russia, the response to the manifold oppressions of Ivan the Terrible's reign (war taxation, disruption of the traditional landholding system, exploitation, indeed sheer plunder by the Tsar's *oprichniki*, Tartar invasion) had been flight to the newly opened up lands of the south and east. The 1590s, strictly interpreted, saw a period of respite; though they saw, too, the perfecting, in 1592–3 of the decrees banning peasant movement and so closing, in so far as it was effective, the safety-valve of migration. It was the murderous famine of 1601–4 that was to unleash the Time of Troubles with its succession of pretenders to the Crown and, in 1606–7, the rebellion of Bolotnikov, first of the series of peasant revolts which punctuate Russian history in the seventeenth and eighteenth centuries.[11]

Most of Germany remained quiet. East of the Elbe, the 'second serfdom' was pressed home intensively. There were isolated instances of resistance in 1593 and 1607 in Lusatia (at Pulsnitz) and in Silesia (Glogau), but very little in Mecklenburg, Brandenburg, and Pomerania, where the second serfdom was pressed most intensively. There was little resistance in Germany west of the Elbe. The exceptions were some isolated peasant risings in Bavaria, each confined to particular lordships in 1596 – in the county of Haag, and in the lordships of Rothenfels and Stanfen, where the peasants succeeded in their protest against the increase of dues and rents until they were crushed by mercenary troops in 1598. Disturbances in fact continued in Bavaria and the Alpine area adjoining Austria (possibly inspired by the Austrian example) into the next decade. Each of these German incidents, however, was confined to a single lordship. There was no hint of a general rising as there had been in 1525, or even of a rising on a regional scale.[12]

Spain, too, is remarkable for an absence of popular revolt, except in the negative sense that the Crown successfully played on the resentment of the Aragonese peasantry against their lords to defeat the Aragonese rebellion.[13] There seems to be nothing in Portugal, although the English did their best to stimulate the still acute nostalgia for independence attested by the phenomenon of pretenders claiming to be King Sebastian, who was killed at the Battle of Alcazar in 1578.[14] There was little popular disorder in the United Provinces in spite of the taxation burden; Leo Noordegraaf talks of fears of food riots and reports of unrest, but instances only some military mutinies as actual disorders.[15] Nor was there much in the southern Netherlands.[16] Even in Italy there seems to be nothing in the way of large-scale revolt after the 1585 insurrection in Naples had been suppressed, although there were attempts to instigate revolts in Naples in 1591 and 1592.[17] In spite of the Marquis of Favara's search for evidence of sedition in Sicily, nothing very serious seems to have happened beyond the circulation of subversive ballads and the barracking of the departing governor.[18]

In general, the tally of disturbances seems less impressive than it was in some earlier periods: the 1520s, the 1540s, the late 1560s and early 1570s especially. And it was, for much of Europe, and particularly for Spain and Italy (let alone the special circumstances of Germany in the Thirty Years War), much less bad than it was to be in the late 1620s. The impression of the 1590s is of an age in which Western Europe as a whole teetered on the edge of the abyss of social disaster but drew back just in time.

In drawing up league tables of disorder, it is very difficult to be sure of comparing like with like. Winfried Schulze, for instance, includes the Oxfordshire rising of 1596 (which did not actually take place) in his list of major risings along with the Croquants and the Austrian peasant revolts.[19] An apparent absence of disorder might (as Faber admits for the United Provinces) reflect an absence of research in the particular field by historians, or perhaps less interest by governments and therefore fewer traces in the records.[20] So Peter Clark can produce a list which consists largely of minor riots. Heinz Schilling can produce disorders in German towns which have been overlooked by other historians. The same meticulousness elsewhere would no doubt unearth a good number of riots in 'peaceful' areas. The non-specialist historian asserting a negative is giving a hostage to fortune.

There are also problems of definition. Most peasant revolts attract some support from members of the higher classes – whether from sympathy and a feeling of *noblesse oblige*, or to use the occasion for their own political ends. An extreme example would be 'a peasant revolt' encouraged by a government against its own rebellious nobles. A striking case is the Finnish 'Club War' in which Duke Charles, then regent of Sweden, encouraged the peasants to rise 'if by no other means, then with stakes and clubs' against Finnish nobles who remained loyal to the displaced Swedish King, Sigismund Vasa.[21] In conditions of foreign domination (Ireland, for instance, or the Balkans under Ottoman rule), a revolt led by ethnic chiefs against the occupying government might have a strong social ingredient. There is something artificial, in sixteenth-century circumstances, in trying to abstract purely 'popular' revolts. It is dangerous, therefore, to use revolts as an index of social discontent; too many variables enter into the question of whether grievances will provoke a revolt, and what form that revolt will take, even if an agreed measuring rod were available.

Two examples from England in the 1590s may illustrate the hazards involved in too mechanistic a correlation between economic crisis and revolt. Cumbria was, as Andrew Appleby has shown, one of the areas of England harder hit by the crisis of 1594–7; perhaps the hardest hit. Yet it saw little if anything in the way of recorded disorder.[22] It might be tempting to explain this in terms of 'areas of stable poverty' being immune to revolt, were it not that Cumbria in 1536–7 had in fact staged a dramatic revolt in conditions of bad harvest, though less bad than those of 1597. The difference lies surely in the absence in the 1590s of the peculiar political circumstances which were present in 1536–7: the unprecedented attack by central government on local landowners, whether monastic or lay-aristocratic, the questioning of traditional popular religious practices, the existence of an easily identifiable scapegoat (Thomas Cromwell and all his works), and the example of widespread rebellion throughout the north of England.[23] By contrast, the so called Oxfordshire rising of 1596 was in fact scotched by government before anything came of it.[24] Had government been less vigilant or had security on the part of the conspirators been less ineffective, it is conceivable that a large-scale revolt against enclosure might have been generated in the Midland counties. Had such a rising taken place it would have been far easier to explain it in terms of the economic *conjuncture* than it is for the 'Midland Rising' of 1607.[25] Explaining why revolts do not happen may not be a very enlightening exercise in itself. But an awareness of the contingencies involved is surely salutary. This is not to deny the general proposition that economic difficulties increase the degree of social tension; it is to suggest that the way that social tension expresses itself is determined not only by structural social factors but by a whole range of apparently extraneous events.

The most important of these is war. The turmoil which raged along the European boundaries of the Ottoman empire – a border dominated on both sides by semi-independent warriors not always to be trusted to direct their attention to the enemy – is striking here. The Cossacks, supported by the Polish crown as a defence against the Turks, upheld or stimulated the resistance of Ukranian peasants against the imposition of Polish landlordism; large-scale revolts took place between 1591 and 1594, under a renegade Pole, Christopher Kosínski, and again under the Cossack Nalewajko (Nalivayko) in 1595–6.[26] The Austrian-Turkish war of 1593–1606 saw ambitious princes taking the opportunity to play off the super-powers against each other, and periodic revolts from below, by peasants goaded by the depredations of rival armies. Several Turkish satellites, Sigismund Bathory of Transylvania, Aron of Moldavia, and, above all, Michael the Brave of Wallachia attempted to establish their independence by playing off the Habsburgs, Poles and Turks against one another.[27] Michael's revolt (1594) produced a resonance through the Balkans, the more especially as it represented militant Orthodoxy against Islam; and revolt sometimes took the form of peasant resistance to the demands of Ottoman lords. Michael's adventurous career began with his annihilation of a troop of Turkish tax-collectors and soldiers in Bucharest. But, although he is sometimes represented as a leader of social protest, his rule depended on the support of the boyars; the peasantry suffered not only increased taxation but the codification of laws binding them to the soil.[28] The Bulgarian 'Turnovo' revolt of 1598 was inspired by Michael's activities. The native landowners had been eliminated following the Turkish conquest some two centuries earlier and replaced by Islamic *timariots*. The revolt, organised by merchants and by upper clergy, may therefore be described as 'social' as well as 'national'. With the withdrawal of Michael's troops it was soon crushed, as were the anti-Turkish revolts in the Balkans.[29]

Meanwhile the Transylvanians, manoeuvred into a pro-imperial position by Sigismund Bathory, found themselves, after several tergiversations by their rulers, eventually occupied by an Austrian army; reaction against its excesses, made worse by famine conditions in 1604, led to the successful revolt by Stephen Boeskay, who returned Transylvania to its traditional position of semi-independence within the Ottoman orbit.[30] In 1605–6 the Hungarian nobles (in alliance with Boeskay) seized the opportunity to win a guarantee of their traditional freedoms from their Habsburg sovereigns, with the result, following a desperate revolt by peasants and ex-soldiers (*haiducks*) in 1607, of an even fiercer imposition of labour services and a definition of serf status in the following year.[31] Similarly successful manoeuvring by Croatian nobles to establish their liberties in 1608 led to an abortive peasant revolt.[32] The net effect of these eastern European movements, everywhere except the Ukraine (where military power was not in the hands of the landlord class), was the strengthening of seigneurial liberties against governments and a decisive step on the road to the 'second serfdom'.

The rapid growth of Istanbul led to frequent and severe grain shortages in the second half of the sixteenth century.[33] It seems, however, to have been the rapid inflation from 1580 onwards, due to debasement, the influx of silver from the west, and the strain of war (with Iran 1578–90 and from 1603–12, and with the Austrians, 1593–1606), that produced the spate of revolts which shook the Ottoman Empire at the turn of the century. The feudalistic (or, in Weber's terminology, 'prebendal') *timariot* system by which the cavalry spahis were maintained was undermined by inflation, while the spahis themselves were becoming militarily obsolete. The more adaptable janissaries needed regular payment; the consequent rapid increase in taxation produced rural depopulation and banditry. Istanbul was shaken by janissary revolts in 1589 (significantly, a famine year), and in 1591–2, and by a spahi revolt in 1593; indeed, the Austrian war may have been undertaken to provide constructive distraction for soldiers. There was another janissary revolt in 1598, and spahi revolts in 1601 and (in association with religious students) 1603. Meanwhile Anatolia, hit by taxation, debasement of the coinage, and military depredation and famine, saw the succession of 'celali' (*jelali*) revolts in 1598 and from 1603–8. These seem to have been on a massive scale (20,000 men were alleged to have taken part in 1598), and to have involved desperate peasants, brigands, and military deserters.[34]

In Austria, the burden of war, the short-term economic crisis, and the longer-term increase of labour services and crushing of peasant status worked together to produce the two risings of 1595–7. The 1590s were certainly a difficult decade in Austria; prices were at record levels (though they rose even higher in the years 1600–1604), and the purchasing power of a Viennese building craftsman was in 1599–1600 at its lowest point (index 33; 100 = 1521–30) for the period 1520–1770.[35] The rebels in upper Austria protested at increased taxes; at increased labour services (*robot*); at rents, dues, and seigneurial monopolies (the sale of wine, use of mills, etc.); in general, at an increasingly intrusive lordship hampering the economic activity of the peasants, and appropriating to the lords the fruits of increased demand for agricultural products. In lower Austria the initial rising was provoked by military service and by taxation. The peasants somewhat unrealistically promised to defend their country (the initial revolt coincided with the great Turkish victory at Mezo Keresztes in Hungary) provided that the troops and dues were raised according to the ancient form, and that they were led into battle by their lords.[36] Bohemia, on the other hand, provides a rather surprising lack of armed risings, due apparently to relative moderation on the part of lords; a situation which of course was to change dramatically after the crushing of Bohemian independence in 1621, and the subsequent imposition of much heavier dues and services.[37]

The effects of war in western Europe are familiar enough, and hardly need elaboration. France provides the most striking example. Reaction against taxation and against the pillaging by troops was obviously the immediate occasion of the Croquant rising, even if, as Greengrass suggests, Bercé's account underestimates the very real underlying social antagonisms.[38] The religious war undoubtedly exacerbated the economic crisis; equally it can be seen, in part, as a result of it. It had been renewed, on a far larger scale, after some thirteen years of relative peace, in 1589. The roots of that renewal obviously lie much further back. Events in Paris provide the immediate cause; and the build-up of that extraordinary populist Catholicism in Paris and in other towns was stimulated by the famine years 1585–7, and perhaps by the plague years of the early eighties. But events would have worked out very differently but for the death of the Duke of Anjou in 1584, which provoked a succession crisis, and the evolution of the international political situation. It would need an extraordinarily naive faith in the possibilities of counter-factual history to guess at what would have been the situation in France if dearth and disease had been the only disturbing factors. In the event, as Benedict suggests, economic disaster, by accentuating the political crisis, strengthened the desire for peace and for social order.[39]

Ireland provides a case in which war appears to be the paramount factor. Certainly, as Outhwaite demonstrates, Ireland shared in full measure in the general dearth of 1594–8; and the climatological determinist might be tempted to associate the outbreak of the Ulster rebellion in 1594 and the adherence of Hugh O'Neill in 1595 with extreme economic desperation. There seems, however, no indication that this was so; rather the policy adopted by both sides, destruction of crops and driving away of stock, made matters much worse. When nature began to relent from 1598, military activity was accentuated. O'Neill was supported by a flourishing agriculture in Tyrone and Tyrconnell; Mountjoy found it 'incredible in so barbarous a country how well the ground was inhabited . . . The wheat we destroyed was valued at above ten thousand pounds . . . the chief treasure wherewith they do entertain their bonaghts'. 'When the plough and breeding of cattle shall cease, then will the rebellion end.' Mountjoy instituted a scorched-earth policy. 'I presumed that man's wit could hardly find out any other source to overcome them but by famine.' He was all too successful: reports flowed in of roaming wolves, of corpses found in ditches, their mouths stuffed with docks and nettles, and even, by hearsay, of cannibalism. Some riots broke out in the towns in 1603. These seem to have been in reaction to the influx of refugees from the stricken countryside, and to a debasement of the coinage in 1601. Catholic hopes were also raised by rumours that James VI was a secret sympathiser.[40]

Taxation for war, the supply of men, and the problems of discharged soldiers and sailors added to the tension in England in the 1590s. War taxation was naturally high in the United Provinces. The southern Netherlands experienced the aftermath of devastation, and suffered military mutinies more frequently and on a larger scale than those which had caused such disastrous results in 1573–6.[41] War taxation told heavily on the Spanish economy, and fell especially on the shoulders of the Castilian peasants. The provision of grain for military and naval forces added to the problems caused by deficient harvest, while the suspension of payments by the Crown in 1596 was a blow to the economy of northern Castile.[42] And yet in none of these cases did strain produce large-scale disorder, any more than it did in countries spared from war, such as most of Germany outside Austria, or Scotland, or indeed Italy after the insurrection in Naples in 1585.[43] The surprising feature about western Europe in the 1590s is not the extent of popular disorder but, by and large, its successful containment.

No single factor will explain the situation. Social disorder or its absence is explicable by particular circumstances, on a national or indeed a provincial or local level, whether these be enduring features of social structure, or such variables as the immediate reaction of those in authority. The usual difficulty of explaining a negative makes this operation particularly hazardous; why the Polish peasantry was so passive in the face of increased exploitation does not seem satisfactorily explained.[44] In the Spanish Netherlands the key to passivity lies, presumably, in the very presence of the Spanish army, complete with the emigration to the United

Provinces which removed the more militant, the more ambitious and the more desperate from the scene; emigration, too, resulted in a labour shortage which helped to keep real wages at the extraordinarily high level characteristic of the Netherlands as a whole during the second half of the sixteenth century.[45] High wages, too, were a feature of the United Provinces, their benefit far from cancelled by the high level of indirect taxation. Price controls were enforced, emergency grain stocks efficiently organised, and control of guilds and militia by the town regents was close. Social conflict seems only to break out in the United Provinces as a by-product of a fracture in the ruling class, and then only on a small scale – for instance, the struggle between Oldenbarnevelt and Maurice, Remonstrants and Counter-Remonstrants, in 1617. The position of Amsterdam as the grain market of western Europe and the ready availability therefore of Baltic grain was a crucial factor here.[46]

Baltic grain, indeed, is a key factor in alleviating local food shortages not only in the Netherlands but also in England, Scotland, and even to some extent in Spain and Italy. Even though the amount of Baltic grain shipped through the Sound was relatively small in aggregate terms (enough to feed about 750,000 people according to one calculation), the margin was invaluable in dearth years; the very much greater fluctuation in prices on, in Wilhelm Abel's words, the inland east-west axis from Lwow to Orleans is very striking. Increased production in Italy, and notably in Lombardy and Sicily, helped, too, to ease the problem in the Mediterranean.[47]

Nevertheless, the apparent quiescence in Spain is one of the most difficult problems in any comparative study, especially given the very real burdens of war in the 1590s on top of what seems to have been dearth in 1593–4 and 1598–9 and plague from 1596 to 1602. To take the obvious comparison with the 1640s, the absence of protest outside Castile is no doubt attributable to the reluctance of Philip II to interfere with provincial liberties; Catalonia, Aragon, Valencia and Portugal were comfortably cushioned from the full burden of the war effort.[48] Nevertheless, this point only accentuates the difficulty of explaining Castilian passivity, especially as grain imports could do little to alleviate a dearth in a largely landlocked kingdom with poor communications. The government, no doubt stimulated by memories of the Castilian *Comuneros* and the Valencian *Germanía*, seems to have decided that, in a society with a dangerously high proportion of landless and often casual labourers, the greatest threat to social stability came from the towns; as James Casey notes, the basic Castilian laws about begging date from 1523. The government imposed price controls, and, probably more effectively, supported municipal granaries and sometimes seed banks (although the importance of indirect taxation, notably the *alcabala*, and from 1590 the *millones* levied on wine, oil, and meat ran counter to this). Private charity and self-help organisations (guilds), conventionally held to be insignificant by historians, may also have been important; so too were relatively high wages (if this traditional point about the Spanish economy is still acceptable). Price controls, however, merely accentuate the problems of harvest failure for peasants, crushed as they are between high outgoings (taxes, rents, dues and tithes, and debt repayment) and low returns. The Castilian peasant seems to have been extremely reluctant to risk armed rebellion, not just in the 1590s but throughout the early modern period. Flight (from the land), not fight was the reaction to intolerable conditions. Their quiescence must therefore be explained by long-term structural factors (among them, no doubt, the strength of the nobility backed by the state), which could outweigh the disasters of the 1590s or even of the 1640s.[49]

In general, western European governments (except in France, where government had in effect broken down) seem to have coped well with the problems of the 1590s. Welfare seems to have been actively pursued, whether from a sense of social responsibility, or as a prophylactic against disorder; attention was paid, too, to effective repression. Elizabethan England, with its Book of Orders for regulating the provision of grain, its poor relief system, its organisation of county militias under Lords-Lieutenant, is a case in point – more efficient, apparently in all these respects (and in its capacity to fight a successful war) than the regime of the 1620s. Elizabethan government feared a repetition of the 1549 revolts. It was also the beneficiary of a century of social experiments, discarding some social regulators (such as blanket price controls, as tried by Thomas Cromwell and his mid-century successors), and refining others, such as the poor law system.[50] The Scottish poor law did not, as is sometimes implied, attain immediate perfection with the introduction of the Reformed Kirk (itself a slower process than in the traditional account); nevertheless, something like a working system was in operation in Edinburgh by the 1590s.[51] Italian towns hastened to establish offices to ensure grain supplies, build up reserves, and regulate prices; Venice had shown the way to buy off social discontent by the provision of welfare on a large scale. In Naples the savage repression of the 1585 insurrection was followed by closer attention to grain supplies and to the improvement of private charity, with success.[52]

German governments, too, had learnt the lessons of 1525 and sought to prevent a recurrence by the practice, both preventive and repressive, of *Gute Policey*. The exception is Austria. Possibly the lack of sympathy between the Catholic and centralising imperial house and the largely Protestant estates prevented the implementation of a purposive policy; while the seclusion of Rudolph II in Prague and the incompetence which led eventually to his replacement by his brother Matthias played its part. The Austrian example underlines the point that circumstances dictate the success or failure of repression. The upper Austrian revolt was one of a series, followed by others in 1610–11, 1626, 1632, and 1634–6; that in lower Austria was the last until 1848.[53]

No student of sixteenth-century popular revolt can neglect the religious factor. Significantly, the religious flame seems to burn at a relatively low level in the 1590s and this, too, helps explain the low level of social disorder. The Cossack revolts in the Ukraine were in part a defence of Orthodoxy against the provisions of the 1596 synod at Brest Litovsk which created an eastern-rite Uniate church – a move of that creeping Polonisation which was also subjecting the Ukraine to Polish landlordism.[54] (Conversely, the Croatian nobility resented Austrian government support for Serbian Orthodox border troops).[55] In Austria the traditional interpretation of the peasant revolts, in terms of a Counter-Reformation attack by the Vienna authorities against still surviving village Lutheranism, is discounted in more recent work. Nevertheless, the protection of Lutheran pastors featured among the demands of the upper Austrians. The fact that the (largely Lutheran) Diets representing the upper orders were active in the repression of the revolts does not, in itself, show an absence of some degree of religious motivation, only that religious solidarity was overtopped, on both sides, by social conflict.[56]

In western Europe, on the other hand, the easy equation of religion with social protest was largely a thing of the past. No doubt this was partly because the religious mould was now set after the fluidity of the mid-century; threats to the existing settlement were now more likely to come from abroad, by conquest, than by subversion from below or imposed by the whim of a ruler from above (although, as Heinz Schilling reminds us, the Religious Peace of Augsburg was far from settling all outstanding problems of German ecclesiastical geography).[57] Even the struggle in the Netherlands had become in some sense an international rather than a civil war. Those tendencies in Protestantism which could inspire iconoclasm as a form of social or economic protest had been superseded by elements making for 'social control'.[58] Protestant leaders had become respectable, and were well aware of the harm done to their cause by such outbursts of socio-religious radicalism as that in Ghent in 1578.[59] Conversely, rulers could turn to their advantage situations in which more extreme Protestants could be associated, however unfairly, with social radicalism; this arguably is true of England in the 1590s, and of Scotland in 1596. Even millenarianism seems to have been at a discount at the end of the century.

France seems to be the exception here; but even in France the high tide of Protestant social radicalism was past, even if Protestantism could still provide ideological justification for the non-payment of tithes. In a sense, Catholic radicalism was a defensive reaction against the threat of change imposed from above by the heretic Henry IV – the more so as such change might be accompanied by revenge for the massacres of 1572. As Benedict notes, religious zeal tended to decline as the crisis was prolonged. Perhaps the League was not as dissimilar from such movements of conservative Catholic protest as the 1536 Pilgrimage of Grace in England or the Småland revolt against Gustavus Vasa in 1542 as at first sight appears.[60]

The social response to the 'crisis of the 1590s' was far from uniform; indeed, with harvests failing at different times (the early 1590s in Italy, 1594–7 in north-west Europe, 1601–4 in Russia), a general reaction was impossible. More important, while the Thirty Years War was to suck most of Europe into a single orbit, that was not the case in the 1590s. On the one hand, we have the confrontation between the Ottoman Empire and its neighbour states, Russia, Poland, Austria, which were also, coincidentally the regions of the 'second serfdom'. On the other, there is the situation in western Europe, involving the French civil war and the related war of Spain in the Netherlands and against England. That most of Germany was at peace, and largely spared social violence, is crucial here in preventing any sense of general social conflagration.

There does in fact seem to have been little conscious imitation from one country to another, except in the various revolts in the Balkans. Bartholomew Steere in Oxfordshire thought 'that the Commons, long sithens in Spaine, did rise and kill all the gentlemen in Spaine, and sithens that time have lyved merrily there'.[61] A Swiss, Lucas Reid, may have been responsible for the references to Swiss liberties in the lower Austrian programme.[62] The overwhelming impression is one of relative passivity, except where, as in the Balkans, the Ukraine, Ireland, and Finland, 'peasant movements' either got caught up in struggles by military leaders against central authority or were stirred up by outside authorities against local lords. Only the Naples insurrection of 1585, the Croquant revolts in France, and the two Austrian revolts – perhaps too the Rappenkrieg against Basle – seem to be examples of unambiguous lower-class rebellion on a significant scale; and even here the Rappenkrieg (in which no blood was spilled) seems more like a large-scale demonstration and taxpayer's strike.[63] It is easy enough to 'explain' disorder in time of crisis; riot or rebellion seem to be a natural, even inevitable, response to high prices, unemployment, and the threat of starvation. It is salutary, perhaps, to be reminded how exceptional such responses were; of how easily they could be contained on a localised level, how quickly defused or repressed. This is not to suggest that sixteenth-century European society was some sort of ideal 'society of orders' in which social solidarity was natural, even unthinking. There is ample evidence of social tension and bitterness, a realisation of the essential injustices of society. Resignation and hopelessness seem, however, the predominant marks of this sombre decade.

Notes: Chapter 13

1 Useful lists are in H. Kamen, *The Iron Century: Social Change in Europe, 1550–1660* (London, 1971), pp. 324–5, 332–46; and by W. Schulze in Schulze (ed.), *Europäische Bauernrevolten der frühen Neuzeit* (Frankfurt-on-Main, 1982), pp. 10–11. For Naples, see R. Villari, *La Rivolta Anti-Spagnola a Napoli* (Bari, 1967), pp. 33–58 (English trans. in E. Cochrane (ed.), *The Late Italian Renaissance, 1525–1630* (London, 1970), pp. 305–30). For the Rappenkrieg, see P. Burckhardt, *Geschichte der Stadt Basel* (Basle, 1942), pp. 43–5. Other references, see below.

2 Clark and Schilling, Chs 3 and 7 above.

3 Kamen, *Iron Century*, pp. 341–6; J. Delumeau, *L'Italie de Botticelli à Bonaparte* (Paris, 1974), p. 229, and the same author's *Vie économique et sociale de Rome dans la seconde moitié du XVIe siècle* (Paris, 1957–9), vol. 2, pp. 543–64. Villari, *La rivolta*, pp. 58–91; Villari suggests that the killing of Baron Orazio Carrafa 'has all the characteristics of rural revolt' involving the entire community; that a refusal of rent and tithe was involved; that the movement was far from being merely a reaction of disgruntled nobles against centralising government. See also Villari, *Ribelli e riformatori dal XVI al XVIII secolo* (Rome, 1979), pp. 69–83; P. Vilar, *La Catalogne dans l'Espagne moderne* (Paris, 1962), vol. 1, pp. 579–86.

4 H. Inalcik, *The Ottoman Empire, 1300–1600* (London, 1973), pp. 50–1; S. J. and E. K. Shaw, *History of the Ottoman Empire and Modern Turkey* (Cambridge, 1976–7), vol. 1, pp. 174, 185–6.

5 J. S. Cockburn, 'The nature and incidence of crime in England, 1559–1625: a preliminary survey', in Cockburn (ed.), *Crime in England, 1500–1800* (London, 1977), pp. 49–71. On the difficulties of interpreting statistics of crime, see B. Lenman and G. Parker, 'The state, the community, and the criminal law in early modern Europe', in V. A. C. Gattrell, B. Lenman and G. Parker (eds), *Crime and the Law: The Social History of Crime in Western Europe since 1500* (London, 1980), pp. 11–49, esp. pp. 46–7.

6 C. Larner, 'Crimen exceptum? – witchcraft in Europe', in Gattrell *et al.*, *Crime and the Law*, pp. 49–75. H. C. E. Midelfort, *Witch-Hunting in Southwestern Germany, 1562–1684* (Stanford, Calif., 1972), pp. 75–7, 121–3; G. Schormann, *Hexenprozesse in Nordwestdeutschland* (Hildesheim, 1977), p. 158. Midelfort and Schormann both stress how much worse were the late 1620s in this respect. For Scotland, see C. Larner, *Enemies of God: The Witch-Hunt in Scotland* (London, 1981), pp. 60–72.

7 Clark, above, Ch. 3.

8 R. Chambers, *Domestic Annals of Scotland* (Edinburgh, 1858–61), vol. 1, pp. 266–75. G. Donaldson, *Scotland, James V to James VII* (Edinburgh, 1965), pp. 195, 201. M. Lynch, *Edinburgh and the Reformation* (Edinburgh, 1981), esp. pp. 218–19. M. Flinn (ed.), *Scottish Population History from the Seventeenth Century to the 1930s* (Cambridge, 1977), p. 109.

9 H. Koht, *Les Luttes des paysans en Norvège du XVIe au XIXe siècle* (Paris, 1929), esp. pp. 75–80. Michael Roberts, *The Early Vasas: A History of Sweden, 1523–1611* (Cambridge, 1968), esp. pp. 366–7. G. Utterstrδm, 'Climatic fluctuation and population problems in early modern history', *Scandinavian Economic History Review*, vol. 3. (1955), pp. 1–47, esp. pp. 26–30.

10 A. Gieysztor, *History of Poland*, 2nd edn (Warsaw, 1979), pp. 190–2; N. Davies, *God's Playground: A History of Poland* (Oxford, 1981), vol. 1, pp. 439–47; W. E. D. Allen, *The Ukraine: A History* (Cambridge, 1941), ch. 3. The importance of grain exports in the development of Polish society is stressed, against recent doubters, by Maria Bogucka, 'North European commerce and the problem of dualism in the development of modern Europe', in V. Zimányi (ed.), *La Pologne et la Hongrie aux XVIe–XVIIIe siècles* (Budapest, 1981), pp. 9–24. For the doubts, see J. Topolski, 'Sixteenth century Poland and European economic development', in J. K. Fedorowicz (ed.), *A Republic of Nobles* (Cambridge, 1982), pp. 70–90.

11 J. Blum, *Lord and Peasant in Russia from the Ninth to the Nineteenth Century* (Princeton, NJ, 1961), esp. ch. 10. P. Anderson, *Lineages of the Absolutist State* (London, 1974), pp. 332–3. R. Mousnier, *Peasant Uprisings in Seventeenth-Century France, Russia, and China* (London, 1971), chs 7 and 8.

12 See Schilling above, ch. 7; also H. Schultz, 'Bäuerliche Klassenkampfe zwischen frühbürgerlicher Revolution und Dreissigem Krieg', *Zeitschrift für Geschichtswissenschaft*, vol. 20 (1972), pp. 156–73; P. Bierbrauer, 'Die Revolten zwischen 1525 und 1789', in P. Blickle *et al.* (eds), *Aufruhr und Empörung: Studien zum bäuerlichen Widerstand im Alten Reich* (Munich, 1980), pp. 50–69. W. Schulze, *Reich und Türkengefahr im späten 16. Jahrhundert* (Munich, 1978), esp. pp. 295–6, makes more of these south German revolts and ascribes them to the pressure of taxes for the Turkish war. See also various studies in W. Schulze (ed.), *Aufstände, Revolten, Prozesse*, Geschichte und Gesellschaft, Bochumer Historische Studien, vol. 27 (1983); see H. Harnisch on Brandenburg (pp. 135–48), R. Blickle on Old Bavaria (pp. 166–87) and C. Ulbrich on the Habsburg territories in south and west Germany (pp. 202–16). All stress the high level of tension and disputes, sometimes violent, but the rarity of rebellion; in Brandenburg, for instance, there was only one rising (1579–80) in a period of acute social conflict between 1560 and 1620 (pp. 140–1).

13 Casey, above, ch. 11; cf. Bartolomé Bennassar on the people of Valladolid: 'Je ne sache pas que ce peuple ait jamais cherché à résister par la violence. A moins que le grand silence des textes ne soit un leurre' (*Valladolid au Siècle d'Or* (Paris, 1967), p. 434.

14 See M. E. Brooks, *A King for Portugal: The Madrigal Conspiracy, 1594–5* (Madison, Wis., 1964); the last pretender actually to gather mass support was Mateus Alvares in 1585 (p. 42).

15 Noordegraaf, above, ch. 4.

16 cf. Paul Janssens on the difficulty of raising popular revolt in the Spanish Netherlands even in the crisis years of the mid-seventeenth century: 'L'échec des tentatives de soulèvement aux Pays-Bas sous Philippe IV, 1621–65', *Revue d'histoire diplomatique*, vol. 92 (1978), pp. 110–29.

17 Villari, in Cochrane, *Late Italian Renaissance*, p. 324. Although the 1585 insurrection was spectacular, Villari's account seems to contradict his argument that 'it was not simply an explosion of wild anger'; there seems no evidence of planning, nor of any other killings by the rioters (ibid., pp. 314–21). Villari, *Ribelli e riformatori*, pp. 72–5, asserts that there was no particular intensity of hunger riots at this time; rather, that banditry was supported by better-off peasants, *contadini agiati*, caught by the ending of the favourable (for producers) price conjuncture of the sixteenth century.

18 T. Davies, above, ch. 10. H. G. Koenigsberger, *The Government of Sicily under Philip II of Spain* (London, 1951), pp. 192–3.

19 Schulze, *Europäischer Bauernrevolten*, p. 10.

20 J. A. Faber, 'Dearth and famine in the pre-industrial Netherlands', in *The Low Countries Historical Yearbook*, vol. 13 (1980), pp. 51–64, esp. p. 60. Compare C. Larquié's warning on the absence of research into popular disorders in Spain in 'Les soulèvements populaires en Espagne au milieu du XVIIe siècle', *Revue d'histoire diplomatique*, vol. 92 (1978), pp. 31–50, esp. p. 41. A notable exception is A. Domínguez Ortiz, *Alteraciones Andaluzas* (Madrid, 1972).

21 Roberts, *Early Vasas*, pp. 366–7.

22 A. B. Appleby, *Famine in Tudor and Stuart England* (Liverpool, 1978), ch. 8.

23 S. M. Harrison, *The Pilgrimage of Grace in the Lake Counties, 1536–7* (London, 1981).

24 See for the moment B. Sharp, *In Contempt of All Authority* (Berkeley, Calif., 1980), pp. 20–1. I am grateful to John Walter for letting me see a forthcoming paper which analyses the Oxfordshire movement in detail.

25 On Hoskins's classification the harvest of 1607 was 'average', following six 'good' years: W. G. Hoskins, 'Harvest fluctuations and English economic history, 1480–1619', in W. E. Minchinton (ed.), *Essays in Agrarian History* (Newton Abbot, 1968), vol. 1, pp. 95–115. Clearly the situation in the Midlands was worse than it appeared to be in London, but it would be impossible to maintain that it was as serious as in the 1594–7 crisis. No doubt enclosure went on apace during the period 1597–1607; see, for instance, L. A. Parker, 'The agricultural revolution at Cotesbach', *Transactions of the Leicestershire Archaeological Society*, vol. 24 (1948), pp. 41–76. Nevertheless, had revolt broken out in 1596–7 historians would have regarded it not merely as natural but as inevitable.

26 See above, n. 10.

27 For useful accounts of these confused events, see G. Parker, *Europe in Crisis, 1598–1648* (London, 1979), pp. 76–81, 86–91, and F. Braudel, *The Mediterranean and the Mediterranean World in the Age of Philip II*, revised edn (London, 1973), vol. 2, pp. 1196–1204.

28 S. Pascu *et al.*, 'Mouvements paysans dans le centre et le sud-est de l'Europe du XVe au XXe siècle', *XIIe Congrès International des Sciences Historiques, 1965, Rapports*, vol. 4, pp. 211–35. S. Fischer-Galati, 'The peasantry as a revolutionary force in the Balkans', *Journal of Central European Affairs*, vol. 23 (1963–4), pp. 12–22. R. W. Seton-Watson, *A History of Rumania* (Cambridge, 1934), pp. 62–74. S. Stefanescu, 'Sozialrechtliche Lage des Bauernstandes in der Walachei . . .', in G. Heckenast (ed.), *Aus der Geschichte der Ostmitteleuropäischen Bauernbewegungen im 16–17. Jahrhundert* (Budapest, 1977), pp. 381–7. Michael's responsibility for the formal introduction of serfdom is disputed; see S. Olteanu, *Les Pays roumains à l'époque de Michel le Brave (l'union de 1600)* (Bucharest, 1975), pp. 51–6.

29 M. MacDermott, *A History of Bulgaria, 1393–1885* (London, 1962), pp. 40–1. S. G. Evans, *A Short History of Bulgaria* (London, 1960), pp. 80–1. Anderson, *Lineages of the Absolutist State*, pp. 371–4. Revolts against Turkish rule were endemic in the Albanian mountains: S. Pollo and A. Puto, *The History of Albania* (London, 1981), pp. 88–91. See, too, the Serbian revolt of 1594, and that of 1597 in Herzegovina and Montenegro: Vladimir Dedijer *et al.*, *History of Yugoslavia* (New York, 1974), pp. 194–6. There is a general survey in Olteanu, *Les Pays roumains*, pp. 15–17.

30 S. E. Rothenberg, *The Austrian Military Border in Croatia, 1523–1747* (Urbana, Ill., 1960), pp. 59–61, 93.

31 The situation is complicated by a three-cornered struggle between landowners, *haiducks* (settled after military service as privileged free tenants of the crown) and peasants. The privileges of the *haiducks* did not benefit the peasants, nor did the *haiducks*' penchant for plunder. See L. Makkai in E. Pamlényi, *A History of Hungary* (Budapest, 1973); I. Rácz, 'Heiduckenfreiheit im System der Zweiten Leibigenschaft', in Heckenast, *Bauernbewegungen*, pp. 131–6; F. Szakály, 'Das Bauerntum und die Kämpfe gegen die Turken bzw. gegen Habsburg . . .', in ibid., pp. 251–66; Z. P. Pach, 'Corvées et travail salarié dans les exploitations seigneuriales de la Hongrie des XVIe et XVIIe siècles', in B. Köpeczi and E. H. Balázs (eds), *Paysannerie française, paysannerie hongroise* (Budapest, 1973).

32 Rothenberg, *Austrian Military Border*, pp. 70–1.

33 M. Aymard, *Venise, Raguse, et le commerce du blé pendant la seconde motié du XVIe siècle* (Paris, 1966), pp. 125–41. Olteanu, *Les Pays roumains*, pp. 39–40.

34 Inalcik, *Ottoman Empire*, pp. 49, 51, 216. Shaw and Shaw, *Ottoman Empire*, vol. 1, pp. 173–4, 185–8. Braudel, *Mediterranean*, vol. 2, pp. 1199, 1203–4. B. McCowan, *Economic Life in Ottoman Europe: Taxation, Trade and the Struggle for Land, 1600–1800* (Cambridge, 1981), chs 1 and 2. H. Inalcik, 'The Ottoman decline and its effects upon the Reaya', in his *The Ottoman Empire, Conquest, Organisation and Economy* (London, 1978), ch. 13. Anderson, *Lineages of the Absolutist State*, pp. 361–96.

35 E. H. Phelps Brown and S. V. Hopkins, 'Builders' wage-rates, prices, and population: some further evidence', *Economica*, vol. 39 (1959), pp. 18–37.

36 A. Czerny, *Der Zweite Bauernaufstand in Oberösterreich* (Linz, 1890). G. Grüll, *Der Bauer im Lande ob der Enns am Ausgang des 16. Jahrhunderts* (Linz, 1969). Schulze, 'Bauerliche Klassenkampfe', provides a useful brief account of the two Austrian revolts. J. Bérenger, 'La révolte paysanne de Basse-Autriche de 1597', *Revue d'histoire économique et sociale*, vol. 53 (1975), pp. 465–92. I must thank Gerhard Benecke for assistance with references and regret the lack of opportunity to make more extended use of them. See also above, n. 12, for south Germany.

37 J. M. Polisensky, *The Thirty Years War* (London, 1971), pp. 38–56, 72–86. A. Klíma, 'Agrarian class structure and economic development in pre-industrial Bohemia', *Past and Present*, no. 85 (1979), pp. 49–67.

38 Y. M. Bercé, *Histoire des Croquants: étude des soulèvements populaires au 17e siècle dans le sud-ouest de la France* (Geneva, 1974), vol. 1, pp. 272–93. Greengrass, above, ch. 6.

39 Philip Benedict, above, ch. 5. See also his *Rouen during the Wars of Religion* (Cambridge, 1981), ch. 10.

40 R. B. Outhwaite, above, ch. 2. R. A. Butlin, in T. W. Moody, F. X. Martin and F. J.

Byrne, *A New History of Ireland*, vol. 3 (Oxford, 1976), pp. 145–7; G. A. Hayes-McCoy, in ibid., pp. 115–17, 125–9. D. B. Quinn, *The Elizabethans and the Irish* (Ithiaca, NY, 1966), pp. 131–40. C. Falls, *Elizabeth's Irish Wars*, 2nd edn (London, 1970), pp. 335–6.

41 G. Parker, *The Army of Flanders and the Spanish Road, 1567–1659* (Cambridge, 1972), ch. 8; and the same author's *Spain and the Netherlands, 1559–1659* (London, 1979); pp. 180 ff; Noordegraaf, above, ch. 4.

42 See Casey, above, ch. 11; I. A. A. Thompson, *War and Government in Habsburg Spain, 1560–1620* (London, 1976), pp. 215–16; J. H. Elliott, *Imperial Spain, 1469–1716* (London, 1963), p. 281.

43 D. Sella, *Crisis and Continuity: The Economy of Spanish Lombardy in the XVIIth Century* (Cambridge, Mass., 1979), pp. 44–7, contrasts the ability of the authorities to increase taxation in the 1590s with the disastrous conditions of northern Italy when war was fought there in the late 1620s.

44 I. Wallerstein, *The Modern World-System*, vol. 1 (New York, 1974), p. 104, suggests, following Braudel, that low density of population makes resistance difficult. M. Malowist, 'The economic and social development of the Baltic countries from the fifteenth to the seventeenth centuries', *Economic History Review*, 2nd ser., vol. 12 (1959), pp. 177–89, believes that the Polish peasants lost their chance in 1525, when the prosperity of the richer peasants prevented a peasant uprising; by the end of the century, the power of the lords was too firmly established, while the towns were too weak to give support to the peasants (p. 188). Topolski, in Fedorowicz, *Republic of Nobles*, pp. 76–7, 87–8, also invokes the benefit to middling and wealthy peasants from the increased demand for grain, but stresses, too, the increase in labour services and in payments of rent in kind which led to serfdom. V. G. Kiernan, *State and Society in Europe, 1550–1650* (Oxford, 1980), p. 206, invokes the possibility of flight to the Ukraine as an outlet for the disaffected. As for townsmen, while both wage-earners and craftsmen were losing from the evolution of prices (see S. Hoszowski, in P. Burke (ed.), *Economy and Society in Early Modern Europe* (London, 1972), pp. 90, 92, 98), Gieysztor, *History of Poland*, p. 199, suggests that small-scale philanthropy was successful in dampening militancy. As in France in 1572, the Church seems to have successfully diverted the wrath of townsmen against the property of Protestants.

45 See, for instance, C. Verlinden, J. Craeybeckx and E. Scholliers, 'Price and wage movements in Belgium in the sixteenth century', in Burke (ed.), *Economy and Society*, pp. 55–84, esp. p. 74. The Spanish army put down disturbances in Brussels in 1619 and in Antwerp in 1659: Janssens, 'L'échec des tentatives', pp. 127–8.

46 Noordegraaf, above, ch. 4; G. Parker, *The Dutch Revolt* (Harmondsworth, 1979), p. 245; Parker, *Europe in Crisis*, p. 143; J. I. Israel, *The Dutch Republic and the Hispanic World, 1606–1661* (Oxford, 1982), pp. 59–60; Faber, 'Dearth and famine' (see above, n. 20).

47 K. Glanman, in C. M. Cipolla (ed.), *The Sixteenth and Seventeenth Centuries*, Fontana Economic History of Europe, vol. 2 (London, 1974), p. 465; W. Abel, *Massenarmut und Hungerkrisen im vordindustriellen Deutschland*, 2nd edn (Göttingen, 1977), pp. 46 ff; Braudel, *Mediterranean*, vol. 1, pp. 570 ff. For Baltic grain and Scotland, see B. Lenman, in C. Wilson and G. Parker (eds), *An Introduction to the Sources of European Economic History, 1500–1800* (London, 1977), p. 145.

48 For Catalonia, Vilar, *La Catalogne*, vol. 1, pp. 575–9, gives qualified support to the argument of lack of peasant revolt owing to the prosperity of the peasantry, the fruit of liberty won during the *Remença* struggle of the fifteenth century and confirmed in the 1486 *Sentencia de Guadalupe*.

49 See Casey, above, ch. 11. For price-fixing and municipal granaries, see Bennassar, *Valladolid*, ch. 2; and A. Domínguez Ortiz, *The Golden Age of Spain, 1516–1659* (London, 1971), pp. 152–3. For private charity, see Casey; Bennassar, *Valladolid*, ch. 3; and Domínguez Ortiz, *Golden Age*, pp. 152–3. M. R. Weisser, *The Peasants of the Montes* (Chicago, Ill., 1976), p. 98, asserts that the total amount of charity was not large. Casey gives guarded support to the classic claims of E. J. Hamilton of a relatively high wage level in Spain. N. Salomon, *La Campagne de Nouvelle Castille à la fin du XVIe siècle* (Paris, 1964), ch. 7, stresses the growing gulf between rich peasants and an increasingly proletarianised rural mass. Weisser, *Peasants of the Montes*, a general discussion of

Castilian peasant passivity before the nineteenth century, also stresses (pp. 113 ff.) polarisation in the villages.

50 P. Williams, *The Tudor Regime* (Oxford, 1979), chs 4 and 6

51 R. Mitchison, 'The making of the old Scottish poor law', *Past and Present*, no. 63 (1974), pp. 58–93. Lynch, *Edinburgh and the Reformation*, pp. 19–20. Lynch observes (p. 11) that Edinburgh, with a population 'approaching 15,000 in the 1590s', was the second or third city of the British Isles, as large as Norwich, and on a level with such towns as Bremen, Delft and Erfurt.

52 Delumeau, *Rome*, vol. 2, pp. 598 ff; B. Pullan, *Rich and Poor in Renaissance Venice* (Oxford, 1971); Villari, in Cochrane, *Late Italian Renaissance*, p. 324.

53 W. Schulze argues that peasant revolt strengthened both repressive and 'social justice' policies by princely states, against the immediate interests of the nobility; he stresses especially the development of legal institutions and, in the long run, of concepts of legal equality. He also suggests that German nobles were less ready to revolt against their princes than those in France and England, and ascribes this in part to the experience of the Knights' War and the Peasants' Revolt: see *Aufstände, Revolten, Prozesse*, pp. 261–85; Grüll, *Bauer im Lande ob der Enns*, p. 239; Bérenger, 'Révolte paysanne', p. 492. Even so, Schulze notes (*Aufstände, Revolten, Prozesse*, pp. 273–4) Austrian nobles complaining in 1596–7 of the imperial authority's readiness to listen to peasant complaints.

54 Allen, *Ukraine*, pp. 83–9.

55 Rothenberg, *Austrian Military Border*, pp. 69–70.

56 Grüll, *Bauer im Lande ob der Enns*, represents an 'economic' reaction against the interpretation of Czerny, *Zweite Bauernaufstand*. The rebellion is traditionally considered to have started with the forcible intrusion of a Catholic incumbent into a Protestant parish at Wimberg in May 1594; but armed conflict did not break out until October 1595. See H. Hantsch, *Die Geschichte Österreichs*, 3rd edn (Graz, 1951), vol. 1, pp. 327–9; G. Mecenseffy, *Geschichte des Protestantismus in Österreich* (Graz, 1956), pp. 89 ff. For the programme, see Czerny, *Zweite Bauernaufstand*, pp. 363–9. The decision of the Protestant lords to oppose the rebels no more disproves the existence of a 'religious factor' than does the opposition of Protestant nobles to the 1525 revolt.

57 Schilling, above, ch. 7.

58 e.g., N. Z. Davis, 'Strikes and salvation at Lyon', in her *Society and Culture in Early Modern France* (London, 1975), pp. 1–16.

59 For Ghent in 1578, see T. Wittman, *Les Gueux dans les 'bonnes villes' de Flandre (1577–84)* (Budapest, 1969). For England, and the successful attempt by Bancroft to associate Puritanism with the activities of Martin Marprelate, see P. Collinson, *The Elizabethen Puritan Movement* (London, 1967), pp. 385–402, esp. p. 397. For James VI's successful counter-coup against the Melvillian party in Scotland, which James successfully tarred with a populist brush, see Donaldson, *Scotland, James V to James VII*, pp. 195–201, and Lynch, *Edinburgh and the Reformation*, pp. 214–22. For the contrast between reformation 'from below' in the early German reformation and reformation 'from above' in Colmar in 1575, see Erdmann Weyrauch, 'Die politische Führungsgruppe in Colmar zur Zeit der Reformation', in W. J. Mommsen (ed.), *Stadtbürgertum und Adel in der Reformation* (Stuttgart, 1979), pp. 215–34.

60 Benedict, *Rouen*, pp. 245–9. For the Småland revolt, see Roberts, *Early Vasas*, pp. 132–6.

61 Steere's interrogation, printed by E. F. Gay, 'The Midland revolt and the inquisitions of depopulation of 1607', *Transactions of the Royal Historical Society*, 2nd ser., vol. 18 (1904), pp. 195–244, esp. pp. 238–9.

62 Bérenger, 'Révolte paysanne', p. 486. On the other hand, the association of Swiss liberties with peasant revolts, usually in a denigratory way, was commonplace. See Bercé, *Croquants*, vol. 1, p. 287.

63 The 'rebels' were eventually dispersed by the eloquence of the humanist city councillor Andreas Ryff, backed by the threat of force: see Burckhardt, *Der Stadt Basel*, pp. 43–5, and Ryff's self-laudatory account of events, edited by Friedrich Meyer as 'Andreas Ryff (1550–1603), Der Rappenkrieg', *Basler Zeitschrift für Geschichte und Altertumskunde*, vol. 66 (1966), pp. 5–131.

14 *The Impact of War*

I. A. A. THOMPSON

I

War was not a defining characteristic of the 1590s. Indeed, on one recent count the 1590s was the decade with the lowest incidence of new wars in the whole of the sixteenth and seventeenth centuries.[1] With the exception of the Ottoman front in Hungary and the complicated manoeuverings of the Poles, the Swedes and the Russians, war in the 1590s was really a phenomenon of Atlantic Europe. For almost all of Germany and Italy the period was one of peace, although Savoy was involved in plots against Geneva (1586, 1602) and in intervention in Provence in pursuance of claims against France; and Milan, Naples and Sicily were compelled to share the burden of Madrid's foreign policies. Even in the Low Countries there was less military activity during the 1590s than in the two previous decades. Holland and most of the Republic, apart from some border provinces, were largely free of fighting after 1576, and in the southern Netherlands the worst phase was over by about 1592. Only for England, with formal involvement in the Netherlands in 1585, intervention in France in 1589, and rebellion in Ireland after 1593, was open war a relatively new experience. For England, however, as for the United Provinces and for Spain (excepting a few unfortunate localities raided by pirates or enemy expeditions), war was experienced in the 1590s largely as a problem of provision. Only in France, among the leading states of Europe, was the direct experience of war in the final paroxysm of the Religious Wars, already a generation old by 1588, more extensive and more acute. Yet even in France war was being phased out in the 1590s – in Languedoc from 1592, in Picardy, Normandy, Maine, Anjou, Poitou and the rest of Aquitaine by 1594, in Champagne, Burgundy and Provence by 1595–6, and only in Brittany not until 1598.[2]

Nor was war greater in scale in the 1590s than it had been in earlier periods, though not since 1559 had so much of Atlantic Europe been involved simultaneously. The army of Flanders was no larger than in the 1570s. The Invincible Armada carried only half the numbers on the Christian fleet at Lepanto. Queen Elizabeth never had an army anything like as large as that of Henry VIII in 1544.[3] War was, however, different in kind.

In the first place, war became global in its implications. The Americas, Asia, Morocco, Algiers, Turkey, and Poland were all seen as part of a single struggle against what Pierre Vilar has called 'the Catholic, feudal empire of Philip II'.[4] 'There is to be seen no maner of hostillitie at this daie in anie part of Christendome, saving in Hungarie, but by his [Philip II's] great armies by sea or land', declared Elizabeth I in a proclamation of September 1597 prohibiting the shipping of strategic materials to Spain.[5] The singleness of the struggle pervaded the political consciousness of Europe, extending the impact of military events in the west into Italy, Germany, Poland and the Baltic. The Swedish constitutional crisis of 1593–8, for example, would not be comprehensible outside this context.[6] Consequently, even where war was not physically present, it was felt to be close. There was an enemy within (papist, Huguenot, *morisco*) and an overpowering fear of invasion from without which magnified and distorted the psychological impact of war in this period.[7]

This was the more particularly so because no state could satisfactorily provide protection for its territories from the sea. The extension of war into the Atlantic in the 1580s compelled governments to the construction of highly expensive coastal fortifications and the creation of high seas fleets, by their nature relatively capital-intensive and logistically demanding compared with armies (a development that in both England and Spain took place mainly after 1588).[8] It also led them to promote a more general militarisation of society as a whole in the interests of national defence, through rearming, retraining and the re-forming of local militias, with all the political, social and jurisdictional problems that that entailed.[9]

For Spain, the war against England meant a fundamental shift of priorities from east to west and a relocation of military bases to the Atlantic coast, with a gradual run-down of her Mediterranean galley defences. The shift from galley to galleon was a shift from a war of aristocratic dash to a war of professional seamanship, and from a war of men to a war of material. The Spanish Armada packed some eight to nine times the firepower of the Spanish galley squadron, doubling the entire ordnance stock of the Spanish war machine, and increased hemp and cordage requirements sixfold.[10]

Parallel changes were taking place on land. The Netherlands war was a forcing-ground for military innovation and a training-school for soldiers of all nations. Although it may be going too far to describe the reforms of Maurice of Nassau in the 1590s as the initiation of a 'military revolution', there were, in fact, crucial changes taking place in warfare which can be summed up as a shift from mass to line, from pike to shot, and, with increasing professionalism in war, a shift from prowess to proficiency and from ascription to achievement in military status.[11] It is not without significance that the Netherlands were the seat of this 'revolution'. What was taking place was a movement, if still a modest one, towards the 'production-line' warfare of an early industrial society.[12] The administrative tasks and skills required of governments, the commercial links and the industrial involvement necessary, were of an entirely new order. Governments were being drawn into an increasing intervention in the control of strategic materials and the promotion of strategic manufactures in the interests of military autarky.[13]

All these considerations are relevant to the nature of the demands made by the wars and their impact on the economies and societies that sustained them. The wars of the 1590s affected different countries in different ways and to different degrees, but it was only Ireland, the southern Netherlands and parts of France that suffered directly war's devastations.

II

Benedict and Greengrass have provided illuminating accounts of the more spectacular ravages of war in the French countryside.[14] The devastation wrought by Parma's campaigns in Flanders and Brabant in the 1580s was no less horrendous. The immediate impact of military events in these areas, particularly on the rural economy, but on the towns as well, is undeniable.[15] The question is, How general were those experiences and what were their long-term consequences? What were the mechanisms by which short-term damage could lead to structural change and how can we distinguish the impact of war from the impact of other factors? How resilient was the early modern economy to sporadic disaster? Was François de la Noue right in saying, admittedly of an earlier and less ferocious phase of the Religious Wars, that France was so prosperous and so fertile that what the war destroyed in one year could be restored in two?[16] The tithe figures for Normandy and Beaune suggest that things were back to normal by the first decade of the seventeenth century. The recovery of cloth production in Amiens was quite spectacular, regaining prewar levels by 1608. In Rheims, recovery in the 1590s, though less sustained, was even more spectacular.[17] The 1590s, therefore, cannot be seen as a period of unrelieved gloom. The war was being wound up in stages and, as Jean Meyer writes, 'comme toujours, destructions et reconstructions se superposent'.[18]

In the southern Netherlands, the decade of crisis was the 1580s; the 1590s was a decade of recovery. Almost all indices mark an upturn after 1589–92 from the extreme low points of the mid-1580s. Recovery, however, was uneven and incomplete. In a few cases the record levels of the prewar period were regained during the 1590s, but for the most part recovery was a slow process, taking twenty, thirty, or more years, and in some cases no substantial recovery took place at all.[19] But the exceptional severity of the late sixteenth-century crisis cannot be attributed solely to war. In some ways, it can be argued, war merely intensified existing endogenous trends towards crisis. The ravages of war in the countryside were exacerbated by the disastrous harvests of 1585 and 1586 which led to the most dramatic famine in over two hundred years, and the process of agrarian recovery was further hindered by another series of bad harvests in 1593–5.[20]

In Ireland, a ferocious war, waged with scorched-earth policies on both sides for much of the ten years 1593–1603, none the less left the country with no long-term economic scars. There was no widespread shortage of cattle or corn; Dublin's trade had collapsed, but more as a result of the coinage debasement of 1601–2, and trade soon revived with the development of new exports of timber and barrel-staves from Wexford, Waterford and Youghal, and beef from Cork. The first decades of the seventeenth century were in fact a period of exceptional buoyancy in the Irish economy.[21]

The immensely varied nature of local responses, both in the southern Netherlands and in France, is not something that can be explained simply by war. Recent studies by Gutmann[22] and by Friedrichs[23] have argued that it was not war alone but a combination of disasters that was necessary to change a region's underlying patterns of economic and demographic growth – war and bad weather and/or pestilence in the Basse-Meuse, a second wave of devastation during the process of recovery in Nördlingen. The evidence of Brittany gives support to Gutmann's central thesis that the impact of war depended not on the nature of the devastation but on the nature of the economy. Brittany's experience was very like that of the Basse-Meuse, and for some of the same reasons, most important, the diversified nature of its economy.

Moreover, on the broader than local perspective, war brought gains as well as losses. The military operations that ravaged the southern Netherlands and led to a massive flight of skill and capital positively benefited the north. Against the difficulties of Antwerp and Hondschoote we have to set the growth of Amsterdam, Leyden, Rotterdam, Haarlem and Delft. The Flanders crisis brought profits to the Liège armaments manufacturers and to the linen industries of Brittany and Normandy.[24] The disruption of the Netherlands trade did Burgos and London no good, but it certainly helped Valencia and Hull,[25] amongst others, whilst the Hanse's direct trade with Spain prospered greatly during the embargo on trade with the Dutch, both before and after the Truce of 1609–21.[26] The French Atlantic ports, Honfleur, Le Havre, La Rochelle, all prospered during the civil wars. There were even profits to be made from privateering, if organised in a businesslike way, to offset against the lost opportunities of England's

Iberian traders – opportunities which in fact were to prove illusory in 1604.[27]

In short, the direct impact of war was too ambiguous and the incidence of warfare too geographically limited to be related too closely to a general European crisis of the 1590s. There are structural shifts of real importance which can be traced to the end of the sixteenth century, but they can by no means be attributed simply to war. War, without doubt, played a major part in the process of economic introversion that was taking place in the southern Netherlands, a process marked by ruralisation, de-urbanisation and regionalisation, with urban capital turned to agrarian investment, a tendency to the concentration of landholding, and a market dominated by domestic demand.[28] But one is describing here a process that was characteristic of other areas where the impact of war was of a very different kind, or not important at all, as in Castile or the Veneto, or, indeed, that characterised the European economy as a whole in the 'general crisis of the seventeenth century'.[29]

The impact of war did not fall only on the areas in which fighting actually took place. The burden of billeting and purveyance, the loss of crops and animals, the levying of contributions in money and kind, and the stopping of trade by the commissariat could be enormously damaging in non-operational areas as well, because they fell selectively on the same military corridors and embarkation dormitory areas for prolonged periods, year after year, and could lead, in the same way, to the destruction of capital, communal indebtedness and peasant expropriation, the main channels through which, it is suggested, war damage might cause structural change.[30] In Spain, where perhaps these pressures were heaviest and most continuous, there is a plethora of complaint during the 1580s and 1590s precisely from those regions newly affected by fleet purveyance and the passage of troops to the Atlantic ports, all reporting a similar situation of abandoned lands, short-range migrations to the more protected larger towns and seigneurial jurisdictions, and communal indebtedness. By 1598, if a statement in the Cortes is to be believed, the villages of Castile were owed 1,600,000 ducats for victualling and billeting expenses, a fivefold increase in only twelve years.[31] Unfortunately, too much of the rather general information we have on these matters is protest-based, and without systematic comparisons it is impossible to say how important these burdens really were. It is perhaps indicative that when an inquiry was conducted into the decay of Castilian agriculture early in the seventeenth century only five of thirty-eight replies mentioned billeting and purveyance as of any significance.[32]

War was also a drain on manpower. Spanish writers, worried by the signs of demographic recession at the end of the sixteenth century, were quick to blame the recruiting officer. We should, however, be careful about giving too much weight to their opinions. Spain maintained no more than 3½ per cent of her adult males in the armed services and recruited, almost entirely on a voluntary basis, about one in a thousand of Castile's population every year.[33] In England, where the contemporary concern was rather with overpopulation, about 0·13 per cent of the population was recruited for foreign service annually between 1585 and 1603.[34] Without knowing the economic standing, the marital status or prospects, the mortality rate, or the length of absence of these soldiers, it is impossible to say what effect this military drain had. Overall, the demographic consequences were probably minimal, even at the local level and in a relatively heavily burdened county like Kent, where the recruiter took 0·38 per cent of the population every year. The recruiting figures that we have for Castile in the 1590s suggest that it was the size of the levy that was contingent upon the state of the population, not vice versa.[35] Cellorigo, for one, recognised that it was not so much the wars but deeper inadequacies in the economy that were responsible for Castile's demographic decline.[36] A comparison of the demographic history of Andalusia, Extremadura and Galicia, the regions most affected by the shift to the Atlantic in the 1580s and 1590s, with that of other parts of Castile, argues against putting too much emphasis on military factors.[37] The prosperity of front-line counties like Norfolk, Kent and Sussex in the earlier seventeenth century tells a similar story.[38] The war disturbed but did not dislocate underlying patterns of growth.

It was through taxation that the impact of war was felt most widely. In general, war doubled state expenditures during the 1590s. Elizabeth spent £4½ million on war in 1585–1603, doubling her prewar expenses. The military budget of the Dutch Republic rose from under 5 million florins in the early 1590s to 10 million florins a year in 1604–6, of which 90 per cent was raised internally. Spain's domestic military budget tripled between the late 1570s and the late 1580s to a peak of around 3½ million ducats. In addition 33 million florins were sent to the Netherlands in the 1570s, 60 million in the 1580s, and 90 million in the 1590s; at the same time, the loyal provinces contributed 7 million florins between 1577 and 1586, and 48 million between 1587 and 1599. By the 1590s Madrid's total annual expenditure stood about 75 per cent higher than in the 1570s, and that in turn was two and a half times as high as at Philip II's accession. By 1600 all governments were in debt, not necessarily, of course, for the first time. Even Elizabeth left about £330,000 owing at her death. The Dutch Republic had short-term debts exceeding a year's income. The capital value of Spanish *juros* increased by some 50 million ducats in the last quarter of the century, the equivalent of four years' gross revenues. In France the *rentes* totalled 50 million *livres* in 1588, 150 million in 1595, half the entire Crown debt.[39]

None the less, even in the 1590s the share of the national income spent on war could have amounted to only about 8 per cent in Castile, perhaps twice that in the United Provinces by the 1600s, and something under 4 per cent in England.[40] This takes no account of direct, local contributions which are almost impossible to assess, but which in England seem to have been considerable and in some cases equalled the value of several subsidies.[41] Compared with a hundred or even fifty years later, these levels were really rather modest.[42] The *per capita* tax burden in the 1590s was the equivalent of about six days of labour in Castile, just over two days in England, The fisc imposed a good deal less than the Church, or the landlord,[43] or indeed than the weather. Even in Castile, the *additional* domestic taxation levied in the 1580s and 1590s was the equivalent in its impact on spending to no more than a 5 per cent rise in the price of wheat. A harvest only 10 per cent below normal would, in theory, have increased grain prices six times as much.[44]

None the less, taxation was unpopular and politically sensitive. Only in conditions of virtual military dictatorship, as existed in France at the local level, could the tax-take be increased five- or sixfold within a decade (St Antoine, Dauphiné; Montpellier). In Castile, where taxes had already tripled between 1559 and 1577, it was possible to increase them by only 30 per cent during the 1580s and 1590s, barely in pace with inflation. In England less than half of expenditure was met by new taxation, which amounted to about 5d per head. Governments, reluctant to risk exacting the entire charge for war directly from existing taxes and unable to get consent for fundamental reforms of the fiscal system (subsidy reassessment, *medio de la harina*), settled for *ad hoc* solutions: borrowing, benevolences and a variety of forms of 'voluntary taxation' and other expedients, sales of offices, noble privileges, lands, jurisdictions, revenues, trading licences and monopolies, as well as forced loans and the exaction of personal and administrative services of different kinds. None of these measures was new, but they were given a new intensity and extension in the 1590s precisely as the traditional forms were becoming exhausted. It was these expedients, much more than the actual levels of extraction, that had profound social, political and economic implications.

The growth of the public debt, offering a still relatively secure alternative for investment, had obvious repercussions on the capital market and drew off funds from potentially more productive employment. The large number of patents of nobility sold by the French Crown was in part a symptom, but also a channel for an unprecendented social mobility.[45] The alienation of ecclasiastical lands effected a wholesale transfer of property to the benefit variously of the *noblesse* (sword and robe), peasant proprietors, and traders and farmers of *seigneuries*.[46] The more than £500,000 of Crown lands sold by Elizabeth between 1589 and 1602 may have had only a limited effect on the actual tenure of the land, but did it not, as James I's Lord Treasurer, Middlesex, believed, seriously weaken ties of obedience to the Crown in the counties?[47] There can be no doubt that Philip II's sales of township status and his extension of the sale of municipal *regimientos* to even the smallest towns and villages after 1581 resulted in the mass transfer of control over communal lands and the village economy from annually elected village councils to proprietary 'village tyrants'. Between 1581 and 1600 more than 400 populations were involved, forty-four of them within the jurisdiction of Seville alone.[48] The effect was to undermine the corporate dominance of the cities over their hinterlands and with it the security of their food supplies. We have here, perhaps, one aspect of the crisis of the cities to which other contributors have drawn attention. The transfer of the usufruct of communal lands and wastes to a narrow plutocracy, most often of pastoralists, dangerously narrowed the margin of subsistence for the population of Castile in the seventeenth century.

Military expenditure involved a transfer from the taxpayer to the soldiery, the supplier and the state creditor. As in the main the new taxation of the 1590s was not levied on commerce and manufacturing,[49] it is tempting to think of it primarily as an expropriation of agrarian resources. Certainly, agriculture does not seem to have been sufficiently compensated by the profits of increased military demand. This was partly because, in global terms, military demand was not very great, and partly because of government interference in the market. The grain purchases of the Spanish commissariat, at their peak of about 400,000 *fanegas*, double what had been required in the early 1580s, drew off perhaps 4 per cent of a normal harvest in Andalusia, which was the principal granary for the fleets.[50] That amount could have been grown twice over on the estates of the Duke of Osuna alone. Harvest fluctuations could have ten times the effect on the market, or more. Moreover, government-imposed price maxima tended to check the upward pressure of prices, as did, in England, the new grain-marketing regulations introduced in 1587, perhaps deliberately to enable victuallers to buy more easily and more cheaply.[51] Compulsory purchases at controlled prices in years of dearth, combined with non-payment or late payment and the discounting of bills, added up to a form of supplementary extraction further disadvantaging the agrarian sector and depressing rural demand.

This is not to say that the net effect of external war on the rural economy was necessarily negative. Locally, and in the short-term, military demand may have had a bullish effect on prices, as may have been the case in East Anglia and in Andalusia, for example,[52] and this would have been particularly beneficial to the agricultural producer in that it did not derive from reduced output. It may also be that the limited evidence of any sustained pull on prices attributable to military demand reflects an adaptation of agrarian production to new demands, fiscal even more than material. García Sanz's work on Segovia has shown how the war taxes of the 1590s were raised, at least in part, by bringing under-utilised land resources into cultivation.[53] This response to fiscal pressure is, of course, a common historical phenomenon, and an analogous process was operative in Ireland where, as Hayes-McCoy writes, 'It was said that Tyrone and Tyrconnell had never been so rich, and had never before produced so much food, as they did in the war years.'[54]

The requirements of the military victualler were, in the broad sense, substitutional. This was not the case with the demand for military hardware, and the manufacturing sector, or at least some branches of it, must have received some stimulus from government and private spending on war. Too much should not be made of this effect, however, nor of its putative implications for the development of capitalism.[55] Only one-third or one-quarter as much was spent on materiel as on victuals, and, despite the concentration of demand in the state and the changes in the nature of warfare, the scale and the demands of war in the 1590s were not substantial enough to be of profound significance at the macro-economic level. Individual industries clearly benefited. There was a lively demand for iron in the war years, and shipbuilders should have done well, not only out of government orders but also out of the accelerated losses caused by the wars, insofar as these outweighed the reduction of carrying capacity required for trade.[56] But it is doubtful whether military demand was sufficient or sustained enough to stimulate any industry as a whole, let alone any economy in which industry was only a small part of the whole. The output of iron guns and shot from the Kent and Sussex foundries increased by about 50 per cent to 800 or 1,000 tons a year between 1578 and 1600, but that was only about 5–7 per cent of England's iron production and probably no more than 1–2 per cent of the iron and steel output of western Europe.[57] In 1621 the royal cannon-founder, John Browne, claimed that the King's service would have occupied his furnaces for only ten days a year.[58] Even in the middle of the seventeenth century it can be calculated that the total productive capacity of cast-iron cannon in Europe could have absorbed only about 3 per cent of iron output.[59] The military demand for textiles was even more marginal. The value of the clothing (of all materials) supplied to the English forces in the Netherlands in 1589 was exceeded fiftyfold by the total value of shortcloth exports.[60] The woollen cloth purchased for the 35,000 men invading Portugal in 1580, one of the largest armies ever raised in Habsburg Spain, could not have exceeded 4½ per cent of the output of the single city of Cordoba.[61]

Moreover, the military supplier and the arms manufacturer suffered from government interference and indebtedness in the same way as the agriculturalist. The business of war did not, therefore, offer either a particularly broad or a particularly easy path to fortune or social advance. Though some achieved a spectacular eminence, rarely was this success lasting. The new noble dynasties were established by lawyers and administrators, not as a rule by government contractors and military profiteers, whose agreements were frequently dishonoured by treasuries and who paid severely for their compensatory malfeasances. Nearly all the most notable of Spain's military contractors were either disgraced or bankrupted within a few years (Pedro de Baeza, Juan Pascual, Gómez de Acosta, Núñez Correa). The Evelyns were one of the few families in England to make a name for themselves from the profits of war. Even Jean Curtius, who did enormously well when the arms industry of Liège benefited from the difficulties of Antwerp and Malines, was forced to move operations to Spain when military activity in the Low Countries died down in the early seventeenth century and to diversify into the manufacture of domestic ironware.[62] The state was too powerful, too dangerous and too unreliable a customer for the ordinary businessman, unless he had powerful protectors at Court.[63]

III

In other ways, however, war contributed to a crisis of the social order which, while neither initiated nor resolved in this period, was made more acute by the events of the 1590s. The exceptional social mobility during the French Wars of Religion, marked by sales of patents of nobility, lands and offices, both distorted and devalued traditional concepts of nobility.[64] In Castile, too, sales of *hidalguía* (few), *regimientos* (many) and *señoríos* closely followed the chronology of war;[65] while in England the inflation of honours under James I must be seen as a deferred legacy of the war years.[66] The fiscal privileges of nobility were beginning to be eroded by benevolences, forced loans and administrative burdens, and challenged in their essence by proposed universal, indirect taxes, like the *millones* or the flour tax in Castile.[67] At the same time, the increasing professionalisation of war was in danger of making traditional nobility a military anachronism.[68]

The wars were thus not merely a cause but also an aspect of the crisis. They were, in part, wars for the restoration of nobility and traditional noble values, wars to recoup fortune, credit and political influence. This is easy enough to see in France where the wars were wars against false nobles, financiers, venal officers, mignons, and what Huppert calls the 'gentry'.[69] In England, as well, the younger generation, arriving in France clad, to the astonishment of their hosts, like knights out of ancient tapestries, was elevating the cult of honour into a challenge to the old men of the gown who held power, patronage and influence.[70] Paradoxically, success, even in war, benefited the bureaucrats. Only in Spain, where the aged counsellors of Philip II's *junta secreta* could be held responsible for the failures of the 1590s, did the military nobility get their victory, with the accession in 1598 of a twenty-year-old king whose idol was the imperial knight, Charles V. In France, the victory of Henry IV was also the victory of the *noblesse de robe* in the King's councils.[71] In England, Essex, with all he stood for, was outmanoeuvred after Cadiz by Cecil's propaganda machine, and the 1590s, which began with the chivalric revival of the Accession Day tilts and the Garter ceremonies, ended with aristocratic treason and conspiracy.[72] Nobility was discredited by its own métier, its respect undermined and its image tarnished by brigandage, profiteering and incompetence.[73] The Duke of Medina Sidonia, returning to be jeered at by street urchins, was seen as the paradigm case of the unfortunate consequences of giving priority to 'precedency' over 'military valour' (Campanella).[74] Faced with the demand for promotion by merit and experience (Brantôme, Valdés, Isaba, Williams, Sutcliff), the nobility had to be rehabilitated by books and military academies, and access to nobility protected by labyrinthine genealogies and ancestral memories of valour.[75]

The nobility may in the end have done well enough economically out of the wars, as Russell Major argues; their local power may have been reinforced, or at the very least not seriously eroded, by the Crown's reliance on their authority; upward mobility may have been checked by 1600 and class lines rigidified with the fossilisation of noble values;[76] but this was achieved only at the cost of raising up the ogre of its own mirror-image. The growth of a distinctive 'bourgeois' consciousness that some historians have discerned about the turn of the sixteenth century[77] was both a reaction to the closing of noble ranks, which made a nonsense of mere titular ennoblement, either by sneering at it or by creating alternative hierarchies within it, and at the same time a recognition of the gulf between the military and the mercantile interest, brought home by the lean years of war which had dramatically straitened the passage through trade to wealth and fortune.[78] Once again, there is a precognition, no more, in the 1590s of the crisis of a later generation.[79]

IV

In his *Méditerranée* Braudel asks of the decade 1600–10, 'l'heure est-elle favorable aux États moyens?'.[80] A crisis of empires seems to be apparent in the 1580s and 1590s. It can be seen in the weakened hold of the Ottomans in north Africa and of the Iberians in north Italy and the East and West Indies, in the failure of Polish imperialism, in Russia's introversion after

Ivan the Terrible. The empires were posited on war. When war ceased to be able to sustain the Ottoman state, the empire fractured, and without the Ottomans the Catholic, Mediterranean empire of Spain that opposed it ceased to cohere.[81] By the late 1590s the Spanish position in north Italy was falling apart, to be saved only by the abandonment of French interests in Italy at the treaty of Lyons (1601).[82] This transformation was rooted in the changed nature of naval warfare in the 1580s and 1590s. With the cheap iron gun and the round-ship coming into the Mediterranean, making the individual corsair as viable an enterprise as he was in the Indies, and with Spain having to maintain an ocean fleet as well, the economics of protection turned against size.[83] The state was not an efficient supplier of protection on that scale, and as protection costs were forced up it was impossible for the state to compete on all fronts.[84] The Armada was fitted out at the expense of a severe tonnage crisis in the Indies trade in 1589–98.[85] The Americas could be protected only at great cost, with the sacrifice of shipping in Newfoundland and North Atlantic waters, and by making the monarchy dependent for its defence on its own enemies.[86] War at sea, therefore, offered the Dutch, 'the most advanced bourgeois nation', and the English both the opportunity and the means to challenge a Spanish imperialism that Pierre Vilar represents as the 'supreme stage of feudalism'.[87] As Wallerstein has written of the Thirty Years War, on the Hispano-Dutch front the concluding phase of the later sixteenth-century struggle, 'The war became one of the modalities by which reallocations of economic roles and intensifications of economic disputes occurred.'[88]

V

Can we also talk of a 'crisis of the state' in the 1590s? 'Already by 1590', Trevor-Roper writes of his Renaissance State, 'the cracks are beginning to appear.'[89] These stresses were largely the consequence of the burdens of war. The effectiveness of the machinery of government was put to the test by the size and the nature of the administrative tasks which war presented in the 1590s. New administrative agencies had to be created or old ones adapted (war secretariats, navy boards, military governors in Spain, Lords-Lieutenant, deputies, muster-masters in England, the Council of State, the provincial admiralties, the audit office in the United Provinces, the development of the secretaryship of state and the intendancies in France). The keynote was to be professionalism, regulation and central control. But military law, prerogative government and 'stranger' commissioners were seen to threaten customary and statutory rights and local interests, and at every level the desire to evade or the attempt to exploit fiscal and military levies and purveyance led to tensions and confrontations, setting communities against each other and reactivating long-standing conflicts of authority and jurisdiction. The administration of war was turned into a battlefield. Control over the militia was fought over by 'county gentry' and 'court gentry', JP and deputy lieutenant, magnate captain and professional muster-master.[90] In Castile the authority of the cities was challenged by the towns of their *partidos*, lords supported by the Council of War were taken to law by their vassals supported by the Council of Castile, and the militia was sabotaged as effectively by the civilian justices there as it was by the JPs in England.

The state, lacking in funds, in internal cohesion, in administrative discipline, in commercial knowhow, far from being strengthened by war was forced to retreat. In Spain the 1580s and 1590s see the most advanced administration in Europe beginning a withdrawal from direct involvement in the administration of war and having to turn from royal officials to contractors, municipalities and local magnates.[91] In England the experiment with direct administration of the customs collapsed and military supply became increasingly privatised.[92] The state had reached the limits of its administrative capacity. In Spain military contracting, the devolution of fiscal and military organisation to the cities and the reinforcement of seigneurial authority, the alienation of jurisdictions and the sale of exemptions that are the legacy of the 1590s, add up to a decentralisation of power and practical authority that is at the heart of the problems of the Spanish state in the seventeenth century. In England, too, the Crown's monopoly of military power was at best partial. Noble retinues continued to be both militarily and socially important, and the influence of the local magnate and gentry remained a real constraint on the appointment of lieutenants, deputies and militia captains.[93] Both Philip II and Elizabeth were forced by the exhaustion of alternative fiscal expedients into increased dependence on parliamentary taxation and into increasing compromises with their parliaments. The war years are critical for the development of parliamentary influence, and perhaps even more so in Castile than in England, where a new *pactismo* was established between *rey* and *reino* as a direct consequence of the *millones* grants.[94] In the United Provinces the centralisation of Leicester was defeated with the curtailment of the powers of the Council of State and its subordination to the States General (1588), the reorganisation of the Admiralty Board (1597), and the efforts of the States to control the armed forces.[95] In France, on the one hand, the reaction against the war strengthened the idea of monarchy; on the other, the postwar settlement built in limitations – the Edict of Nantes, the capitulations with the grandees, which cost more than 32 million *livres*, the concessions to municipal self-government, the *paulette*, the failure of Sully's *élections*.[96] Faced with a crisis of government which threatened to turn into a crisis of the constitution, princes were compelled to defer internal conflict by compromise or retreat if war was to be pursued or concluded satisfactorily. None of the issues raised during the 1590s was resolved. It was left to their successors a generation later to face up to the same issues in a more resolute way.

VI

War was undoubtedly one element in the epidemic of popular disturbances and discontents in the 1590s, but it was only one element, and opposition to the wars, as such, though not unknown, was not widespread. Protests against high taxes, the export of grain to the army and the depredations of the soldiery characterised the peasant rebellions in Upper Austria and Hungary, the Gautiers and Croquants in France, popular discontents in the southern Netherlands, and other isolated disturbances, like those in Ipswich in 1586[97]. A growing war-weariness, and even a rejection of basic policy aims, can be seen, but expressed usually in indirect and sometimes surprising ways: the reluctance of gentlemen and commoners to join up for the wars, the pro-Spanish utterances of ordinary people in Kent and Oxford,[98] the celebrated 'let them be damned' speech of the representative of Madrid in the 1593 Cortes,[99] the extraordinary resistance of Avila and other cities of Old Castile to the *millones*, the disaffection of the Portuguese, smarting at the pillaging of their empire and their shipping, which found one outlet in false Sebastians and another in the murder and mistreatment of the Spanish soldiers garrisoning Lisbon.[100]

In some ways it was the soldier, owed months of back pay and left starving by the incompetence or rapacity of the commissariat, who was the real sufferer in the 1590s, and it was the military mutiny that was the characteristic popular revolt of the decade.[101] The returned soldier, often sick, starving and maimed, clearly posed a problem for governments to which they responded with welfare policies, hospitals and pensions which went some way, at least, to meet the need.[102] But was the returned soldier the serious and widespread problem that the panic reactions of some contemporaries have led us to believe? Did war really turn young gentlemen, yeomen, artificers and other lusty young fellows into rogues and thieves, as Sir John Smythe thought, or were his opponents right when they claimed that the levies were 'the very scum, thieves, and rogues of England, and therefore have been very well lost, and that the realm, being too full of people is very well rid of them, and that if they had not been consumed in those wars they would have died under a hedge'?[103] Given the underlying social problems of the 1590s, it may be doubted whether war contributed as much to the problem of poverty or to the increase in vagrancy as is commonly said.[104] If it was overwhelmingly the landless, the unemployed, the marginal who went into the armies and navies, then the recruiter was doing the community a service by exporting vagrancy, or at least transferring the burden of poor relief from the locality to the exchequer and bringing some of the starving within the orbit of an organised procurement system with access to the international market. There is something to be said for the commonplace contemporary view of war as a social safety-valve – 'Foreign War serving', as Sir Walter Raleigh wrote, 'like a Potion of Rhubarb to waste away Choler from the Body of the Realm'.[105] The Turkish invasion of Hungary not only drew off the dangerous throng of unemployed soldiers in Istanbul, it also did a lot to check the growth of banditry, notably in Catalonia and the Romagna, that may be associated with the preservation of a formal peace in the Mediterranean after the 1570s.[106] One reason for the formation of a special Catalan galley squadron in 1600 was to divert the young from a life of banditry.[107] If the means did not exist to socialise the deviant, they had to be created.

In some sense, then, war had a conservative function in the 1590s, damping down discontents, deflecting internal hostilities against external enemies and domestic scapegoats (foreigners, *moriscos*, witches, gypsies),[108] and periodically reinforcing loyalty to the regime in response to victory, disaster or threat. It was the fate of the Armada that induced the Cortes to concede Philip II the *millones*, and the sack of Cadiz in 1596 that persuaded them to recommend its regrant after protracted resistance, just as in England it was the threat from Spain that underwrote the cult of Gloriana, completed the collapse of the Puritan opposition in Parliament, and sustained the sometimes prickly co-operation between Elizabeth and the Commons. It was left to James I to deal with the fiscal archaisms and the political and social frustrations papered over by the Elizabethan myth. The Bye Plot, the Gunpowder Plot, the disaffection of Raleigh were all, it has been argued, manifestations of a revolt of the 'mere gentry' against *peace*.[109] The legacy in England of the dissatisfactions of the 1590s was an expectation of reform with the peace that, unfulfilled, led to a growing alienation of the local community and polarisation between Court and Country.[110] So too, it was only with peace that the profound constitutional and religious differences within the United Provinces were released, and only after peace with Russia in 1595 that Charles of Sweden was able to turn inwards against Fleming in Finland. In many respects peace turned out to be rather more dangerous than war.

VII

Not the least of the crises of the 1590s was a crisis of war itself. The wars of the 1590s were wars which nobody really won. Reputations evaporated, even of the greatest (Essex, Parma, Medina Sidonia). Universal failure exposed the pitiless waste of resources. Even the wealth of the Indies could achieve nothing; nor could divine providence be relied upon to defend its cause. The interests of true religion seemed no longer to be forwarded by expensive and inconclusive butchery. The Sainte Union degenerated into brigandage and tyranny. There was a shrieking dissonance between means and ends. Anthony Wingfield bemoaned the paradox that the military profession was despised just at the moment when it was 'never so necessary' (1589).[111] Cynicism was everywhere. Old Sir John Smythe was convinced that the gentry of England were packing off their tenants to certain death in the wars in order to cash in on entry fines.[112] The captain and the colonel were condemned as callous profiteers of their men's lives.[113] The common soldier had to be forced to the wars. Any man with any substance would buy himself out. Even to be a soldier was coming to be shameful.[114] It was for this reason, above all, that the many attempts to bring about a general militarisation or re-militarisation of society for the purposes of national defence, through the reactivation or the reform of local militias, trained-bands, weapons practice, or horse-breeding, inspired by the invasion psychosis of the 1590s, proved to be largely ineffective. The glowing chivalric revival had burnt out. The '1590s' began with Philip Sydney; they ended with Don Quixote.

There is a spiritual crisis of the 1590s, a 'traumatisme de fin de siècle',[115] a loss of meaning and purpose, a debilitating dejection that one finds in surprising places, as in the letter written to a patron by Philip II's secretary of war, Esteban de Ibarra, a man who had worked with Alba in the golden days:'Everything is in such a state that it takes away one's will to work and serve just to see the way things are going.'[116] Perhaps it is this spirit which goes some way towards explaining the muted nature of the political crisis of the 1590s. Discontent and disillusion seem to channel themselves away from active opposition. Bitterness is turned into verse. Dissidence is displaced into *desengaño*. 'Melancholia', scepticism, atheism, withdrawal from the active world of politics and a picaresque rejection of established values, on the one hand, and, on the other, a 'moralizing puritanism', the revival of Augustinian salvationism, and neo-Stoicism have all been seen as responses to the wars.[117] For Lipsius and Quevedo, at least, the link was explicit.[118] But neo-Stoicism was important because it was much more than an escape. It offered a new social ethic and a rehabilitation of the military ethos. It civilianised the military virtues and pointed the way towards a new perception of the role of nobility in the service of the state.[119] It was to be one of the principal means by which the traditional social order overcame the 'crisis of the 1590s.'

Notes: Chapter 14

1 F. A. Beer, *How Much War in History: Definitions, Estimates, Extrapolations and Trends* (Beverly Hills, Calif., 1974), pp. 12–15.

2 J. Meyer, 'Le paysan français pendant les guerres de la Ligue', in B. Köpeczi and E. H. Balázs (eds), *Paysannerie française, paysannerie hongroise, XVIe–XXe siècles* (Budapest, 1973), p. 66, for France. For Holland, A. Th. van Deursen, 'Holland's experience of war during the Revolt of the Netherlands', in A. C. Duke and C. A. Tamse (eds), *Britain and the Netherlands*, vol. 6 (The Hague, 1977), pp. 31, 34; and, for Flanders, E. Thoen, 'Warfare and the countryside: social and economic aspects of military destruction in Flanders during the late Middle Ages and the early modern period', *The Low Countries History Yearbook*, vol. 13 (1980), p. 25. On the campaigns of the 1580s and 1590s in the Netherlands, see G. Parker, *The Dutch Revolt* (London, 1977), pp. 208–35.

3 G. Parker, *The Army of Flanders and the Spanish Road, 1567–1659* (Cambridge, 1972), p. 271; C. S. L. Davies, 'The English people and war in the early sixteenth century', in Duke and Tamse, *Britain and the Netherlands*, vol. 6, p. 2.

4 P. Vilar, 'The age of Don Quixote', in P. Earle (ed.), *Essays in European Economic History, 1500–1800* (Oxford, 1974), p. 105; G. Parker, 'The Dutch Revolt and the polarization of international politics', in G. Parker, *Spain and the Netherlands, 1559–1659* (London, 1979), pp. 65–81.

5 J. Payne Collier (ed.), *The Egerton Papers*, Camden Society, 1st ser., vol. 12 (1840), p. 260, an attitude mirrored in Castile by the *procurador* for Murcia in the Cortes in 1593: *Actas de las Cortes de Castilla*, vol. 12 (Madrid, 1887), p. 463.

6 M. Roberts, *The Early Vasas* (Cambridge, 1968), pp. 333, 373.

7 P. Williams, *The Tudor Regime* (Oxford, 1979), p. 15; P. Benedict, *Rouen during the Wars of Religion* (Cambridge, 1981), p. 170; F. Braudel, *The Mediterranean and the Mediterranean World in the Age of Philip II* (London, 1973), vol. 2, p. 1223, for Spanish and Venetian fear of the Turk; and, for Spanish fears of *morisco* treachery, see *Actas de las Cortes* (hereafter *Actas*), vol. 9, p. 28, vol. 11, p. 542, vol. 13, p. 95, and F. Pérez Mínguez, *Don Juan de Idiáquez* (San Sebastián, 1934), p. 262.

8 C. S. R. Russell, 'Monarchies, wars, and estates in England, France and Spain, *c.*1580–*c.*1640', *Legislative Studies Quarterly*, vol. 7, no. 2 (1982), p. 210.

9 See L. Boynton, *The Elizabethan Militia, 1558–1638* (London, 1967); I. A. A. Thompson, *War and Government in Habsburg Spain, 1560–1620* (London, 1976), ch. 4. Proposals for national militia training were made in the United Provinces also but dropped in 1600 by the States as 'contrary to the liberty and character of these lands': Van Deursen, 'Holland's experience', p. 31.

10 P. W. Bamford, *Fighting Ships and Prisons: The Mediterranean Galleys of France in the Age of Louis XIV* (Minneapolis, Minn., 1973), pp. 24–5; Thompson, *War and Government*, pp. 32–3.

11 M. Roberts, 'The military revolution, 1560–1660', in M. Roberts, *Essays in Swedish History* (London, 1967), pp. 195–225; G. Parker, 'The "military revolution, 1560–1660" – a myth?', in Parker, *Spain and the Netherlands*, pp. 86–103; M. D. Feld, 'Middle-class society and the rise of military professionalism: the Dutch army, 1589–1609', in M. D. Feld, *The Structure of Violence: Armed Forces as Social Systems* (Beverly Hills, Calif., 1977), pp. 169–203; J. R. Hale, 'Armies, navies and the art of war', in R. B. Wernham (ed.), *The New Cambridge Modern History*, vol. 3 (Cambridge, 1968), p. 178. For parallel developments in the Ottoman army, see V. J. Parry, 'The Ottoman Empire, 1566–1617', in ibid., pp. 365–6.

12 The concept comes from Feld, 'Middle-class society', p. 179.

13 'In Western history war has always made it necessary, to a lesser or greater extent, for the governments which wage it to control or seize the sources of trade and production': J. U. Nef, *Western Civilization since the Renaissance: Peace, War, Industry and the Arts* (New York, 1963), p. 18.

14 See their contributions to this volume, and Benedict, *Rouen*, pp. 221–6.

15 See Thoen, 'Warfare and the countryside', H. van der Wee, *The Growth of the Antwerp Market and the European Economy (fourteenth–sixteenth centuries)* (The Hague, 1963), vol.

2, ch. 8, and the essays by Daelemans, De Wever, Jansen and Tits-Dieuaide in H. van der Wee and E. van Cauwenberghe (eds), *Productivity of Land and Agricultural Innovation in the Low Countries (1200–1800)* (Louvain, 1978). G. Parker, 'War and economic change: the economic costs of the Dutch Revolt', in J. M. Winter (ed.), *War and Economic Development* (Cambridge, 1975), pp. 49–71, surveys the data on the southern Netherlands at pp. 50–4.

16 J. Russell Major, 'Noble income, inflation, and the Wars of Religion in France', *American Historical Review*, vol. 86 (1981), p. 48; G. Livet, *Les Guerres de religion (1559–1598)* (Paris, 1962), p. 87: 'Si bien qu'on peut poser la question de l'interprétation de cette dépression finale (longue ou courte durée? guerre ou crise aiguë de subsistances?).'

17 Above, pp. 86–7. For Amiens, see P. Deyon, 'Variations de la production textile aux 16e et 17e siècles', *Annales ESC*, vol. 18 (1963), pp. 948–9. See Livet, *Guerres de religion*, pp. 85, 90, on the limited demographic effect of the war.

18 Meyer, 'Paysan français', p. 66. Rouen was recovering from 1594 (Benedict *Rouen*, p. 230), Marseilles from 1596 and Lyon in the 1590s (J. N. Ball, *Merchants and Merchandise: The Expansion of Trade in Europe, 1500–1630* (London, 1977), pp. 94, 77), while Languedoc in general escaped relatively lightly. E. Le Roy Ladurie, *Histoire du Languedoc* (Paris, 1967), p. 69, writes that after the final truce in 1596 'la reprise est rapide, générale, vigoureuse'; the crisis of the Religious Wars checked economic growth but did not reverse it and was nothing like as severe as that of the fourteenth century.

19 Thoen, 'Warfare and the countryside', p. 29 ('economic recovery . . . always occurred with amazing rapidity') and pp. 30–8 on the range of experiences; C. Verlinden, 'En Flandre sous Philippe II: durée de la crise économique', *Annales ESC*, vol. 7 (1952), pp. 28–9; Van der Wee, *Antwerp*, vol. 2, p. 271, vol. 3, p. 70; Van der Wee and Van Cauwenberghe, *Productivity of Land*, pp. 13, 48, 84–6; H. van der Wee, 'Typologie des crises et changements de structures aux Pays-Bas (XVe–XVIe siècles)', *Annales ESC*, vol. 18 (1963), p. 223, on the rapidity of agrarian and economic recovery after 1587 and 1588.

20 Van der Wee, *Antwerp*, vol. 2, p. 260; H. van der Wee, 'Structural changes and specialization in the industry of the southern Netherlands, 1100–1600', *Economic History Review*, 2nd ser., vol. 28 (1975), p. 218; C. Verlinden, J. Craeybeckx and E. Scholliers, 'Price and wage movements in Belgium in the sixteenth century', in P. Burke (ed.), *Economy and Society in Early Modern Europe* (London, 1972), p. 60.

21 T. W. Moody, F. X. Martin and F. J. Byrne (eds), *A New History of Ireland*, vol. 3 (Oxford, 1976), pp. 140–1.

22 M. P. Gutmann, *War and Rural Life in the Early Modern Low Countries* (Princeton, NJ, 1980).

23 C. R. Friedrichs, *Urban Society in an Age of War: Nördlingen, 1580–1720* (Princeton, NJ, 1979).

24 Van der Wee, 'Structural changes', p. 217, and *Antwerp*, vol. 2, p. 262.

25 R. Davis, *The Trade and Shipping of Hull, 1500–1700* (York, 1964), pp. 7, 11; E. Salvador, 'En torno al comercio y a la economía valenciana del quinientos', *Estudis*, vol. 1 (1972), pp. 36–40.

26 P. Dollinger, *The German Hansa* (London, 1970), pp. 350–1. England's Baltic trade also increased by 150 per cent between 1575 and 1595, but it was carried overwhelmingly in foreign bottoms after 1585: H. Zins, *England and the Baltic in the Elizabethan Era* (Manchester, 1972), pp. 274, 289.

27 K. R. Andrews, *Elizabethan Privateering* (Cambridge, 1964); H. Taylor, 'Price revolution or price revision? The English and Spanish trade after 1604', *Renaissance and Modern Studies*, vol. 12 (1968), pp. 5–32, and at p. 20: 'our countrymen exclaim and wish nothing but wars, alleging that no merchandise but victual is in any request to yield profit'.

28 Van der Wee, *Antwerp*, vol. 2, pp. 270, 279, 308, 397; Van der Wee and Van Cauwenberghe, *Productivity of Land*, pp. 14, 47, 85; Verlinden, 'En Flandre', p. 60; Van der Wee, 'Typologie', p. 222.

29 I. Wallerstein, *The Modern World-System*, vol. 2 (New York, 1980), pp. 14–16.

30 The impact in England is discussed by A. Everitt, 'The marketing of agricultural

produce', in J. Thirsk (ed.), *The Agrarian History of England and Wales*, vol. 4 (Cambridge, 1967), ch. 8, p. 523, and by Outhwaite, above, pp. 24 ff.

31 *Actas*, vol. 15, p. 759

32 Biblioteca Nacional, Madrid, MS 9372, fos 31–40*v*, reproduced in C. Viñas Mey, *El problema de la tierra en la España de los siglos XVI–XVII* (Madrid, 1941), pp. 215–26.

33 Thompson, *War and Government*, pp. 103–6.

34 C. G. Cruickshank, *Elizabeth's Army* (Oxford, 1966), pp. 290–1. This calculation assumes a population of *c* 4½ million for England and Wales or *c* 1 million households.

35 Thompson, *War and Government*, p. 104, table 4.1.

36 *Memorial de la política necesaria y útil restauración de la república de España* (1600), fo. 4, cited in M. Colmeiro, *Historia de la economía política en España*, vol. 2 (Madrid, 1965), p. 604.

37 For a survey of some of the recent demographic literature, see A. W. Lovett, 'The Golden Age of Spain: new work on an old theme', *Historical Journal*, vol. 24 (1981), pp. 739–49; for Andalusia, J. I. Fortea Pérez, *Córdoba en el siglo XVI: Las bases demográficas y económicas de una expansión urbana* (Cordoba, 1981), ch. 3; for Galicia, J. Ruiz Almansa, *La población de Galicia (1500–1945)* (Madrid, 1948); for Old Castile, L. A. Ribot García *et al.*, *Valladolid, corazón del mundo hispánico – siglo XVI* (Valladolid, 1981), p. 76.

38 J. T. Evans, *Seventeenth-century Norwich* (Oxford, 1979), pp. 4–5, 19; P. Clark, *English Provincial Society from the Reformation to the Revolution: Religion, Politics and Society in Kent, 1500–1640* (Hassocks, 1977), ch. 10; A. Fletcher, *A County Community in Peace and War: Sussex, 1600–1660* (London, 1975), p. 21.

39 Williams, *Tudor Regime*, p. 75; Parker, *Dutch Revolt*, pp. 237, 249; Thompson, *War and Government*, pp. 69–71; F. Ruiz Martín, 'Las finanzas españolas durante el reinado de Felipe II (alternativas de participación que se ofrecieron para Francia)', *Cuadernos de historia: anexos de la revista 'Hispania'*, vol. 2 (Madrid, 1968), pp. 109–73; Braudel, *Mediterranean*, vol. 1, pp. 510–17, on the 1596 'bankruptcy' in Spain, vol. 2, p. 694, for a graph of *asientos*; R. Briggs, *Early Modern France, 1560–1715* (Oxford, 1977), p. 220.

40 For estimates of national income in Castile, G. Gentil da Silva, *En Espagne, développement économique, subsistance, déclin* (Paris, 1965), p. 92; A. Domínguez Ortiz, *The Golden Age of Spain* (London, 1971), p. 198. The Dutch and English figures are guesses extrapolated from wage rates on the basis of 400,000 families in the United Provinces and 1 million in England. Taking a soldier's pay of 130 florins a year in Holland (P. Zumthor, *Daily Life in Rembrandt's Holland* (London, 1962), p. 337, n. 6), and 8d a day in England (Cruickshank, *Elizabeth's Army*, p. 88), for comparability, a figure of 52 million florins is reached for the United Provinces and £12 million for England. For a justification of the method, see P. Bairoch, 'Estimations du revenu national dans les sociétés occidentales pré-industrielles et au XIXe siècle', *Revue économique*, vol. 28 (1977), pp. 177–208.

41 Williams, *Tudor Regime*, p. 75; Clark, *English Provincial Society*, pp. 225, 228; A. Hassell Smith, *County and Court: Government and Politics in Norfolk, 1558–1603* (Oxford, 1974), pp. 278–9.

42 C. Wilson, 'Taxation and the decline of empires, an unfashionable theme', in C. Wilson, *Economic History and the Historian* (London, 1969), p. 120.

43 N. Salomon, *La Campagne de Nouvelle Castille à la fin du XVIe siècle d'après les 'Relaciones topográficas'* (Paris, 1964), ch. 6, esp. pp. 234, 243.

44 B. H. Slicher van Bath, *The Agrarian History of Western Europe, AD 500–1850* (London, 1963), p. 118. Castilian wheat prices at the *tasa*.

45 D. Bitton, *The French Nobility in Crisis, 1560–1640* (Stanford, Calif., 1969), ch. 6.

46 Livet, *Guerres de religion*, pp. 91–5; H. Drouot, *Mayenne et la Bourgogne: étude sur la Ligue (1587–1596)* (Dijon, 1937), vol. 1, p. 45.

47 R. B. Outhwaite, 'Who bought crown lands? The pattern of purchases, 1589–1603', *Bulletin of the Institute of Historical Research*, vol. 44 (1971), pp. 18–33. Cranfield is reported to have told the King often that 'in selling land he did not only sell his rent, as other men did, but sold his sovereignty, for it was a greater tie of obedience to be a tenant to the King than to be his subject': M. Prestwich, *Cranfield: Politics and Profits under the Early Stuarts* (Oxford, 1966), p. 339.

48 Data from Archivo General de Simancas, Dirección General del Tesoro (Inventario 24),

legajo 323. *Actas*, vol. 18, p. 583, Alonso Muriel (Madrid): 'es poner en los regimientos tiranos perpetuos'.

49 This was probably not true of Holland, where the main tax, the *verponding*, was levied as a percentage of the rental value of real property: J. de Vries, *The Dutch Rural Economy in the Golden Age, 1500–1700* (New Haven, Conn., 1974), p. 210. In England, although the subsidy may have fallen more heavily on the towns and the merchants, the Book of Rates was unchanged since the reign of Mary, and the effective rate was very low: Williams, *Tudor Regime*, pp. 78–9.

50 The estimate of Andalusian grain output was made by Don Juan Chacón de Narvaez in 1583: Archivo General de Simancas, Guerra Antigua, *legajo* 155, fos. 46, 49, 53, 57, 62, 65, 66.

51 B. Pearce, 'Elizabethan food policy and the armed forces', *Economic History Review*, 1st ser., vol. 12 (1942), p. 41; Cruickshank, *Elizabeth's Army*, p. 82.

52 The data in E. J. Hamilton, *American Treasure and the Price Revolution in Spain, 1501–1650* (Cambridge, Mass., 1934), app. 6, pp. 390–2, support this conclusion, as does the generally high level of wheat prices in Norwich during the 1590s: see above, p. 28, and local complaints, like that of the mayor of Chester in March 1595, in Pearce, 'Elizabethan food policy', p. 45.

53 A. García Sanz, *Desarrollo y crisis del Antiguo Régimen en Castilla la Vieja: Economía y sociedad en tierras de Segovia, 1500–1814* (Madrid, 1977), p. 145; *Actas*, vol. 15, pp. 655–7: 'las tierras son más que nunca han sido por las que de nuevo se han rompido que eran dehesas concejiles y baldíos' (26 August 1598).

54 Moody *et al.*, *New History of Ireland*, vol. 3, p. 125. See also W. W. Rostow, *The Process of Economic Growth* (Oxford, 1953), pp. 149, 153–4; De Vries, *Dutch Rural Economy*, p. 210; P. Deane, 'War and industrialization', in J. M. Winter (ed.), *War and Economiç Development*, pp. 91, 98.

55 J. U. Nef, 'War and economic progress, 1540–1640', *Economic History Review*, 1st ser., vol. 12 (1942), pp. 13–48.

56 R. Davis, *The Rise of the English Shipping Industry in the 17th and 18th Centuries* (London, 1962), pp. 5, 7, on the ambivalent impact of war in the 1590s and the excessive emphasis on big ships. L. A. Clarkson, *The Pre-Industrial Economy in England* (London, 1971), p. 163, argues that the leather industry also benefited from military demand: 'government contracts were a forcing-house of entrepreneurship'.

57 C. Cipolla, *Guns and Sails in the Early Phase of European Expansion, 1400–1700* (London, 1965), pp. 39–40, for the Kent and Sussex figures. M. Oppenheim, *A History of the Administration of the Royal Navy and of Merchant Shipping in Relation to the Navy* (London, 1896), p. 159, gives a figure of 2,500 tons a year. For English iron output in the 1570s (*c.* 13,000 tons), D. C. Coleman, *Industry in Tudor and Stuart England* (London, 1975), p. 42, and for the European figures see Nef, *Western Civilization*, pp. 35, 80. See also Fletcher, *County Community*, p. 19.

58 Cipolla, *Guns and Sails*, p. 44.

59 Collating Cipolla's estimate for cannon production in ibid., p. 73, with Nef. Similarly for copper, the demand for coin after 1599 seems to have been much more important than the demand for guns, doubling copper prices between 1599 and 1610: Ball, *Merchants and Merchandise*, p. 120.

60 Cruickshank, *Elizabeth's Army*, p. 99; D. C. Coleman, *The Economy of England, 1450–1750* (Oxford, 1977), p. 64. See also Nef, *Western Civilization*, p. 101.

61 Calculated from the accounts of Diego de Postigo and Andrés Sanz de Portillo, 1577–81, Archivo General de Simancas, Contaduría Mayor de Cuentas, 2a época, *legajos* 556, 530, 558; Cordoba's output from Fortea Pérez, *Córdoba*, p. 311.

62 On Curtius, J. Lejeune, *La Formation du capitalisme moderne dans la principauté de Liège au XVIe siècle* (Liège, 1939), pp. 279–304; Alcalá Zamora y Queipo de Llano, *Historia de una empresa siderúrgica española: Los altos hornos de Liérganes y La Cavada, 1622–1834* (Santander, 1974), p. 82, On Evelyn, J. W. Gough, *The Rise of the Entrepreneur* (London, 1969), p. 206. According to L. Stone, 'The nobility in business, 1540–1640', in *The Entrepreneur: Papers Presented at the Annual Conference of the Economic History Society* (Cambridge,

1957), p. 19, Lord Robartes was the only peer who achieved his wealth and thus his title mainly as a result of industry (tin).

63 Nef, *Western Civilization*, pp. 98–9, for some general observations. Note the close ties between Pascual and Lerma, Núñez Correa and Franqueza, Cranfield and Buckingham. Conversely, the success of the Tripp family of Dordrecht took place in a state with a 'weak' court: Ball, *Merchants and Merchandise*, p. 120.

64 J. H. M. Salmon, *Society in Crisis: France in the Sixteenth Century* (London, 1975), p. 326; Benedict, *Rouen*, pp. 182, 225, 250; Bitton, *French Nobility*, p. 95; Ladurie, *Languedoc*, p. 68; Drouot, *Mayenne*, vol. 1, p. 45; J. H. Mariéjol, *Histoire de France illustrée*, ed. E. Lavisse, vol. 6, pt 2 (Paris, 1911), p. 3.

65 M. Ulloa, *La hacienda real de Castilla en el reinado de Felipe II* (Madrid, 1977), ch. 22; I. A. A. Thompson, 'The purchase of nobility in Castile, 1552–1700', *Journal of European Economic History*, vol. 8 (1979), pp. 313–60.

66 L. Stone, 'The inflation of honours, 1558–1641', *Past and Present*, no. 14 (1958), pp. 45–70, and his *The Crisis of the Aristocracy, 1558–1641* (Oxford, 1965), pp. 66–82.

67 It was precisely this that inspired the sedition in Avila in October 1591: A. Merino Alvarez, *La sociedad abulense durante el siglo XVI: La nobleza* (Madrid, 1926), p. 99. See also the Ligue manifesto of 31 March 1585: Salmon, *Society in Crisis*, p. 238.

68 Reflected in the hostile reactions to modern warfare of traditionalist apologists for nobility, like Sir John Smythe, *Certain Discourses Military*, ed. J. R. Hale (Ithaca, NY, 1964), or Sir Henry Knyvett, *The Defence of the Realme*, ed. C. Hughes (Oxford, 1906), as well as in the many contemporary expressions of the social futility of nobility, e.g. Ford's 'Ye're fat in no felicity but folly' or Raleigh's 'fools and therefore insufficient for charge, or cowards and therefore uncapable of lieutenancy': see W. Notestein, *English People on the Eve of Colonization* (New York, 1954), p. 40; H. R. Trevor-Roper, *The Gentry, 1540–1640*, Economic History Review Supplement, vol. 1 (1953), p. 38. For the decline of the French *noblesse* as a military class, J. Bérenger, 'Noblesse et absolutisme de François Ier à Louis XIV', in B. Köpeczi and E. H. Balázs (eds), *Noblesse française, noblesse hongroise, XVIe–XIXe siècles* (Budapest, 1981), pp. 20–1.

69 G. Huppert, *Les Bourgeois Gentilshommes* (Chicago, Ill., 1977), pp. 169–70; Salmon, *Society in Crisis*, pp. 237, 241; Mariéjol citing Robert Dallington (1598), *Histoire de France*, vol. 6, pt 2, p. 19; Drouot, *Mayenne*, vol. 1, p. 43.

70 A. Esler, *The Aspiring Mind of the Elizabethan Younger Generation* (Durham NC, 1966), pp. 93, 174, 108–11, 124. Essex's personal challenge to the duke of Villars, the governor of Rouen, was very much in the same vein: Benedict, *Rouen*, p. 218.

71 Salmon, *Society in Crisis*, p. 316; Bérenger, 'Noblesse et absolutisme', p. 18.

72 Esler, *Aspiring Mind*, p. 139. For the chivalric revival, see R. Strong, *The Cult of Elizabeth* (London, 1977), chs 5 and 6.

73 H. Kamen, *The Iron Century* (London, 1971), pp. 132–3; Salmon, *Society in Crisis* pp. 270–1; François de la Noue (as cited by Sir John Smythe, *Certain Discourses Military*, p. lvii) 'doth in terrible sort blame and disable almost the whole nobility of France of this time, imputing unto them many imperfections'; Bérenger, 'Noblesse et absolutisme', p. 21. Williams, *Tudor Regime*, p. 439, argues that the proletarianisation of war pushed the aristocracy to the exploitation of offices at Court, at the cost of both reputation and popularity.

74 Fray Jerónimo de Sepulveda, 'Historia de varios sucesos', in J. Zarco Cuevas (ed.), *Documentos para la historia del monasterio de San Lorenzo el Real de El Escorial*, vol. 4 (Madrid, 1924), p. 59.

75 J. R. Hale, 'The military education of the officer class in early modern Europe', *Renaissance War Studies* (London, 1982), pp. 225–46. For some of many government attempts to remilitarise the nobility, see Bérenger, 'Noblesse et absolutisme', p. 21, and A. Rodríguez Villa, *Ambrosio Spínola, primer marqués de los Balbases* (Madrid, 1905), p. 44.

76 Russell Major, 'Noble income', pp. 42–3; Salmon, *Society in Crisis*, pp. 323, 325. For some, of course, it was peace that was a financial disaster: see, for example, R. W. Kenny, *Elizabeth's Admiral* (Baltimore, Md, 1970), p. 265. For the ossification of noble values, see Huppert, *Bourgeois Gentilshommes*, pp. 18, 170; Drouot, *Mayenne*, vol. 1, pp.

52–3; R. B. Grassby, 'Social status and commercial enterprise under Louis XIV', *Economic History Review*, 2nd ser., vol. 13 (1960–1), reprinted in R. F. Kierstead (ed.),. *State and Society in Seventeenth-Century France* (New York, 1975), pp. 200–32, on the revival of *dérogation* in the early seventeenth century at p. 201. For Spain, Thompson, 'Purchase of nobility', p. 354.

77 See R. Villari, 'Rivolte e coscienza rivoluzionaria nel secolo XVII', *Studi Storici*, vol. 12 (1971), Spanish trans. in R. Villari, *Rebeldes y reformadores del siglo XVI al XVIII* (Barcelona, 1981), at pp. 29–32; Huppert, *Bourgeois Gentilshommes* pp. 8–10, 21, 33, 173, on Loyseau; Salmon, *Society in Crisis*, pp. 323–4; Grassby, 'Social status and commercial enterprise', pp. 203–6; Drouot, *Mayenne*, vol. 1, p. 53.

78 Of all admissions to the chartered companies, 1575–1630, only 6 per cent date from 1585–1603: T. K. Rabb, *Enterprise and Empire: Merchant and Gentry Investment in the Expansion of England, 1575–1630* (Cambridge, Mass., 1967), p. 72. See also Prestwich, *Cranfield*, p. 52, and Benedict, *Rouen*, p. 182.

79 Villari, 'Rivolte e coscienza rivoluzionaria', *passim*.

80 F. Braudel, *La Méditerranée et le monde méditerranéen à l'époque de Philippe II*, vol. 2 (Paris, 1966), p. 46. The rendering in the English translation is '1600–1610: the comeback of the smaller state?' (vol. 2 (London, 1973), p. 701).

81 Braudel, *Mediterranean*, vol. 2, p. 1200; Parry, 'Ottoman Empire', pp. 351–2; A. C. Hess, *The Forgotten Frontier* (Chicago, Ill., 1978), ch. 6, 'North Africa in revolt', pp. 100–26.

82 Braudel, *Mediterranean*, vol. 2, p. 1219; J. L. Cano de Gardoqui, 'España y los estados italianos independientes en 1600', *Hispania*, vol. 23 (1963), pp. 524–55.

83 J. F. Guilmartin, *Gunpowder and Galleys: Changing Technology and Mediterranean Warfare at Sea in the Sixteenth Century* (Cambridge, 1975), ch. 6, on the decline of the 'Mediterranean system'. See also A. Tenenti, *Piracy and the Decline of Venice, 1580–1615* (London, 1967); G. Fisher, *Barbary Legend: War, Trade and Piracy in North Africa, 1415–1830* (Oxford, 1957), pp. 127, 176.

84 The 250–300 ships plundered in and out of Venice, 1592–1609, and insurance rates to the Levant of 25 per cent were symptoms of that: Braudel, *Mediterranean*, vol. 2, pp. 887, 880.

85 H. and P. Chaunu, 'The Atlantic economy and the world economy', in P. Earle (ed.), *Essays in European Economic History, 1500–1800* (Oxford, 1974), p. 119.

86 By 1598, 400,000 pesos (35 per cent of remittances to Seville) were being held back in Mexico for defence: I. Sánchez Bella, *La organización financiera de las Indias* (Seville, 1968), p. 59 and n. 155; Andrews, *Elizabethan Privateering*, pp. 224–6.

87 Vilar, 'Age of Don Quixote', p. 105.

88 Wallerstein, *Modern World-System*, vol. 2, p. 23.

89 H. R. Trevor-Roper, 'The general crisis of the seventeenth century', in T. Aston (ed.), *Crisis in Europe, 1560–1660* (London, 1965), p. 78.

90 J. Hurstfield, 'County government: Wiltshire, *c.* 1530–*c.*1660', in J. Hurstfield, *Freedom, Corruption and Government in Elizabethan England* (London, 1973), pp. 237–44; W. B. Willcox, *Gloucestershire: A Study in Local Government, 1590–1640* (New Haven, Conn., 1940), pp. 73–102; Hassell Smith, *County and Court*, pp. 242–6, 277, 280–93; Clark, *English Provincial Society*, ch. 8; Williams, *Tudor Regime*, p. 123.

91 Thompson, *War and Government*, ch. 10.

92 F. C. Dietz, *English Public Finance, 1558–1641* (New York, 1932), pp. 308, 312 n. 17, 325; A. P. Newton, 'The establishment of the Great Farm of the English customs', *Transactions of the Royal Historical Society*, 4th ser., vol. 1 (1918), pp. 129–55; Cruickshank, *Elizabeth's Army*, p. 85; Andrews, *Elizabethan Privateering*, p. 238.

93 Williams, *Tudor Regime*, pp. 128, 436–7.

94 C. Jago, 'Habsburg absolutism and the Cortes of Castile', *American Historical Review*, vol. 86 (1981), pp. 307–26; I. A. A. Thompson, 'Crown and Cortes in Castile, 1590–1665', *Parliaments, Estates and Representation*, vol. 2 (1982), pp. 33–4. For parallel developments in France during the Assembly of Notables, 1596–7, see Salmon, *Society in Crisis*, pp. 302–4.

95 Parker, *Dutch Revolt*, pp. 242, 247; J. den Tex, *Oldenbarnevelt*, vol. 1 (Cambridge, 1973), pp. 61–5.

96 'Majestas major ab igne' (the motto on a royal medallion of 1604) sums up one side of this equation, with an accentuation of absolutist theory and the discrediting of the Estates, general and provincial; for the other side of the equation, see Salmon, *Society in Crisis*, pp. 301, 317–18, 320; *Cambridge Modern History*, vol. 3 (1907), pp. 665–6; Mariéjol, *Histoire de France*, vol. 6, pt 2, pp. 12–20.

97 Kamen, *Iron Century*, pp. 337–41; Livet, *Guerres de religion*, pp. 95–7; Salmon, *Society in Crisis*, pp. 277–91; Benedict, *Rouen*, pp. 172, 249; Parker, *Dutch Revolt*, p. 230 and, for anti-tax riots in the United Provinces, p. 237; Williams, *Tudor Regime*, p. 326.

98 B. Sharp, *In Contempt of All Authority* (Berkeley, Calif., 1980), p. 39; Clark, *English Provincial Society*, pp. 249–50.

99 *Actas*, vol. 12, p. 473: 'y que pues ellos se quieren perder, que se pierdan'.

100 *Calendar of State Papers, Venetian*, vol. 8, nos 327, 550, 616, 739, 790, 828; Museo Naval, Colección Navarrete, vol. 8, doc. no. 28, 'Relación de arbitrios propuestos para la defensa de la Monarquía de España . . . por Alonso Gutiérrez en el Consejo de Estado', Aranjuez, 1 May 1602, at fos 183–4; *Colección de documentos inéditos para la historia de España*, vol. 43, pp. 530, 538–9, Don Juan de Silva, Lisbon, June and July 1594.

101 G. Parker, 'Mutiny and discontent in the Spanish Army of Flanders, 1572–1607', in Parker, *Spain and the Netherlands*, ch. 5, pp. 106–21; P. van Isacker, 'Les mutineries militaires aux Pays Bas à la fin du XVIe siècle', *Annuaire*, University of Louvain (1909), pp. 469–80. There were more than forty mutinies in the Spanish Netherlands, 1589–1607. Kamen, *Iron Century*, pp. 337–41; Cruickshank, *Elizabeth's Army*, p. 79, on the Ostend mutiny of 1588, caused by poor victuals at high prices; Outhwaite, above, pp. 30–2, on the sufferings of the troops in Ireland and Berwick. Parry, 'Ottoman Empire', p. 371, revolts of janissaries 1589, spahis 1592 and 1603 over pay.

102 J. Pound, *Poverty and Vagrancy in Tudor England* (London, 1971), p. 5; Willcox, *Gloucestershire*, p. 106; C. Viñas Mey, 'La asistencia social a la invalidez militar en el siglo XVI', *Anuario de historia económica y social*, vol. 1 (1968), pp. 598–605.

103 Smythe, *Certain Discourses Military*, pp. 25–6; M. Lewis, *The History of the British Navy* (London, 1959), p. 188; 'the navy is for the greatest part manned with aged, impotent, vagrant, lewd and disorderly companions; it is become a ragged regiment of common rogues' (1608).

104 But cf. Pound, *Poverty and Vagrancy*, pp. 4–5: a band of 500 soldiers back from Portugal threatened to loot Bartholomew Fair; F. Aydelotte, *Elizabethan Rogues and Vagabonds* (London, 1967), p. 71 and n. 6, attributing the increase in vagabondage after 1588 to returned soldiers and sailors, and p. 170, citing Hext. However, it is clear from the six proclamations against vagrant soldiers, 1589–98, that many vagrants were pretending to be soldiers. In fact, poor relief paid by the corporation of Winchester through St John's Hospital *fell* between 1585 and 1592. In Warwick in 1587 only *c.* 10 per cent of the poor were in the age group 15–30, and in Ipswich in 1597 only 6 per cent. In neither town is there any indication of returned soldiers among the vagrants or the poor: A. Rosen, 'Winchester in transition, 1580–1700', and A. L. Beier, 'The social problems of an Elizabethan county town: Warwick, 1580–90', in P. Clark (ed.), *Country Towns in Pre-Industrial England* (Leicester, 1981), pp. 144–95 and 46–85, at pp. 159 and p. 63 respectively: Clark, *English Provincial Society*, p. 235.

105 For this and other quotations in similar vein, see E. Silberner, *La Guerre dans la pensée économique du XVIe au XVIIIe siècles* (Paris, 1939), ch. 2.

106 Kamen, *Iron Century*, pp. 341–6; Braudel, *Mediterranean*, vol. 2, p. 1199.

107 Archivo General de Simancas, Estado, *legajo* 1945, *consulta* of Consejo de Estado, 16 November 1600.

108 As Livet, *Guerres de religion*, p. 101, puts it: 'La foi remplace le pain.' In Valencia the upsurge of persecutions against the *moriscos* by the Inquisition in the years 1585–95 (coinciding with the fears of a Huguenot-*morisco* axis) is quite remarkable, with the numbers of *procesados* peaking in 1589–92 at 1,124, compared with an average of 60–80 up to 1585: R. García Cárcel, *Herejía y sociedad en el siglo XVI: La inquisición en Valencia, 1530–1609* (Barcelona, 1980), p. 211 and chart p. 210. In Essex the peak period for

witchcraft prosecutions coincides with the threat from Spain (A. D. J. Macfarlane, *Witchcraft in Tudor and Stuart England* (London, 1970), pp. 28, 70) and in France there is a direct connection between the prosecution of witches and the fortunes of the Ligue (A. Soman, 'The parlement of Paris and the Great Witch-Hunt (1565–1640)', *Sixteenth-Century Journal*, vol. 9 (1978), p. 39. In the Nord, on the other hand, the upsurge comes in the immediately postwar years, 1590–1620: R. Muchembled, 'Sorcières due Cambrésis: l'acculturation du monde rurale aux XVIe et XVIIe siècles', in M.-S. Dupont-Bouchat, W. Frijhoff and R. Muchembled, *Prophètes et sorciers dans les Pays-Bas XVIe–XVIIIe siècles* (Paris, 1978), p. 177.

109 Trevor-Roper, *Gentry*, pp. 37–40.

110 R. C. Munden, 'James I and "the growth of mutual distrust": King, Commons, and reform, 1603–1604', in K. Sharpe (ed.), *Faction and Parliament: Essays on Early Stuart History* (Oxford, 1978), pp. 43–8; Hassell Smith, *County and Court*, pp. 242, 275, 277, 333–4; Clark, *English Provincial Society*, pp. 256–7, 259, 265–6. For suggestions of a comparable court-country divide within the French nobility, see J. H. M. Salmon, *The French Wars of Religion* (Boston, Mass., 1967) p. 90.

111 R. Hakluyt, *Voyages*, vol. 4 (London, 1907), p. 352.

112 Smythe, *Certain Discourses Military*, pp. xxxiv, 21.

113 Knyvett, *Defence of the Realme*, p. 30.

114 Hakluyt, *Voyages*, vol. 4, p. 350; Knyvett, *Defence of the Realme*, p. 19: 'of late yeares all pryvate soldiers have bin so lightlie regarded, yea so uncharitablie and cruellie used as were it not for theire extraordinarie obedience and loyall love which they beare to yor most sacred Matie they would more willinglie be hanged at there dores then abyde shamefull martirdome with sundrie extremities abrode'; Smythe, *Certain Discourses Military*, pp. xxxviii, lxxx, 19, 22.

115 Meyer, 'Paysan français', p. 70.

116 Museo Naval, MS. 505, no. 91, Esteban de Ibarra to Don Pedro de Toledo, S. L. de El Escorial, 21 August 1597: 'y todo está de manera que quita la gana de travajar y servir, ver como y por donde se camina'.

117 Esler, *Aspiring Mind*, pp. 194–5, 208, 232 and 228, quoting G. B. Harrison: 'a ... progress from romance to realism, from realism to satire, from satire to nausea': O. H. Green, *Spain and the Western Tradition*, vol. 4 (Madison, Wis., 1966), p. 363; Parker, *Dutch Revolt*, p. 204; Huppert, *Bourgeois Gentilshommes*, pp. 166, 169; M. Defourneaux, *Daily Life in Spain in the Golden Age* (London, 1970), p. 228; J. H. Elliott, 'Self-perception and decline in early seventeenth-century Spain', *Past and Present*, no. 74 (1977), p. 47; Salmon, *Society in Crisis*, p. 273; H. Ettinghausen, *Francisco de Quevedo and the Neostoic Movement* (Oxford, 1972), p. 8; and, for other penitential and devotional responses to war, Benedict, *Rouen*, pp. 191, 194, 202.

118 Ettinghausen, *Francisco de Quevedo*, pp. 21, 128–9.

119 For this interpretation, see, especially, G. Oestreich, *Neostoicism and the Early Modern State* (Cambridge, 1982).

15 *The Roles of the State and the town in the General Crisis of the 1590s*

BRIAN PULLAN

The contributors to this volume present the state in many forms. Let us call it, in general, the legitimate public body which exercises the highest effective authority and power available within a particular territory. Sometimes the state is a town, or at least a town senate or council, ruling an actual or former city state with an empire appended, ranging in extent from the compact hinterlands of the imperial free cities in Germany to the sprawling mainland and island empires of the Republic of Venice. But sometimes the state is a none-too-impartial umpire between towns competing for all too scarce supplies of food, and sometimes, as in Spain, it is an oppressor of towns, which loads them inefficiently with the responsibility for collecting taxes. In the shape of the Dutch Estates-General the state may be the representative organ of a military union composed of very diverse entities, heavily urbanised or largely rural, republican or princely in their sympathies. Sometimes the state has appeared as an intimate, paternalistic, territorial principality such as Hesse-Kassel, drawing into a closer relationship with petitioning village communities. Or it can be seen as a pocket monarchy encroaching on the autonomy of towns and thrusting bureaucratic tentacles into peasant communities formerly managed by village elders. Sometimes the state is the Church, as in the prince-bishopric of Dillingen, where ecclesiastical discipline is synonymous with good order; sometimes the lay state recognises the Church as a formidable rival in a contest for sovereignty. Sometimes the state manifests itself as a distant dynasty making ill timed demands for exports of grain from a dearth-stricken island, as the Spanish monarchy made them of Sicily about the year 1590. Sometimes the monarch himself becomes a faction leader in a civil war, as did Henry III when he engineered the assassination of the Duke of Guise; with Henry IV he becomes the conciliator who seeks to rise above faction. Sometimes the state seems held in abeyance, or overshadowed by a counter-state as formidable as the Holy League. Organs of the state as vital as the parlements in the French provinces are divided by faction and geography, splitting themselves between, say, Rouen and Caen, and sometimes magistrates can be routed by the plague, which produces (as in Grenoble and Lyons in the later 1590s) a temporary collapse of government even at a local level.[1]

What generalisations can possibly be framed about the activity of these so diverse entities in the 1590s, and can the decade be seen to mark something more than an exceptionally severe outbreak of famine and disease? These are, after all, the recurrent scourges of a heavily populated continent, and of an economy ill equipped with defences against weather and microbes. Can the decade be seen as a turning point in which the state reacts to natural or man-made catastrophe and to the consequent dislocations of the people in a distinctive and original way?

First, perhaps, the state ought to be considered as a cause of catastrophe, and not as a defence against it. Among the larger dynastic states examined in this volume, only the Elizabethan monarchy has been clearly represented as a capable protector, which adequately maintained domestic law and order in return for the taxation it levied. By contrast the French and Spanish monarchies have been portrayed as extractors and to some extent exporters of wealth, channelling a high proportion of the shrinking resources of their countries into waste and destruction, taxing inexorably on the basis of unrealistic or obsolete assessments, and shifting responsibility for extortion to intermediate agencies which range from military captains to urban oligarchies. Taxation swells the burdens of individual or communal indebtedness borne by peoples who have also to contend with dearths, and doubtless it encourages those with capital to invest it in unproductive loans, to the state itself or to its debtors, rather than in more creative forms of agricultural, commercial, or industrial venture. The Spanish state's increased reliance on the *millones*, on the indirect taxation of foodstuffs, seems calculated to weigh most heavily on the poor in whose budgets food inevitably bulks largest. Sale of office, that favourite expedient of the French monarchy, multiplies the number of privileged exemptions from the payment of direct taxation.

To complement these accounts of states involved in war, it is worth considering the pressures exerted by the government – for good or ill – within a country free at this time from both civil and from foreign warfare: the Republic of Venice. Here neutrality, on the part of a state whose Italian dominions were once described as 'nothing but frontier', went hand in hand with very high defence costs, both for territorial possessions and for commerce. After 1593 these were enhanced by the Senate's decision to erect the show-piece fortress and new town of Palma in the impoverished region of the Friuli, a strategic area through which the Terra Ferma Stato was threatened by two potential aggressors, the Germans and the Turks.[2] Its governors were well aware of the burdens thrown on peasants, both within and outside Friuli, by demands for labour services in shifting nearly half a million cubic yards of earth, and conscious, too, of the damage inflicted on agriculture by the diversion of human and animal muscle-power into excavation and haulage. Wretched conditions at the site brought desertion and death on an alarming scale, although one commissioner saw the fortifications as a splendid source of maintenance for poor but feckless labourers migrating during the dearths of the 1590s from within a radius of forty or fifty miles.[3] The war fleet and the arsenal imposed heavy burdens, if only because the Republic maintained large numbers of galleys specifically designed as warships and unable to earn their keep in peacetime by serving as merchantmen.[4] Venetian ambassadors to England in King James's time would soon be looking, with some envy as well as contempt, upon a state which could allow its fortifications to decay and its navy to dwindle.[5]

In a recent forceful contribution to debate on the decline of Venice, blame for this process has been shifted away from the bloody-minded conservatism of the guilds, where it once seemed to belong, and towards the fiscal policies of the state itself. These are held responsible for pricing Venetian goods, and especially high-quality textiles, out of the competitive international market. In 1587, trade taxes accounted for 36 per cent of Venice's revenue, and between 1588 and 1630 some 42 per cent of the price of each broadcloth could be expected to disappear into the public coffers.[6] Even if the city's guilds were to blame after all, the Venetian state must be held responsible for extending and strengthening them, for they were highly valued as administrative devices for recruiting a reserve force to row the galleys in time of war. According to the revised quotas imposed in 1595, this was to consist of 8,882 men, of whom 4,947 would be furnished by the guilds.[7] In practice the main task of the peacetime navy, heavily dependent not on guildsmen but on convicts, was to protect merchant shipping against pirates, and it is not thought to have performed it so efficiently as to justify government spending on warships or the arsenal's overriding claims on short supplies of timber.[8]

What can be set against this negative record? In the context of the late sixteenth century, what is it reasonable to expect a state to do for its subjects in the face of dearth, plague and war, and how well does it carry out its brief? It will be best to include in the discussion town governments as well as central ones, for the public authority which immediately confronts these disasters tends to be the town's council and its executives, or the representatives of royal or republican government resident in the town (*parlements, rettori, corregidores*). These two bodies may act simultaneously, either in competition or in collaboration with each other. Central governments tend, on the whole, to receive petitions from towns on which they may or may not act, or to try to co-ordinate the actions taken in towns. The English Privy Council may be an exception to the rule; its interventions during the 1590s were more vigorous than they came to be in the middle and later seventeenth century.[9] Towns, in the 1590s, were centres of attraction and repulsion for population movement and for movements of grain; they were places of shelter for the starving and the victims of war, and places to shun for those rich enough to flee from epidemics. Much social action was concerned with regulating these movements of people and food, and had to be undertaken at their focal points.

Within the towns, the public authority – in the 1590s, as in previous decades – strove to mediate in a society which threatened to split into the two camps of those whose interest lay in the high prices of cereals and of those who might starve if hoarders, speculators and exporters got their way. Big loaves at constant prices for the poor seemed the surest bastion of good order. Max Weber once wrote of an almost eternal form of class conflict, concerned not with wages but with commodity prices,[10] and the state can be seen as the regulator of this contest in times of greatest danger. States were often consciously preoccupied with preserving a large population for their own service, with preventing its reduction by the emigration of the oppressed, and with attracting useful settlers, even while they tried to get rid of idle *fainéants* by the crudest possible means. Their obligation to protect their subjects clearly extended to saving them not only from invaders and rebels but also, through quarantine and other measures, from the assaults of disease – which brought in its wake looting, disorder, and prolonged unemployment through the mutual banning of cities and the paralysis of the textile trades.[11] All these considerations led them into a concern with poverty. It seems possible that the crisis of the 1590s bred, at least in some parts of Europe, a certain sensitivity on the part of those who governed, not just to the problems of the vagrant or of the *menu peuple* in the towns, but also to those of the rural poor. Perhaps the crisis fostered a belief that some of these could be alleviated by new kinds of legislative action, which would go beyond the mere palliation of the symptoms of poverty, beyond relieving the refugees who rushed to the city. At the same time, one effect of widespread famines was to impose an almost intolerable strain on existing administrative arrangements, and to place the utility of some of them in serious doubt.

In two widely separated countries at least, the crisis of the 1590s provoked vigorous debate on the desirability of elaborate public intervention in the management of vital food supplies, and particularly on the usefulness of trying to regulate the movement of breadstuffs within a state's boundaries rather than merely prevent exports. Did price controls and other provisos serve a useful purpose, or did they merely encourage fraud and theft, interfere with the market, and upset the natural and inevitable movement of grain to wherever the price was best for the seller?

In England the Book of Orders was challenged by leading townsmen in London and the provinces, a lord mayor pleading to the Privy Council that the high price of corn would 'soon abate if it were left free to men to buy and sell as themselves should think good'.[12] In Verona, the heartland of the Venetian mainland state, there was heavy criticism in 1598 of the cumbersome bureaucratic machinery which governed the Mercato Vecchio. Here, bread baked from grain commandeered from producers at a fixed proportion was exposed for sale at a controlled price to poor persons who had proved their need and been issued with printed certificates or metal tokens, entitling them to buy in this way. A freer market, the Mercato della Brà, where foreigners could sell to citizens at whatever prices they chose, had been established by its side in 1591.[13] Governors of other Venetian towns and fortresses, at Bergamo or on the Riviera di Salò, bitterly complained of regulations which allowed the populous towns of Verona and Brescia to hog supplies of grain far in excess of their normal needs, and to interfere with its flow towards Desenzano, the great grain market to the south of Lake Garda. One of them, Alvise Priuli of Bergamo, delivered to his government in Venice what has rightly been called a remarkable paean of praise to smugglers and others who defied the law, and so kept the foodstuffs moving to where they were most required.[14]

It has to be said, none the less, that debate is one thing and radical changes of policy another; in the two countries discussed, such changes came about in the 1630s or later, rather than in the 1590s. It was well into the seventeenth century before anti-dearth measures in England were relaxed into the hands of local communities. And it took the north Italian plague of 1630–1, savagely depleting the population of Verona and eliminating the persistent risk of famine, to bring in a new system based on a substantial monetary deposit at the city's public loan bank. This could be invested according to need in a suitable quantity of cereals or 'lesser crops', and sold off at cost price.[15]

It was surely true, however, that Italian governments in particular were compelled by the famines of the 1590s to turn at least temporarily away from depleted traditional sources of supply, elsewhere in Italy, in Sicily, or in the Ottoman Empire. Where necessary they would use diplomatic machinery, or contract with their own trusted agents, to make substantial purchases in Germany or the Baltic countries.[16] To any reader of Braudel, the crisis of the 1590s implies the invasion of the Mediterranean by grain ships from northern Europe, bearing their cargoes from Amsterdam, Middelburg, Danzig, Hamburg, Lübeck, London, and elsewhere.[17] And these moves may foreshadow certain deep-seated changes in the structure of Mediterranean commerce – even, perhaps, the great seventeenth-century shift in the economic hegemony of Europe from the

Mediterranean countries towards the United Provinces and England. For the northerners, accustomed once more to Mediterranean markets, remained to take over a part of the Mediterranean carrying trade from Italian merchants and captains, and there is a certain shift in the fortunes of Mediterranean ports. In general, those well placed geographically to receive Dutch, Hanseatic or English shipping, and those readiest to encourage foreigners by the abandonment of high customs duties, anchorage taxes and tiresome discriminatory regulations, might well find themselves on a long rising curve of activity, handling more and more tonnage – as did Livorno and Genoa. The price of such concessions was a partial surrender of the economy to alien control. Venice, which certainly received northern grain fleets from 1594 but persisted in trying to maintain advantages for its indigenous or long-resident merchant population, was far more dubiously placed. Livorno was very much a new town, conceived, planned and privileged by the personal policies of the Medici grand dukes. Decisions to introduce the free port at Genoa were carried through by the government against the opposition of the Banco di San Giorgio, the association of state creditors whose income was secured partly by customs dues.[18] If the subsistence crisis of the 1590s started a train of events which eventually altered the mechanisms of Mediterranean trade, the Italian state in various forms – both princely and republican – had to make choices which strongly influenced the process.

Disasters such as those of the 1590s may seem to demand a transfer of responsibility for the poor from the sphere of private charity, where it normally belongs, to the domain of communal or public action, financed by rates, taxes, or forced loans. Dependence on relief for survival will surely begin to spread from the inner circle of the permanent or 'structural' poor, the cripples, widows, orphans and foundlings who must always live on charity, to a second and much larger circle of *menu peuple*, the 'crisis poor' or *pauvres conjoncturels*, who are low-paid casual workers, street traders, unskilled labourers, and journeymen with families to support. In time it may even reach the outer circle of skilled artisans and wage-earners whose reserves are insufficient to equip them to withstand long stoppages of work coupled with soaring prices.[19] The problem, joined with that of strangers and refugees flooding in from beyond the ramparts and suburbs, quickly becomes too vast for private charity to handle.

A difficulty here is that there is seldom a clearly identifiable point at which charity cuts off and public assistance intervenes. One often encounters hospitals, confraternities, charity banks, grain deposits and almonries which are financed by a mingling of public and private funds. Some of these may come from gifts and bequests, some from allocations of public money, such as fines levied on criminals.[20] Such institutions may be subject to close supervision from magistrates who see them as guarantors of public order too important to be neglected, or even as potential sources of subversion and corruption which have to be rigorously controlled. Often the primary duty of the public authority is not to tax but to exhort, and so to squeeze the largest possible sums both out of private individuals and out of long-established charities. Compulsory assessment is there in the background, but kept as a last resort. In Rouen in 1595 and 1596, as on several earlier occasions, counsellors of the Parlement, together with curés and parish treasurers, are instructed to carry out house-to-house visitations of the citizenry and invite them to give to the support of the needy. 'And should any of the said citizens and inhabitants show so little charity that they will not assess themselves in a free and reasonable manner, then they shall be taxed and assessed according to their property and means by the said counsellors, curés and treasurers'.[21] Anxiety to uphold the principle of voluntary giving was not confined to Catholic societies in search of spiritual merit for the donors. Some years ago W. K. Jordan contended that in no year prior to 1660 was more than 7 per cent of the sum expended on the poor in England derived from parish rates. He has since been criticised for basing his estimates on discontinuous parish records and on arguments from silence, for confusing the aspirations of donors and testators with the actual achievements of private philanthropy, for unfairly comparing gifts which led to endowments with rates which were immediately expended on the poor.[22] But James Casey (Chapter 11) is surely right to be sceptical about the importance of public policy and the effectiveness of institutions such as workhouses in early modern Spain.

Severe dearths and savage epidemics of plague or typhus had in the past promoted innovation in the field of public poor relief and social policy, especially where they happened to coincide with debates over religious belief and practice, or with related outbreaks of intense puritanism and evangelical fervour of the kind that flourished in the France of the Holy League. The holy city must care for its poor; their neglect would be a blasphemy; but it must also cure them of idleness, which was a sin as well as a social offence, and must expel its vagabonds and tricksters, perhaps also its prostitutes and its Jews. The giving and withholding of relief could be an instrument for inducing an insecure and dependent population, consisting perhaps of 20 per cent of the city's inhabitants, to conform to the religious and moral standards of those who controlled relief. In Lyons, in the last quarter of the sixteenth century, every year was a 'necessitous year' in which the lower-paid workers with dependent children could survive only by resort to private charity or public relief for several months.[23]

None the less, although the conditions were right, the 1590s cannot as an originator of new principles compare with the 1520s and early 1530s, or even perhaps with the 1560s. In the 1520s the municipal poor laws had spread across western Europe from town to town, from Saxony and Flanders in the early and middling years of the decade to northern Italy and eastern France a few years later, to England soon afterwards, and eventually to Spain in the early 1540s. It was then that the towns began to codify and systematise their procedures in such a way as to discriminate between inhabitants and outsiders, to pool revenues in common chests, to appoint overseers for the poor, to find at least rough work for the able-bodied, to correct the idle, and generally to spread the burden of caring for the poor across the entire community.[24] In Rouen, during the 1590s, the town authorities and the Parlement were repeating a number of well-tried procedures to which they had been resorting at intervals throughout the previous sixty years. They organised a descriptive census of the poor; they set the able-bodied to labour on the fortifications and river quays during the months of spring and early summer, but expelled them during the autumn; they forbade all begging on pain of a flogging; they were ready, as usual, to move from exhortation to taxation of the richer citizens; and they tried to exact all arrears of interest payments due to the *bureau des pauvres*.[25] Perhaps it is only in 1617 that clear signs appear of an intention to devise new approaches to the problem of poverty in Rouen, when the heavily indebted *bureau* thinks of constructing 'des maisons fermées'. In some of these they might establish 'des manufactures' to employ poor people of all ages, and others would be places of punishment both for the 'refractory' poor of the town and for vagabonds.[26] These would be something different from the temporary *ateliers* for public work gangs set up during the famine years of the sixteenth century, and less crudely penal and more reformatory than the 'towers' which awaited the sturdy rogues of that period.

It has of course been argued that the distinctive contribution of the later sixteenth and the seventeenth centuries to the treatment of poverty lay in new measures to concentrate all beggars, paupers and undesirables within the walls of such 'closed' institutions. There they could be subjected to an intensive discipline and be forcibly educated in piety and habits of work to a degree hardly possible in older and looser systems – for these had depended on forced apprenticeships to local tradesmen, assignment as cabin-boys to merchant ships, or condemnation to penal terms in the galleys.[27] The performance of the masters and overseers involved in such a system might prove to be very variable. There are indeed some striking examples of particular cities resorting, as a result of public initiative, to expedients of this kind during the 1590s – whether their actions were a direct response to famine and the threat of disease, or whether they were inspired by distaste for the sins and blasphemies of idle, masterless men ignorant of Christian truth. Two of the most enduring institutions of the decade were the hospital of San Lazzaro e Mendicanti, founded in Venice in 1594,[28] and the workhouse of Amsterdam, established in 1589 and extended to women in 1596. The Amsterdam workhouse certainly had great influence as a model, since it seems to have been adopted in the seventeenth century by no fewer than twenty-six Dutch towns, and to have crossed frontiers into the Spanish Low Countries, north Germany, Sweden and France. It should be said, however, that the Amsterdam workhouse constituted only a small-scale experiment, not clearly attuned to awareness of any massive increase in the problem of urban poverty, and that it was directed against juvenile crime as much as against vagrancy. It contained sixty or seventy prisoners in 1597–8,[29] although it is impossible to assess its powers as a deterrent, or its impact on those who kept out of it. The implementation of principles is often as remarkable as their conception, but it should be said that the Venetian beggers' hospital was a successful realisation of ideas that had been formulated, at least in Italy, in or about the 1560s. Carlo Borromeo, Cardinal Archbishop of Milan, had in that decade urged the foundation of general beggars' hospitals; the general hospital of Bologna, advertised by an Augustinian friar, had been a model for Cremona in 1569 as it was for Venice twenty-five years later. The Venetian measure, funded in part by the revenues of a decayed leper colony in the lagoon, was an application by the Senate of the principles embodied in one of the more radical of the Tridentine decrees. This allowed the conversion of outdated charities to more immediately useful ends.[30] But the famines of the 1590s had demonstrated the need.

In the Mediterranean countries at least, the effect of the famines of the 1590s was often to expose public institutions of this type to overwhelming demands which they could not possibly meet. Famines in Rome in the early years of the decade plunged the newly established hospital of Sixtus V into grave financial difficulties, and attempts to curb begging in the city proved altogether vain.[31] For some years the regents of the hospital of Santo Alessio in Cremona had been complaining of uncontrollable influxes of beggars into the town. Numbers of inmates rose from 160 poor in 1587 to 450 or more in 1592–3; by 1598 there was a threat not just of bankruptcy but of starvation within the hospital's walls.[32] In Genoa the number of internees in the Lazzaretto, the public pest-house which had since the 1580s been used for the enclosure of some of the town's poor, increased from some 200–400 in 1584–6 to peaks of 665 in 1591 and 870 in June 1592.[33] In Toledo, a new beggars' hospital had been opened in 1581, and success had been claimed at least for its capacity to galvanise the idle who did not want to be confined in it. But by 1589 it had collapsed for lack of funds. Attempts were then made to revive it, to stave off crowds of beggars expelled from Madrid; but when, in March 1598, a board of royal and civic officials inspected 356 beggars they were clearly reverting to an older and less elaborate system of expelling some and granting others licences to solicit alms.[34] Significantly, when in that year Cristóbal Perez de Herrera wrote about beggars' hospitals, he chose to speak of *albergues* for the genuinely poor which would provide shelter and sermons only: the inmates would have to venture out and support themselves by begging during the day.[35]

Throughout the decade one encounters endless stories of towns struggling against heavy odds. Cities pursuing grain for the vital town stock are still condemned to compete anarchically with one another, as are Abbeville and Amiens in Philip Benedict's contribution, whilst London and York, in Peter Clark's, are constantly invading the catchment areas of lesser towns. Central governments are seldom strong enough to regulate these contests; they are often too susceptible to pressure from their voracious capitals, too readily alarmed by the prospect of disorder in their immediate vicinity, to prove capable of acting as impartial referees. Towns, it seems, can win no victories, for the more generous their charities or relief organisations the greater the 'swarm and surcharge of poor' they are liable to attract; the cheaper their grain the more rapidly they incur the charge, as in Spain *circa* 1600, of putting the private producer out of business; the more freely public relief is granted, the more gravely they risk (as in Leicester in 1599) diverting resources from trade and taxing those who are themselves in need of assistance. At the root of such problems lies the imbalance of resources and privileges between town and countryside, the uneven distribution of fiscal and military obligations between townsmen and country-dwellers, the location of the larger almonries, grain stores, controlled markets, and loan banks in towns. It is true, of course, that townsmen accused of enjoying excessive advantages might well retort by expressing disquiet at the spread of industries in the countryside or the suburbs, as the tailors' guild in Leicester complained of those 'who like drone bees to the hive, paying neither scot nor lot, lie lurking in the suburbs and other secret places in and about this town, and rob your suppliants of the work which they should do to their great disgrace and utter undoing'.[36] And it is also true that towns were not the only points of convergence for unwelcome migrants: they could fling the problem back on to villages. Codogno in the Lombard plain complained bitterly in the 1590s of Piacenza discharging its burdens on to them by a one-way service which ferried beggars across the Po and refused to take them back.[37]

Were central governments and their representatives ever capable of rising above the interurban contest, or of tackling at its roots the fundamental problem of rural poverty? It can perhaps be argued, in accordance with Peter Clark's fairly optimistic account of a 'crisis contained', that at least in England there were effective moves towards systematic national legislation on poor relief. It may be that English statutes of the

1590s were essentially codifications of previous laws and advertisements of devices already adopted by such cities as London and Norwich.[38] But moves from municipal to national legislation are certainly not to be despised. These arguments can perhaps be balanced by some evidence from southern Europe, from a former city state with a high reputation for stability and good government: the Republic of Venice. To some extent, the patriciate or sovereign nobility of Venice saw themselves as representing an interest which competed with those of a league of subject cities, rather than as a government which promoted the general good of an integrated state. However, when pressed by petitions from the locals, the Venetian Senate was ready to make loans to subject communities to enable them to purchase grain,[39] and even to finance some new initiatives in the Friuli designed to have the effect of preserving peasant communities as well as townsmen against famine. Here there were moves to locate publicly managed grain stores well away from the provincial capital of Udine. It might be possible to eliminate the insuperable difficulties of travel for thirty or forty miles to Udine, and to exert a more evenly distributed influence over small-town markets such as Porcia or Spilimbergo, which were both notorious for unscrupulous speculation and for 100 per cent profiteering. The state was acting as a central treasury which would give nothing away, but could be approached for advances of ready cash; the 5,000-ducat loan to float the new warehouses would be secured on a hearth tax spread over the next five years.[40] Much of this concern for peasant well-being seemed to be prompted by the fear of emigration into Germany, and hence of the depletion of a people famous for its services to the state as taxpayers, galley oarsmen, pioneers, and transporters of oaks to the government shipyards. In 1599 the population of the province was said to have fallen from 196,000 thirty years before to a mere 97,000.[41] Towards the end of the decade the reports and recommendations of the Venetian Lieutenant of Udine do hatch some ideas of what legislation might do to tackle the root causes of rural poverty, rather than merely relieve its refugees when they were desperate enough to make for the towns. Stefano Viaro suggested that the law could be used to encourage landlords to consolidate scattered holdings: at this moment every peasant paid rent to a considerable number of proprietors, and none felt any sense of responsibility for maintaining him. Such consolidation of ownership, or *ingrossatione*, was universally desired and would be beneficial to all social strata. But only the sovereign state of Venice would be able to rise above local squabbles in such a way as to bring about significant improvements.[42]

Another region of notorious rural poverty was the Bergamasco, on the western edge of the Terra Ferma dominions of Venice. Here the town of Bergamo attracted and fed from a mixture of charitable and public funds anything from 14,000 to 30,000 mouths in the early 1590s. Here again the *Rettori* showed awareness of certain fundamental problems of rural poverty, and up to a point they took action. In this province, heavily dependent on seasonal migration to large cities in search of work, villagers could resort to local almonries called *Misericordie*. The Venetian government authorised the *Rettori* to improve the service by ensuring that revenues should no longer be distributed to all the inhabitants, but only to those who could prove poverty. Here, too, there was a growing fear of population losses through emigration of the poor, and the *Rettori* in the 1590s laid particular stress on the need to control the appropriation of common lands by private enclosers, whilst to some extent they entertained the possibility of improving cultivation by irrigation schemes and of extending the system of public cereal deposits. It may be that the decade was more remarkable for the diagnosis than for the cure of ills, but famine and depopulation had helped to envisage, if not to enact, a social policy less unquestioningly biased towards the towns.[43]

One last point arises from the remarks of Philip Benedict about the impact of the Wars of the Catholic League on the conception of monarchy in France, and from those of Heinz Schilling about the movement of refugees and the establishment of religious conformity within the German states. A real crisis ought to be a turning point or a crossroads. It is possible that we can in the 1590s discern a parting of the ways in the attitudes of governments towards clericalism and strict religious conformity, and that they were brought nearer to this crossroads by the nature of the conflicts in France and the Netherlands. In Leaguer France especially, the clergy had acquired an unprecedented influence over government, and (as Benedict has written) the League was marked by the 'tendency to abolish divisions between cleric and layman, the secular realm and the sacred, so that priests became magistrates and magistrates sanctified their power by priestly rite'.[44] It may be that in the late sixteenth and early seventeenth centuries states and societies tend to drift more decisively towards one of two poles. At one of these stands what can very crudely be called the 'closed' society which sets religious values above economic calculation and is ready to carry out expulsions of religious minorities – Lutherans from re-catholicised regions of Germany, Jews from several German cities, *moriscos* from Spain in 1609. At the other pole is a more 'open' type of society, where the state, be it Dutch or Italian, Calvinist or Catholic, holds firmly to an official religion and upholds the higher standing of those who adhere to it, but is none the less prepared to grant extensive toleration (sometimes by express agreement) to religious minorities so long as they cause no scandal and so long as their presence confers economic benefits. A small but significant example is that of Marrano or *converso* emigrés from the 'closed' societies of Portugal and Spain, for whom these years were certainly a turning point. Though in theory liable to prosecution for heresy or apostasy when they openly adopted Judaism in Italy, they won express guarantees of toleration in Venice in 1589 and in Livorno in 1593. To these they may even have added some implicit encouragement from the Pope himself to settle in Ancona in 1594.[45] It is at least arguable that the circumstances of the 1590s made the Venetian state, for one, exceptionally conscious of the need to resist those kinds of clerical intrusion that threatened its sovereignty and its economic and fiscal well-being. Hence, for example, its opposition to the Clementine Index of Prohibited Books which menaced the hard-pressed book trade in 1596,[46] and its determination to curb the acquisition of landed property on the Terra Ferma by ecclesiastical institutions after the liquidation of government consolidated loan funds which began the same year.[47] Clerical power might become a threat to the state at least as strong as Protestant heresy.

Of course, the 'open' or 'closed' character of states and societies, and their tendency to accept or reject useful minorities possessed of capital, skill and valuable connections, were not determined solely by the religious attitudes of governments. 'Closure' can be brought about by the resistance of established citizens and guildsmen to the economic competition of alien immigrants. A city such as Venice can be receptive to Flemish, English and Sephardic Jewish merchants, but still cling to her ancient and restrictive laws on citizenship, and refuse to become a free and open port in the same sense as Genoa, or Livorno, or even papal Ancona.

In general, the 1590s may well have called for the more efficient application of relief measures conceived in the second quarter of the sixteenth century. Dearth often demonstrated the shortcomings and limitations of more recent devices, such as comprehensive beggars' hospitals, though it could also lead to further experiments with them, which were sometimes successful and sometimes not. There was some debate about principles, including the broad question of the role the public authorities ought to play in the regulation of the grain trade. But there were relatively few moves actually to apply drastically new ideas on a significant scale. Examples can, however, be found of ability on the part of governments – or at least of individual governors – to analyse the problems of rural poverty; to confront those abuses which caused losses of the people through starvation and emigration, and which choked the towns in time of dearth with thousands of unwelcome petitioners for relief; to think of attacking causes, rather than merely of devising palliative measures. Religious war and persecution made *politiques* and *politici* aware of the state's need to maintain its own integrity against *diacatholicon* and to rise above the savagery of confessional conflict. The Wars of Religion in France and the Netherlands, and the activities of the Inquisition in Portugal and Spain, stirred a great cauldron and produced a significant redistribution of capital and skills across Europe. Famine in the Mediterranean countries in the early 1590s demonstrated the potential of the northerners as long-distance carriers of grain, and of the east European serf economies as producers of wheat and rye for export. Those countries which were open enough to take advantage of these developments were most likely to prosper in the seventeenth century, and government policy played an important part in bringing this openness about.

Notes: Chapter 15

1 For the last points, see P. Benedict, *Rouen during the Wars of Religion* (Cambridge, 1981), p. 185 ; J.-N. Biraben, *Les Hommes et la Peste en France et dans les pays européens et méditerranéens* (Paris, 1976–7), vol. 2, pp. 162, 166–7.

2 See J. R. Hale, 'Terra Ferma fortifications in the Cinquecento', in S. Bertelli *et al.* (eds), *Florence and Venice: Comparisons and Relations* (Florence, 1979–80), vol. 2, pp. 172, 177–9.

3 *Relazioni dei Rettori Veneti in Terraferma*, ed. A. Tagliaferri (Milan, 1973–9), vol. 14, pp. 42–4.

4 cf. esp. W. H. McNeill, *Venice, the Hinge of Europe, 1081–1797* (Chicago, Ill., 1974), pp. 129–31.

5 See *Calendar of State Papers, Venetian*, vol. 10, pp. 504–6; vol. 15, pp. 466–8.

6 R. T. Rapp, *Industry and Economic Decline in Seventeenth-Century Venice* (Cambridge, Mass., 1976), pp. 6, 112–14, 138–40.

7 AS, Venice, Milizia da Mar, *fascicolo* 707. On Venetian guilds, see now R. S. Mackenney, 'Trade guilds and devotional confraternities in the state and society of Venice to 1620', unpublished PhD thesis, University of Cambridge, 1982.

8 See A. Tenenti, *Piracy and the Decline of Venice, 1580–1615* (London, 1967).

9 See R. B. Outhwaite, 'Dearth and government intervention in English grain markets, 1590–1700', *Economic History Review*, n.s., vol. 34 (1981), pp. 394–6.

10 M. Weber, 'Class, status, party', in H. H. Gerth and C. Wright Mills (eds), *From Max Weber* (London, 1948), pp. 185–6.

11 For a summary of measures taken by public authorities against plague, see Biraben, *Les Hommes et la Peste*, vol. 2, pp. 85–181.

12 Outhwaite, 'Dearth', pp. 399–400, 402.

13 See F. Vecchiato, *Pane e politica annonaria in Terraferma Veneta tra secolo XV e secolo XVIII (il caso di Verona)* (Verona, 1979), pp. 38–45, 159–60, 170–2.

14 *Relazioni dei Rettori Veneti*, vol. 10, pp. 22–5; vol. 12, pp. 192–3.

15 Vecchiato, *Pane*, pp. 167–8, 209–17.

16 cf. F. Braudel and R. Romano, *Navires et marchandises à l'entrée du Port de Livourne (1547–1611)* (Paris, 1951), pp. 52–3; M. Brunetti, 'Tre ambasciate annonarie veneziane', *Archivio Veneto*, 5th ser., vol. 58 (1956), pp. 110–15; M. Aymard, *Venise, Raguse et le commerce du blé pendant la seconde moitié du XVIe siècle* (Paris, 1966), pp. 156 ff.; B. Pullan, *Rich and Poor in Renaissance Venice: The Social Institutions of a Catholic State, to 1620* (Oxford, 1971), pp. 355–9; *Relazioni dei Rettori Veneti*, vol. 2, pp. 30–1.

17 F. Braudel, *The Mediterranean and the Mediterranean World in the Age of Philip II* (London, 1975), vol. 1, pp. 599–602.

18 Braudel and Romano, *Navires*, pp. 15–28, 50–1; E. Grendi, 'I nordici e il traffico del Porto di Genova, 1590–1666', *Rivista Storica Italiana*, vol. 83 (1971), pp. 23–71.

19 For degrees and definitions of poverty, and for the terms *pauvres structurels* and *pauvres conjoncturels*, cf. esp. J. P. Gutton, *La Société et les pauvres: l'exemple de la généralité de Lyon, 1534–1789* (Paris, 1971), pp. 7–11, 53; for some further developments of the idea, B. Pullan, 'Poveri, mendicanti e vagabondi (secoli XIV–XVII)', in *Storia d'Italia. Annali I. Dal feudalesimo al capitalismo* (Turin, 1978), pp. 988–97.

20 An example close to the 1590s is that of the new flour deposit, or Fontego delle Farine, for the poor of Vicenza: see AS, Venice, Senato, Terra, *filza* 110, 19 March 1589.
21 See G. Panel (ed.), *Documents concernant les pauvres de Rouen extraits des archives de l'hôtel-de-ville* (Rouen, 1917–19), vol. 1, pp. 166 ff.
22 W. K. Jordan, *Philanthropy in England, 1480–1660* (London, 1959), pp. 126–42; among his recent critics, note especially J. Hadwin, 'The problem of poverty in early modern England', in T. Riis (ed.), *Aspects of Poverty in Early Modern Europe* (Alphen aan den Rijn, 1981), pp. 236 ff.
23 See R. Gascon, *Grand commerce et vie urbaine au XVIe siècle: Lyon et ses marchands (environs de 1520-environs de 1580)* (Paris, 1971), vol. 1, pp. 402–3; cf. also vol. 2, pp. 752–5, and Gascon's article 'Économie et pauvreté aux XVIe et XVIIe siècles: Lyon, ville exemplaire et prophétique', in M. Mollat (ed.), *Études sur l'histoire de la pauvreté (Moyen Âge-XVIe siècle)* (Paris, 1974), vol. 2, pp. 747–60.
24 Literature on these early poor laws includes: J. Nolf, *La Réforme de la bienfaisance à Ypres au XVIe siècle* (Ghent, 1915); Panel, *Documents*; F. R. Salter, *Early Tracts on Poor Relief* (Cambridge, 1926); N. Z. Davis, 'Poor relief, humanism and heresy – the case of Lyon', in her *Society and Culture in Early Modern France* (Stanford, Calif., 1975), pp. 17–64; Gascon, *Grand commerce*, vol. 2, pp. 797 ff.; Gutton, *La Société*, pp. 266 ff.; Pullan, *Rich and Poor*, pp. 239 ff.; C. Lis and H. Soly, *Poverty and Capitalism in Pre-Industrial Europe* (London, 1979), pp. 88 ff.
25 Panel, *Documents*, vol. 1, pp. 166 ff.; cf. esp. the *ordonnances* of 1534, printed at pp. 19–27, and the description of the *bureau des pauvres* at pp. 79–90.
26 ibid., vol. 1, pp. 199–200.
27 The theme is especially familiar from the work of M. Foucault, *Folie et déraison: histoire de la folie à l'âge classique* (Paris, 1961), pp. 57 ff.; cf. also B. Geremek, 'Renfermement des pauvres en Italie (XIVe–XVIIe siècle): remarques préliminaires', in *Historie économique du monde méditerranéen, 1450–1650: mélanges en l'honneur de Fernand Braudel* (Toulouse, 1973), vol. 1, pp. 206–17.
28 Pullan, *Rich and Poor*, pp. 364–70.
29 T. Sellin, *Pioneering in Penology: The Amsterdam House of Correction in the Sixteenth and Seventeenth Centuries* (Philadelphia, Pa, 1944), pp. 25 ff., 47, 102–6; Lis and Soly, *Poverty and Capitalism*, pp. 118 ff.
30 For Borromeo's recommendations, *Acta Ecclesiae Mediolanensis* (Milan, 1583), fo. 21*v*; cf. also M. Fantarelli, *L'istituzione dell'Ospedale di S. Alessio dei poveri mendicanti in Cremona (1569–1600)*, ed. G. Politi (Cremona, 1981), pp. xxiv, 3–4, and Pullan, *Rich and Poor*, pp. 330 ff., 362 ff.
31 J. Delumeau, *Vie économique et sociale de Rome dans la seconde moitié du XVIe siècle* (Paris, 1957–9), vol. 1, pp. 414–16; C. B. Piazza, *Eusevologio Romano, overo, Delle opere pie di Roma* (Rome, 1698), vol. 1, pp. 56–9.
32 Fantarelli, *L'istituzione*, pp. 28–31.
33 E. Grendi, 'Pauperismo e Albergo dei Poveri nella Genova del Seicento', *Rivista Storica Italiana*, vol. 87 (1975), pp. 630–5.
34 L. M. Martz, 'Poverty and welfare in Habsburg Spain: the example of Toledo', unpublished PhD thesis, University of London, 1974, pp. 172–91.
35 M. Jiménez Salas, *Historia de la asistencia social en España en la edad moderna* (Madrid, 1958), pp. 103 ff.; Martz, 'Poverty and Welfare', pp. 115–19.
36 Quoted in P. Clark and P. Slack, *English Towns in Transition, 1500–1700* (London, 1976), p. 108. On rural competition with town industries, see (for example) Benedict, *Rouen*, pp. 13–14; on inequalities between town and countryside in northern Italy, see esp. D. Sella, *Crisis and Continuity: The Economy of Spanish Lombardy in the Seventeenth Century* (Cambridge, Mass., 1979), pp. 30–3.
37 Sella, *Crisis*, p. 36.
38 cf. Jordan, *Philanthropy*, pp. 96 ff.; J. Pound, *Poverty and Vagrancy in Tudor England* (London, 1971), pp. 50–7.
39 For examples, see AS, Venice, Senato, Terra, *filza* 115, 18 and 31 August 1590; *filza* 116, 15 September 1590; *filza* 117, 20 October 1590; *filza* 118, 6 and 13 December 1590; *filza* 119, 9 and 29 March and 4 April 1591; *filza* 122, 5 and 15 December 1591, 11 January 1591–2.

40 ibid., *filza* 115, 11 August 1590, and *filza* 117, 25 October 1590.
41 ibid., *filza* 104, 31 December 1587; *Relazioni dei Rettori Veneti*, vol. 1, p. 115. A census of 1579 had estimated the population of Friuli at 148,780 souls.
42 *Relazioni dei Rettori Veneti*, vol. 1, pp. 115–16.
43 ibid., vol. 12, pp. 183–4, 186–7, 196, 248. The great survey of the Bergamasco, conducted by Giovanni de Lezze in 1596, lists and describes the *Misericordie* of the province (AS, Venice, *Sindici Inquisitori in Terraferma*, b. 63). The account of the *Misericordie* in the Valle Brembana Superiore (fos 199*r*–208*v*), and particularly that of Sanbusita, suggests that not all maladministration had been eliminated, and that in some places the income from the *Misericordie* was used partly for the support of the clergy.
44 Benedict, *Rouen*, pp. 186–7.
45 For Venice, see B. Ravid, 'The first charter of the Jewish merchants of Venice, 1579', *Association for Jewish Studies Review*, vol. 1 (1976), pp. 187–222; for Venice and Ancona, B. Pullan, 'Religious toleration and economic decline: Venice and the Marranos', forthcoming in *Journal of Italian History*, and B. Pullan, *The Jews of Europe and the Inquisition of Venice, 1550–1670* (Oxford, 1983). For Livorno, G. Laras, 'I Marrani di Livorno e l'Inquisizione', *Atti del Convegno 'Livorno e il Mediterraneo nell' età medicea'* (Livorno, 1978), pp. 3–25. For changing attitudes towards Jews in England and Europe, *c.* 1590–1600, see S. Ettinger, 'The beginnings of the change in the attitude of European society towards Jews', *Scripta Hierosolymitana*, vol. 7 (1961), pp. 193–219; T. K. Rabb, 'The stirrings of the 1590s and the return of the Jews to England', *Transactions of the Jewish Historical Society of England*, vol. 26 (1974–8), pp. 26–33.
46 See P. F. Grendler, *The Roman Inquisition and the Venetian Press, 1540–1605* (Princeton, NJ, 1977), pp. 225 ff.
47 cf. Pullan, *Rich and Poor*, pp. 139–40. For the possible effects of the famines of the 1590s on the Venetian state's attitude towards clerical proprietors, see M. J. C. Lowry, 'The Church and Venetian political change in the later Cinquecento', unpublished PhD thesis, University of Warwick, 1971, pp. 273 ff.

16 Yet Another Crisis?

J. H. ELLIOTT

Exactly twenty years have passed since the publication of my *Imperial Spain* with a section entitled 'The Crisis of the 1590s'. In the same year, in a brief note published in *Past and Present*, I urged my colleagues to impose a moratorium on the word 'crisis' before it became yet one more piece of debased historical currency.[1] This notable example of doublethink suggests that words have their own destiny, and that 'crisis' has responded to too many of the central concerns of the twentieth century to let itself slip gracefully from circulation or be summarily pensioned off.[2]

Yet readers of this volume will be conscious of a vein of scepticism running through it. A number of contributors have obvious doubts about the applicability of the notion of crisis to the decade of the 1590s, and there are some indications that historical analysis couched in terms of 'crisis' is no longer regarded as quite as useful, or as conclusive, as it was even a few years ago. The time may now be approaching when, surfeited by crises, historians seek other, and perhaps more precise, explanations of the process of historical change. In the meantime, readers of this volume may well have come away with the impression less of another full-blown 'general crisis' than of an unusually interesting case of *fin de siècle* malaise.

The signs of trouble, as presented and discussed in this volume, are all around: famine and epidemics, vagrancy and unemployment, riots and revolts. But these were hardly unusual phenomena in the life of early modern Europe, and the difficulty comes when we try to rank them on a scale that spans two or more centuries of European history. Is there really any case for singling out the 1590s as a decade in which conditions were such as to warrant a special degree of attention?

The classic case of crisis-oriented historiography remains the great debate over the 'General Crisis of the seventeenth century', in which the 1640s were identified as a critical period in the political and economic development of modern Europe.[3] There is no need to rehearse yet again the arguments which brought a new historiographical celebrity to that agitated decade; but what seemed to give special plausibility to the case for the 1640s was the conjunction of major political and social upheavals with a set of economic conditions which could be interpreted as marking a decisive moment in the transition of Europe from feudalism to capitalism. As the debate proceeded, however, some of the problems inherent in the original formulation of the argument became apparent, even while the study of conditions in seventeenth-century Europe was notably enhanced. The generality of the alleged 'general crisis' was disputed; doubts were expressed as to whether the continental upheavals of the 1640s were really comparable in their long-term significance to those of other 'revolutionary' decades, notably the 1520s and the 1560s; and arguments were put forward for locating Europe's economic crisis not in the 1640s but twenty years earlier, between 1619 and 1622. Above all, it remained a persistent weakness of the 'crisis' interpretation that the mechanism by which economic adversity was translated into revolutionary political action was never convincingly explained. Indeed, throughout the entire debate there ran an assumption which was never systematically challenged, that economic and social conditions were the prime determinants of political change.

As the case for the 1640s falters, so other decades of early modern history step forward as promising candidates for re-examination. But what are the criteria required? Some of the contributions to this volume spell them out. For R. B. Outhwaite, definitions of the term 'crisis' are bound to differ, 'but necessarily embodied in it is the notion of a turning point'.[4] 'A real crisis', writes Brian Pullan, 'ought to be a turning point or a crossroads'.[5] Peter Burke, recalling the medical definition of crisis, opts for 'a short period of acute difficulties, leading to long-term structural changes',[6] a phenomenon which some may consider to be as elusive as crisis itself.

Where 'acute difficulties' are concerned, a forceful claim can be made for the 1590s. Although some of the contributors might wish to qualify Kamen's assertion that 'the conditions of the 1590s were catastrophic',[7] the accumulated weight of the evidence here presented is undeniably impressive. To judge from the chapter by Leo Noordegraaf,[8] even the Dutch Republic, which has a remarkable capacity for defying alleged general trends, does not on this occasion remain immune.

What, however, are we to make of these difficulties? Is their multiplicity and their gravity indeed such as to make the decade as much of a 'turning point' as proponents of the general crisis theory assumed the 1640s to be? Here the contributors seem far from certain, and even the notion of a mortality crisis begins suddenly to look surprisingly insubstantial after the critical scrutiny given it by David Souden.[9] If, as he concludes, 'the 1590s occupy a prime position in the mortality peaks of the sixteenth century', this does not of itself necessarily make them a turning point. Indeed, 'the occurrence of mortality crises may well disguise the true demographic turning points in populations which did decline'.[10]

The problem is compounded when we move from population statistics to the general indicators of Europe's economic health. Here, as in demographic history, there is some common ground about the kind of turning point to be sought. If, as has come to be widely assumed, an expansionist sixteenth century was followed by a stagnant seventeenth, then the challenge is to find the moment of transition from one period to the next. For Ruggiero Romano, writing in 1962, this moment was located between 1619 and 1622. These were the years of true economic crisis, when the long expansionist phase that had begun at the end of the fifteenth century was finally brought to a close.[11]

Where Romano provides figures for industrial production and international trade reaching back into the sixteenth century, the 1590s look a reasonably healthy decade. The value of Seville's trade with America, which played such an important part in generating and sustaining the economic vitality of sixteenth-century Europe, rose to its maximum between 1596 and 1600. The number of ships engaged in that other great branch of international commerce, the trade between the Baltic and western and southern Europe, was at its highest in the 1590s, and Romano argues the case for a steady increase in the value and volume of this trade until the early 1620s. The records for European industrial production are spotty, but again Romano managed to identify in several European centres 'a boom during the last few years of the sixteenth century' which continued through the first two decades of the seventeenth. It is only when we turn to agrarian life that the sombre depiction of the 1590s in this volume is fully vindicated. Romano's 'agrarian depression' begins in the last decade of the sixteenth century, and indeed serves to precipitate the post-1620 general depression, as the commercial and industrial sectors, deprived of the support of agriculture, lose their driving force.

The 1590s might, from this perspective, be justifiably regarded as a turning point. But, assuming that the agrarian depression did give rise to a depression affecting other branches of the European economy, the evidence for the universality of that depression is by no means uncontested, while its real character is still the subject of debate. In an important reassessment of the 'general crisis' controversy, Niels Steensgaard argued that 'the seventeenth-century crisis was a distribution crisis, not a production crisis'.[12] If he is correct, some of the explanations so confidently advanced for the economic problems of the middle years of the seventeenth century immediately become suspect. They can be faulted, in particular, for ascribing an excessive degree of autonomy to economic trends, and underplaying in the process the economic impact of the state as a redistributor of public income in pursuit of its own political and military ends. In this reading the 'absolutist' state would resume the position which it traditionally occupied at the centre of the historical stage. It was the state which, by its extravagant pretensions and its exaggerated fiscalism, aggravated the economic problems of the times, exacerbated the social injustices, alienated the governing classes and provoked the revolutionary/reactionary upheavals that swept the Europe of the 1640s.

Such a reinterpretation of the 'General Crisis of the seventeenth century' has its implications also for the 1590s, since it tends to reduce their importance as a potential economic turning point. For a variety of reasons – climatic and man-made – economic conditions in the 1590s were undeniably harsh; but in a society like that of early modern Europe, in which population and resources were always in unstable equilibrium, a number of self-regulating mechanisms came into play when the equilibrium was seriously disturbed. Unusually high mortality rates, like those of the 1590s, helped to redress the balance between production and consumption. It could be argued that the process of recovery was getting under way in the first two decades of the seventeenth century, but that in some areas (like Richelieu's France) it was then interrupted by a sharp increase in the fiscal demands of the state, which – by interfering with patterns of distribution and arrogating to itself a larger share of limited resources – stopped the self-regulating mechanism in its tracks, and provoked a new and violent disequilibrium, with sometimes revolutionary results.

It is one of the encouraging features of this volume that the contributors have not been seduced into pursuing the chimera of a general crisis to the neglect of the phenomena in their own backyards. Sensing the elusive nature of their quarry, they have paid meticulous attention to local conditions, and in so doing have helped to justify this kind of cooperative historiographical enterprise by pointing research in new directions. In particular, they have drawn attention to the need to pay more regard to the varieties of human response in the face of adverse conditions.

On the principle of Occam's razor, crises are not to be unnecessarily multiplied. This desirable result could be achieved if instability were more widely recognised as a constant in the life of early modern Europeans. Such a recognition would in turn reduce the tendency to think in excessively mechanistic terms about the 'conditions' which allegedly give rise to revolts and revolutions. For if conditions in early modern Europe were in general such as to leave society precariously poised between dearth and sufficiency, order and disorder, the human equation at any given moment becomes of paramount importance. Operating in a world in which a single poor harvest could have cataclysmic social and even political consequences, sixteenth- and seventeenth-century Europeans were required to make continuous adjustments in a situation in which they had only limited room for manoeuvre. At some moments and in some places they adjusted with greater success than at others, by containing disorder, alleviating distress, or actively righting wrongs. The problem then becomes to determine why a particular generation or a particular society displayed more or less skill in the process of adjustment.

It is here that the 1590s, as discussed in this volume, acquires a special interest. For the impression conveyed by these essays in less bleak than their general theme might suggest. It is true that the conditions depicted by the contributors were almost universally sombre. The already intense strains imposed by the pressure of population on limited resources were aggravated not only by poor weather and bad harvests, but also by the burden of warfare, both between and within states. Yet this Europe, which seems so close to disaster, proves strikingly resilient. In many parts of the continent there was serious unrest; but C. S. L. Davies, after chronicling the revolts, can still arrive at the conclusion that 'in general, western European governments . . . seem to have coped well with the problems of the 1590s',[13] while Peter Clark, discussing the England of the 1590s, can write of 'a crisis contained'.[14]

How was it that this generation of the 1590s succeeded in negotiating with a fair degree of success the difficulties of those undeniably difficult years? A variety of answers emerges from this volume – some no more than hinted at, others discussed in some detail. Inevitably, responses occurred simultaneously at many different levels, individual, collective and governmental. Of the options discussed by Albert Hirschman in his book *Exit, Voice and Loyalty*,[15] there are manifestations of all three.

The option of exit is one which deserves more systematic attention than it receives in this volume. Exit can take the form of overseas emigration, internal migration and migration between states. It is difficult not to see some connection between the notable absence of 'generalised unrest' in the Castile of the 1590s[16] and the opportunities for 'exit' available to Castilians. This indeed was a commonplace of the times. The Huguenot La Popelinière, lamenting in 1582 the disorders of his native France, advocated a great colonial venture as the answer to his country's problems, on the analogy of Spain, which had succeeded in exporting its disorderly elements overseas.[17] The available evidence points to a considerably higher rate of Spanish emigration to the Indies in the seventeenth than the sixteenth century – perhaps an annual rate of 4,000–5,000, as compared with 2,000–3,000[18] – and it would not be surprising if the miseries of the 1590s made overseas emigration an increasingly attractive option to many Castilians. In the early seventeenth century an illegal passage to America could be bought from a ship's captain for twenty or twenty-five ducats – a month's wages for a skilled workman – 'and as many go who want'. It was as easy, remarked a contemporary, as 'buying bread or meat'.[19]

Internal migration was even easier – that 'widespread subsistence migration' which Timothy B. Davies notes in the Sicily of the 1590s.[20] Destitute labourers who flocked into the cities all over western Europe in the 1590s came in the expectation that city life offered them at least a chance of food. They were often cruelly disappointed, but the expectation was not unreasonable, given the traditional preoccupation of city magistrates with building up stocks of grain and keeping food prices pegged at artificially low levels. Although European cities of the late sixteenth century were liable to be overwhelmed by the sheer magnitude of the problem, they held out at least a prospect of salvation and in this way did something to reduce tensions in the countryside. Where mobility was to some extent restricted by legal restraints, as in Austria, the chances of a major rural upheaval were correspondingly increased.

There were possibilities, too, for migration across frontiers – as from the southern Netherlands to the United Provinces,[21] or from southern France across the Pyrenees into Catalonia;[22] and even the armies which did so much to add to the widespread distress of the 1590s can be seen from another standpoint as agencies of institutionalised migration, which absorbed the surplus population of one region and transferred it to another.[23] 'Exit', by one or other of these methods, could help to moderate 'voice' – the cries of outraged protest which understandably alarmed the upholders of authority. But 'loyalty', too, could mute the voices of dissent. For potential dissidents the price of patriotism was self-imposed restraint. It is difficult to gauge the degree of loyalty which European monarchies had succeeded in generating among their subjects by the later sixteenth century: it is likely to have been strongest in those societies, like the England of Elizabeth and the Spain of Philip II, where national and religious interest had coalesced in a prolonged war against a foreign power closely identified with an alien faith. But even in the France of the 1590s, torn as it was by religious vendettas, Henry of Navarre could take advantage of collective resentment at Spanish intervention to mobilise support for the Crown.

As the example of Henry IV suggests, the late sixteenth-century state was not without resources for containing and reducing discontent, but everything depended on good management – on the capacity, for instance, to combine in judicious measure repression and reward. If the 1590s were the age of Justus Lipsius, with his neo-Stoic counsels of persistence and fortitude in the face of individual adversity,[24] they were also the age of Botero, whose *Reason of State* (1589) was designed to instruct rulers in the art of preserving their states. To the question 'whether it is a greater task to extend or to preserve a state', he answered: 'Clearly it is a greater task to preserve a state, because human affairs wax and wane as if by a law of nature, like the moon to which they are subject. Thus to keep them stable when they have become great and to maintain them so that they do not decline and fall is an almost superhuman undertaking.'[25] In the climate of pessimism generated by the miseries of the 1590s, the highest aim to which hard-pressed governments could aspire in their management of states was to 'keep them stable'.

The best way to stabilise conditions was to return to peace. By the 1590s the western monarchies were vastly over-committed. Wartime taxation and deficit financing had imposed enormous additional strains on society, while compounding the endemic difficulties of royal treasuries. There were many indications that the late sixteenth-century state was reaching the limit of its administrative capacities, and was being forced, whether in England, Spain or France, to make expensive concessions to individuals, corporate bodies and representative assemblies in its attempt to keep the war-machine running[26] – concessions which would strengthen the power of local oligarchies, and make the tasks of seventeenth-century governments correspondingly harder. As the decade progressed, circumstances began to impose their own remorseless logic. In 1596, for the third time in the reign of Philip II, the Spanish Crown was forced to suspend payments to its bankers. With Philip himself approaching death, a progressive disengagement of Spain from its expensive foreign ventures could no longer be avoided. France, too, was in desperate need of peace – domestic peace, and peace with Spain. The settlements of 1598 – the Edict of Nantes, the peace of Vervins between France and Spain, and Philip II's transfer of sovereignty in the Netherlands to Albert and Isabella – all signalled the beginnings of a general movement in western Europe towards the reduction of national and international tensions. Serious international problems remained, but, as the new century opened, even these seemed to be approaching some form of resolution. By the end of 1600, having almost extinguished Tyrone's rebellion, England was close to checking, at least temporarily, its running 'ulcer of Ireland'.[27] Spain and England were finally to make peace in 1604; the long war in Hungary between the Habsburgs and the Turks was formally ended in 1606; and the failure of Spain's last major effort to subjugate the Dutch drove it reluctantly to the negotiating table and the truce of 1609.

Peace would bring its problems no less than war, but the gradual return of Europe to a precarious peace around the turn of the century helped to ease the pressures that had accumulated in the 1590s. 'Prudence' – that great virtue which Botero so extolled[28] – was much in evidence among rulers as they sought to reduce the military commitments which had inflated their budgets and brought such widespread distress. But it was also manifested in the attempts made at different administrative levels to mitigate suffering and reduce the possibilities of social unrest. Through welfare schemes and poor relief, provisioning policies and policing, the public authorities made strenuous efforts to contain and control social evils which they seemed unable to prevent.[29]

But was there no way to move beyond mere containment and to break out of the constricting mould through enterprise and innovation? The contributions to this book hint at missed opportunities, as in the Castile of the early seventeenth century, where the malady was effectively diagnosed, but the remedies not applied.[30] But they also point to signs of creative action, sometimes in unexpected places, as in Sicily at the turn of the century, with its construction of new model villages.[31] In his study of the peasants of Languedoc, Le Roy Ladurie observes that it was not simply 'natural' economic forces, but also cultural and even spiritual forces which blocked the road to recovery and growth.[32] There were Frenchmen – Olivier de Serres, Laffemas, Sully – who glimpsed what might be done to foster improvement and expansion, but they were thwarted, like the more intelligent among the *arbitristas* or economic projectors of seventeenth-century Spain, by a combination of traditional mental attitudes and vested interests. The Europe of the 1590s was a world in which 'novelty' was by definition unacceptable. 'If novelties must be introduced', wrote Botero grudgingly in the section of his book devoted to 'the avoidance of novelty', 'let this be done gradually and almost imperceptibly'.[33] The acceptance of the idea of novelty as a desirable possibility was to be one of the hardest-won achievements of early modern Europe.

It was practice rather than preaching which would slowly lead to a change of attitude, and already in the 1590s the way forward was being indicated by those pragmatic pioneers, the Dutch. The single most important economic development of the decade was the irruption of Dutch shipping into the Mediterranean, carrying Baltic grain. The importance of this lay not only in the alleviation of hunger in a Mediterranean world which was finding it increasingly difficult to feed its own peoples, but also in the long-term economic and political transformations which followed in its wake. Having once secured a foothold in Mediterranean ports as suppliers of grain, the Dutch followed up their advantage by extensively penetrating the Mediterranean markets as purveyors of a wide range of northern and colonial commodities, and developing a north-south trade which turned Amsterdam into the focal point of the European commercial system.[34]

The resulting influx of wealth into the United Provinces helped to pay for their prolonged struggle for independence from Spain, and gave them an opportunity to develop a unique society with its own unique form of political organisation – a society that, by contemporary standards, was free, tolerant, innovative and experimental beneath its traditionalist trappings. Above all, it was a society that worked, and not only worked but prospered. The true reasons for that prosperity might be ignored or dismissed by the monarchical states of the west, but none could fail to be impressed by the achievement. The Dutch showed that it was possible, even for a society with very few natural advantages, to enhance wealth, and with it power, by pursuing the proper policies. How else was it possible to explain their achievement in holding at bay the massed forces of the Spanish monarchy?

For a Europe which had been able to do little more than attempt to hold the line in times of trouble like the 1590s, the example of the Dutch held out unanticipated hopes of wresting advantage even from adversity. Through a more rational organisation of resources, through the encouragement of agriculture, trade and industry, it lay within the capacity of rulers to augment impressively the power of their states. But if the climate of opinion in the first two decades of the seventeenth century was turning towards acceptance of the idea that it was possible for men and societies to secure some degree of control over their collective destinies, the practice of government still lagged far behind. The very return to peace at the start of the new century helped to diminish the sense of urgency. As the pressures generated in the 1590s lessened, so the need for 'prudence' receded, and the courts of the western monarchies – the England of James I, the Spain of Phillip III, the France of Marie de Médicis – embarked blithely on their peacetime spending sprees. These were the locust years, in which old problems were left unresolved, new problems began to accumulate, and a new generation of court favourites, lacking the sense of responsibility of their immediate predecessors in government, squandered the opportunities for retrenchment and reform provided by the return of peace.

But the age of the activists was at hand. The relative peace of the opening years of the new century was, at least in part, a peace of exhaustion. An ageing generation of princes and statesmen had been anxious to settle the differences and balance the accounts before it was too late. But there were younger and more impatient men waiting in the wings – some, like the Earl of Essex, too impatient to survive. In the German and Habsburg lands in particular, the religious and political balance so precariously achieved in the second half of the century was beginning to collapse as it reached its close.[35] A new generation, less dedicated to the preservation of consensus, was arising – a generation with strong religious convictions which assumed aggressive political forms. As a result, the lines of division – between Catholic and Protestant, between monarchs and estates – began once again to harden, presaging the new age of international conflict that would open in 1618.

The demands of this new and harsher age would call forth a new generation of statesmen of a tougher breed. These men – a Richelieu, an Olivares, a Strafford – were scornful of the inadequacies and irresponsibility of their immediate predecessors, and determined to show themselves of a different mettle. Power was to be used to the full, and used above all for a purpose. Reform was, to their minds, long overdue, and made all the more pressing by the costly requirements of defence and rearmament as

Europe lurched back into war. In order to maximise the strength and international competitiveness of their states, they were prepared to apply the lessons that had been taught by the Dutch. Interventionist and protectionist in their economic policies, they would deploy the full panoply of the royal authority to achieve what the Dutch had achieved under the relatively benign auspices of their republican and constitutionalist political system.

These statesmen of the 1620s and 1630s, unlike those of the 1590s, were more impressed by the possibilities than the limitations of power. Members of a generation born in the 1580s and 1590s, they combined an austere sense of personal responsibility with an exalted sense of the majesty of kingship. They had come to maturity in a world which had felt the influence of Bodin's transcendent views of sovereignty, and knew the meaning of the divine right of kings. If they had learnt from Botero and Justus Lipsius the need for 'prudence' in government, they had gone to Tacitus – often mediated by Lipsius – for their historical lessons in statecraft, and had learnt the value to be attached to the Roman virtues of discipline, command and obedience. They belonged, moreover, to a generation open to the conviction that man, by organising and systematising his knowledge into 'science', could unlock the mysteries of government, economic management, and the universe itself, and so seize control of his destiny.

It was in the confidence of their belief that they could somehow set the world to rights that the men who held positions of supreme authority in the 1630s differed most sharply from their predecessors of the 1590s. There was nothing very heroic about Lord Burghley's vision of the world. Essentially a prudent helmsman, he devoted his energies to keeping the ship of state on an even keel. This was a far cry from the visionary idealism of the men of the 1630s, who would push the powers of the state to its limits, and beyond, in their determination to reach their chosen destinations.

It was this new assertiveness of the state which made the 'crisis' of the 1640s very different in kind from that of the 1590s. The pressures generated by war had indeed made the state increasingly intrusive in the last decades of the sixteenth century. But it had compromised, bargained, and been forced to make major concessions in order to get its way. In so doing, it may have created new problems for succeeding generations, but its compromises and concessions had allowed it to maintain some control over the immediate course of events. The statesmen of the 1630s, by contrast, were less prepared to compromise. Oblivious of – or isolated from – public opinion, and confident that they alone had the answers, they rode roughshod over the opposition, and refused to moderate the demands they were making on society in the name of the state and its needs. In so doing, they tilted the balance between society and the state more violently than the scales could bear. In the revolts of the 1640s, they, or their successors, paid the penalty.

It may be, then, that the time has come to pay fresh attention to changing aspirations and expectations – to the new ambitiousness of power – as a key to the troubles, and achievements, of the seventeenth century; to scrutinise more carefully the differences in the thinking of sixteenth- and seventeenth-century Europeans about the potential of the state, and the capacities of man. In this story, the 1590s may come to assume a position of critical importance. For it was in this dispiriting decade, as Europe's rulers worked their way as best they could through the problems created by war, famine, poverty and endemic social disorder, that the Dutch finally succeeded in establishing on permanent foundations one of the most radical collective experiments in European history. They proved – through their trade, their agriculture, their industry, and their technical ingenuity – that it was possible for a society to break out of the straitjacket to which the iron laws of geography, climate and demography had apparently condemned it in perpetuity.

In 1644, in the early years of the revolt of the Principality of Catalonia against the government of Philip IV of Spain, a Catalan who was visiting the United Provinces found encouragement for his compatriots in the shining example of the Dutch: 'the Dutch at the beginning of the war were much poorer and more broken down than us, but in a short time by means of trade they have made themselves the richest and most powerful people in the world'.[36] The success of the Dutch in creating prosperity and its concomitant, power, profoundly changed the contours of European discussion about policy and action. But there were other important lessons, too, to be learnt from the Dutch. In establishing a state that was in some respects an anti-state, with its loose political structure, its free play of institutions, its spirit of tolerance and critical inquiry, they had offered the model of a successful anti-authoritarian society to a Europe simultaneously tempted and frightened by the possibilities of power. The men of the 1640s who struggled to resist and throw back the encroachments of monarchical authority were to find in that supreme creation of the troubled 1590s, the Dutch Republic, an exemplary source of encouragement for their own still more troubled times.

Notes: Chapter 16

1 *Past and Present*, no. 25 (1963), p. 96.
2 See R. Starn, 'Historians and "crisis"', *Past and Present*, no. 52 (1971), pp. 3–22 for the historiography and use of the word.
3 There are two convenient and complementary anthologies of articles which bear on this

debate: T. Aston (ed.), *Crisis in Europe, 1560–1660* (London, 1965); and G. Parker and L. M. Smith (eds), *The General Crisis of the Seventeenth Century* (London, 1978).
4 Above, p. 40.
5 Above, p. 296.
6 Above, p. 177.
7 H. Kamen, *The Iron Century* (London, 1971), p. 335.
8 Above, ch. 4.
9 Above, ch. 12.
10 Above, p. 240.
11 'Between the sixteenth and the seventeenth centuries: the economic crisis of 1619–1622', in Parker and Smith, *General Crisis*, ch. 7.
12 'The seventeenth-century crisis', in ibid., ch. 2. See esp. p. 42.
13 Above, p. 253.
14 Above, ch. 3.
15 Cambridge, Mass., 1970.
16 Above, p. 221.
17 Cited in J. H. Elliott, *The Old World and the New, 1492–1650* (Cambridge, 1970), p. 83.
18 F. Chiappelli (ed.), *First Images of America*, vol. 2 (Berkeley, Calif., 1976), p. 708.
19 R. de Vivero, *Du Japon et du bon gouvernement de l'Espagne et des Indes*, trans. and ed. J. Monbeig (Paris, 1972), p. 93.
20 Above, p. 200.
21 Above, pp. 76–7.
22 See J. Nadal and E. Giralt, *La Population catalane de 1553 à 1717* (Paris, 1960).
23 Above, p. 275.
24 See in particular G. Oestreich, *Neostoicism and the Early Modern State* (Cambridge, 1982).
25 Trans. and ed. P. J. and D. P. Waley (London, 1956), pp. 5–6.
26 Above, p. 273.
27 Sir Francis Bacon in the Parliament of 1597–8, quoted by J. E. Neale, *Elizabeth I and Her Parliaments, 1584–1601* (New York, 1978), p. 360.
28 *Reason of State*, bk II.
29 Above, ch. 15.
30 Above, p. 224.
31 Above, pp. 202 ff.
32 E. Le Roy Ladurie, *Les Paysans de Languedoc* (Paris, 1966), vol. 1, pp. 640–1.
33 *Reason of State*, p. 52.
34 J. de Vries, *The Economy of Europe in an Age of Crisis, 1600–1750* (Cambridge, 1976), pp. 120–1. See also, for the Dutch system and its impact, C. Wilson, *Profit and Power* (London, 1957).
35 R. J. W. Evans, *The Making of the Habsburg Monarchy, 1550–1700* (Oxford, 1979), p. 39.
36 Cited by J. Sanabre, *La acción de Francia en Cataluña en la pugna por la hegemonía de Europa, 1640–1659* (Barcelona, 1956), p. 355.

List of Contributors

PHILIP BENEDICT is Associate Professor of History at Brown University. He is the author of *Rouen during the Wars of Religion* (1981), as well as of articles on the political, economic and demographic history of France in the later sixteenth century.

PETER BURKE taught at the University of Sussex from 1962 to 1978 and now lectures at the University of Cambridge. Among his publications are *Culture and Society in Renaissance Italy* (1972) and *Venice and Amsterdam* (1977).

JAMES CASEY is the author of *The Kingdom of Valencia in the Seventeenth Century* (1979) and is currently engaged in research on family structure in early modern Spain. He is a Lecturer in History at the University of East Anglia.

PETER CLARK is Reader in Social History at the University of Leicester. He has written and edited a number of books on urban and social history, including *The English Alehouse* (1983) and *The Transformation of English Provincial Towns 1600–1800* (1984).

NICHOLAS DAVIDSON was formerly a Research Fellow at Girton College, Cambridge, and at present teaches at Leicester University. He is preparing a book on Venice and the Inquisition in the sixteenth century.

C. S. L. DAVIES taught Economic History at Glasgow University; since 1963 he has been Fellow and Tutor in Modern History at Wadham College, Oxford. He wrote *Peace, Print and Protestantism* (1976) and his research interests lie principally in the field of popular reaction to the Reformation.

TIMOTHY DAVIES did his postgraduate research at the University of Reading and has taught for several years at the University of Palermo. He is at present writing a general history of Sicily in the early modern period.

J. H. ELLIOTT, who was formerly a University Lecturer in History at Cambridge and then Professor of History at King's College, London, is now a Professor in the School of Historical Studies at the Institute for Advanced Study, Princeton. He has written a number of books on Spanish and early modern European history, including, most recently, *Richelieu and Olivares* (1984).

MARK GREENGRASS is lecturer in Modern History at the University of Sheffield. He has written *France in the Age of Henry IV: The Struggle for Stability* (1984) and is working on a study of French provincialism in the sixteenth century.

LEO NOORDEGRAAF teaches in the Economisch-Historisch Seminarium of the University of Amsterdam. He has published several articles on economic and social developments in the Dutch Republic during the sixteenth- and seventeenth-centuries.

R. B. Outhwaite is a University Lecturer in History and a Fellow of Gonville and Caius College, Cambridge. His publications include *Inflation in Tudor and Stuart England* (2nd edn, 1982) and, as editor, *Marriage and Society: Studies in the Social History of Marriage* (1981).

B. S. Pullan undertook his undergraduate and doctoral studies at Cambridge University. He was a Research Fellow of Trinity College, and later an Official Fellow of Queens' College and a University Lecturer in History. Since 1973 he has been Professor of Modern History at Manchester University.

Heinz Schilling completed his doctoral research at Freiburg University and held the Chair of Early Modern History at Osnabrück University, 1980–2. He is currently Professor of Modern History at the Justus-Liebig-University of Giessen. He has written extensively on the social and religious history of Germany and the Netherlands in the early modern period.

David Souden was previously a Research Fellow at Emmanuel College, Cambridge. He is completing a major study of migration in early modern England and is also preparing a television documentary series on English agrarian society before 1800.

I. A. A. Thompson has taught at Reading and Flinders Universities and is now Senior lecturer in History at the University of Keele. He is the author of *War and Government in Habsburg Spain 1560–1620* (1976) and he is currently working on the Cortes of Spain in the Habsburg period.

Index

BOSTON PUBLIC LIBRARY
3 9999 00322 122 1